Using the Stanislavsky System

A Practical Guide to Character Creation and Period Styles

Using the Stanislavsky System

A Practical Guide to Character Creation and Period Styles

by

Robert Blumenfeld

LIMELIGHT EDITIONS

An Imprint of Hal Leonard Corporation

New York

Published in 2008 by Limelight Editions
An Imprint of Hal Leonard Corporation
19 West 21st Street, New York, NY 10010

Printed in the United States of America

Book design by F. L. Bergesen

Library of Congress Cataloging-in-Publication Data is available upon request.

ISBN 13: 978-087910-356-9

www.limelighteditions.com

With love, admiration, and appreciation,
I dedicate this book
to my mother, Ruth Blumenfeld;
her brother, Seymour Korn;
and her sister, Bertha Friedman

Contents

Acknowledgments

Among those dear friends who have contributed directly and indirectly to this book are Christopher Buck, Albert S. Bennett, John Guerrasio, Michael Mendiola and Scot Anderson, Peter Subers and Rob Bauer, Tom and Virginia Smith, Paul and Joanna van Mulder, Alice Spivak, Stephanie and Russell Cowell-Clay, William and Lynn Carter, Buford and Elizabeth Norman, Kenneth Cohen and Doug Lerner, Anthony G. Henderson, Derek Tague, Jacob Knoll, Wesley Stevens and Jack Horner, Mikhail Shirokov, Dan Truman, Peter Kingsley, Blanche Buffet, and François Roulmann. And I express my gratitude and thanks for their love and support to my wonderful family, and most especially to my father, Max David Blumenfeld (1911–1994) and my mother, Ruth Blumenfeld; my brothers, Richard Blumenfeld and Donald Blumenfeld-Jones; my wonderful sister-in-law, Corbeau, and my nephew Benjamin and niece Rebecca; as well as my aunts, uncles and cousins— among them, my cousin Jonathan Blumenfeld; Shirley Korn (1919– 2004) and Seymour Korn; my cousins Rita Korn and Billy Korn; Bertha Friedman (1913–2001) and her husband Morton Friedman (1911–1981); my cousins Allan Friedman and Margery Friedman Loewer; and Nina Koenigsberg. Many thanks are owed to my very helpful copy editor, Joanna Dalin; my editor, Gail Siragusa; and the graphic designer of this book, F. L. Bergesen, who has done such a beautiful job. Lastly, I want to thank my publisher, John Cerullo and editorial director Carol Flannery, who, as always, have been terrifically supportive and helpful throughout. I owe an incalculable debt to all the authors in the bibliographical sections throughout the book. Translations from French, German, and Italian, unless otherwise noted, are my own.

PART ONE

The Stanislavsky System

The Great Debate:
To Be or Not to Be

Acting is full of paradoxes: the actor plays out intimate, private scenes in front of an audience and projects his or her voice, almost shouting memorized words that must seem never to have been uttered before. Every moment must appear to happen spontaneously, although it has been planned and rehearsed thoroughly and performed a hundred times.

Yet everyone agrees that actors must convince the audience of the truth and reality of what they are doing. Marie-Françoise Dumesnil (1713–1803), known for her sensitive, realistic acting in an age of declamatory external playing, wrote in her memoirs, "The height of theatrical art is without doubt to appear to recite not others' thoughts, but one's own." The problem is how best to do that: should actors feel the characters' emotions and live through them, or should they imitate them by external, technical simulation?

For Constantin Stanislavsky (1863–1938), the answer to the question was obvious: only the former is real acting; the latter is shallow and inartistic. He would have agreed with the dramatist and stage manager, Aaron Hill (1685–1750), who published a periodical called *The Prompter*, in which he wrote:

> An actor who assumes a character wherein he does not seem in earnest to *be* the person by whose name he calls himself, affronts instead of entertaining the audience.

Acting Styles Before Stanislavsky:
Ancient Greece Through the Eighteenth Century

Polus, the most famous tragedian of Ancient Greece, known for the dignity, intelligence, and clarity of his acting, was prostrate with grief at the death of his dearly loved son. Having gone through a period of mourning, he found the courage to return to the stage to play the title role in a revival of Sophocles' *Electra*. Taking the urn with his son's ashes from its tomb, Polus carried it on stage with him and, in tears, embraced it as if it held the remains of Electra's brother Orestes, filling the whole theater "not with simulated or imitated sorrow, but with genuine grief and heartfelt lamentation."

So says the Roman writer Aulus Gellius (ca. 125–ca. 180 CE), who tells this story centuries after the fact in *Noctes Atticae* (Attic Nights). It is the first example that has come down to us of an actor really living through the emotions of a part, and using the technique of substitution to help him do so. And Polus had done exactly what Stanislavsky would recommend centuries later to actors using emotional recall: only use emotions that have been assimilated and are no longer raw and traumatic, so that some aesthetic distance and self-control are possible.

In ancient writings on rhetoric and poetry, the question of how to move the audience is taken up extensively. The Greek philosopher Aristotle (384–322 BCE) maintained in his *Poetics* that since we all share a basic human nature, actors, like orators and poets, can make us feel emotion most effectively by feeling it themselves. In his widely read treatise on rhetoric, the *Institutions of Oratory*, designed to educate children, the Roman pedagogue Quintilian (ca. 35–ca. 96) says it would be inappropriate and even ridiculous to simulate such feelings as anger or sorrow merely by assuming certain facial expressions and using certain gestures; these feelings should be heartfelt and real. And the most famous orator of ancient Rome, Cicero (106–143 BCE), studied oratory with Roscius—Quintus Roscius Gallus (126–162 BCE)—Rome's most famous actor. Cicero said that when he wanted to make a strong impression, he first aroused strong feeling in himself, as he had seen actors do, their eyes appearing through their masks to be "inflamed with fury." Furthermore, he maintained that real emotion is more effective in oratory than an imitation of feeling.

Centuries later, William Shakespeare (1564–1616) wrote Hamlet's well-known and oft-quoted advice to the players. Hamlet admires the emotional realism of the old actor and tells the actors to "hold, as 'twere, the mirror up to nature," but this may be in the context of using standardized conventional gestures—"Nor do not saw the air too much with your hand, thus"—and a declamatory style. It is by no means certain that such a system was actually in use, and even if it were, not all actors may have agreed with such a way of working: from descriptions of his acting, Richard Burbage (1567–1619), the first Hamlet, Othello, King Lear and Richard III, seems to have eschewed such a style and was much praised for the power and naturalness of his art.

In *A Short Discourse of the English Stage*, written in 1664, the traveler and dramatist Richard Flecknoe (1600–ca. 1678) had this to say about Burbage's acting, which he may have seen in his youth:

> He was a delightful Proteus, so wholly transforming himself into his part, and putting off himself with his clothes, as he never (not so much as in the tiring-house) assum'd himself again until the play was done. . . . He had all the parts of an excellent orator, animating his words with speaking, and speech with acting; his auditors being never more delighted than when he spoke nor more sorry than when he held his peace; yet even then he was an excellent actor still, never failing in his part when he had done speaking, but with his looks and gestures maintaining it still.

In 1747, the journalist and playwright Pierre Rémond de Sainte-Albine (1699–1778) published *Le comédien* (The Actor), in which he expounded his theories on the actor's art and maintained the necessity for the actor to experience emotion. He is a remarkable precursor of Stanislavsky; in part 2, chapter 2, "On Truthful Actions," he has this to say:

> To be truthful in [playing] actions is to do exactly what the character would or should do in each of the circumstances through which the author has successively had him go.

The actor/dramatist Antoine François Riccoboni (1707–1772), member of a well-known theatrical family, disagreed with Sainte-Albine, and he wrote in *L'Art du Théâtre* (1750) that the actor had to imitate and not feel emotion, and that everything should be calculated and predetermined. In this he disagreed with his own father, the actor and writer Luigi (Louis) Riccoboni (1676–1753), who took the opposite point of view—and who, incidentally, wrote the first history of theater in Europe, an excellent book, published in 1740. In his essay "Pensées sur la déclamation" (Thoughts on Declamation), he writes that voice, intonation patterns, gesture, and physical expression should be all of a piece and should arise naturally from the inner workings of the mind. Nature, he says, has made each person an individual, and each person therefore expresses everything individually, despite the necessity of good diction and heightened expression. But above all, one must declaim using "the notes of one's own soul":

> The great thing on the stage, as I have said, is to create the illusion for the spectators that Tragedy is not a fiction, but that it is the Heroes who act and speak, and not actors who represent them.

Even Antoine François decried the misuse of technique and counseled moderation of gesture and voice as well as "simplicity and truth." Here is how he describes the current fashion of declamation, which both he and his father found objectionable and which he characterizes as "a rooted evil" (among others) in the French theater:

> To begin low, to speak with affected slowness, to draw out the sounds languorously with no variation, to raise the voice on one sound suddenly, taking a half pause for meaning, and to return promptly to the note on which one began; in moments of passion, to express oneself with superabundant force, without abandoning the same sort of modulation—that is how one declaims.

Interestingly enough, he discusses the idea of intentions in terms we can readily understand, even though his advice is full of calculated, non-specific stereotypes:

> You have to say "hello" in a scene. This is a simple word and everyone understands it. But it is not enough to understand that it is a polite way of addressing people who arrive and whom one approaches: there are a thousand ways of saying "hello," depending on the character and the situation. A lover says "hello" to his mistress with that sweetness and affection that communicate his feelings to the one he is saluting. A father says it with tenderness to the son he loves, and with a coldness mixed with sorrow to the son with whom he is disappointed.

The idea that actors, to be effective, should only imitate and not feel emotion is clearly expressed in the philosophical dialogue *Paradoxe sur le comédien* (The Paradox of the Actor) by the Enlightenment encyclopedist and playwright Denis Diderot (1713–1784), who disagreed emphatically with Sainte-Albine and Louis Riccoboni. He was convinced, for instance, that Aulus Gellius was wrong, and that Polus could only have been imitating grief, however really and expertly, since this was not how he would actually have behaved in the privacy of his own home. Diderot was very curious about how actors actually worked, but he tended to view things as an outsider, although having written dramas, he was close friends with some major actors of his day.

Two of the famous rivals of the period, Marie-Françoise Dumesnil and Hyppolite Clairon (1723–1803), were publicly and jealously on opposite sides of the great debate. Mlle. Clairon, who cruelly tears Dumesnil apart, was extremely technical in her approach, as she makes clear in her *Memoirs of Hyppolite Clairon the celebrated French Actress: With Reflections Upon the Dramatic Art: Written by Herself.* Here, in the original unaccredited translation published in 1800, is some of her advice about how to play Phèdre in Racine's tragedy:

> I would advise for the expression of remorse, a simple diction, noble yet tender accents, a profusion of tears, a countenance deeply affected; and, for the expression of love, a sort of delirium and insensibility...
>
> In the scene, in the second act, with Hyppolite, I would recite the first couplet in a low and trembling voice, and without daring to raise my eyes. At the moment the sound of his voice struck my ear, my whole person should evince that pleasing trepidation, which souls of real sensibility [sensitivity] experience...
>
> The second couplet should be expressed by a different emotion. My words should appear to be interrupted by the violent palpitation of my heart.

As you can see, this is all a question of calculated effects—nothing organic here, whereas Mlle. Dumesnil was known for the reality of her emotions. In her own *Memoirs of Mlle. Dumesnil in Reply to the Memoirs of Hyppolite Clairon*, she espouses the point of view that emotions should be expressed spontaneously and really, without calculation.

Clairon, says Dumesnil, with as much cruelty as Clairon displayed toward her, is pompous where she should be truthful. She does not create, she recites. Clairon, on the other hand, thought Dumesnil's acting inconsistent and maintained that she had reality without art. As one might expect, Diderot was convinced that Clairon's methods were superior to those of Dumesnil: "What acting is more perfect than that of Clairon?" he writes. As for Dumesnil, "Half the time she doesn't know what she is saying, and then comes a sublime moment."

And Diderot's point of view—shared by some actors even now—is succinctly summed up:

> All of his [the actor's] talent consists not in feeling, as you suppose, but in rendering so scrupulously the exterior signs of feeling, that you could mistake them [for real feeling]. His ear has remembered

the sounds of sorrow. The gestures of despair are in his memory, and have been prepared before a mirror. He knows the exact instant when he will take out his handkerchief and when his tears will begin to flow: expect them at this precise moment, on this syllable, no sooner and no later. This trembling of the voice, those words that hang suspended, those stifled or drawn out sounds, that shuddering of the limbs, those shaking knees, those fainting spells, those furors [are] pure imitation, lessons recorded in advance, pathetic grimaces, sublime imitation.

For Diderot, the actor should not only be detached from feeling; he should not even want to experience or live through a character's emotions, because doing so is the enemy of the actor's art. Finally, the actor "is not the character: he plays him and plays him so well that you would take him for the character, but the illusion is only for you; he knows very well that he is not the character." Of course he does, but Diderot does not realize that this does not preclude his feeling the emotions he is portraying.

David Garrick (1717–1779), the great reformer of the English stage in the eighteenth century and the true father of modern acting, was acquainted with Diderot, who knew him and admired his work. At a private party to which they had both been invited, Diderot witnessed Garrick's exhibition of a rapid-fire succession of emotional states, and he simply did not believe that Garrick could really have felt all the emotions he displayed. But the fact is that Garrick was, by all accounts, a virtuoso, and could indeed change rapidly from one feeling to another as he wished. His main idea about acting was that actors should thoroughly understand the inner workings of their roles and live through them, not simply calculate their effects or pose in accordance with general ideas of how, for instance, fear or overwhelming joy were expressed.

Technique and Artificiality: Nineteenth-Century Acting and François Delsarte

In the 1947 Ealing Studio version of Charles Dickens's *Nicholas Nickleby*, there is a supremely funny excerpt from the last scene of *Romeo and Juliet*, performed by that consummate actor and comedian, Stanley Holloway (1890–1982), as the actor-manager Vincent Crummles. He captures perfectly the common romantic conception of how to do

Shakespeare. The hilarious, completely unconvincing ham acting is from the pre-Delsarte era, but it strikes us as Delsarte nonetheless: grand gestures, and the lines delivered with pear-shaped tones. The calculated, exaggerated vocal effects are priceless.

Enthusiastic and inspired by lofty aesthetic and religious ideals, the highly popular French teacher François Delsarte (1811–1871) thought he had discovered the science of how actors could be real and psychologically truthful in their performances. But the thoroughgoing system Delsarte thought so scientific had no grounding in depth psychology or the realities of behavior, and it was ultimately a superficial attempt to codify what cannot be codified: the expression and physical manifestations of emotion, which are subject to innumerable individual variations.

Delsarte divided the human body into zones: the head, seat of the mind and the intellect; the trunk of the body, seat of the emotions; and the limbs, which would express the body's emotions and the mind's thoughts. He felt that all emotion, all nuances of feeling, all ideas could be expressed on stage by using beautiful elocution and specific, meaningful gestures and poses, which, however calculated and studied they might be, must appear to be spontaneous and natural. Emotion gave rise to movement—indeed, the Latin root of the word is *emovere* (to move outward or away from)—and his elaborate system described in minute detail the movements associated with each emotion.

Delsarte also emphasized the teaching of calisthenics intended to make the actor powerful, supple, poised, and graceful, so that the movements Delsarte had devised could be smoothly executed. And the student studied voice production and how to produce pear-shaped tones as well as exercises meant to teach grace and elegance, such as the correct and most beautiful way to point the finger or to gesture with the arm, or to lift a significant eyebrow.

One of the problems, as Stanislavsky saw it, was that the kind of approach Delsarte proposed and the kind of acting that prevailed even before Delsarte—what Stanislavsky called "mechanical acting"—actually led to a series of hackneyed clichés and generalized ideas, presented as truth to a public that accepted them because they were usually exposed to nothing else. A worried character would wring his hands and perhaps bite a finger. If a character were sick, she coughed or shivered. If a character were supposed to be nervous, he opened a letter with a trembling hand or let a glass knock against a water jug as he tried to pour a drink. A drunk staggered about the stage. If a character were agitated, she paced furiously up and down. Someone dying clutched at his chest or tore at his shirt collar. If all this was what the imitation of emotion amounted to, Stanislavsky wanted none of it.

Delsarte's ideas on the performing arts had a great influence in the United States through his enthused American disciple, the theater manager, prolific playwright, actor, and director Steele MacKaye (1842–1894). He taught Delsartian technique at the Lyceum Theatre School for Acting, which he founded in New York in 1884. It was the first such school in the United States; its name was later changed to the American Academy of Dramatic Arts.

Neither MacKaye nor Delsarte wrote books about the system, although Delsarte did begin to write a huge tome, but he had only finished five chapters by the time of his death. They were published in *Delsarte System of Oratory* (Edgar S. Werner, 1882), which contains writings by some of his disciples as well. His daughter, Madame Marie Delsarte-Géraldy, gave a series of lectures and lessons on a visit to the United States, and published them as her contribution to the book:

Lesson VI.
Basic Attitudes.

1. Weakness. Feet close together, weight of body on both. This attitude is that of childhood and old age.

2. Perfect calm and repose. Rest weight on one foot (settling at the hip), bend the knee of the other leg and advance the foot.

3. Vehemence. Move the body forward so that the weight rests on the foot that is in front; the heel of the foot that is behind is thus raised.

4. Prostration. Throw one foot far behind the other, with the knee bent and the weight of the body upon it. This attitude, when properly taken, leads to the kneeling position.

5. Transitive position. In walking, stop midway between two steps and you have the 5th attitude or transitive position. It is the one that leads to all kinds of walks, and especially to the reverential or oblique walk.

6. Reverential walk. Let the foot which is behind take a step forward in this manner: With the toe describe on the ground a semicircle that bends inward toward you; this will cause the heel to pass over the instep of the other foot. The other foot now takes a straight step forward, and you pause in a respectful attitude

before the personage of importance whom you wish to salute. Several steps may be taken in succession before the final pause. The ceremonious step is always taken with the foot you begin with (the one toward the person you salute); the other foot always takes natural steps. This walk is only meant for men, and only on grand occasions.

Among François Delsarte's pupils, perhaps the most illustrious was Rachel (1820–1858), the most idolized French actress before Bernhardt. She died young of consumption (tuberculosis), which killed so many of the romantics at a young age, among them the composers Bellini and Chopin. The daughter of impoverished French Jewish itinerant peddlers, Rachel was born Élisa Félix in Switzerland. Her family moved to Paris when she was still a young girl, and her talent was quickly recognized. In fact, she and her sister sang in the streets in order to earn money to keep the family together, and her six siblings all went into the theater. She played leading roles at the Comédie Française when she was still in her teens. Among other things, she was known for her superb diction and an economy of gesture. She used what she learned from Delsarte, but she made it her own, so that her performances were not exaggerated or extravagant but infused with ardor and passion that came from the heart.

Euripides' tale of intrigue and incest, *Hippolytus*, as adapted by Racine in 1677 for his play *Phèdre*, provided her with a great tragic part. The polymath, philosopher, literary critic, amateur actor, and noted biographer of Goethe, George Henry Lewes (1817–1878), best known now for his then scandalous relationship with Mary Ann Evans (George Eliot), wrote an eyewitness account of mid-Victorian theater, *On Actors and the Art of Acting*, in 1875. He describes her in the role, which he calls "the finest of all her performances":

> Nothing I have ever seen surpassed this picture of a soul torn by incestuous passion and struggling conscience; the unutterable mournfulness of her look and tone.... What a picture she was as she entered! You felt that she was wasting away under the fire within, that she was standing on the edge of the grave with pallid face, hot eyes, emaciated frame—an awful ghastly apparition.

The French actor Constant Coquelin (1841–1909), who created the role of Cyrano in *Cyrano de Bergerac*, said that he could see an image of his character in his mind's eye and that all he had to do then was imitate what he saw. His two books, *Art and the Actor* and *The Art of the*

Actor, are in agreement with Diderot's concepts and with some of Delsarte's ideas; he provoked an outraged reaction from Henry Irving (1838–1905), whom he critiqued and who believed in a realistic approach to the creation of character, even in the second-rate melodramas he often starred in. The recordings Coquelin made seem very mannered and stylized and not at all natural vocally; so do Irving's. But how can one really tell what the effect would have been in the theater? The long-unavailable original cast recording of Edward Albee's *Who's Afraid of Virginia Woolf?* which seemed so startlingly, uncannily real when I saw it on stage in 1962, sounds surprisingly stagy and artificial and not at all like what I remember experiencing. In any case, the great American actor, Joseph Jefferson (1829–1905) wrote in his autobiography that as far as he was concerned, they were both correct: each actor was using the methods that were right for him, and that was the important thing.

The famous French actress and matinee idol Sarah Bernhardt (1844–1923) performed in many silent films, and she recorded excerpts from some of her most acclaimed stage roles. Her acting—which is actually quite unforgettable, very impressive, and even haunting in those old films—appears in some ways to be an embodiment of the Delsarte system, but her own originality, charisma, and genius must have been major factors in her sensational success. Not everyone was impressed, of course. Although he kept her framed photograph in his study, Chekhov felt that her art was too calculating and gave too great an impression of lessons learned by heart. Stanislavsky thought she was more interested in fame than in art.

Bernhardt's book, *The Art of the Theatre* (The Dial Press, 1925), sets out her basic approach to acting. Elegance and refinement of gesture, a well-modulated but powerful trained voice, and superb diction are the most important tools of the actor, she tells us. The psychology of a character can be conveyed vocally and with the use of appropriate gestures. And you have to have a good jaw and teeth so you can articulate clearly—very important, according to la grande Sarah. If you don't, you might almost as well forget acting, although with hard work you can overcome the handicap if your teeth aren't *too* small! And since looks and what the audience sees are all-important, you have to know how to apply makeup—more elaborately for women than for men, she informs us—so as to mitigate or overcome the defects of nature: "An insipid face with small eyes is especially to be dreaded." The remedy? "An enlargement of the eyes effected by means of a blue or chestnut-colored pencil."

It is interesting to note that she thought she was being absolutely real in her acting and felt emotionally involved in her performances. Her perfervid tears and her hysterical laughter were genuine, as far as she was concerned, and every musical tremor of the voice arose from authentic feeling. Indeed, she counsels young people going into the theater that an absolute identification with the role, and with every emotion the character experiences, is essential. Without that, there is no great acting.

Here is what *la voix d'or* (the golden voice) has to say in an appendix entitled "Hints on the Voice":

> To forget one's personality and live the part, with real tears and laughter, to link even the breathing of the attentive crowd to the inflexions of one's own emotions——this is what is required. And this cannot be taught.

Bernhardt's great rival, the Italian star Eleonora Duse (1858–1924)—considered the mother of modern, realistic acting—aspired to be absolutely real in her performances. "I do not use paint," she said, "I make myself up morally." George Bernard Shaw (1856–1950) wrote that "she immeasurably dwarfs the poor little octave and a half on which Sarah Bernhardt plays such pretty canzonets and stirring marches," and that "with a tremor of the lip, which you feel rather than see, and which lasts half an instant, she touches you straight on the very heart."

The point is this: both these towering *monstres sacrés* thought they were being real in their acting, and yet their approaches to the art, like Irving's and Coquelin's, were quite different.

Mikhail Shchepkin and Nineteenth-Century Realistic Acting

Mikhail Semyonovich Shchepkin, born into serfdom in 1788, purchased his freedom in 1821 with the help of wealthy friends. He was already a famous actor, known for the realism of his approach to the art. And for several decades, he was director of the famed Maly Theater in Moscow. In ways precursive of Stanislavsky, he wrote about the art of acting in his voluminous correspondence and memoirs.

Shchepkin died in 1863, the year Stanislavsky was born. But the parents of one of his school friends had been Maly Theater actors: Alexander Fedotov, and Fedotov's wife, Glikeria Fedotova. They were students of Shchepkin, who, as was usual in established theaters, trained actors for his company. She gave Stanislavsky penetrating critiques of his acting. And when Fedotov directed him in a semiprofessional production of Gogol's *The Gamblers* in 1888, his work methods made a profound and lasting impression on the young actor.

Shchepkin analyzed thoroughly every role he worked on, and he brought characters to life with specificity, elegance, and passion. Once he had decided how to play a character, he never deviated from his playing, and he would not pander to the crowd by crudely overdoing comic effects or elaborating on comedic business in the inspired heat of the moment simply to get a cheap laugh. He was committed to being the character. Even after rehearsals were done, he would frequently stay up all night before a performance working on a role. Then he would arrive at the theater hours before it was supposed to begin in order to prepare.

In the great debate, he was firmly on the side of the actor really entering into the character's emotional life and living through the character's experiences. He decried the general practice of mechanical declamation and artificial posing that was so widespread in the theater of his day, and he felt that actors should eliminate their own personalities and take on that of the author's character.

Shchepkin believed that actors should be great observers of life and develop their imaginative abilities. He despised imitative acting and called it "actoring." His approach to a role began with rigorous script analysis so that he could understand the author's main idea, which it was the actor's job to fulfill. All important for him was the search for the way to bring the text to life naturally. The actor should think about how to be specific in his characterization and dynamic in his performance, with every thought of the character able to be read in the character's eyes and heard in the character's voice. Shchepkin was very "unstagey on stage," according to the writer Alexander Herzen (1812–1870), who knew him well and saw him perform many times.

Stanislavsky was inspired not only by the writings of Shchepkin but also by the famous performances of great actors. Among them was Tommaso Salvini (1829–1916), whom he saw in *Othello*, a role Stanislavsky had played himself. Conscientious to a fault, Salvini, like Shchepkin, would arrive at the theater three hours before a performance to begin getting into character. Salvini's aim, as he tells us in his autobiography, was to identify himself with the character so completely that the audience would believe it was seeing the real person and not an imitation.

George Henry Lewes was less impressed than Stanislavsky was with Salvini, whom he saw on tour in London in the 1870s. He regrets that

Salvini as Othello did not have "tears in his voice," and he found his suffering as the character too personally felt, too individual. "Tragic pathos to be grand should be *impersonal*," writes Lewes. "Instead of our being made to feel that the sufferer is giving himself up to self-pity, we should be made to see in his anguish a general sorrow." Still, Lewes thought that in some ways Salvini surpassed Edmund Kean (1787–1833), known for the thoroughness and realism of his Shakespearean characterizations.

Henri-Louis Le Kain (1729–1778), a famous Comédie Française tragic actor known for his naturalistic playing; the Irish actor and playwright Charles Macklin (1697–1797), first celebrated for his realistic Shylock and then for many other roles he played on the London stage; Adrienne Lecouvreur (1692–1730) of the Comédie Française; Talma (1763–1826), the great French tragedian of the Napoleonic era; and the American Edwin Booth (1833–1893; see pages 279, 280) were all for realism in acting. Talma even wrote an essay in which he deplored the sing-song, declamatory style prevalent in the French theater.

In short, contemporary realistic acting had many precursors, but even those actors who had written about the art had not discussed their systems of working in a way that would be useful for actor training. And nobody had yet written down a systematic method or process that actors could use in a practical way to bring their characters to life on stage.

CHAPTER ONE

Understanding the System: Basic Principles and Acting Techniques

After years of playing Dr. Stockman in Ibsen's *An Enemy of the People*, his favorite part and one for which he was much praised, Stanislavsky was distressed to find that there were many times when he was no longer feeling the part at all. "I mechanically repeated . . . the physical signs of absent emotion," he says in *My Life in Art* (Little, Brown and Company, 1924). He found himself indicating: "copying the outer appearances of experiencing my part and of inner action." "I copied naïveté, but I was not naïve." Even though he continued to garner applause, the part had gradually and unaccountably slipped away from him, and he relied more and more on intuition and inspiration to help him get through his performances.

During his long vacation, "sitting on a beach in Finland and examining my artistic past, I suddenly struck on the feelings of Stockman long lost in my artistic soul." He was astonished. And he asked himself how he could awaken those feelings every time he performed. He felt inspired to search for the solution to the problems of how to free the actor's imagination, how to bring characters to life with truthfulness, and how to feel fresh and vital at every performance. Exhilarated, he returned to Moscow for the 1906–07 season at the Moscow Art Theatre, the company he and the littérateur, stage director, and playwright Vladimir Nemirovich-Danchenko (1858–1943) had founded in 1898. The logical "system," based in reality, which he would work on developing for the rest of his life, was about to be born.

The Fundamental Ideas and Basic Principles of the System

The System's Fundamental Ideas: Fundamental to the system is the idea that there are basic components, or elements, common to any play and any character; these will be discussed in the next chapter in connection with script and character analysis. Work on creating a character begins with the system's *basic procedure*, or technique, of *deconstruction*—that is, of breaking down the play and the role into their elements. This is followed by the process of *reconstruction*—of putting the elements of the play and the role back together. You can study what a character wants (*objectives*), and why he or she wants it (*motivation* and psychology), separately from what is in the character's way (*obstacles*): they condition what the character does (*actions*), and how he or she does it. But all these things ultimately exist inseparably, in the finished character.

Who am I—the character? Why do I do what I do? The deterministic theory underlying the Stanislavsky system is that every action the character takes has an emotionally based psychological reason: a motivation, a logic, and a justification that cause someone to act in a particular way. This theory involves the corollary idea that people's motivations involve interaction with others in an attempt to fulfill wants, needs, and desires. You have to discover the character's motivations, which are hidden in the text; these motivations give rise to the *intentions* with which the words are said. Motivations and intentions taken together constitute the *subtext*. As Stanislavsky tells us, the subtext is what makes us say the words.

All the steps in the preparation and rehearsal process involve making choices, which are your particular, individual interpretations of the subtext and the character as a whole. The author has provided a sketch or a blueprint of the character, but it is you who will complete the sketch and construct the character. You will be using your powers of logic and deduction to invent those parts of the character's life that the author has not directly depicted, such as what happened before the play began and what happens between the scenes. And you alone will supply the character with an internal life.

But the very first principle, as you begin your work, is *Tell the truth*.

Truthfulness and Reality: Everything in acting starts with the self-evident truth that life on stage is artificial. And you are always and forever yourself, not a character in a work of fiction. You don't have to *be* someone else (how could you be?) but rather to *behave as if* you were the character. You know you are saying memorized words somebody else wrote. The stage set around which you move in a pattern set in rehearsal is not a real desert island or prison cell or your own living room, or indeed any actual living room; it may even be abstract, or you may be performing on a virtually bare stage. The costume you wear is not your actual clothing. The sunlight is artificial, and so is the rain falling outside the fake window. But what would you do *if* all of that were real, *if* you really were that person living through those circumstances, *if* the words you say were really yours? How would you behave? "*If* is the starting point," says Stanislavsky, "the *given circumstances* build the basis for *if* itself.*" In *An Actor Prepares* (Theatre Arts Books, 1936), Stanislavsky defines given circumstances as "the story of the play, its facts, events, epoch, time and place of action, conditions of life." He also includes the production elements: "the actors' and regisseurs' interpretation, the mise-en-scène, the production, the sets, the costumes, properties, lighting, and sound effects."

In order to give yourself the necessary *feeling of truth* and of living within the given circumstances, in order to find the *inner truth*—yours and therefore the character's—you have to have a naïve faith in the reality of what is happening. To achieve this, you have to use your imagination to project yourself into the life of the play. You have to use *your* mind and *your* emotions to bring the character's mind and feelings to life, *your* body to make the character's physical life real.

Another truth that Stanislavsky knew well and that had often been previously stated: the actor when performing is living a kind of double reality, playing a character, while always aware that he or she is an actor acting on a stage and always aware of the audience's energy, which the actor takes in and gives back. As Stanislavsky says, "Scenic truth is not the truth of life; it is peculiar to itself."

Specificity—Here, Today, Now, This Very Minute: And the corollary to the principle of truthfulness and reality is *Be specific*, not general. As Stanislavsky said, "In general is the enemy of art." You don't exist in general. Nothing exists in general. It is therefore not truthful or real to be general. To achieve specificity, you should know every detail of your character's life.

Place has an enormous influence on what you do and how you feel. Dining at home alone in front of the television feels very different from an intimate dinner with a friend or loved one either at home or in a neighborhood restaurant, which will be different again if that restaurant is in Paris, London, or Rome.

Historical time and place are also determining factors. The banquet given to honor an ambassador at the court of Louis XIV requires quite different deportment and manners than one given in Charlemagne's castle centuries earlier or a Roman feast in the time of Augustus or a presidential reception in contemporary Washington, DC. How would you behave *if* you were in any of those places? Or *if* you were in a cell in the Bastille in 1789 or the Tower of London in 1568 or a contemporary American prison? You would have as an actor to explore in depth and detail what those places are like.

And nothing takes place at just any old time. You go to the theater, and the curtain rises at eight, or perhaps ten minutes after. You know exactly when your birthday is and when America's Independence Day is. But more than that, you know how you behaved at specific moments of your life, and this is of paramount importance. In a play, you know exactly when something is happening: the first scene of *Hamlet* takes place just before and then a few minutes after midnight during the changing of the guard at Elsinore castle.

In her acting class, which I had the pleasure of attending, Uta Hagen did a very instructive and entertaining exercise to demonstrate the specificity of time's conditioning of behavior: She was in her apartment on Washington Square and was about to go teach a class at the HB Studio across town on Bank Street. Looking at her watch she discovered she had only ten minutes to be there on time. Could she make it? She hurriedly packed her purse, put on her coat, and ran out the door, shouting, "Taxi! Taxi!" The second time she did the exercise she looked at her watch and saw that she now had only five minutes to make it to her class on time. Now she was really in a hurry! She rushed around like a mad person and frantically shouted, "Taxi!" as she almost fell. She did the exercise a third time. Now it was already the exact time the class was supposed to begin. So, what's the use? She was already late. In disgust, muttering obscenities, she packed her purse and got the necessary things together, then walked fairly swiftly out the door, and suddenly broke into a run and yelled, "*Taxi!*"

When you talk of characters who never appear on stage—such as Protopopov, with whom Natasha is having an affair in Chekhov's *Three Sisters*; or Vera Petrovna, Vanya's dead sister, whom all the other characters knew well; or any person in a character's past or present life whom we will never see—you as an actor must know specifically who that person is. You must know your relationship to and events you remember involving him or her.

The principle of specificity also means that you will avoid preconceptions and stereotypes about the character, as well as uninteresting mechanical theatrical clichés. Clichés and stereotypes are facile, nonspecific approximations, and they never depict reality but only a semblance of it.

And this same principle means that you must listen to your fellow actors and hear what they say and how they say it, in order to be specific in your reactions and responses at every moment.

Stanislavsky said to Vasili Toporkov, during rehearsals for Bulgakov's adaptation of Gogol's *Dead Souls*, "You need to know down to the last detail what is the specific purpose of everything you do." And you need to know what happens at each specific moment, and why: why does it happen "here, today, now, this very minute?" That phrase became the watchword of the Moscow Art Theatre actors, as it should be for you.

Through the Conscious to the Unconscious: In *An Actor Prepares*, Stanislavsky wrote about one of "the fundamental principles of our art: 'unconscious creativeness through conscious technique.'" This "psycho-technique" is the foundational bedrock, the basic premise, of the Stanislavsky system, and of the *method of physical actions* that is the heart of that system. In order to awaken unconscious feelings and emotions, you must work by conscious means. As Stanislavsky says:

> We cannot directly act on our emotions, but we can prod our creative fantasy, and it stirs up our *emotion* or *affective memory*, calling up from its secret depths, beyond the reach of consciousness, elements of already experienced emotions, and regroups them to correspond with the images which arise in us.

Like Sigmund Freud, Stanislavsky knew that most mental processes take place unconsciously. And he knew as well that the actor had to understand and create not only the character's conscious life but also his or her unconscious mind, which is what really drives the character to want certain things and take certain actions. But how do you get to the character's unconscious? By using conscious techniques of script and character analysis and by rehearsing with your fellow actors, in the course of which you will determine what the character actually does.

Doing what the character does will awaken the unconscious, and emotions will arise naturally: your own unconscious, of course, which responds to the given circumstances, and which therefore becomes the character's unconscious; your own emotions, in response to the imaginary given circumstances that you posit as real—these emotions and responses are therefore the character's. You cannot work by trying to force emotions to the surface because you think they should be there. You must work without worrying about what emotions the unconscious will bring forth as a result of the action taken by the character (you). In fact, the emotions and exact responses will vary from performance to performance, although they will all be within the parameters and the architectonics that were set up in rehearsal.

Once the unconscious is awakened, you must let it be and trust that it will do its work based on the given circumstances you have set up for it to work with. You must allow it to do its work unhindered. You can give it instructions, on which it will act in its own good time. Suppose, for instance, that you wish to play a certain moment that is not coming to you naturally, that you are just not finding. "What do I do about that moment? I just don't see things clearly." If you "sleep on it," you may find it is there for you in the next rehearsal.

We learn things about ourselves and others, and about the character we want to bring to life, as we go along. Much of what we have learned will recede into the unconscious to be recalled as necessary—or to remain repressed and unrecalled unless a concatenation of circumstances summons it to return to consciousness, as it does for the protagonists in countless plays from *Hamlet* to Henrik Ibsen's *A Doll's House* to Tennessee Williams's *The Glass Menagerie* to Eugene O'Neill's *Long Day's Journey into Night*. If it did not, the brain would be so bombarded with knowledge that we would be unable to live in the present moment. How often, in any case, do we live in the past or the future in our minds, while remaining perforce fixed physically in the present moment? Characters such as Blanche DuBois in Williams's *A Streetcar Named Desire* and Amanda Wingfield in *The Glass Menagerie* do exactly that.

The character's emotional state influences the actions taken, and the actions taken in turn influence the character's emotional state. External circumstances also influence the emotional state: temperature, place, and time, for instance, have an effect of which people are not always conscious. And physical states, such as drunkenness or illness, influence both emotion and behavior.

You can only understand something outside yourself by analogy with something inside yourself—something you have a mental image of and an emotional attachment to. Using these analogies, which are usually called *substitutions* (about which, more later), summons your unconscious to do its work. In other words, when you substitute something analogous in your own life and imagination for the persons, places, events, or situations in the play, you are fusing your own circumstances with the character's given circumstances in a way that makes the latter real, and therefore playable, to you. You are *personalizing* and *particularizing* them.

For the purposes of acting, Stanislavsky distinguished between what he called "primary emotion"—that is, immediately experienced feelings, such as anger or love at first sight—and "repeated emotion"—that is, emotions from the past that could be recalled and that are filtered not only through memory but also through the interpretation of past events that have been dealt with, assimilated, and absorbed into the unconscious. It is repeated emotion, through the use of *emotional recall*, that the actor will find useful.

Primary emotion can be dangerous: if the actor playing Hamlet is really furious with Claudius, he might actually kill him. As Stanislavsky said, emotions on stage are a "poetic reflection of life's emotions," as the sensitive actor, attuned to the character and the moment—and always aware that he or she is acting and playing the character—goes through them and experiences them.

Discovering Through Doing: As corollary to the previous principle, the most important way to get to the unconscious through the conscious is by doing—that is, by actually performing a psychophysical action. Only in that way will you really discover what is going on with the character both physically and emotionally. You will also find out how much time it takes to go from here to there—literally and figuratively. You will see how you relate to the other characters. Discovering through doing is at the heart of the method of physical actions as it is of *active analysis*.

Evolving out of the method of physical actions, active analysis was the last, unfinished stage of Stanislavsky's theory and practice. The two ways of working are not substantially different from each other. Active analysis—somewhat of a misnomer, since little actual analysis is involved—incorporates the method of physical actions and concentrates on its last step: discovering through doing. It was principally used as a streamlined rehearsal method, and it is not to be confused with the system of thorough script and character analysis discussed in these pages. Instead of sitting around a table talking endlessly about the play—as had been the case—the MAT actors would get on their feet almost immediately, by the second or third rehearsal, and begin exploring the objectives and psychophysical actions of their parts through improvisations based around the text. Such improvisations had always been used at the MAT, but with active analysis, the actors would also start working with the text itself much sooner than before.

Discovering through doing is essentially what rehearsal is all about. The answers you seek will not be there at the beginning. In fact, the answers should never be predetermined or decided: "Never begin with results," says Stanislavsky. Analysis only takes you to the door of the rehearsal room; you have to enter it and rehearse to see what is really going to happen. True understanding and the discovery of the correct actions, based on the character's psychology and on what the character wants and what the character does to get what he or she wants, all take time. Yes, you have to think first about what to do, but then you have to do it, and what you do will have results, which may be quite different from your original vision.

Acting is doing and not thinking, even though it is thinking that gives rise to doing. And "thinking" itself may be a perfectly valid action, as it is in a famous episode from the old Jack Benny television series. He is accosted by a mugger with the cliché "Your money or your life!" Benny hesitates. The mugger wants to know what he is doing! "I'm thinking."

The Basic Acting Techniques of the System

Relaxation, Concentration, and Public Solitude: Professional actors have to arrive at an organic, spontaneous, felt performance that is psychologically truthful and, most importantly, repeatable, even though no emotional moment is or ever can be repeated exactly. The framework that has been set up, including the blocking and the sequence of actions, is repeatable; however, these will be experienced differently every time, as the actor lives through them from moment to moment, concentrating on the task at hand.

The key that unlocks the door to the creative mood is *concentration*. The creative mood includes a desire to perform, a heightened awareness of the circumstances and the environment in which they unfold, energy directed to the performance, and the ability to have that sense of being alone (with your fellow actors) in a public place (the stage) that Stanislavsky called *public solitude*. By the use of concentration, actors can arouse the creative mood every single time they have to perform, whether they arrive at the theater feeling buoyant and wanting to act or not really wanting to be there.

This is how to concentrate: First of all, in order to shed life outside the theater and begin to relax physically, the actor, who should ideally arrive at the theater two hours before the performance, has to begin by centering his or her attention on the reality of the self; on the body's actual physical sensations and the mind's present, real thoughts; and on the environment backstage and in the dressing room. As the actor prepares by putting on costume and makeup, he or she should simultaneously prepare the character's inner life. Concentrate on the character's circumstances, which will have been thoroughly understood and rehearsed, and allow the imagination to revolve around the play. Concentration on the character's specific circumstances just before the first entrance—Where have I just come from? What have I just been doing? What is the first thing I want?—will solidify the actor's entering into the character, and the actor's impulses and instincts will by then have been aroused. And once the performance begins, the actor will find that he or she is almost automatically able to continue concentrating on the work. When you are concentrating and relaxed, you are alert at the same time and in the creative state that is the prerequisite for rehearsal and performance.

Stanislavsky talked about a *circle of concentration* that the actor builds around him- or herself. You can do this by concentrating on an *object of attention*, whether it is the actor you are playing opposite, a thought, or an external object such as the coffee cup you are supposed to be drinking from. You have to have a sense of privacy, of being as alone and unobserved as the character is—or thinks he or she is.

Relaxation when performing involves an absence of nervousness about performing accompanied by a readiness to perform. The actor is in a state of creative tension and heightened energy—the creative mood—that allows him or her to be free and flexible at every moment. Feeling the truth of what is happening, feeling the inner justification for what you are doing as the character, enables you to relax, quite literally, and to feel muscular flexibility that will enable you to respond to whatever happens. Although we know as actors what is coming next, we must appear not to know, not to anticipate, the next moment, since the character does not know what will take place. Concentration on living through the circumstances serves to prevent anticipation, which would be untruthful and unreal. If you think about it, we do not, in any case, really know what will happen next, no matter how much we may have rehearsed. The scenery could collapse, or the theater catch on fire.

One of the devices used to bring about that sense of being in private in a public place is called the *fourth wall:* that invisible, transparent partition through which the audience is watching the play. The term alludes to the proscenium stage sets in which a room consisted of three walls, with a missing fourth wall at the front of the stage. As an actor, you are free to help your concentration by furnishing the fourth wall with whatever object of attention might be on it: a mirror, a window, an oil portrait, furniture, the ocean you see from the deck of a ship, and so forth.

The convention of the fourth wall can be broken in certain period plays, from Shakespeare through nineteenth-century drama, with two other conventions: the *soliloquy* and the *aside* (see pages 140–141). The convention has also been broken in modern theater pieces, such as those of the Living Theater that include the audience in the action.

Communication: Relating, Listening, and Hearing: According to Stanislavsky, there are three categories of communication. First, you communicate directly with your fellow actors—you are in "communion" with them; second, you communicate directly with an object that is absent, as when you think of a loved one; and, third, you communicate indirectly with the audience, of whom you have to be aware, but who are never to be objects of your attention except when you address them directly, as in the conventional aside. On the stage, you have always to find your real object of attention, with which you communicate at any given moment, with or without words.

People can and do communicate wordlessly as well as verbally, and one can often sense another person's mood and feelings. You communicate in the way you look at someone or something, and your love or hate will be apparent. In order to do this, you must have developed the character's internal life, which will then also communicate itself to the indirect object of your attention: the audience.

On stage in 1971 in Ibsen's *A Doll's House*, Claire Bloom as Nora communicated with absolute clarity and specificity: I could read her thoughts as if I were reading a book, so complete was her internal life. The same thing was true of Vivien Leigh's performance as Anna Petrovna in John Gielgud's 1966 production of Chekhov's *Ivanov*. The effect was extraordinary. They were simply there, in the moment, and thinking the character's specific thoughts—all prepared for by hard, detailed, specific work. This kind of communication of a character's inner life is something for every actor to strive for.

It also shows us another difference between life on stage and real life: We go through life doing everything we have to do in a relatively unconscious manner. We routinely get up and make breakfast and perform our ablutions while thinking about other things, just as characters sometimes do. But on stage, we have to be more aware of the character's directed inner life and thoughts than we ever are of our own.

You do not act in a vacuum but with your fellow actors; therefore, you must learn to listen to them; to hear what they say and, importantly, how they say it—their intentions—and to respond as your character. You must relate to your fellow actors as people. And you must also relate to them as your character relates to their characters. Giving and receiving information is essential. Without that give and take, that "communion" with your fellow actors, as Stanislavsky called it, you cannot react or respond. You cannot be specific, and you cannot live in the moment.

Important Questions When You Listen: Did you understand what the other actor wanted to communicate (his or her intention)? What did he or she want from you? Did what the other person say really have an effect on you? Was it the effect the other person wanted, or its opposite?

Important Questions When You Communicate: What do you want to communicate (your intention)? Did what you say really have an effect on the other person? Did it have the effect you wanted, or its opposite?

We automatically, unconsciously react in life. And these reactions affect the way you as your character will proceed in the scene, because whether you got what you wanted or not, the scene, or at least the play, goes on, and the next thing in your character's life must be dealt with—unless, of course, it is your last scene in the play.

The "Magic If": All acting depends entirely on what Stanislavsky called in *My Life in Art* "the magical, creative *if.*" It is the first concept he discusses when describing the evolution of his system. Without it, in fact, there is no acting. You behave *as if* the character had a past and *as if* the character has a future, unless, of course, the character dies in the course of the play. But before that happens, you continue to behave *as if* it were not going to. And you behave *as if* events have taken place when the character is not there, between the scenes of the play, and *as if* you have reacted to those events. You have to act *as if* the present time in which the character lives is your own (it is, actually). Most important of all, you have to behave *as if* every moment had never happened before and were occurring spontaneously.

Using the "Magic If," I: The Imagination, Sense Memory, and Endowment: "Not a step should be taken on stage without the cooperation of your imagination," said Stanislavsky. It is through your imagination that you can enter into the life of the character, and into the character's mind and emotions.

One of the most important techniques of the imagination used in bringing a character to life and in allowing inspiration to function is the conscious use of affective memory, which is a kind of re-imagining. *Affective memory* means the visceral memory of emotions and feelings (emotional memory) and the memory of physical sensations: hot, cold, drunk, sick, tired, attracted to something or someone, and so forth (sense memory). Emotional and sense memories can overlap.

You can recall the melody of a beloved piece of music or the smell of coffee or the look on someone's face or any other kind of sense memory merely by conjuring up the sensory image of those things. So vivid and specific are these pictures that we react to them physically: we may beat time to music that is there only in our imaginations; or our mouths may begin to water as we remember that delectable dish we had at last night's or even last year's dinner; or we may begin to breathe hard and perspire at the terrifying image of a nightmare or the recollection of a traumatic or unpleasant event, or to smile and flush with pleasure at the image of a fulfilling daydream or fantasy of love. Such pictures either come from the willed or involuntary recollection of experience or are created anew from the recombination of experiential elements when we decide unconsciously that we desire or want something we don't yet have, or when we want to re-experience something, for whatever reasons. We don't always consciously know that we have made the decision to see something, but we clearly must have done so unconsciously, or the image would not have appeared to us.

And this faculty of being able to recall external stimuli and re-experience them even when they are not there is of paramount importance, and it is even heightened for actors, who can train themselves to use it— hence all the sense-memory exercises in acting classes that are meant to sensitize you. If you have to pretend to drink a hot cup of coffee when the actual cup is cold, you need sense memory, just as you do if you are supposed to be drunk or ill or in pain or basking in the sun when the only light is supplied by artificial stage lighting.

To do these things, you have to use the technique of *endowment*. An endowment is the attribution of particular qualities to an object or person. You then behave *as if* that object or person has those qualities: That (cold) coffee is hot! It's freezing (under those hot lights)! That whiskey (it's really cold tea) packs quite a punch! At this particular moment, that character behaves exactly like someone I know, and I react as I do in real life: the character has become that someone, but only for that moment, not for the entire play. If you have to lift a heavy suitcase that is in reality a stage prop with nothing in it, you have to endow it as being fully packed. How would your character lift it? If you are a spry athlete, you could lift it easily, but we in the audience still have to know it is heavy. If you are a weaker character, you might have difficulty getting it off the ground.

Using the "Magic If," II: Emotional Recall and Substitution: Emotional *recall* involves the idea that the actor needs to find emotional analogies drawn from his or her own experiences and then apply them to the character's experiences in order to grasp completely what is happening in the play. The actor's experiences are used as a rehearsal tool, as a way into playing the character. This process, called *substitution*, is partly unconscious and intuitive. Using substitution, the actor is able to behave as if the given circumstances in the play were real and as if they were his or her own. Stanislavsky says in *An Actor Prepares:*

> Once you have established this contact between your life and your part...you will see how easy it will be for you sincerely to believe in the possibility of what you are called upon to do on the stage.

The way it works is this: You think of a past experience and imaginatively project yourself into it, feeling as if you were actually involved in it, while doing the actions and saying the words of the script. If the character is waiting for some result, such as a verdict in a trial, then the substitution might consist of remembering the frustration you felt on a visit to the doctor when you were kept waiting for news of your health. If the character is in love, the actor substitutes someone he or she is or was in love with, endowing the other actor as if he or she were that person. But that is only a way into being in love with the character you are playing opposite. In performance, you have to forget the substitution and relate to your fellow actor. Every substitution is meant to bring the actor into the situation presented by the given circumstances.

CHAPTER TWO

Using the System: Script and Character Analysis; the Method of Physical Actions

Stanislavsky's Method of Script Analysis

First, read the play for its story. Look for the *facts* of what happens, what the characters do, and how the plot unfolds. The story includes everything that happened before the play began—the *before-time*. Look at the play's given circumstances: it is essential to understand its historical and sociocultural background and ethos. If you are unfamiliar with the period in which the play is set, you must begin now to study it, immerse yourself in it, and familiarize yourself with its history, manners, culture, clothing, style of movement, and behavior.

Next, break the story into major *episodes*. Give the episodes titles to help concretize them: "Hamlet sees the Ghost" in *Hamlet*, "The Gentleman Caller Visits" in *The Glass Menagerie*. What is the broad line of what happens in each episode? Break the episodes down into *events*. What happens in each event? The episodes and events constitute the *external circumstances* of the play.

Here is an analysis of the first episode of *Uncle Vanya*, which corresponds to act 1, followed by a list of the events in it:

> "The Fateful Meeting": In the garden near the Professor's house, Astrov meets Yelena for the first time, and they are attracted to each other. (Dr. Astrov has been sent for to minister to the ailing Professor, who is married to Yelena. They are spending the summer on the Professor's estate, inherited from his first wife.)
>
> 1. "Waiting and Reminiscing": Astrov waits outdoors for the return of the Professor, Yelena, and Sonya (the Professor's daughter by his first marriage) from their walk, and he passes the time reminiscing with the old Nurse, who has prepared tea for the family.

2. "Jealousy Revealed": Vanya (Sonya's uncle and the estate manager), comes out of the house, having just awakened from a nap. He and Astrov talk. Vanya's sarcastic, disapproving attitude toward the Professor and his obvious feelings for Yelena are clear.

3. "The Return and Taking Tea: Making Connections": The family returns from the walk. The Professor goes in, asking that his tea be served in his study. The rest take tea outdoors; Maman (Vanya's mother) reads her political pamphlets. She criticizes Vanya for having lost his ideals. Astrov tries to connect with Yelena, to whom he is attracted, by interesting her in his ecological ideas, offering to show her the local forest preserve. Sonya, in love with Astrov, enthusiastically supports the doctor's philosophy, but Vanya makes fun of him, knowing he will get his goat. The company disperses.

4. "Love Rejected": When they are alone together, Vanya renews his vows of love for Yelena, who can't stand it and flees into the house.

Next, break the story into smaller, more manageable, easily studied *units*, such as the different happenings in event 3 above. But as Stanislavsky warned, "Do not break up a play more than is necessary." Keep the big picture in mind even when studying the units. Examine the play scene by scene in order. What happens in each scene? What happens between the scenes—the *between-time*?

Stanislavsky would want to know what was at the heart of a play, the things without which its story would not exist. If Hamlet's father had not been murdered, and if Hamlet had not been called upon to avenge the murder, there would be no play. If Richard, Duke of Gloucester, did not desire the crown, Shakespeare's *Richard III* would not exist. If Nora had not lied to protect her husband, the story of *A Doll's House* would not happen. Stanislavsky would examine the other elements necessary to the story: Claudius's desire for the throne and for Gertrude, the unstable political situation in England during the Wars of the Roses, Helmer's rigidity and obtuseness. And he would take note of the general impression the play made on him, of its atmosphere and moods.

Finally, examine your character's place and role in the story. You can then describe the episodes and events as briefly as possible from your point of view. For instance, if you were playing Astrov in *Uncle Vanya*, you might say, "This is the episode where I meet Yelena, and I am immediately attracted to her. This is the event in that episode where I try to connect with her. How do I do that specifically? I launch into a speech about the Russian forests falling under the axe. I invite her to go with me the next day to see what is going on for herself."

After understanding the story, Stanislavsky could trace its *throughline*, also called the *throughline of action*, which is the main thrust of the action as it proceeds from its beginning to its end. The throughline is analogous to a road along which you travel: it will take you where you want to go. You may pause or turn aside, but you must always resume the journey along that road.

Stanislavsky would then begin to understand the author's themes and the superobjective. The *superobjective* is the main theme, giving the play its overall meaning. It is the play's subject and its main philosophical or moral point. The themes give the play its life and reason for being. What is the playwright trying to say? Why did he or she write the play?

A play also has a *counter-throughline*. The throughline, which leads to the fulfillment of the superobjective, is opposed by actions that constitute a counter-throughline. The throughline is represented by the protagonist, and the counter-throughline by the antagonist. Hamlet is opposed by Claudius, whose actions counter his. Iago represents the counter-throughline for all the other characters in *Othello*.

Stanislavsky informs us in *Creating a Role* (Theatre Arts Books, 1961) that a play exists on many interrelated "planes":

1. The "external" plane, discussed above: the events, facts, and so forth.

2. The "social" plane, which includes sociocultural and historical facts and background, such as nationality and social class.

3. The "literary" plane, which includes the playwright's style, and the language.

4. The "aesthetic" plane, having to do with the production elements, such as costumes and scenery.

5. The "internal" plane, which informs the external plane and constitutes the characters' inner lives and psychology: their goals, objectives, tasks, and motivations.

6. The "physical" plane, which includes external physical characterization—the "plastic" of the character, meaning the way the character

looks (helped by costume and makeup), moves, and talks. The plastic of a role is ideally the logical, organic result of psychological processes, and has to do with the character's social class, upbringing, profession, age, sex, state of health, and sometimes national and cultural attitudes. The plastic features of a role are also determined by genre and by style: people in a farce will often be required to move quite differently from people in a Shakespearean tragedy; and period styles are of paramount importance for behavior, deportment, movement, and appearance.

An example of the plastic of a character is provided by Stanislavsky himself: in descriptions of his portrayal of Dr. Stockman in Ibsen's *An Enemy of the People*, we read that he modeled the character physically on several people. The makeup was drawn from portraits of the composer Nicolai Rimsky-Korsakov (1844–1908). His idiosyncratic walk—neck and chest thrust forward because of myopia—was in imitation of people he had observed in the street. And his gesture of sawing the air with his right hand—thumb extended, forefinger and middle finger held together—was taken from those the realist playwright Maxim Gorky (1868–1936) used when making a point. Another example is provided by Henry Irving, whose somewhat eccentric walk on stage (as opposed to his normal walk in real life) has often been described: he virtually danced his way through roles, moving as the character, and calculating movements and steps in a technical way, despite his realistic approach to character creation.

All these planes are conditioning factors, but not all of them are "immediately accessible," nor are they all of equal importance for an actor creating a character. But "eventually all of the planes coalesce in our creative feelings and presentation."

Studying the Character: What to Look For and How to Approach the Role

The system of analyzing a character follows the same basic procedure as that for analyzing the play: the role is broken down into its components, then put together again. When you first approach the role, as Stanislavsky points out in *An Actor Prepares*, you must gather together and study "all the materials that have any bearing on it," including information on the historical epoch in which the play is set. Use your imagination continually as you work, projecting yourself more and more into the given circumstances in order to make them come alive. "In the beginning, forget about your feelings. When the inner conditions are prepared, feelings will come to the surface of their own accord."

Objectives: An *objective* is what the character wants: the character's goal; the character's aim; the problem the character has to solve. The character has an objective in each scene, as well as an overall objective: the superobjective.

What does Hamlet want? He says he wants to avenge his father's murder. He then proceeds to do everything but that. In fact, he avoids taking revenge and does nothing about carrying out his stated purpose, aside from killing Polonius by mistake, until the end of the play. We are entitled to assume that there is an unconscious objective standing in the way of his conscious, stated goal—or perhaps a number of them. According to Ernest Jones, in *Hamlet and Oedipus* (Doubleday & Co., 1949), Hamlet's Oedipus complex interferes with his stated desires. Unconscious motivations play an even greater part in characters' objectives than conscious motivations, just as they do in real life.

And just like people in real life, characters are always involved with the past, the present, and the future. The past has shaped them and conditioned their behavior. They want something and they go after it, or they don't, and this behavior determines future possibilities.

Objectives, says Stanislavsky, should be clear-cut and active. They are a result of the character's thoughts, will, and feelings; therefore, they should propel the character forward. An objective should be personal, specific, dynamic, and alive; something that has value for the character and that the character really wants; something magnetic; something expressed in terms of an active verb: "I want to ____." Objectives should attract the actor, as well as the character, so that the actor really wants to go after them.

Some of the important questions in regard to objectives are as follows:

1. What do you want—specifically?
2. How much do you (the character) want something—that is, how much importance does it have for you? A simple, small physical task or problem (two of Stanislavsky's other words for "objective"), such as getting a glass of water, is not interesting: it is merely there. A pang of thirst must be satisfied; it is a temporary

and insignificant need or want, unless you are lost in a desert, when it may assume overwhelming importance. But the desire to fulfill love or to attain power—ah, that is the stuff from which stories are made. Since we all want love and power, those stories continue to engross us and to hold the stage, whether they are ancient Greek tragedies, Shakespearean dramas, or Wilde's nineteenth-century comedies.

3. What is your opinion of the person from whom you want something? How much do you respect that person? If you are in love, you already know something about what you want, but what are your basic opinions about that love object? The answers will condition the way you behave: they will determine how you go after what you want.

4. How much do you feel entitled to have what you want?

Every character throughout a script is maneuvering and manipulating and attempting to control the situation he or she is in. Everyone wants to feel justified. Everyone wants to survive. In the case of people or characters who commit suicide, survival is no longer a viable option, as they see it. But even in committing suicide, people often want something besides ending an untenable situation: Constantine's vengeful message to the other characters in *The Seagull* is, "You will finally realize how you have failed me, and you will be as unhappy as I have been!"

Stanislavsky analyzed scenes in terms of who was leading the scene and who was following or being led: one of the characters in a two-character scene wants the scene to take place, in pursuit of an objective, and the other character is involved without having willed the scene to happen. In the last scene of act 1 in *Uncle Vanya*, Vanya wants to tell Yelena how much he adores her. Vanya is leading the scene, which would not take place without him, and Yelena is forced to respond.

A character may be a leader in one scene and a follower in another. In act 3 of *Uncle Vanya*, Vanya is the follower in the scene where the Professor, who leads the scene, has summoned the family in order to hold a conference on the future of the estate.

Obstacles: An *obstacle* is something that is in a character's way, preventing him or her from accomplishing an objective. The obstacle may be internal (psychological) or external; it may be physical; it may be another character. Without obstacles, there is no play, because there is no conflict. There is no place for the character to go, nothing to fight against.

Working on the obstacles to a character's objectives is imperative. What they are may not always be obvious, particularly if they are internal and unconscious. Also, since obstacles come not only from inside ourselves but also from external circumstances and other characters, we cannot know what they are fully without working with the other actors, who will surprise us by what they do to get what they want and for whom we may constitute an obstacle.

When trying to surmount obstacles, you can never behave as if the game is lost in advance. Nobody does in real life. Where there's a will, there's a way, and you have to find it. If we in the audience perceive Vanya's love for Yelena as hopeless, he doesn't. On the contrary, he lives in hope, until he is rudely disillusioned in act 3 by the shock of seeing Astrov and Yelena kissing.

Physical, Psychological, and Verbal Actions: An *action* is something a character does at a specific moment in furtherance of an objective. Actions may be verbal: each utterance has an intention and is designed to accomplish something. They may be actual external physical actions, such as embracing the person one loves. Actions may be internal: something that is going on in the character's mind. They are experienced in the form of an *interior monologue*, which is a running series of thoughts that may or may not lead to external action—should I or shouldn't I do something?

Maureen Stapleton as Amanda Wingfield in the first Broadway revival of Tennessee Williams's *The Glass Menagerie* in 1965 sat immobile on the tatty, faded couch in her shabby living room. Stanislavsky wrote in *An Actor Prepares*, "Frequently physical immobility is the direct result of inner intensity." She was just thinking, and we in the audience could see that she was miserable. And we supplied her thoughts for ourselves; we interpreted her expression. Her internal action, her inner life, and her intensity were riveting, because she was dynamic and full of energy even though she never uttered a word and never moved. She wanted to be happy; she wanted to be surrounded by a happy family and admirers, just as she had been when she was a girl, before everything went wrong and she married beneath her station and lost everything. She wanted to return to that state of bliss that the infant experiences before it knows any better, before it detaches itself from its parents and begins to become an individual, the state Freud talks about as "primary narcissism." In short, she wanted the impossible. The obstacles to her happiness were internal as well as external: her own inability to cope with the reality she found so distressing and distasteful, the shabby gentility in which her economic circumstances had forced her to live. And her psychophysical action in that moment was simply "to sit there and think." What would she do next?

The *method of physical actions* involves the actor doing a necessary series of specific actions in order to achieve something the character desires; and the actions are not to be done mechanically, but with real purpose. At the same time, once again, the actor must not worry about feelings or emotions, but trust that they will be aroused when the action is performed. For instance, if Romeo is determined to see Juliet, he has to overcome the obstacles that are in his way: he must climb the garden wall; creep across the open lawn until he finds someplace to conceal himself, since he would be in danger if he is noticed; actually proceed to conceal himself; and bide his time. When Juliet appears on her balcony and he hears how she feels, he knows he can safely approach her, but he has to climb up the balcony, and he might be observed, so he has to climb quickly yet carefully.

Romeo has always to ask himself in the situation in which he finds himself, "What would happen if...?" For example: "If I were caught by Capulet; if I made noise and he heard me and came after me...would I have to fight him? What would I do? Would I fight, or would I run away?" This inner life and these real considerations lend reality to the actions and condition how they are played.

In *The Seagull*, Arkadina is bandaging her son Constantine's head, and she is full of rage, so the manner in which she carries out the action is far from calm. Her impatience and fury, her anger at her son, shows in her manner and in how she deals with the material objects—the props—so that the audience clearly sees what is going on in her mind. In Stanislavsky's elaborate plan for the 1898 production, he has Arkadina impatiently tapping her foot and sometimes dealing a bit roughly with the bandage. Her objective is to try to repair the damage not only to his head but to their wounded relationship, but she is nearly incapable of understanding him and his aspirations, and she feels that he despises her. That feeling is an inner obstacle to her objective, the desired reconciliation. The thought "He is impossible" keeps interfering with what she tells herself she wants.

Actions that are externally static—for instance, waiting to hear a verdict or news from a doctor—nevertheless involve internal tension, and they have a tempo and rhythm of their own. Actions that are externally dynamic, such as fighting a duel, also have an internal aspect, and an inner as well as an outer rhythm. You will find these rhythms, and emotions, as you do the actions.

Verbal actions, which are done with the voice, involve the desire to communicate something to someone in a specific way—that is, with a specific intention. You can use the playwright's punctuation as a guide: it provides clues to intentions and subtextual meaning. For instance, in act 1 of *The Seagull*, Masha says to Dr. Dorn, "I want to tell you—I—I wanted to before. I have to talk to someone . . . (*Agitatedly*.) I dislike my father . . . but I—I like you a great deal." What did Chekhov mean to convey with those dashes and suspension marks? What do they tell you about Masha's action and how to play it? The punctuation tells you all you need to know to figure out the subtext and Masha's interior monologue here. Even a comma or a semicolon can be important: Stanislavsky wrote that taking the slight pause indicated by a comma "can make people listen to you." He always emphasized the fact that vocal technique—which includes knowing when and how much to stress certain words in order to have an effect on the other character—is essential. Once again, you can use the playwright's punctuation as a guide. In general, you should not have to think about such things as which words to stress. But there are times when you must. When you do, they must always come from an inner feeling and an inner logic and become organic.

The Throughline, the Counter-Throughline, and the Superobjective: Just as a play has all these elements, so does a character. Stanislavsky makes clear in *An Actor Prepares* that the superobjective is "life-giving" and unifying, and that if an actor has not found the character's "ultimate purpose," all the actions will be disjointed, fragmentary, and unrelated to a central idea: the actor will go off the road and make detours that are meaningless. Each particular action may be well performed, but if there is no overall purpose towards which they tend, there is no shape to the part, and no play.

What is driving the character overall? What does the character want out of life?

Hamlet's endless ruminating and philosophizing are verbal actions "that a man might play." The ruminations serve to solve problems in the short term, and sometimes to avoid fulfilling his stated objective. His objective in a particular speech might be stated as "I want to understand" or "I want to decide." Hamlet's superobjective, on which all his speeches depend, may be "to understand life and what we human beings, including me, are all about; to know what the idea of destiny means and what is the correct, moral course."

In Ibsen's *A Doll's House*, the superobjective of the play is "to establish women's inalienable right to absolute equality with men." Nora's throughline is that she tries everything to get her husband to see reason and treat her as an equal marriage partner, but she does it obliquely and constantly accommodates him, not daring to state her case. The ambivalence that causes her discomfort and that results in her lack of daring is an internal obstacle.

The counter-throughline is represented by the general societal pressure to conform and fulfill the role society has decreed for your gender, no matter what the adverse circumstances of the marriage might be. This external pressure forces Nora to try to adjust to her situation, to be accommodating, and to give in against her true desires. Helmer's actions throughout, as he treats his wife like a little doll, not taking her seriously as a human being, are part of the play's counter-throughline.

Nora's superobjective is to have the freedom to be who she is as a person. Eventually, she discovers the necessity to be assertive and to make clear to her husband what she needs and desires, and then to take the consequences.

Bits: Finding the Subtext, Understanding the Intentions, and Scoring the Actions and the Beats: Stanislavsky used the word *bit* to mean the small unit of a scene during which an action is played out. A *beat* is the beginning of a new action. When one action stops, another immediately begins.

You can write out a *score*, which is a list of the beats—the actions you do—in each scene, in the order in which you do them. This will help you find the throughline.

You have to consider the character's individual intentions. With what specific intention do you say something? Are you merely passing the time in polite conversation? Do you wish to convey by your tone of voice how you feel about your interlocutor? Are you ordering someone to do something? The lines are there to help fulfill what the character wants. Remember, too, that words may conceal as well as reveal.

You want to avoid preconceptions and calculated line readings. The words should arise organically from the situation. How they are said is not something that should be predetermined. Predetermined readings are mechanical and stifling. Stanislavsky was against them, although when an actor was stuck, he would resort to a discussion of which words to emphasize and how to read a line.

Activities: Activities, also called *stage business*, are physical tasks that reinforce the psychological objectives, to which they are secondary. They constitute the character's physical life. And they arise logically out of the given circumstances of the play. Do not confuse them with the character's objective(s).

If a physical action becomes the primary objective in a scene, it is no longer an activity; it is an action. When Romeo climbs the garden wall and hides, what he does is a psychophysical action in furtherance of his objective, not a secondary activity that he might or might not do if he wished. But when the French princess works at her embroidery while Henry V is wooing her, she is performing an activity. The manner in which she embroiders may say much about her inner state.

In Chekhov's plays, there are always many activities either directly stated in the text or implied in it. In *Uncle Vanya* there is all the activity revolving around the samovar in act 1. Maman reads her pamphlets, which is her action, her way of escaping while remaining there as the others sit or stand around talking. Taking tea is her activity. In *The Seagull*, the workmen are finishing their job of constructing the makeshift stage at the opening of act 1, and this is their physical action, not simply an activity, because their psychological objective is to get the work done so they can go for a swim in the lake.

The Physicality of the Character: Voice and Movement: Tommaso Salvini said, "All you need is the voice—voice, voice and more voice." Stanislavsky always stressed that it was by means of the word, of language, that the character's objective would be fulfilled. He said, "An actor above all must operate through words. On stage the only important thing is the active word." The psychophysical verbal action, the *active word*, is part of the character's behavior as much as nonverbal physical actions are. If you play Shakespeare, you must speak the words beautifully and find the correct verbal action. You must give the lines in any kind of play shadings, nuances, mood, coloration, emotional reality, and energy, all of which should ideally arise organically, without your having to do anything preconceived or intellectually conceptualized. The words you say are the result of thought processes; they are the expression of the character's will and desires.

The physicality of a character, too, should be organic and not preconceived or calculated. A certain physicality may be immediately suggested by the character: Richard III's crippled gait; the stately, dignified movement of Julius Caesar; the gracefulness and agility of Juliet.

But these do not have to be predetermined. There are actors who work on this aspect of a character first, as Olivier often did. But even he, who was known for taking great pains over a character's appearance, wrote in his book *On Acting* (Sceptre, 1986) "[looks] must come from the head and the heart first."

Tempo, Rhythm, and Timing: Internal and external tempi work together simultaneously. A character may be hurrying physically but thinking of something slowly. Or a character may be walking slowly, or even standing still, and thinking rapidly. The combination of opposite tempi lends immediacy and reality to a scene; they should be organic, not predetermined.

Tempo and rhythm have to do not only with pace but with the way in which a scene, and the play as a whole, build to a climax. Pauses are included in tempo, as they are in music, and the beats in a scene are, in a sense, musical beats. It is essential that all pauses be filled with life—namely, the character's internal life. As Stanislavsky stressed, a pause, which is an action, must always be justified, motivated, and logical, like all actions.

Correct timing, which includes pacing, tempo, and rhythm, is one of the two essential components of comedy style, the other being absolute realism of intentions. Cyril Ritchard (1898–1977) was a master of comic timing. As General Burgoyne in the 1970 American Shakespeare Festival production of Shaw's *The Devil's Disciple*, he could elicit two or even three laughs on a line where another actor might get only one. He would stop speaking at the end of a clause as if he had finished a thought, and the audience would laugh. At the right moment, just when the laughter was dying down, he would say the rest of the sentence, as if he had just thought of it as an addendum to his previous thought, and the audience would burst out laughing again. He never telegraphed the joke. And although he knew he was funny, he never let the audience know he knew: he was always deadly serious, unless the character was supposed to be knowingly witty.

The Method of Physical Actions: An Actor's Step-by-Step Guide to Analyzing and Working on the Character

Some of the steps in this schematic outline will take place simultaneously; for instance, relationships should be considered along with objectives. Even though you will do the preliminary work on the script by yourself, the intellectual work and character analysis that allow you to know the character's biography, psychological history, and beliefs will only take you so far—to the door of the rehearsal studio, in fact. It is only in rehearsal with the other actors that you will really find your character, as you *discover through doing*. While you are doing the work, allow your imagination to work with *affective memory*, both emotion and sense memory, using substitution and endowment as necessary. Leave room for revelations that will come out of your unconscious mind. Remain open. Allow feelings to happen.

Steps 2, 3 and 4 are the heart and soul of the *method of physical actions* of character creation. Objectives and obstacles must be determined and actions decided upon, not only for the play as a whole, but for each unit in it. The basic method is as follows: analyze and define the given circumstances, find the objective, find the actions taken to fulfill it, then bring the actions to life by doing them.

1. First, read the play in the way suggested at the beginning of this chapter.

2. Define the *facts* that are the *given circumstances* for your character: place, time, weather, historical epoch, and all the circumstances that go with them. You begin to answer the question *"Who am I, the character?"* What are the character's age, state of health, profession, economic circumstances, marital status, living arrangements, educational background, religious beliefs, and political ideas? Is the character pessimistic or optimistic? How does he or she feel about sex and sexuality, his or her own and other people's? What is going on with the character emotionally? Analyze each event provisionally in terms of your character's general *inner life* and *state of mind* during the event. Be open to the answers changing as you explore these aspects of the character in rehearsal.

3. Determine provisionally the character's *objectives* (Stanislavsky also used the words *wishes, aim, goal, problem,* and *task*) and *obstacles* (which are part of the *counter-throughline*). What is the character's *superobjective*—that is, what does the character want overall as a general life objective (provisionally defined at this point in the work)?

4. What *actions* does the character take? Think in terms of verbs: I fight a duel. I propose marriage. I threaten, I scold, I make love,

I plan a battle, I organize an event, I go swimming. Why do you do any of these things? How or why is the action motivated by the inner state? In what order are the actions done?

5. In order to determines the character's objective(s) and actions, begin to analyze the *relationships* with the other characters. What does your character want from each of the other characters? How does your character feel about each of the other characters? How well does your character understand the other characters? How well does your character understand him- or herself? Does the character relate well to him- or herself—that is, does the character have a good self-image? How does your character relate to other people (loving, needy, giving, taking, dominating, submissive, masochistic, complaining, sadistic, sarcastic, seductive, dismissive, withdrawn, shy, timid, outgoing, extroverted, controlling, manipulative)?

6. *Read and analyze each scene*, in order, in which your character appears. You can give the scene a title, just as you do the episodes, or describe the scene briefly: "This is the scene where I ____."

7. What happened before the scene began—the *before-time*?

8. The following elements are included in your *entrance into a scene:* Before you enter, you should know where you are, where you have just been, and what you have just been doing. What do you immediately want when you enter? What is the *moment of orientation*—that is, the moment in which you orient yourself to where you are and to the other character, if that character is present on stage as you enter, or to the other character or characters when they enter? If you are already in the place, what is your immediate want in that place at the point in time where you are in the scene?

9. Break the scenes down into smaller units, which are the *beats* in the scene from your point of view (they will be different and individual for every character). What does your character *do* in each scene (the *actions*)? What is the character's *objective* in each scene (provisionally defined)? What are the *obstacles* for the character in each scene? What is the *moment of absorption*, when you take everything in, seeing if you have had the effect you want to have and if you have attained your immediate objective for each scene? What is the *moment of reversal*—that

is, the moment when the beat changes because you are continuing to pursue the objective, and you take a step backward, as it were, to regroup? When does one beat changes to the next beat?

10. Who is the *leader* in the scene and who is the *follower*? Which is your character? (A character may lead in one scene and follow in another; see page 36.)

11. What is the *spine* of the scene—the *throughline of action* that drives each scene—from your character's point of view?

12. What are the *activities* in the scene? How is the activity integrated into the scene? When do you perform the activity, and in what manner?

13. Explore the *relationships* further. What does your character want in each of the relationships with the characters in each scene? Does the character succeed in getting what he or she wants in each scene? What does the character do when he or she does or does not attain an objective?

14. What happens to your character after the scene ends—the *after-time*?

15. What happens in the time between the scenes when the character is offstage—the *between-time*?

16. Consider further the *intentions* of the lines, which will have been organic (unconscious) but may have had to be studied individually if you have a problem. All the psychophysical actions require *justification*; if you have not justified the actions and intentions logically, you will immediately have the impulse to do so.

17. As a result of the previous steps, you will be able to begin to determine more clearly the character's underlying, subtextual, unconscious *motivations* and *ambivalences*, which will add depth to your characterization as they gradually dawn on you and emerge because of your work on the script.

18. The character's *physicality*—appearance and way of moving, talking, and gesturing—should have emerged spontaneously as a result of the process. Does the character have a particularity, such as Richard III's humpback or Cyrano de Bergerac's large nose? Is the character vain about his or her looks, and does this influence how the character moves and walks? Is the character athletic, spry, limber, or slow with heavy movements? How does the character wear his or her hair? Is the character comfortable

or uncomfortable in his or her clothing? How has period clothing conditioned movement?

19. As a result of the rehearsal process, you will be able to *score* the actions and the beats in each scene. And you will allow yourself to "forget" what you have chosen (because it has been assimilated and absorbed into the preconscious area of the unconscious) as you act organically when you actually perform the rehearsed piece, at which point all the work on the role is pushed away from conscious awareness and acting it—performing it—takes over.

20. By this time, too, you will have found the correct *rhythm* and *tempo* for each scene and for the play as a whole. This means that once you begin performing, you will find these things there for you.

Ideally, your lines will simply stay with you, as a result of the process. But in professional working situations, you are often asked to come into rehearsal with the lines already memorized, partly because of time considerations. Every actor will have his or her own way of doing this, but it is still a good idea not to predetermine, calculate, or set line readings, but to wait to listen to the other actors.

Adding Dimension to Psychophysical Actions and Character: The Technique of Playing Opposites

Stanislavsky put it succinctly in *My Life in Art:* "When you play a good man look for the places where he is evil, and in an evil man look for the places where he is good." This creates reality and a contrast that Stanislavsky called *heroic tension*—that is, the existence of contradictory positive and negative character traits, desires, and impulses even in a heroic character. Also, find the moments that are opposite to a character's usual way of behaving. When is Hamlet jocose or jubilant as opposed to serious or melancholy?

"A man may smile and smile, and be a villain," remarks Hamlet of Claudius. This is a good indication as to how to play some of Claudius's actions when he is in public, making speeches to the court or attending the play within the play. His ingratiating manners and nods to courtiers that flatter their vanity are an important part of how he maintains power. If he were merely horrible, he would be overthrown in a minute.

He has to be charming and even seductive in order to attract the support of his courtiers, not to mention Gertrude, who has indeed found him so and whose relationship with him is based on sexual attraction. And he is a murderer who acts as if he has not committed any crime.

"Playing opposites" also means juxtaposing two contrary impulses and playing them at the same time, as in the phrase "smiling through tears." As Theodore Roosevelt famously said, "Speak softly and carry a big stick." Threatening someone in low tones, instead of screaming at them; crying at a wedding because you are so happy; laughing when you are frustrated or resentful—this is how we actually behave, very often.

Playing opposites arises organically when an emotion is threatening in some way to the person who feels it. The emotion therefore has to be suppressed. Someone may, for instance, act as if he or she is quite well when we can see that the person feels ill, or be cold and hateful to a person he or she secretly loves in order to avoid the disappointment of a feared rejection. Or someone may smile and hold him- or herself back because of really wanting to assault the person he or she is talking with. This attempt to control oneself and situations is behavior that we see all the time: playing opposites adds reality to the playing of actions.

In *The Merchant of Venice*, Shylock, before telling Antonio that he will lend him the three thousand ducats, confronts the merchant with the way he has treated him. "Many a time and oft on the Rialto, you have rated me," he begins, and perhaps he has a smile on his face and speaks in a low tone of voice, because he does not dare to scream in rage at his persecutor, whose treatment he bitterly and deeply resents.

George Henry Lewes describes the playing of Charles Matthews (1803–1878), a Victorian actor with "an innate sense of elegance" and a mastery of playing opposites. In the role of an aristocratic villain in *The Day of Reckoning*, "a French melodrama never worth much, even on the Boulevards," Matthews played the part of a man "destitute alike of principle and of feeling, the incarnation of heartless elegance, cool yet agreeable.... Instead of 'looking the villain,' he looked like the man to whom all drawing-rooms would be flung open." And in *The Game of Speculation*, another forgotten Victorian melodrama, the "artistic merit" of his performance "was so great that it almost became an offense against morality, by investing a swindler with irresistible charms, and making the very audacity of deceit a source of pleasurable sympathy."

Ambiguity and ambivalence represent inner conflict: if you feel one way about something, assume you feel the opposite way as well. People's motivations are ambivalent. Ambivalence is unconscious: love

and hate exist side by side. Vanya unconsciously hates Yelena for reject-
ing him, so he tortures her by continuing to tell her about his love for
her. Yelena does not hate Vanya completely because she is flattered by
his attentions, however impossible she finds him.

Ambiguity is ambivalence made conscious. People are consciously
ambiguous in their attitudes: they want something but are afraid to go
after what they want. One reason may be that they are unconsciously
ambivalent about the consequences of having it. Exploring the ambivalence and ambiguity of a character's motivations will add depth and
reality to your portrayal. To put it another way, what is the correct
psychophysical action to play? In order to get what he or she wants, a
villain may behave in a charming and ingratiating fashion, but when the
time comes, the true nature of the character is bound to be revealed.

Using the Method of Physical Actions:
Analyzing and Playing Scenes

The same method of analysis, the same basic procedure of deconstruction followed by reconstruction set out previously for plays and characters also applies to scene analysis:

1. Read the scene through for its *story*.
2. What happened before the scene began that led to it—the
    before-time?
3. What is the *main event* in the scene?
4. Who is *leading* the scene and who is *following*? That is, who is
    the catalyst for the scene? At whose instigation or behest is it
    taking place? Who wants it to happen: you or the other charac-
    ter?
5. Where does the scene *take place*?
6. What are the other *given circumstances*—time of day, weather,
    your physical condition?
7. What does your character actually do—the *actions*?
8. What is your character doing just before entering into the scene?
    Where have you come from, and how did you get there?
9. What is the *moment of orientation* when you enter the scene?
10. What is the first thing you want?

11. What do you want in the scene overall—your *objective*?

12. What is in the way—the *obstacle(s)*?

13. What are the *beats*—that is, where does your small objective, on the way to the larger one, change—the *moment(s) of absorption* and the *moment(s) of reversal*—as you meet the small or large obstacles? You have to play each beat from moment to moment, without anticipating the next beat.

14. What do you do at each change of beat? What new action do you take? You discover much of this in the course of working with the other actors in the scene.

15. Do you attain your objective by the end of the scene?

16. Whether you reach your goal or not, what do you do next—the scene's *after-time*?

17. What happens between the scenes—the *between-time*?

Your playing of the beats involves your paying attention to the other actors: listening not only to what they say but to the way they say it, and gauging the effect of what you have said to them. That is the moment of absorption, of seeing if you have had the effect you want in order to obtain your objective, or if you will have to try another approach involving a new and different action.

It is important to understand as well that each character has his or her own set of beats, and that the beats in a scene are therefore different for each character. This difference is one of the things that gives the scene its life.

Vasili Toporkov, a Moscow Art Theatre actor who worked with Stanislavsky on several productions, has left a fascinating account of what Stanislavsky was like as a director: *Stanislavsky in Rehearsal* (Routledge, 2004). Mikhail Bulgakov's adaptation of Nikolai Gogol's *Dead Souls* was one of the great productions he oversaw—it was directed by someone else, but under Stanislavsky's supervision. Toporkov played the leading role of the swindler, Chichikov.

Before serfdom was abolished in Tsarist Russia in 1861, there was a census of serfs every ten, or sometimes twenty, years. Owners had to pay taxes on every serf on the census list up until the next census, even on those serfs who had died; they could not be removed from the list until the next census. On the other hand, owners could borrow money using the serfs as collateral, and they did this even using the names of the dead ones in order to obtain larger loans.

Chichikov has thought up a fantastic, preposterous scheme: with the little money he has, he travels around the country buying up lists of dead serfs at reduced rates, thus saving their owners from paying the government tax. He plans to become rich by taking out loans on the dead serfs, whom he will pass off as still alive. He will then buy land. Along the way, he is obliged to bribe government officials, who realize what he is doing, and to pull the wool over the eyes of the dead serfs' owners.

Chichikov is a very difficult role because it is so repetitious: in scene after scene, he is trying to buy up those dead souls from "a gallery of typical Gogol characters," who can become far more interesting to the audience than he is, even though the story revolves around him. Stanislavsky asked searching questions that made Toporkov think of all that was motivating Chichikov, all the subtlest aspects of his desires. What would you do, Stanislavsky wanted to know, if you were in Chichikov's shoes and you wanted to make a profit? And he told Toporkov he would have to learn how to bargain, even if that was alien to his own nature. He would have to learn what bargaining was all about. And he would have to assess every character he wanted dead souls from so that he would know exactly how to bargain with that person specifically. This would add variety to what could otherwise be a series of monotonous conversations. And this is also the way such a con man works. He is a master psychologist and knows how to control and manipulate people. He has an endless variety of tricks up his sleeve, and he keeps them in reserve for when he needs them.

In the first scene, Chichikov wants to talk with a government official whom he has followed to the restaurant where he is dining. He wants him to stay, and he wants to get him interested in talking with him. Therefore, he goes through a series of maneuvers designed to keep him there. The actor/character had to perform truthfully a logical series of physical actions that would awaken complicated feelings and emotions and keep him alive in the circumstances of the role. "In life," said Stanislavsky, "if you really needed to stop him, you would." And he told Toporkov, "Every physical action must be dynamic, and lead to the accomplishment of some goal or other, and that includes every line you speak on stage."

In *Stanislavsky: A Biography* (Routledge, 1990), Jean Benedetti has published a section of the prompt books of Stanislavsky's 1904 production plan for *The Cherry Orchard*, which he directed before he had even come up with his system. He set forth in detail exactly what the actors were supposed to do in psychophysical terms, and he goes so far as to give characters a psychological background based in childhood experience—a very Freudian approach.

He even gives directions about tone of voice and audibility. When the nearly impoverished Madame Ranevskaya asks Lopahin if her beloved cherry orchard has been sold, Stanislavsky has Lopahin—the former serf on the estate, whom she knew as a boy and who has now turned entrepreneur—examine his handkerchief, look down, and pause briefly before answering "guiltily" that "It has." When she then asks in a voice that is "barely audible" who bought it and Lopahin tells her he did, shouting the line, she "sinks down and remains in that position for some time." Lopahin, even more embarrassed, "pulls at his handkerchief" as the situation grows even more awkward. Soon, "he tears his handkerchief in two and flings it away."

Stanislavsky continues to describe all the characters' feelings, and their actions, based on his own visualization of everything that was happening in the scene. The actions and the use of props are all motivated. Later in his career as a director, when he had ceased to dictate such things to his actors, he might have allowed the actors playing Ranevskaya and Lopahin to find such stage business on their own and to say the lines as they wished. Perhaps the use of a handkerchief is not really necessary, for instance, and indeed it feels a bit obvious, tacked on, and even amateurish when you read about it, although it could certainly work in performance.

The Opening Lines of Othello

The physical actions listed below in brackets are based on Stanislavsky's direction in the prompt books that have been translated and published in *Stanislavsky Produces Othello* (Geoffrey Bles, 1948); those actions in quotation marks are directly from the prompt books. He goes into great technical detail on the physical aspects of the 1929 production, by which time the system had been well thought out, and also into rich psychological detail about who the characters are and what they are thinking about.

The political, historical background for this play involves the war between the Ottoman Turks and the Venetian Republic, run autocratically by the Doge and the Council of Senators. The Turks are an immediate danger to the republic in 1570–71. As we learn shortly into the play, the council has had to summon the great general Othello to take command in besieged Cyprus, a Venetian enclave. Political and personal tensions are palpable: Senator Brabantio's daughter, Desdemona, has eloped with Othello.

What does Venice look like? There are innumerable picture books that will show you, and it has not changed that much in appearance since Shakespeare's day. Where is Brabantio's palazzo located? The play doesn't tell us, so the actors and director are free to decide.

It is late at night, dark and gloomy. In Stanislavsky's production, we first hear the splash of oars as Roderigo and Iago are rowed in a gondola to the quay where Brabantio's house is located. The play begins with "two subdued voices in heated argument." Stanislavsky states that "Roderigo is *very, very* angry with Iago." Iago is extremely embarrassed over what has happened, and he may be losing the friendship of the man who supplies him with money so that Iago can plead Roderigo's case with Desdemona. Also, Iago does not want to be seen "in Roderigo's company," because people might ask embarrassing questions about what he is up to, so he is obliged to calm Roderigo down.

Iago's throughline of action for the scene is to manipulate and control Roderigo so he can continue to use him for his own ends. For Roderigo, the throughline is to obtain satisfaction and the assurance that he still has a chance to win the love of Desdemona, and since he hears what he wants to hear, he is easy prey for Iago and his willing tool. His superobjective for the play is to achieve happiness by marrying the woman he is obsessively in love with. The counter-throughline is all the actions taken by Iago to keep Desdemona and Roderigo apart while pretending Roderigo has a chance to obtain her love, which is precluded, of course, by Desdemona's involvement with Othello.

Iago's superobjective, like that of all psychopaths, is to attain power, and again like the typical psychopath, he doesn't even know why he wants it or what he would really do with it. But his narcissism has been deeply wounded and his ego called into question by various circumstances—including being passed over by Othello for the ensignship, which has fallen to Cassio, whom Iago now loathes because Othello has preferred him. Iago's paranoia is reawakened as he fails to understand why. His throughline of action for this brief section is to proceed to put a vague, half-formed plan into action for making Othello uncomfortable at the very least.

SCENE I. Venice. A street.

Enter RODERIGO and IAGO

[They try to maintain their balance in the gondola as they argue. What was Iago's previous line? Perhaps he said that they were going to rouse Brabantio, because Othello has eloped with Desdemona and might even have married her by now. The argument has to have been proceeding for some time, probably in much the same vein, as the gondola is rowing towards the landing. Roderigo has had a moment of absorption before he says his first line.]

RODERIGO: Tush! never tell me; [Roderigo "turns his back on IAGO." First beat: I will get you to do what I want under threat of abandoning you—no more money for you!] I take it much unkindly / That thou, Iago, who hast had my purse / As if the strings were thine, shouldst know of this.

IAGO: [Moment of absorption. Moment of reversal. This does not mean the actor should take a pause: these moments are instantaneous, and simultaneous with the lines. First beat: I will make you listen to me!] 'Sblood, but you will not hear me: / If ever I did dream ["PAUSE"] of such a matter, / Abhor me. [Stanislavsky writes, "THEY arrive {at the landing}. The gondolier steps out, rattles the chain. IAGO checks him. Act the pause to the end. THEY look round—nobody is watching from the window."]

RODERIGO: [Second beat, starting again after the pause: I'm not giving up on this, but I will listen.] Thou told'st me thou didst hold him in thy hate. [His impulse is to grab Iago, but he doesn't dare to do so.]

IAGO: [Moment of absorption; second beat: I know I have him now!] Despise me, if I do not.

The rest of the speech is probably delivered in subdued tones and with urgency, because of where they are and the main objective of the scene: to rouse Brabantio and the household and inform them of what has happened. Iago succeeds in his immediate objective at the beginning of the scene: to calm Roderigo.

The actors' preparation should include where they are coming from in immediate terms—that is, where the gondola has departed from. Do they know the gondolier and can they trust him, or is he simply one of the many who ply their boats up and down the canals? What have they been doing prior to taking the gondola to the landing? Has Roderigo sought Iago out to reproach him with not making fast enough progress, only to be informed about the elopement? It would seem that this is the case. Is Iago's plan to rouse her father Brabantio one conceived at the last minute, an inspiration that would serve to calm Roderigo's anger, or had he thought about it as soon as he heard the news and is now pretending it is a plan off the top of his head?

The Opening Lines of *The Seagull*

The physical actions listed below in brackets are based on Stanislavsky's prompt books for the 1898 production that made history and put the MAT on the theatrical map. They have been translated and published in *The Seagull Produced by Stanislavsky* (Theatre Arts Books, 1952). Those in quotation marks are directly from the prompt script; the translation of the dialogue is mine. As you will recall, this production was mounted before Stanislavsky had come up with his system, which we see here in germination.

Act 1 opens on the grounds of Sorin's country estate. In the background is a lake, and in the foreground a bench. A makeshift stage has been erected, and there is a curtain across the front of it, which obscures the view of the lake. There are bushes and trees, a table and some chairs. The time is just after sunset. What are the exact day and time? We hear hammering and coughing as workmen finish constructing the stage. Masha, the daughter of the estate manager, and Medvedenko, a local school teacher, enter. They will be in the audience of the play that is about to be presented by Constantine, nephew of the retired senator Sorin, who is the brother of Constantine's mother, the famous actress Arkadina. Medvedenko is in love with Masha, but she does not requite his affection.

They may be walking without saying anything at first, and their moments of orientation occur at the beginning of the walk, perhaps before we ever see them. They hear the noise the workmen are making as they finish the stage, and they hear the sounds of nature. Medvedenko is thinking. Finally, he says what is on his mind. His first beat: I want to find out what she is thinking deep down:

> MEDVEDENKO: Why do you always go around in black? [He is smoking a cigarette: Stanislavsky tells us that "HE smokes a lot during the whole of the play." This is an activity, as opposed to an action. He also carries a small club—"not a walking stick." Why? Because he is not a gentleman about town but a country schoolmaster. On his walk over, he might run into an animal he has to scare away.]
>
> MASHA: [Moment of absorption. First beat: What is he talking about? Isn't it obvious why I wear black?] It's mourning for my life. I'm unhappy. ["MASHA is cracking *nuts*." This is also an activity,

and not an action. From the audience point of view, cracking a nut after you say you are unhappy might be quite funny—Chekhovian, or at least Stanislavskian, humor. Also, people often eat when they are unhappy.]

MEDVEDENKO: [Moment of absorption.] Why? (*Pensively.*) I don't understand. You're healthy. Maybe your father isn't rich, but he's not poor either. My life is much harder than yours. I earn a total of twenty-three rubles a month, and they take deductions out of that. But for all that, I don't wear mourning.

They sit.

"They sit" is Chekhov's stage direction. But Stanislavsky, who was directing the production, had other ideas. He crossed out the stage direction and had the two actors take an after-dinner stroll among the trees as their dialogue continued, and only later on did they sit. "Pensively" is Chekhov's direction to the actor, and it is just the kind of direction that an actor might wish to ignore when finding the life of the character. It may well be that the actor will end up speaking the lines in a pensive tone, but he has to play the scene without thinking about that stage direction. The line will come out organically in whatever way it happens to be uttered.

The schoolteacher's superobjective is to live a moral, virtuous life and to find love. Hopefully Masha will come round to loving him. He is not, however, very passionate or strong-willed, but is rather timid. The throughline of action in this little opening scene is simply to express himself to Masha. The counter-throughline is her resistance to him.

Masha's superobjective is to understand life so she can overcome her despair and accept the circumstances of her unhappiness. She is flattered by Medvedenko's affection for her, but she cannot return it, does not find him attractive as a man, and feels he is too conventional and limited for her. She would ideally want someone who is adventurous and a romantic artist, like Constantine. Her throughline of action in this brief dialogue is simply to pass the time until the play begins and she can see Constantine. And she does not wish to be disagreeable, but if Medvedenko were to press his suit further, she would easily become so and put him off less gently than she does, even driving him away. In other words, he is not really important to her but is rather simply someone with whom to pass the time for the moment. Since he is not too insistent, she can put up with him. The counter-throughline for Masha is his insistence on his affections.

Some of the questions about specific activities and actual physical actions include: When did Medvedenko light that cigarette? What brand is it, or did he roll his own? (Probably he did.) What kind of nuts are Masha eating? Is she carrying them in a little bag or in a small bowl? How does she dispose of the container, whatever it is? These small activities that are not part of the main objective, or even of the objective for the scene, have to be dealt with. A while later she will take snuff and offer some to Medvedenko. Presumably she has a pocket from which she can take the snuffbox. If so, perhaps she puts the paper bag that contains the nuts into it; she certainly would not litter.

These activities, which are physical actions, have psychological motivations. Perhaps Medvedenko smokes to calm himself down in the presence of the woman he loves, because he is nervous when he is with her, especially since he knows she does not feel the same way about him that he does about her. Perhaps Masha cracks nuts and takes snuff out of boredom, simply to while away the idle hour before the play begins; or perhaps she too is feeling nervous, and maybe even guilty, because she is taking a walk with the man she knows loves her.

Here are some of the basic facts about the historical, sociocultural background of the play: *The Seagull*, first produced in 1896, takes place in the autocratic Czarist Russia of Nicholas II (1868–1918), with its rigid class system and formal ways of behaving. The protocol and etiquette of the period would be well known to each character, and the actors have to research those aspects of the social life of the times, even though the characters are relaxing on a country estate. There are different social classes represented in the play. How does this condition the way the characters relate to each other? The Petrograd riots of 1905 will be virtually a rehearsal for the 1917 revolution, and feelings of general discontent and unrest are in the air. What are the characters' political opinions?

You can invent the exact details of the estate income and of the characters' economic situations. What are the markets like where they sell the estate's products? How close are they to the estate? What products do they sell? People ride horses and get about in horse-drawn carriages or buggies, and in horse-drawn sleighs in winter. How many horses are there? How many dogs do they have (one at least, who barks and prevents people from sleeping)? What are their names? Who are the peasants who work Sorin's land? What is the daily routine of each of the characters? What is the house like? How many rooms does it have? How are they furnished? Rooms in Russian homes of this period were heated by wood in decorative, tile-covered floor-to-ceiling stoves with closed doors, rather than by fireplaces. There were sleeping platforms above some low stoves. Some beds might have curtains. The windows would be heavily curtained, and there would be area carpets on the wooden floors.

For More Information

Benedetti, Jean. *The Art of the Actor*. New York: Routledge, 2007.

————*The Moscow Art Theatre Letters*. Selected, edited, and translated by Jean Benedetti. New York: Routledge, 1991.

————*Stanislavski: A Biography*. New York: Routledge, 1990.

————*Stanislavski and the Actor*. London: Methuen Drama, 1998.

————*Stanislavski: An Introduction*. New York: Routledge, 1982.

Carnicke, Sharon M. *Stanislavsky in Focus*. London: Harwood Academic Publishers, 2003.

Chekhov, Anton. *The Complete Plays*. Translated, edited, and annotated by Laurence Senelick. New York: W. W. Norton & Company, 2006.

————*Letters of Anton Chekhov*. Translated by Constance Garnett. New York: Macmillan, 1920.

————*The Seagull Produced by Stanislavsky*. Production score for the Moscow Art Theatre by K. S. Stanislavsky. Edited with an introduction by Professor S. D. Balukhaty. Translated from the Russian by David Magarshack. New York: Theatre Arts Books, 1952.

Gorchakov, Nicolai. *Stanislavsky Directs*. Foreword by Norris Houghton. New York: Limelight Editions, 1991.

Gordon, Mel. *The Stanislavsky Technique: A Workbook for Actors*. New York: Applause Theatre Books, 1987.

Houghton, Norris. *Moscow Rehearsals: The Golden Age of the Soviet Theatre*. With an introduction by Lee Simonson. New York: Grove Press, 1936.

Merlin, Bella. *The Complete Stanislavsky Tool Kit*. Hollywood, CA: Drama Publishers, 2007.

————*Konstantin Stanislavsky*. New York: Routledge, 2003.

Moore, Sonia. *The Stanislavsky Method: The Professional Training of an Actor*. Preface by Sir John Gielgud. Foreword by Joshua Logan. New York: The Viking Press, 1960.

Nemirovich-Danchenko, Vladimir. *My Life in the Russian Theatre*. Translated by John Cournos. With an introduction by John Logan, a foreword by Oliver M. Saylor, and a chronology by Elizabeth Reynolds Hapgood. New York: Theatre Arts Books, 1936.

Rayfield, Donald. *Anton Chekhov: A Life.* New York: Henry Holt, 1997.

Senelick, Lawrence. *The Chekhov Theatre: A Century of the Plays in Performance.* Cambridge: Cambridge University Press, 1997.

——*Serf Actor: The Life and Art of Mikhail Shchepkin.* Westport, CT: Greenwood Press, 1984.

Stanislavski, Constantin and Pavel Rumantsev. *Stanislavski on Opera.* Translated and edited by Elizabeth Reynolds Hapgood. New York: Routledge, 1974.

Stanislavsky, Constantin. *An Actor Prepares.* Translated by Elizabeth Reynolds Hapgood. New York: Theatre Arts Books (1936, 23rd printing), 1969.

——*Building a Character.* Translated by Elizabeth Reynolds Hapgood. New York: Theatre Arts Books (14th printing), 1949.

——*Creating a Role.* Translated by Elizabeth Reynolds Hapgood. New York: Theatre Arts Books (6th printing), 1969.

——*My Life in Art.* Translated by G. Ivanov-Mumjiev. Moscow: Foreign Languages Publishing House, n.d.

——*My Life in Art.* Translated by J. J. Robbins. Orig. pub. Little, Brown and Company, 1924. New York: The World Publishing Co. Meridian Books, 1966.

——*On the Art of the Stage.* Introduced and translated by David Magarshack. New York: Hill and Wang, 1961.

——*Stanislavsky Produces Othello.* Translated from the Russian by Dr. Helen Nowak. London: Godfrey Bles, 1948.

Toporkov, Vasili. *Stanislavski in Rehearsal.* Translated and with an introduction by Jean Benedetti. New York: Routledge, 2004.

PART TWO

Doing Period Styles

Style Is Behavior

A play's era is part of its given circumstances. In order to portray the characters convincingly, actors must do extensive research and immerse themselves in the history and sociopolitical and artistic culture of the period. Associated with each era are general beliefs about the world and religion (whether shared by the character or not), customs, manners, deportment, salutations and greetings, decorum, and a societal hierarchical structure that demands particular behavior in the form of etiquette and protocol. All these things, like the language and technology of the period, are second nature to someone from that time. They are part of a character's mental world. A period's style is what we see as external behavior, which is the result of inner attitudes and motivations.

Dress and the use of certain accessories—wigs, hats, gloves, fans, snuffboxes, watches, lorgnettes, swords, canes—are particularly important factors in period style. Stanislavsky tells us in *My Life in Art* that the MAT actors "studied costumes, their patterns, and the methods of wearing them," not only in a theoretical but in a practical way. You should know the clothing of the relevant era as well as you know your own.

You usually have to deal with dress rather late in rehearsals, although costume fittings will have taken place fairly early, and you will probably have seen the designs at the first or second rehearsal. But you should wear rehearsal clothing that will help you. If you are a Victorian lady, wear a long skirt; often, a skirt that can be worn over your own clothing will be supplied for rehearsal purposes. If you are a Restoration or Edwardian gentleman, wear a sport jacket or long coat. Once you get the actual costume, you will, of course, have to adjust your movement.

In 1970, when I was a fellowship student at the American Shakespeare Festival in Stratford, Connecticut, I played the King of France's Major-Domo in *All's Well That Ends Well*. Michael Kahn's production was set in sixteenth-century France. I led the court processions in and participated in elaborate dances, for which we had lessons from an expert choreographer. The costumes were exceptionally beautiful. My gorgeous suit was blue with silver filigree and included an unwieldy feathered cylinder hat. I could only move my head very carefully indeed, especially since I was also wearing a large ruff. Both men's and women's costumes were well padded and contained inner ribbing (metal, to be sure, and not the whalebone that was used at the time). For many of the men, including me, arms encased in padded sleeves had to rest on the tops of padded balloon trousers; gestures were very limited in such an outfit. High-heeled shoes obliged us to walk slowly and carefully and in the most stately, ceremonious manner. Keeping one's balance could be difficult, but I was lucky, because as Major-Domo I always carried a long jewel-headed staff that helped me maintain my poise. Shoes were supplied to us very early on in the process so that we got used to them, but naturally, we had to wait until we had the costumes to know how moving in them would feel.

Knowing the mores, customs, and culture of the country and era in which a play is set is as important as wearing the clothing. These things form part of the ethos—the general sociocultural background—embedded in the character's mental world. How Norwegians celebrate Christmas in Ibsen's *Doll's House* or what the customary behavior is at a Spanish bullfight are simply part of a character's inner constructs, ingrained from an early age, like table manners. The symbolic meaning of the samovar Chebutykin presents to Irina in act 1 of Chekhov's *Three Sisters* on her "name day" or saint's day is something that all the characters would know: it is an extravagant, inappropriate, and much too personal gift for the nature of the relationship between the doctor and the youngest of the three sisters—and for the simple occasion, which is very much like that of a birthday party in the United States of our own day. When you do Russian or French plays or films, you have to know what a "saint's day" means, as opposed to a birthday, just as you may have to know what a menorah is used for in a Jewish home and how the Jewish Sabbath or a Passover Seder is celebrated.

In Paddy Chayevsky's *The Tenth Man*, I played the *shammes*, or sexton, of the little Orthodox *shul* (synagogue) where the play takes place. In one scene, I had to conduct a service in the background while the main dialogue was taking place in the foreground. Every once in a while, the audience would hear parts of the service, which therefore had to be real and in the correct order, so that those who might be familiar with the liturgy would accept what they were hearing as being true to life. In order to prepare, not only did I attend some services at an

Orthodox shul, but I also learned the relevant parts of the liturgy (which are not in the script, but which we worked out with the director and a technical adviser). I had to learn how to put on the *tallis* (prayer shawl) and the phylacteries that are ritually donned every morning, and how to use a *yad* (hand, in Hebrew), which is a pointer with the shape of a small hand, forefinger extended, at its tip, used for keeping one's place when reading from the scrolls ceremoniously removed from the ark. Clearly, all the stylistic elements were part of my character's mental world. The correct gestures, intonation patterns, and manner of vocal delivery; the way the religious garments are worn; and the way the ritual implements for the service are handled were habits that would not even have to be given a second thought.

The best way of getting to know an era is through its literature. Novels, epics, and stories are very instructive as sociological and cultural documents, and they show the relationships, manners, social classes, and behavior of a period better than almost any other source. Literature also includes primary historical source materials such as letters, memoirs, diaries, journals, autobiographies, legal documents, trial transcripts, logbooks, prison and church records, archives, period newspapers, and minutes of legislative and other meetings. Secondary sources include well-researched histories and biographies.

From 1890 on, recorded audio material allows us to hear what such people as Edwin Booth, Henry Irving, Joseph Jefferson, Ellen Terry, Leo Tolstoy, Johannes Brahms, Sir Arthur Conan Doyle, Gilbert and Sullivan, and Presidents Theodore Roosevelt, William Howard Taft, and Woodrow Wilson sounded like. And there are recordings of artists who worked with Offenbach, Gilbert and Sullivan, Verdi, Puccini, and Wagner, among others, so that we are in a position to get at least an impression of the authentic style in which their works were performed. On the other hand, as Philip Gossett amply demonstrates in his indispensable *Divas and Scholars: Performing Italian Opera* (University of Chicago Press, 2006), it is difficult at this remove in time to know exactly what composers' intentions were, considering the problematic and contradictory state of manuscripts and published scores; or what opera performance practice was, if we are to judge by incomplete contemporary accounts of what took place on stage. Nineteenth-century composers wrote for specific singers, and they often revised scores for revivals with different singers, composing music that would suit their voices.

Listening to music will arouse a wonderful feeling for the era. The rhythms of seventeenth-century baroque composers such as Albinoni,

Bach, or Vivaldi contrast strikingly with the more sprightly, but still ornate, elegant classical music of Haydn and Mozart—and more strikingly still with the tempestuous romantic music of Beethoven; the effervescent, moving melodies of Schubert; the rhythmic variety of Mendelssohn and Offenbach; and the brooding melodies of Brahms, or the haunting, broad cadences of Tchaikovsky in the late romantic period. The musical idioms in which these composers wrote are as different from each other as the styles in which their works are performed.

Folk and pop music, including operettas and musicals, are just as valuable and in some cases even more so than classical music, because they have taken the pulse of the people. The music of every country and every era gives you the tone, the mood, the temper, and the feeling of the times. For example, the Scottish songs and ballads of the 1745 rebellion—when the clans rose in support of Bonnie Prince Charlie against the Hanoverian regime—are sometimes wistful, sometimes tragic, always fiercely patriotic and often mordantly satiric. In them, the period comes to life.

The visual art, paintings, drawings, engravings, and photographs of a period are extremely important resources. And early motion pictures show us how people moved in their sometimes cumbersome clothing.

The information in the following chapters about specific period styles assumes that the plays would be set in their time frame, but abstract productions in modern costumes or set in other periods are not uncommon. Of course, if the plays are done in period, knowledge of attitudes and ideas on sexuality and propriety, manners and the niceties of etiquette, and how costume and accessories condition movement is crucial. Without it, actors simply seem displaced in time or behave as if they were at a costume party. Also, it is possible that a Restoration comedy, for instance, could be set in an abstract décor with modern dress but still retain such props as snuffboxes and fans, so that the actor must be prepared to use those props in an appropriate stylistic way that will give an impression of the period rather than an actual recreation of it.

Finally, remember always that what is history to us were current events to the living, breathing people who experienced them. Today's history is yesterday's news, and yesterday's people were modern and up to date. Even the ancient Roman historian Tacitus refers in his *Annals* to "we moderns." Every character in a historical play would know the news of his or her day just as well as we know the news of ours.

What You Should Know:
Actor's Essential Questions for Period Styles

Aside from the answers to the following questions, which are part of the character's background and given circumstances, there are also particular activities you may need to concern yourself with for particular periods, such as riding horses or fencing with various kinds of swords; using such accessories as fans or snuffboxes; or practicing a particular profession, such as blacksmithing. Such matters as legal procedures and medicine may need to be delved into. You may have to learn the style and method of playing an instrument in a particular era. Professional coaches, music experts, and dance and fight choreographers will usually be brought in by the theater or film company.

Clothing, Accessories, and Movement
Conditioned by Clothing

1. What did people wear? You should know the names of every garment.
2. How did clothing condition movement?
3. How did clothing condition posture?
4. How did clothing condition the positions one could stand or sit in?
5. What was people's deportment like—that is, how did they walk, stand, and sit?
6. What were the accessories of the period (cane, sword, fan, lorgnette, eyeglasses, pince-nez, snuffbox, wigs, hats, gloves, muffs, wristwatches, pocket watches, jewelry)?
7. How were the accessories carried or worn, and how were they used?

The Social and Political Systems, Relationships,
Manners, and National Culture

8. What was the system of government?
9. Who were the ruler(s) and other important, well-known figures at the time when the play takes place?
10. What was the social class system?

11. What were working conditions like?

12. How was the work system organized (apprenticeship, guilds, unions, serfdom, slavery)?

13. How rigid was the class structure—that is, how easily could someone's social class be changed?

14. How did this system condition behavior and the way people were with each other?

15. What was the protocol of the period, and how did it condition behavior?

16. Who took precedence over whom, and why?

17. What were the particular typical ways of showing reverence, such as bowing or curtseying or saluting?

18. How did people greet each other (shaking hands, kissing each other on both cheeks, bowing slightly or more fully, etc.)?

19. What are your character's attitudes and beliefs about the system of class structure?

20. What is the character's national culture?

21. What are the aspects of the culture that are taken for granted as part of the character's mental world? You should know literary and geographical allusions to commonly known works; folk tales; folk dances; well known songs, such as folk songs and national anthems; national costumes, such as the Scottish kilt with its accoutrements (the sporran and dirk) and the kimono and obi of Japan; food, including the most well known national dishes; the ceremonies, celebrations and holidays of the particular culture, including how they are celebrated; religion, religious attitudes and rites and rituals; and rules of etiquette, such as the Russian idea that a guest should refuse an offer of food and drink at first, then accept after the host politely insists.

The Public and Private Environments; Food and Table Manners

22. What were people's houses like? You should know every room and its purpose in a house you are supposed to live in.

23. What were the private environment and living spaces like?

24. What was the furniture of the period like?

25. Was it comfortable?

26. How did furniture condition the way people sat, taking the clothing of the period into account as well?

27. What was the technology of everyday life (cooking; fireplaces; stoves; laundry; household procedures, such as making fires; lighting; heating; water supply; furnaces; air conditioning)?

28. How did people cope with cold and heat?

29. What was the public environment like?

30. What was the urban environment like?

31. What was the rural environment like?

32. What did people eat?

33. How was food cooked?

34. Who cooked it?

35. What sort of implements did people use to eat with? This often depended on social class.

36. What were the table manners of the period?

37. Were there particular table manners typical of a specific social class?

38. How many meals a day did people usually have and at what times?

39. Does the household of the play have servants?

40. What were the specific jobs servants had to do, and how did they do them?

Time

41. How was people's time spent, depending on social class?

42. What is the order of events in a typical day for the particular character?

43. What was people's sense of time?

44. How did people tell time (clocks, watches, etc.)?

Education

45. What was the educational system like?

46. Was education widespread or limited to a few?

47. What did people learn, and what did they know?

48. Were women educated as well as men?
49. What does your character know, as far as general areas of knowledge are concerned and as far as a particular area of expertise?

Family Relationships and Relationships Between the Sexes

50. How did people define and view marriage and the family?
51. What was the relationship with the larger community?
52. How were children raised?
53. Who was in charge of bringing children up, depending on social class as well as on the period in question?
54. What were the relationships between parents and children?
55. What were the sexual attitudes of the time?
56. What was the ideal of beauty, masculine and feminine?
57. What was the social position of men?
58. What was the social position of women?
59. How did the sexes view each other?
60. Were there gender-related stereotypes?
61. What was the attitude of women towards their position in society?
62. What was the attitude of men towards their position in society?
63. How did men and women treat each other?
64. What were the courtship rituals of the period?
65. How was marriage entered into (e.g., arranged or by agreement between the partners)?
66. How was friendship viewed?
67. How was homosexuality viewed?
68. What was the attitude towards age?
69. What was the attitude towards youth?

Arts and Entertainment

70. What were the recreation and entertainments of the period?
71. How did people behave at public events?
72. What was the music of the period?

73. How were plays performed and in what circumstances?
74. What were the painting, graphic arts, and sculpture of the period?
75. What were the games and sports of the period?
76. What were the dances of the period?
77. What was the social dancing of the period like—decorum, manners?
78. What was the architecture of the period?
79. Who were the well-known artists, musicians, and performing artists?

Transportation

80. What were the methods of transportation?
81. How did transportation condition the way people behaved (in a public coach, in a private carriage and horses, in an automobile, etc.)?

Money

82. What was the monetary system of the place and period?
83. What were the names of the coins, and what was each one worth?
84. What is their value by today's standards?
85. What is your character's attitude about money?

Belief Systems

86. Are there ideals or principles that were widely believed in and taken for granted as being self-evident?
87. What was the role of religion in the period?
88. What are the rites and rituals of the characters' religions?
89. What are your character's religious, political, and philosophical beliefs?
90. What was the proverbial lore of the period?
91. How was nature viewed, and what was people's relationship to nature?
92. What are your character's beliefs about the world as it exists, including its political and social relationships?

Scientific, Technological, and Medical Matters

93. What was the state of science?
94. What were the latest scientific advances and discoveries?
95. What was the technology of the warfare like (naval and military procedures, ships, weapons)?
96. What was the workplace and its technology like (blacksmith's shops, factories construction, arts and crafts)?
97. What were the medical practice and procedures of the period, and how were diseases treated?

Legal and Institutional Matters

98. What was the legal practice and procedure of the period?
99. What were the legal institutions (Victorian workhouse, debtor's prison)?
100. What were the prison system and prisons like?
101. What were the usual punishments, and how were they carried out?

Language and History

102. How is the language of the period different from your own contemporary language? You must make its grammar and vocabulary yours.
103. Who were the well-known political figures, rulers, and leaders of the period?
104. What are the current events that form the background to the script?
105. What are the events of the immediate past that form the background to the script (wars, explorations, discoveries, advances in science)?

For More Information

Boehn, Max von. *Modes and Manners*. Translated by Joan Joshua. 4 vols. London: Harrap, 1932.

————*Modes and Manners Ornaments: Lace, Fans, Gloves, Walking-Sticks, Parasols, Jewelry and Trinkets.* London: J. M. Dent & Sons, Ltd., 1929.

Boucher, François. *20,000 Years of Fashion: The History of Costume and Personal Adornment.* Expanded Edition. With a new chapter by Yvonne Deslandres. New York: Harry N. Abrams, Inc. Publishers, 1987.

Carson, Gerald. *The Polite American: 300 Years of More or Less Good Behavior.* London: Macmillan and Company, Limited, 1967.

Clark, Kenneth. *Civilization.* New York: Harper and Row, 1969.

————. *Civilization—the Complete Series (1969).* New York: BBC Warner DVD, 2006.

Cole, Toby and Helen Krich Chinoy, eds. *Actors on Acting: The Theories, Techniques and Practices of the World's Great Actors Told in Their Own Words.* New York: Three Rivers Press, 1970.

Crompton, Louis. *Homosexuality and Civilization.* Cambridge, MA: The Belknap Press of Harvard University Press, 2006.

DeJean, Joan. *The Essence of Style: How the French Invented High Fashion, Fine Food, Chic Cafés, Style, Sophistication, and Glamour.* New York: Free Press, 2005.

Gossett, Philip. *Divas and Scholars: Performing Italian Opera.* Chicago: The University of Chicago Press, 2006.

Grant, Gail. *Technical Manual and Dictionary of Classical Ballet.* Illustrated by the author. 3rd revised edition. New York: Dover Publications, Inc., 1982.

Guy, Christian. *An Illustrated History of French Cuisine: From Charlemagne to Charles de Gaulle.* Translated by Elizabeth Abbot. New York: The Orion Press, n.d.

Hartnoll, Phyllis, ed. *The Oxford Companion to the Theatre.* 3rd edition. London: Oxford University Press, 1967.

Hindley, Geoffrey, ed. *The Larousse Encyclopedia of Music.* New York: Crown Publishers, Inc., 1971.

Horne, Alistair. *Seven Ages of Paris.* New York: Alfred A. Knopf, 2003.

Hudson, Roger, ed. *The Grand Tour, 1592–1796.* London: The Folio Society, 1993.

Januszczak, Waldemar, consultant ed. *Techniques of the World's Great Painters.* Secaucus, NJ: Chartwell Books, Inc., 1980.

Johnson, Paul. *Art: A New History.* New York: HarperCollins, 2003.

Kennedy, Dennis, ed. *The Oxford Encyclopedia of Theatre and Performance.* New York: Oxford University Press, 2003.

Merriam-Webster's Encyclopedia of Literature. Springfield, MA: Merriam-Webster, Inc., 1995.

Nagler, A. M. *A Source Book in Theatrical History (Sources of Theatrical History).* New York: Dover Publications, Inc., 1952.

Oxenford, Lyn. *Playing Period Plays*. Woodstock, IL: Dramatic Publishing Company, 1957.

Racinet, Albert. *The Historical Encyclopedia of Costume*. New York: Facts on File Publications, 1988.

Radice, Mark. *Opera in Context: Essays on Historical Staging from the Late Renaissance to the Time of Puccini*. New York: Amadeus Press, 1998.

Randel, Don Michael. *The Harvard Dictionary of Music*. 4th edition. Cambridge, MA: The Belknap Press of Harvard University Press, 2003.

Robb, Graham. *The Discovery of France: A Historical Geography from the Revolution to the First World War*. New York: W. W. Norton & Company, 2007.

Róheim, Géza. *Psychoanalysis and Anthropology*. New York: International Universities Press, 1950.

Schechner, Richard. *Performance Theory*. New York: Routledge, 1988, 2003.

Schlesinger, Arthur M. *Learning How to Behave: A Historical Study of American Etiquette Books*. New York: The Macmillan Company, 1946.

Schonberg, Harold. *The Lives of the Great Composers*. 3rd edition. New York: W. W. Norton and Company, 1997.

Smiley, Jane. *Thirteen Ways of Looking at the Novel*. New York: Alfred A. Knopf, 2005.

Strong, Roy. *Feast: A History of Grand Eating*. London: Pimlico, 2003.

Trevelyan, G. M. *English Social History: A Survey of Six Centuries/Chaucer to Queen Victoria*. New York: David McKay Company, Inc., 1942.

Wildeblood, Joan. *The Polite World: A Guide to the Deportment of the English in Former Times*. London: Davis-Poyntcr, 1973.

Williams, Hywel. *Cassel's Chronology of World History: Dates, Events and Ideas that Made History*. London: Weidenfeld & Nicholson, 2005.

Wood, Melusine. *Historical Dances, 12th to 19th Century: Their Manner of Performance and Their Place in the Social Life of the Time*. Princeton, NJ: Princeton Book Company Publishers, 1982.

Internet Resources

The Costume Page: www.costumepage.org
>An invaluable listing of web sites dealing with costumes and costume history from all eras, links to reference and museum web sites.

Google: www.google.com
>Doing a book search will sometimes yield a scanned copy of a rare eighteenth- or nineteenth-century memoir or other work.

The Internet Movie Database: www.imdb.com

Information on just about every movie ever made.

The Jewish Virtual Library: www.jewishvirtuallibrary.org

An invaluable source for Jewish history and biography.

Project Gutenberg: www.gutenberg.org

More than twenty thousand free downloadable books in the public domain, including the memoirs and diaries of individuals from various historical periods and the complete plays of any number of playwrights.

Society of Dance History Scholars: www.sdhs.org

A directory of specialists in early dance, links to web sites for dances of all kinds.

Wikipedia: www.wikipedia.org

The free online encyclopedia.

CHAPTER THREE

The Beginning
of European Theater:
Athens and Rome

Ancient Greece and Its Theater

The origins of ancient Greek theater remain obscure, but there is little doubt that it started in the independent city-state of Athens and derived from religious festivals and ceremonies. Peisistratos (607–528 BCE), a general who had made himself ruler of Athens in a coup d'état and was twice deposed, sought on his third accession to the seat of government to secure his authority and gain the support of the populace by exalting the hereditary priests of Dionysus: god of wine and revelry, and symbol of all that was wild, untamed, and lustful in humankind. Around 546 BCE, Peisistratos established the Dionysia, transforming what had been a minor rural rite celebrating the wine harvest into a major urban religious festival that would become an annual drama contest in honor of the lubricious deity.

With great pomp and ceremony, Athenian citizens, metics (resident aliens), and representatives from the Athenian colonies processed to the theater of Dionysus on the Acropolis, bearing a statue of the god as well as numerous phalli—some of them animated mechanically. A cart transported a huge ritual phallus, and wine and food carriers accompanied the parade. Bulls were sacrificed, musicians played, obscene songs were sung and danced, and beautifully costumed choruses competed in performing dithyrambs—passionate songs on mythological themes. The priests of Dionysus sat in the front row. They presided over an opening ritual purification, and libations of wine were offered to the god by city officials before the performances took place.

Several ancient sources tell us that it was at this time too that Thespis of Icaria, considered the father of tragedy, started conversing with the chorus, and so began the tradition of playing characters. At the first

Dionysia, where he sang his own dithyrambs with answering choral refrains, he won first prize, which was a goat—one of Dionysus's symbols—hence the word *tragoidia* (tragedy), which literally means "goat song" (the ancient Athenians had a sarcastic sense of humor). His acting was considered so startlingly real that Peisistratos's friend and sometime opponent, Solon (638–558 BCE)—the great Athenian lawgiver who had established timocracy (rule by the wealthy)—thought him a very dangerous man. As Plutarch (46–127 CE) tells us in his *Lives*, Solon was shocked at a tragedy he had just seen, and he confronted Thespis. Was he not ashamed to tell so many lies in front of so many people? Why no, replied the actor, because it was all in play! But Solon was not convinced. He thought theater was inherently seditious and had the power to corrupt the people.

Tales of ancient days appealed to the sophisticated Athenian audience, centuries removed from the events they depicted. Athens had become a democracy, but Greek drama took as its subjects the days of the kings and the events of the Trojan War—traditionally said to have ended in victory for the Greeks under Agamemnon in 1184 BCE after a ten-year siege of Troy—and other myths and legends, such as the story of Oedipus.

When Albert S. Bennett, a New York City actor, was studying at the Yale Drama School in 1950, he remembered the performances of tragedies by Aeschylus (525–426 BCE) and Sophocles (496–406 BCE) that he had seen at the Greek Theatre on the Berkeley campus where he did his undergraduate work. Those plays were done in an extremely artificial style. The actors declaimed rather than acted their parts, and the chorus often posed in imitation of ancient Greek statues. Any psychological subtlety or depth was lost in the attempt to appear as graceful as a carving in a bas-relief frieze.

Reacting against this deadly way of presenting such plays, Albert directed his thesis production, Euripides' (5th c. BCE) *Hippolytus*, the story of Theseus's queen Phaedra's doomed love for her stepson, in a completely different style from what he had seen in Berkeley. The play was framed by the two goddesses who are at odds over the fate of Phaedra and Hippolytus, and who were always positioned at opposite sides of the stage: hot-blooded Aphrodite—goddess of love, prurient and voluptuous—and cold, self-contained, distant Artemis, goddess of the hunt. He used David Greene's translation, a very speakable adaptation, rather than a literal rendering. It allowed the actors to play their parts with great freedom and fluidity. And he directed them to act their roles realistically but without losing the sense of the play's poetry and heightened emotion. There was a chorus of only three women, who spoke chorally without artificial gestures.

There were no women in ancient Greek choruses: they were not allowed on the stage. Women were not allowed in the audience either. And the rule instituted by Aeschylus for the Dionysia was that all roles were to be apportioned to only three actors. All parts were played by men, who probably often performed in the nude, their bodies glistening with oil, in the early days. Later, costume pieces such as cloaks for shepherds or messengers were worn. The costumes worn by the chorus consisted of the short *chiton* (tunic), revealing the phallus. Women characters were costumed in a long chiton that could be elaborately decorated. Floor-length tunics were worn by royal characters, with a train for female personages, and the gods and goddesses had their own special insignia. The actors' faces were hidden by masks or half masks that indicated the kind of character they were playing, and they wore calf-length, heavy boots, called *cothorni*, to give them stature, limiting their movement enormously and requiring athletic strength. They had to project their voices to the uppermost rows of the raked amphitheatre; the sound was often crystal clear without the actors having to shout. In Epidaurus, where plays are still performed after two thousand years, the acoustics are perfect, and if the actor stands in a certain spot, even his or her whisper can be heard in the back row. Unfortunately, the secret of the construction of the ancient theaters has been lost to us.

The ancient Greek theater consisted of a *theatron*, the semicircular tiered stone auditorium built into a hillside where the spectators sat; the *orchestra*, a space in front of the stage where the chorus danced; the *skene*, a building at the back of the raised stage, where dressing rooms were located behind the *proskenion* (which, so it is conjectured, was decorated with painted scenery representing a palace entrance, temple, or other appropriate place); and the *parodoi*, aisles through which the audience entered, as well as actors playing messengers or returning travelers.

Greek tragedy followed a strict, formal order in its exposition of a story: There was a *prologos*, an introduction delivered by one or more characters; followed by a *parados*, the entrance of the chorus, which told the audience how it was supposed to feel and which would fill in details it needed to know and comment on the action at various points; then the *episodes* that constituted the events of the story; which alternated with the *stasimon*, a choral ode sung and danced by the chorus at the end of each episode; and finally an *exodus*, a concluding section that always followed the chorus's last utterances.

In accordance with the Aristotelian analysis of "classical unities" (misinterpreted by the seventeenth century neoclassicists as being sacrosanct prescriptions rather than analytic templates), the stories of Greek plays deal with one major event and unfold within the conventional period of a day. The plays are usually set in one place, most often a public place, which could be either a street or square or an area in front of a palace. For an actor considering the given circumstances of place and time, this is extremely important: there is room only for the kind of behavior that happens in a public setting at a specific time. This means immediately that everything takes place in a more formal manner than it would otherwise. The chorus of citizens, warriors, or councilors listens with respect to its leaders and to the other characters, although it may become a threatening, unruly mob on occasion, as it does in Aeschylus's *Agamemnon* and Sophocles' *Oedipus the King*.

Greek comedies also had to follow the classical rules of construction. They were looser in their formats than tragedies, and they included elements of clowning and burlesque. Aristophanes (448?–380? BCE), the only comic poet whose plays have come down to us intact (and then only eleven out of the forty he wrote), did not hesitate to use outrageous, malevolent invective and licentiousness in his parodies of the established order. He not only mocked political figures and satirized certain pretentious ways of behaving, but also parodied other writers, albeit good-humoredly.

The Stylistic Elements: Clothing, Accessories, Movement, Manners, and the Art of Living

Clothing, Accessories, and Movement in Costume: Both men and women in ancient Greece wore comfortable, loose-fitting, graceful clothing meant to show the beauty of the human form. It also allowed for free movement, both in general and in the ritualized dancing that was part of religious and martial ceremony, as well as part of every play in the theater. There was no front opening, as there is today: clothing was fitted over the head or fastened at the shoulders. Rather than being fitted or tailored, ancient Greek clothing was draped over the body and consisted mostly of one or two large square pieces of cloth arranged in various ways.

In early Athens, women wore the *peplos*, a large, almost shapeless, sleeveless wool garment that fitted over their heads. But the most basic ancient Greek garment, worn by both men and women, is the long tunic known as the *chiton*, which could have sleeves or not. The *talaris* was another kind of tunic that both genders wore. It had wide sleeves that could be long or short, and it was fastened with a belt at the waist. The sleeves draped elegantly when the arms were resting at the sides. There was also another kind of floor-length tunic or dress called a *podere*, worn by women and children and made of nearly transparent material that was often ornamented with embroidered stars or other symbols. The usual footwear for both men and women was sandals. Soldiers wore tightly laced boots in battle.

For outer garments, cloaks were worn, fastened with a brooch at the neck. Earrings, bracelets, and necklaces were also worn. The *palla* was fastened with brooches or clasps at both shoulders and secured with a belt at the waist. Leaving the arms bare, it hung down gracefully at the sides. The *chloene*—a square of cloth with a hole in its center, similar to a modern poncho—fitted over the head and had metal hangings at all four corners so that the garment could hang down.

Soldiers wore armor, mostly made of leather or metal, and metal helmets as well. Although the armor could be heavy, their movement was free, as they rode on horses or in chariots and fought with lances, short swords, or bows and arrows.

Among the accessories used in Greek homes were gorgeous Phoenician imported luxury goods. The Phoenicians, who colonized parts of the Mediterranean and founded the North African city of Carthage, used money and a monetary system derived from that of ancient Egypt and adopted in Greece, like the Phoenician alphabet that the Greeks adapted. From their bustling port cities, Sidon and Tyre, they exported gold and silver jewelry and dishes, furniture and clothing, and perfumes in fancy little bottles.

Greetings and Salutations: In the army, a strict hierarchy and ceremony was observed: A salute with one arm raised was given to those in authority to whom one was reporting.

On special occasions, men bowed with one hand held to the heart. On emotional occasions, men would greet each other with kisses, as would women, or men and women. Otherwise, there was no particular form of greeting, simply a smile or a nod, and men did not shake hands in the ordinary course of events. That gesture was reserved for sealing a pledge or an oath, or as a special greeting. Women did not curtsey, but they inclined their heads in greeting and sometimes decorously kissed each other, if they were intimates or family members. To plead in supplication, sometimes both knees of the lord or king who granted a favor were grasped by the suppliant.

Living Spaces and Furniture: Athenian democracy was established around 462–58 BCE. There had arisen a system of self-governing city-states—the *polis*—based on commerce. All the necessities of life were enclosed within an area where everything was within easy reach, so that one could walk, for example, from one of the two ports of Corinth to the temple area, or go to the theater or the sports arena, and return home on foot. The ruins of ancient Corinth are Roman, because the Romans destroyed the Greek city when they conquered it. They rebuilt it because of its great commercial importance, since it was on a narrow isthmus that straddled the Aegean and Ionian seas.

Much of life in ancient Greek cities took place publicly, in the *agora*, which was a marketplace as well as a meeting area. In Athens the streets were narrow and winding, with ramshackle houses. But the rural Greek homes, constructed of brick and with walls covered in whitewashed plaster, were in general airy and gracious, and built around a central courtyard. Wealthier houses often had two central inner courtyards, each one surrounded by rooms: the first courtyard, the *andronitis* (the men's quarters), was entered from the street, while the *gunakonitis* (the women's quarters) was entered from the far end of the *andronitis*. The rooms were built around all four sides of the living area(s), onto which they opened. Courtyards could also serve for cooking, unless that was done outside the house in the open space surrounding it. A wealthy house excavated in Piraeus, the seaport of Athens, had one central courtyard, with all the rooms on one side of it and a long open hall with columns on the other.

At night, there were oil lamps for light. Furniture consisted of stone benches, but there were also wooden stools, chairs with arms, and low tables. Beds were made of stone, and cushions were thrown on them and on the stone benches. There were no bathrooms, except perhaps in the larger palaces, and only the aristocratic class or wealthier people took full baths at home; but there were country ponds and streams, and there were the Aegean and Ionian Seas, and the Greeks bathed often. You will recall that the first thing Agamemnon wants after his long journey home from Troy is a hot bath. The Greeks also paid attention to hygiene in general, but there was no toilet plumbing, so they relieved themselves where they pleased—often in public, on streets or in alleys—and nobody thought anything about such common practices. Nobody was embarrassed to be seen doing such things. In the Roman ruins of ancient Corinth, there is a line of public toilets that were simply open to the sky and to all and sundry. They are near one of the entrances to the city and could be used immediately upon entering or before leaving through the city gates. Apparently, merchants thought nothing of conducting business while seated on the toilet.

Food and Table Manners: Food has been very important in Greek culture from its earliest days, and it is talked about even in the *Iliad*. Banquets, called *symposia*, were elaborate and lengthy. Plato's (late 5th century BCE) dialogue about love, the *Symposium*, takes place against the background of just such a feast. There were two meals a day: the *ariston*, or lunch, and the *deipnon*, or dinner. Fish, poultry, or meat (the latter was rare in urban settings), prepared on wood or charcoal fires; kettles of stew; and fresh fruits such as apples, figs, and cherries, as well as fresh vegetables, beans, and grains (from which breads were made), were all part of the Greek diet. The arts of making honey, wine, and cheese were practiced very early. Among the foods mentioned by Athenaeus of Naucratis (in Egypt, late 2nd c. CE) in book 4 of his philosophical dialogues, *The Deipnosophists* (The Learned Banqueters), in which the banqueters discuss everything under the sun—including, of course, gastronomy— are stewed meats with sauces, barley cakes, wheat bread, ham, venison, lamb, sausages, fish, geese, pheasants, and figs. People ate with spoons and knives and sometimes with their right hands while reclining on couches before low tables, which had been brought in already laden with food. After the main course, the tables were taken out, cleaned, and reset with sweets and other delicacies. At a large banquet, there was usually one table per one long couch. Although forks existed, they were used for cooking and religious ceremonies but not for individuals to eat with. Table manners were decorous, and people even washed their hands before a meal and changed their shoes before entering the dining room.

The most ancient cookbook—known only in fragmentary form, and much cited in other works, especially *The Deipnosophists*—is an epic poem entitled *Hedypatheia* (Gastronomy, or The Art of Dining), written around 360 BCE by Archestratus of Gela in Sicily, renowned even then for its magnificent cuisine. One of his simple recipes calls for roasting fish in an oven, the fish sprinkled only with salt and cumin and basted with olive oil. The fish is to be served with a dipping sauce of an unspecified nature.

Athenaeus seems rather to disapprove of Archestratus's attitude that life is to be enjoyed in the most hedonistic manner possible, for he says in book 8:

> What, I ask, has this noble epic poet omitted, that is calculated to ruin one's morals? He is the only man who has emulated the life of Sardanapalus, the son of Anacyndaraxes, who, as Aristotle says, was sillier even than you would expect from his father's name.

Sardanapalus was the (probably) fictional last king of Babylon, known for his debauchery and slothfulness. The ancient Greek historian Ctesias of Cnidus (5th century BCE) no doubt invented him as a character in his now lost *Persica*, a history of ancient Persia known through later Roman accounts. It was said to have been based on information in Persian royal archives but was possibly entirely made up. Athenaeus, however, quotes Sardanapalus's supposed epitaph, which reads in part, "Though knowing full well that thou art but mortal, indulge thy desire, find joy in thy feasts. Dead, thou shallt have no delight. Yes, I am dust, though I was king of mighty Nineva."

The important ancient Greek physicians who explored many medical subjects and phenomena, Hippocrates of Cos (460–370 BCE) and, next in importance to him, Galen (129–200 or 216), physician to the Roman Emperor Marcus Aurelius (121–80), were influenced by Aristotle's (384–322 BCE) theory that the body had four humors. These corresponded to four temperaments: blood/sanguine, phlegm/phlegmatic, yellow bile/choleric, black bile/melancholic. Food was viewed as relating to these, so that, for instance, the sanguine temperament, associated with heat and humidity, could be soothed and cooled by eating something cold and dry; and the melancholic temperament, associated with cold and dryness, could be helped by eating something hot and wet, such as a nice broth or soup. The Greeks recognized the relationship between diet and health. Hippocrates recommended taking other factors besides the humors into account in deciding what someone should eat: age, physique, strength, and season; hot weather called for different foods from cold. Moderation in all things was his guiding principle.

Greek Time Keeping: The sense of time in ancient Greece must have been quite different from ours, although they used water clocks, which they had learned to do from the Babylonians. Archimedes (287?–212 BCE), for instance, invented quite an elaborate *clepsydra* (the word is a combination of the words *water* and *thief:* time steals away the life of man). They reckoned time by the rising and setting of the sun, the time of which changed seasonally, of course. The day was divided into twelve hours, and sundials were used from the sixth century BCE onwards.

In the law courts of ancient Athens, accurate time keeping was demanded, and justice required that speeches be of the same duration for all parties. Using a system instituted by Peisistratos, there were at one point forty circuit judges who made the rounds of the Athenian provinces, so that people did not have to make the journey to Athens to have their cases heard. Each Athenian judge had his own courtroom while his term of office lasted. And there was a jury system: jurors were drawn by lot, and juries were very large; there could be as many as 2,000 jurors or more trying a case. The *clepsydra* was used to insure equal time: a clay vessel was filled with water, and a plug allowing the water to drip out slow drop by slow drop was removed when someone began a speech, which had to stop when all the water had dripped out.

Natural signs, such as the appearance of leaves on trees or their changing color, were used to determine the seasons. But there was no universal standard for the length of a year, and each region and city-state had its own measure.

The Dance: The muse of the dance was Terpsichore, and dance and dancelike movement were important in stage presentations. The ancient Greeks believed that dancing was a gift from the gods, and the art of the dance evolved from ritualized movements used in religious ceremonies. There were also war dances, again connected with religious rites, appealing to the gods for victory. And there were dances used in the theater, as well as in peaceful religious ceremonies and in mourning rites.

The chorus in plays sometimes moved in ritualized unison in a kind of rhythmic dance. Each type of play had a characteristic dance: some were solemn and stately, some were more pantomime than dance, and some dances involved lewd miming with phallic props, as in Aristophanes' *Lysistrata*. But usually Greek dances were done from the waist up, with ritualized movements of the arms and feet and the pelvis area as still as possible.

We know what Greek dances must have looked like principally from sculptures and friezes, but we don't really know very much about how they were actually performed. The dances were apparently done in a circle, whether open or closed, and there were sometimes serpentine and spiraling movements as well, as the dancers wove in and out. There were also chain dances. Very often, the dancers held each other's hands in the circle, releasing them in order to perform twists and turns and arm waves in unison. As usual in the ancient Greek culture, men and women danced separately. There were dances for women only, which they danced among themselves, and martial dances for men only. Very often, the dancers chanted as they danced.

These are some of the dances that have come down to us:

1. *Emelia* was the name of the dance used in tragedy; it was danced by the chorus to illustrate its emotional reaction to the events of the story.

2. *Kordax* was the name of the dance used in comedy; it involved mime as well as dance movement, and it could be grotesque and obscene.

3. *Sikkinis* was the dance of the satirical comedy; it imitated animal movements, and it must have been the kind of dance seen in such plays as Aristophanes' *Frogs*.

4. *Pyrrhic* dance, which could involve rhythmic marching, was a military dance and was part of basic training for warriors in both Athens and Sparta.

5. *Gymnopaedia* was another Spartan dance and involved calisthenics in unison, gymnastic movements, and displays.

6. *Epilinios* was a Dionysiac dance meant as a tribute to the god of wine. Grapes were treaded using ritualized movements, so that the wine would turn out to be good.

7. *Imeneos* was a solemn woman's marriage dance. Apparently it was danced quickly in a twisting, turning circle by the bride and her female relatives.

Painting and Sculpture

Greek civilization produced vast public buildings, the trained architects and engineers to design and construct them, and artists to decorate the pediments with sculptured friezes and statues. Wherever the Greeks held sway, they set the standard for aesthetic excellence, and built their rectangular temples with triangular pediments and sloping roofs, all supported by Ionic or, later, Doric columns.

As a visual way into the period, looking at Greek sculpture, from the idealistic to the realistic, will give you a feeling for the Greek aesthetic ideals of harmony, balance, and proportion. There are friezes in bas-relief, for instance, of horses and chariots that give a sense of the fierce athletic prowess of the soldiers or athletes who rode them. Greek statues of men and women are elegant and sophisticated, as well as light and graceful. Among the subjects of Greek sculpture are mythological heroes and gods, all quite human, and there are portrait busts as well as statues of athletes. Statues can also be quite formal, and certain sculptures follow a standard sort of format, such as that of the *kouros*, a smiling naked boy who stands in a semi-military posture. There are also amazing, complex, detailed group sculptures, such as the Vatican Collection's the *Farnese Bull*, which shows three young men trying to subdue the raging beast. One of the men is fully clothed, the other two almost naked, and the sculptor has given everything such a sense of motion that you would almost not be surprised if the bull were to leap off its pedestal pursued by the young men.

Studying the paintings on Greek pottery can also be quite instructive. Everything from banquets to games of checkers to athletic events to hunting and farming is portrayed on the ancient vases, of which approximately 4,000 have survived. Sculptures too were sometimes painted, as the famous statue of Zeus by Praxiteles (4th c. BCE) is said to have been, but that statue, one of the wonders of the ancient world, no longer exists.

Paints were made from various substances. Vermilion, for instance, one of the oldest paint pigments in existence, was manufactured from a combination of mercury and sulphur, melted together. Egyptian blue was manufactured from soda, lime, and copper carbonate, heated to extremely hot temperatures. If green was wanted, the heating process was continued until the desired color was obtained. Or copper was allowed to corrode in vinegar, then ground into a powder and mixed with more vinegar, yielding a green called *verdigris*. White was made from soaking powdered lime for a week, and reds and browns were obtained from clay and rocks containing rusted iron ore.

Music

Music was studied as part of general education. It held an important place in all public arenas, including the Olympic Games and the presentation of stage plays. Most music in the theater was unaccompanied vocal melody that followed closely the rhythm and pitch accents of the verse. The chorus sang in unison or in octaves. There was also instrumental accompaniment as incidental music to both tragedies and comedies. And there were musical contests at which prizes were awarded. It is conjectured that the authors of plays were also the composers of music for their own works.

As we know from the account of his student Philolaus, Pythagoras (580?–500? BCE) is credited with discovering the relation between mathematics and music, and with defining the idea of intervals to which strings should be tuned. Greek music was supposedly composed in seven modes of an octave each, similar to our contemporary scales. However, not much is known about how Greek music sounded, as there are only some fifty surviving fragmentary records, despite such Greek authors as Aristoxenus, who wrote a treatise entitled *Harmonics* around 330 BCE. But there was no harmony, although there were semitonal intervals and ornaments that Aristoxenus describes, which may have sounded something like contemporary Middle Eastern music. Interpreting what Aristoxenus means, however, has proved quite difficult for expert musicologists. There was no system of notation as far as we know, and the music was taught and memorized directly, without a written reference.

We know what musical instruments looked like, because there are vase paintings depicting instrumentalists and instruments. Greek instruments were percussion, stringed, or wind. Among them, most importantly, were the *lyre*, a stringed, unfretted instrument; the *kithara*, a kind of harp; the flute; and the *aulos*, a kind of double recorder. There were also cymbals, bells, and drums of various kinds. And there were instruments made of seashells as well.

For a cogent and concise explanation of the modes, and the debate about whether or not they were actually used in ancient Greek music, consult *The Harvard Dictionary of Music* (The Belknap Press of Harvard University Press, 2003).

Literature

Composed somewhere around 850 BCE by one or more poets known as Homer, traditionally said to be a blind individual, the *Iliad* and *Odyssey* are basic and necessary reading. I recommend especially the translations by Robert Fagles, published by Penguin and available in paperback. The *Iliad* recounts events in the Trojan War; Ilion (*Ilium* in Latin) was another name for Troy. And the *Odyssey* is the story of Odysseus's adventurous journey home to the isle of Ithaca after the war.

Read the philosophic dialogues of Plato, especially the *Symposium* and those relating to the death of Socrates, accused and convicted of corrupting the youth of Athens by his teachings. He drank hemlock in the presence of his dearest friends, thus carrying out the death sentence imposed on him by the Athenian authorities. The *Dialogues* show us that the moral climate of the Athenian democratic age was more puritanical than one might suspect. *The Deipnosophists* by Athenaeus, rambling and discursive, provides more information about manners, morals, and customs of daily living than almost any other book even could, so immense an undertaking is it. Even the theater is discussed by the learned banqueters, as they recline, feasting around low tables. And all the works of Aristotle, especially the *Poetics*, are still influential, and in many ways unsurpassed for both their profundity and their breadth.

Original sources for mythology include Hesiod's *Cosmogony* and Apollodorus's *The Library of Greek Mythology*, the latter written somewhere between the first and second centuries BCE. Both are indispensable, as is the classic *Fables* by Aesop. They are available in excellent translations, with extensive explanatory notes, from Oxford University Classics paperbacks.

The geographer Pausanias's (2nd century CE) lengthy *Description of Greece* covers the entire country, and his extensive travels took him far and wide through the Mediterranean area. It is essential reading if you want a firsthand account of what the ancient world was like. Historians generally consider him a reliable source. He saw the ruins of Troy and Egypt, went to Italy, and journeyed through what are now Syria and Israel. He describes customs and religious rites and makes frequent reference to mythology, but he also delights in descriptions of nature, places, and architecture.

For history, read the first great historical narrative by the father of history, Herodotus (5th c. BCE): the *History* of the Greco-Persian Wars. It is extremely inaccurate, as we now know, but fascinating nonetheless. The story of the wars between the two great rival city-states—refined, cultivated Athens and militaristic, stern, athletic Sparta—the *History of the Peloponnesian War* by Thucydides (471?–400? BCE) is often considered the greatest masterpiece of ancient historical writing.

Since he actually served in the Athenian army and lived through the events of the period, his narrative has the ring of truth. The *Hellenica*, which recounts the history of the final seven years of the Peloponnesian Wars, and the *Anabasis*, describing the journey to conquer Persia, by Xenophon (431–355 BCE), who accompanied the soldiers there, are two of the most important primary sources for the history of the era.

Film and Television

Despite the popularity of Greek mythology, there is not a great wealth of really good filmed material. There is a 1961 Italian film, *The Trojan Horse*, with Steve Reeves as Aeneas. The 2004 film *Troy* is in some ways an accurate presentation of the Trojan War period, especially in what it shows us of soldiers' armor and the way battles were conducted, as well as the boats and chariots and details of feasts and soldiers' encampments. *The Trojan Women* (1971 and 2004) and *Helen of Troy* (1956 and 2005), *The Odyssey* (a 1997 television film), and the Greek films *Iphigenia* (1977) and *Electra* (1962), both with Irene Papas, are available on videotape and DVD.

Other Greek myths and tragedies have been filmed as well: Laurence Olivier plays Zeus in *Clash of the Titans* (1961), which largely concerns Perseus and the Medusa. Also available on DVD are the Oedipus plays: *Oedipus Rex* (1957) with Douglas Campbell, *Antigone* (1951) with Irene Papas, *Antigone* (1974, Broadway Theatre Archive) with Fritz Weaver and Genevieve Bujold, and *Oedipus the King* (1967) with Christopher Plummer and Lili Palmer.

The story of Jason and Medea is retold in *Jason and the Argonauts* (1963) and *Medea* (1987). Aside from Steve Reeves's Italian films from the 1950s based on the myth of Hercules, there is a 1990s television series, but that is strictly for adolescent viewing.

There have been a number of films based on the life of the ambitious world-conqueror Alexander III of Macedonia, known as the Great (356–323 BCE). He ruled all of Greece and conquered Persia, the Middle East, and Egypt, where he founded Alexandria; his empire extended as far as northern India. The most well-known films about him are *Alexander the Great* (1956), starring Richard Burton in the title role, and Oliver Stone's *Alexander* (2004), starring Colin Farrell. Both films are sumptuous period pieces and quite ahistorical.

Ancient Rome and Roman Theater

Edward Gibbon (1737–1794), one of the most urbane and polished of English writers and a brilliant historian, spent twenty years writing his masterpiece, *The Decline and Fall of the Roman Empire*. It takes the reader from 180 BCE to 1453 CE, from the time of the republic's conquests and the founding of the empire to its fall. Its decline began with its founding and with the ominous murder of the republic's last great hero, Julius Caesar (b. 100 BCE), assassinated in 44 BCE. The first emperor, Augustus (63 BCE–14 CE), reigned from 27 BCE, and the empire continued on into the decadent reigns of such hedonistic psychopaths as Caligula (12–41) and Nero (37–68). When the Visigoths sacked Rome in 410, and the last Western Roman emperor, Romulus (b. 461?), a puppet ruler, died in 476, Greek Byzantium became the Eastern Roman Empire. This ceased to exist in 1453 when the Moslem Ottoman Turks conquered its capital, Constantinople.

Roman theater, like much of Roman culture, derived directly from Greek, and it was performed in the same kind of open-air amphitheater. But the Romans, who enjoyed the circus and such sports as chariot racing and bloody gladiatorial combat, added another typical dimension: the execution of condemned criminals, who were on stage as characters that were supposed to die. The Romans loved their theater. That murderous tyrant, the infamous emperor Nero, was an amateur practitioner of the arts, who overestimated his abilities as a singer and the beauty of his voice, according to that amusing gossip and scandalmonger, Suetonius. Both Tacitus (55?–117?) and Suetonius (2nd c.) tell us that Nero was rumored to have played his lyre and sung his opera *The Fall of Troy* against the background of a burning Rome, which he had caused to be set aflame so that he could raise funds for his new palace through a scheme of compulsory fire insurance, imposed on all citizens after the fire.

Securing its borders but imperfectly against the barbarians who were always threatening to overrun Rome, the empire became cosmopolitan in its culture, as it pursued its imperialistic conquest of other nations. Rome incorporated a diverse population and adopted alien traditions, making them its own, as it did with the ancient Greek religion. The Romans simply changed the names of the gods and goddesses. These names are part of the mental world of every character in a play set in Rome, even if most of the names are never mentioned: The Greek king of the gods, Zeus, became Jupiter; and Hera, queen of the gods, Juno.

Aphrodite became Venus; Artemis, Diana; Athena, (goddess of wisdom), Minerva; Poseidon (god of the sea), Neptune; Ares (god of war), Mars, and so forth. Apollo was so popular that he remained Apollo; and Pluto was so feared that he retained his name as god of the underworld, Hades, where the shades of the dead wandered restlessly in the shadow of cypresses by the banks of the river of forgetfulness, Lethe. The Fates oversaw the destiny of humans and had charge of the threads of life and death. And the nine Muses, daughters of Zeus/Jupiter, danced on Mount Helicon and dwelt on the towering slopes of Mount Parnassus. To humankind they gave the gifts of history, music, dance, tragedy, comedy, sacred song, singing, epic and lyric poetry, and astronomy.

At Delphi, on Mount Parnassus, the ancient Greek shrine of Apollo, god of the sun and of masculine beauty, is serene and solemn. Crowds of tourists who gaze down at the sea, far, far below, meander through the sacred ruins that once were vibrantly alive, thronged with celebrants and presided over by priests and prophetesses. In a trance, these women sat on golden stools amidst the swirling vapors emanating from the underworld and uttered the prophecies of the arbiter of man's fate, whose decrees none could escape. People consulted the oracle well into the Christian era, until the Byzantine Emperor Theodosius I (347–395) put a stop to the practice by closing it down in 393. In that same year, the last Olympic Games were played. The emperor banned them henceforth as a survival of paganism.

The Romans added little to Greek mythology, aside from their myth of the founding of Rome by Romulus and Remus, and by Aeneas, the prince of Troy who escaped the carnage at the end of the Trojan War. Otherwise they adopted Greek myths wholesale, only changing some names as was their habit—so that, for instance, the wily and weary world-traveler Odysseus, returning to his home island of Ithaca after the Trojan War, assumed the name Ulysses.

Skepticism, impiety, hypocrisy, irreligion, and even sacrilege were not unknown in the ancient Greek and Roman worlds. Valerius Maximus (1st c.), an author about whom nothing is known beyond his work, *Memorable Doings and Sayings*, tells us that Pythagoras maintained that even if there were gods, we could know nothing about them. He also tells us that Dionysius the Elder (ca. 432–367 BCE), the cruel tyrant of Syracuse, after despoiling the temple of Persephone (Proserpina to the Romans) at Locri, quipped to his friends as propitious breezes blew their boat along, "You see with what fair sailing the immortal gods themselves pay tribute to the sacrilegious?"

Roman tragedies were more or less adapted from the Greek plays, but their comedies were more original and quite domestic, with characters who were always recognizable human beings—your neighbors and friends—and their dilemmas could be yours any day of the week. There were also one-person shows. Valerius Maximus relates that "the poet Livius," who was known for his satires, "acted his own work and was often called back by the public, which made his voice hoarse, so he brought on a boy and a flute player, who made music while he silently went through miming."

Roman comedies were freer in form than their Greek antecedents, and there were scenes and devices, such as the soliloquy, the aside, and the eavesdropping scene (see pages 140–141), that were used through the following centuries. These are found in Renaissance Italian commedia dell'arte, in Shakespeare and Molière, and in eighteenth- and nineteenth-century plays, melodrama, and opera, where the soliloquy becomes the solo aria. Even twentieth-century vaudeville and television sketches derive unwittingly from Roman comedy.

As Niall W. Slater informs us in *Plautus in Performance* (Princeton University Press, 1985), we don't really know much about Roman theaters or performance practice beyond the texts of the plays themselves, in which there are some indications as to how they were done. In fact, we don't even know what the theaters themselves were like; there is "no satisfactory visual record (in the form of vase paintings or other artistic representations) or verbal description." We don't know much about Roman acting style or theater costumes either, but we do know that Roman actors performed in masks. And we know that plays were accompanied by music and performed against elaborate sets.

And we know as well that there were claques, presumably hired by actors to applaud them and boo their rivals, which says a great deal about how sophisticated and popular theater was in ancient Rome. Tacitus in book 1 of the *Annals*—his history of the reigns of Tiberius (42 BCE–37 CE), Claudius (10 BCE–54 CE), Caligula (much of the account of his reign is missing), and Nero—tells us that on the death of Augustus and the accession of Tiberius as *imperator* (emperor, or commander), there was a short-lived soldiers' mutiny, a strike for better working conditions and higher pay. One of its leaders was "Percennius, formerly leader of a theatrical claque." He had a good, strong voice and could deliver speeches to crowds of his fellow mutineers. Tacitus also tells us that actors were very competitive and that Nero himself, who loved to sing, studied with "voice-trainers" and had his own claque. Roundly applauded in the Roman fashion—hands clapping, fingers snapping, linen cloths waving—he was always awarded first prize at competitions, after kneeling before the judges in mock terror, lest he should lose.

Some wealthy nobles built theaters to celebrate political appointments to such offices as consul, Rome's supreme magistrate, of which two were elected annually for a year's term. Seating at the theater was by rank, and fourteen rows were reserved for the nobility. As in Greece, only men performed. The actors were usually specially trained slaves or former slaves who had purchased their freedom. Many plays were spectacles combining mime, dance, spoken dialogue, and vocal music, as well as instrumental concerts. Pantomime actors who performed in obscene plays and frequently performed in the street for money were banished from Rome, so Tacitus informs us; but they seem to have returned periodically, only to be banished again.

One of the great spectacles, presented intermittently, was *Troy*; it consisted of military parades and mock battles, in which nobles rode horses and displayed their skills. And there were many other games at which plays and spectacles, including mock naval battles, were presented, among them the Juvenalian games instituted by Nero, so that he should not incur the dishonor of appearing in public theaters but could sing in relatively "private" performances. Indeed, for his debut on the public stage, he discreetly avoided Rome and went to Naples, largely a Greek settlement in those days, where a temporary wooden theater was erected for him; many such were built for a specific show and immediately torn down after it. A show was given for him the night before he was to perform, and afterwards, when everyone had left the theater, it collapsed—a not unusual occurrence with these poorly and hastily constructed edifices, in which whole audiences met their deaths, according to Tacitus. The Neapolitans, aghast, considered that a bad omen, but Nero thought otherwise: he had been saved by the gods and was inspired to write songs about collapsing theaters.

The Stylistic Elements: Clothing, Accessories, Movement, Manners, and the Art of Living

Clothing, Accessories, and Movement in Costume: Roman clothing during the ancient period was more ornate and less relaxed than Greek, which it nevertheless more or less imitated. Tunics were worn, long or short; and the toga, draped gracefully by itself or over a long tunic, was the best-known garment. It too was of varying lengths. Magistrates and priests wore an official toga, called a *praetexta* or *pretexta*; it was white and decorated with a wide purple border. The *praetexta* was also worn by boys until they were mature enough to wear the *toga virilla* (man's toga) and by girls until they were married, when they wore gowns that could be quite elaborately dyed and decorated. Another garment, worn by the equestrians (knights) and augurs at such ceremonies as funeral processions was the *trabea*, a white gown with scarlet stripes and a purple seam.

At one point during the reign of Tiberius, so Tacitus informs us, sumptuary laws—laws restricting clothing, food, and other articles of consumption—were enacted. These forbade silk clothing for men as being too luxurious and leading to corruption; gold dinner vessels were forbidden for the same reason. On the other hand, Tiberius scolded his son Germanicus, who had gone to Egypt ostensibly "to become acquainted with antiquity," for going around in a simple Greek tunic and open sandals, instead of in the patrician Roman toga, to make himself popular with the people.

A corner of the toga was often draped around the arm, and the left hand was politely concealed within its folds. Without both hands at the sides to act as a balance, movement could be somewhat slow, impeded by the garment. Women glided on their soft slippers, but men strode in boots and sandals.

In *My Life in Art*, Stanislavsky describes some of the preparation process for the 1903–04 production of *Julius Caesar*, in which he played Brutus, directed by Nemirovich-Danchenko, who recreated the Roman forum on stage in exact and vivid detail:

> We went around in uniforms the whole day.... This experience
> taught us a great deal which one cannot learn in books, or from theories
> or drawings. We learned to handle a toga and its folds, to gather
> them in the fist, to throw the toga over the shoulder or head, to ges-
> ticulate, holding the tip of the toga. We thus created a system of
> movements and gestures that we borrowed from ancient statues.

Women and some emperors were very fond of wigs. Women liked blond hair imported from Germany. Suetonius tells us some revealing details about Julius Caesar's vanity; this is from Philemon Holland's (1552–1637) marvelous Elizabethan translation:

> About the trimming of his body, he was over-curious [fastidious]: so
> as he would not only be notted [have his hair clipped short] and

shaven very precisely, but also have his hair plucked, insomuch as some cast it in his teeth and twitted him therewith. Moreover, finding by experience, that the deformity of his bald head was oftentimes subject to the scoffs and scorns of back-biters and slanderers, he took the same exceedingly to heart; and therefore he both had usually drawn down his hair, that grew but thin, from the crown toward his forehead; and also, of all honors decreed unto him from the senate and people, he neither received nor used any more willingly, than the privilege to wear continually the triumphant laurel garland.

Jewelry and adornments were very popular, and brooches, rings, and necklaces were ostentatiously displayed.

Both men and women could write, which they did on wax tablets with pointed styluses. The tablets were rectangular wooden boards surrounded by raised rims, with black wax spread evenly in the central space of the board.

Social Customs, Greetings, and Salutations: According to Valerius Maximus, when walking in the street, the man of highest rank was followed by someone of lower rank. However, the small son of the person of rank could precede him. One of the many customs showing ranking and precedence even in the republic is that the ten Tribunes of the Plebs (people), whose function was to protect the people by protesting against injustices, were not allowed in the Senate House in the Forum, but sat on a bench outside to examine the decrees of the senators. The plebs are distinguished from the mass of the people as being a class, or order, of people wealthy enough to vote.

Male friends greeted each other by clasping elbows, not hands—and if they were very close, by embracing, and sometimes by kissing on the cheek as well. The hand-clasp, as in Greece, was reserved for the sealing of an oath or promise. As Suetonius informs us in his biography of the emperor Claudius, that worthy tried to be a man of the people on occasion, in order to be popular. When distributing prizes after gladiatorial games or to soldiers, "Putting forth his left hand, he together with the common sort would both by word of mouth tell, and with his fingers also number the pieces of gold when he tendered them unto the winners; and many a time by way of exhortation and entreaty provoke the people to mirth; ever and anon calling them Sirs, yea, and between whiles intermingling bald and far-fetched jests." The patrician Roman custom was to keep the left hand decently concealed; only plebeians "put forth" their left hands. This could prove useful in a production of *Julius Caesar*, where the conspirators' daggers can be concealed in the left hand during the assassination scene.

Tacitus describes Germanicus's friends swearing an oath to avenge him and "touching the right hand of the dying man" in token of their fealty, which is just what Mark Antony might do when he kneels over the corpse of Caesar. He also tells us of military leaders meeting with a right hand clasp and parting with a kiss. In describing the meeting of two "barbarian" kings, Tacitus informs us that it was their custom when sealing an alliance to grasp and entwine their right hands with the thumbs so tightly held that blood would spurt forth, which they would then lick in a mystic treaty.

The bloodthirstiness of the games in which gladiators fought each other to the death or fought animals—or in which, later, Christians were massacred and mauled by lions—is well known. Thumbs up, thumbs down was the well-known indication that a gladiator could live or die in the arena. Gladiators saluted the emperor before the games with the phrase, "We who are about to die salute you." Salutes were given with the right arm, which was extended full length at a ninety-degree angle from the shoulder.

Bows and curtsies, with the right hand over the heart, were customary when entering the presence of the emperor or when leaving it.

Tacitus describes the customs at funeral processions. The ashes of Germanicus, for instance, were carried on the shoulders of tribunes and centurions, preceding "unadorned standards, reversed fasces," which were rods bound together with an axe protruding (a symbol of high office; the axe normally pointed outwards). The plebs, or people, wore black clothing in mourning, and the equestrians the trabea. They "cremated" the clothing and burned incense to the gods as funeral offerings in every town through which the procession passed.

Living Spaces and Furniture: Rome—with its vast infrastructure of roads, bridges, aqueducts, and stone and marble houses and temples—was a sprawling city that housed more than one million inhabitants by the time Augustus ruled over the newly created Empire. Much of the life of ancient Rome took place in the teeming streets of the metropolis, with its endless commerce and traffic.

On the coast near Rome, the wealthy had villas with long, covered corridors affording a view of the sea, and the emperors and highest nobles built palaces. But there were two basic types of Roman houses:

the *domus* (or private house, belonging to patricians or middle-class entrepreneurs) and the *insula* (the equivalent of a modern apartment house; the word also means "island"). Houses could be elaborately decorated, and frescos were painted with great art using a variety of colors; dark red was a favorite. The richly painted rooms, which also contained sculptural ornamentation, were decorated with such motifs as urns and arabesque designs, mythological scenes, and pictures of individual gods and goddesses. And landscapes could be painted high up on a wall. Walls could be very high, and some rooms were surrounded at the top by loggias. Over the centuries, there were different styles of decoration. All of these—like the houses themselves, their rooms, and the rooms' functions—are wonderfully described and discussed by John R. Clarke in his gorgeously illustrated book *The Houses of Roman Italy, 100 B.C. to A.D. 250: Ritual, Space, and Decoration* (University of California Press, 1991), with examples from Pompeii; Herculaneum; and Ostia Antica, the ancient seaport of Rome; among others.

The basic, original design of the *domus* comprised a central courtyard surrounded by rooms. It was a one-story, and usually a one-family, house, which could have a separate area reserved for women and, in the larger houses, a bath area with dressing rooms and hot and cold rooms, and even a daytime reading room. The outer wall facing the street had a narrow entrance, on either side of which were small rented shops opening onto the street; the shops had no back exit. From the street, one entered a roofed corridor that led to the open, central *atrium* (interior courtyard), which could be furnished with marble tables. There was a fountain, or catch basin, called an *impluvium*, directly below the atrium's *compluvium*, its square roof opening. The basin's function was to collect rainwater that the family used for cooking and washing. Surrounding the atrium were the rooms: a dining room, which could be a *biclinium* or a *triclinium*, meaning that it had either two or three tables and stone benches, on which diners reclined during meals (not every domus had a dining room), and *cubicula* (bedrooms). Continuing along through the atrium, one reached the *tablinum*: a reception room, sometimes used as a dining room and often with a raised platform, where the *dominus* (the master of the house) received guests, clients, and dependents, all of whom were expected to bow on entering. Running the length of the back wall of many *domi* was an enclosed garden, onto which the *tablinum* opened. Windows and doors opened onto the atrium; there were no openings to the outside of the house, except for the entrance. *Domi* were built in various styles, including one with wings of rooms off the central wing, each surrounding its own atrium.

Rooms could contain alcoves that were used for various purposes—for instance, to place the beds in the *cubicula* or as a frame for a statue or as the area where the *lares* (the household gods) were worshipped. The floors were sometimes made of red cement, which was manufactured from crushed terra cotta.

The houses of the middle class were smaller versions of the *domus*—and those of the less wealthy artisans, shopkeepers, and freedmen were sometimes quite small—but with two stories, a covered atrium, and no *tablinum*, unnecessary for them in any case. The patrician *domus* was not a private house as we think of houses today. Rather, it was an open establishment that was the nub of the family's activities, including the *dominus's* business. Not only did invited guests stop by, but the uninvited were also free to make an appearance if they had any business to attend to or just wanted to pay their respects. The family and slaves slept in the house at night, but during the day it could be freely entered, just as stores are now, and people came and went all the time.

The *insula*—a much larger establishment, sometimes housing wealthier people, but more often middle-class or poorer Romans—had doors and some windows on the outside wall. It too was constructed around four sides of a central courtyard, but it was built up and usually had two or three, or even more, stories. The *insula* was often divided into apartments. Even with all the windows, the lighting was poor, and oil lamps gave limited light at night.

The furniture was sparse, and there were few armchairs, even in rich houses. Most seating was on benches or stools, some more elaborate than others, without arms. There was a kind of folding seat, the backless "curule" chair. These were used only by officials of the highest rank, who as a general class were called *curules*, meaning that they alone were entitled to use such a chair; it had curved legs and arms, in semicircles that rested on top of each other, and was often ornately decorated with ivory.

Without proper toilet facilities, people did the necessary in public. Although they built vast aqueducts and knew the art of bringing water into fountains in the center of a city, they had no concept of sanitary plumbing, even though the patrician *domus* had latrines; and the gutters of Rome ran with raw sewage. But the Romans were known for their cleanliness, and the ruins of huge public baths attest to the constant attendance and luxury enjoyed by the citizens of the most powerful empire in the European world.

In the many soldiers' camps throughout the empire, living conditions could be quite rough and primitive. In book 1 of the *Annals*, Tacitus describes the soldiers living in tents on the northern borders having to do the extra work, besides that of soldiering, of putting up ramparts, digging ditches, "and haulings of pasturage, fuel and wood, and anything else which was required out of necessity and to combat inactivity in the camp."

Food and Table Manners: The first Roman cookbook that has come down to us was written by Apicius (14–37). Meals were eaten, as in Greece, while leaning on the left arm when reclining on low couches set before low tables. The seat of honor was to the left of the host, on the side nearest his heart. According to Valerius Maximus, it was an ancient custom for the younger diners to await the arrival of their elders before reclining, and to allow the elders to rise and leave before rising themselves. He also tells us that the older banqueters sometimes gave poetry recitations to flute accompaniment, and that men and women used to dine together, a custom that was discontinued. Gold and silver table services were often elaborate and ornately decorated, and the presentation of dishes was lavish. Romans ate with their hands and with spoons and knives. As in ancient Greece, forks were used for cooking and for serving, but nobody used a small fork for dining. Romans dressed for dinner, changing their tunics and shoes. They were gourmets and could be gluttonous gourmands. Belching was considered a sign of politeness.

Aristocrats such as the general Lucullus (1st c.), known for the lavish feasts he provided to his guests, ate very well and even ostentatiously. Such delicacies as snails and roast peacock graced their tables. Julius Caesar loved asparagus with melted butter. But most people ate a limited diet of wine, bread, and grains; some olives, greens, and other vegetables made with olive oil; and occasionally fruit, especially figs, pears, and apples. Meat was a rarity, particularly within the city, but poultry was fairly common, and in seacoast areas, fish was eaten all the time. Cooking was often done outdoors. One of the most popular dishes was a fish sauce called *garum*, made from decaying fermented fish. It was inexpensive, and people could buy a bowl of this nutritious concoction with a slice of bread at a marketplace food shop.

Roman Time Keeping: The Romans carved their calendars into the sides of public buildings. They divided the year into twelve months. However, they did not refer to the years by number but, in the days of the republic, by the names of the consuls who had been elected, or by the years it had been since the founding of the city of Rome.

The Roman year lasted three hundred and fifty-five days, with occasional extra months added to make up for the problem they perceived when months did not occur when they were supposed to, which meant that a month meant for planting could come round at the wrong time of year and confuse the farmers. But the priests added a month every so often, and all was set to rights. It was Julius Caesar who added ten days to the year, making it three hundred and sixty-five days long and eliminating the necessity of having the priests arbitrarily insert a month. But his action was itself deemed arbitrary and was one more reason to get rid of someone who thought he could assume priestly functions and play with time. The Roman year began on March 1, and that is why December, which means the tenth month, was not the twelfth month.

The concept of measuring time by specific units had been around since at least the era of the ancient Babylonians—who, like the ancient Egyptians and Greeks, had used water clocks, and to whom we owe the idea that there are sixty seconds in a minute and sixty minutes in an hour. But although the Romans had water clocks also, they may not generally have used this system of minutes and seconds. However, they did divide the daylight time into twelve hours, and every third hour had importance: after the first one (*prime*), the next significant time was *terce* (the third hour), then *sext* (the sixth), and then *none* (the ninth hour). The hours in between those changed in length with the season and the duration of sunlight, so that time was irregularly measured: summer hours could be considerably longer than winter hours. Nevertheless, *prime* was reckoned as beginning directly after sunrise, and *sext* was then at noon, when the sun was at its highest. At the twelfth hour came sunset. It was all guesswork, even though the Romans used sundials and town criers announced the setting of the sun, and it must have been difficult to make appointments in any exact way. At night there was no set way of telling time, particularly if the moon was clouded over.

The Romans considered certain days lucky and others unlucky. The ides of March, the middle day of the month that began the new year, was unlucky; hence the Soothsayer's warning to Julius Caesar, who scoffs at such superstitions. The *ides* was the middle of a month; the *calends*, its beginning.

The Dance: Dance was important for both ceremonial and theatrical purposes, and in general, we may assume that Roman dance was modeled on the Greek system (see above), but not much is known about it.

Painting and Sculpture

Aside from its amazing architecture, the portrait sculpture of Rome is one of its great glories. The elegance of the Greeks is often lacking in Roman sculpture, which imitates Greek models but is somehow heavier and less graceful. Many Roman sculptures are portraits of political figures or busts of wealthy patrons; studying the realistic faces on the busts of those who could afford to have their portraits done is wonderful for character.

The paintings in the ruins of Pompeii are very instructive about daily life and the style of costumes and decors, even though they are often commonplace. But they do depict real people at real activities, such as writing, dressing, and dining.

Music

Music was important in the life of the ancient Romans, but we don't know much about what it sounded like. To the Greek wind and stringed instruments, they added brass: the *cornu*, a curved horn held around one shoulder with the mouthpiece conveniently placed, used in public ceremonies; the *litnus*, a shorter, hand-held horn also used in ceremonies; and the *tuba*, which was a long narrow tube—a horn totally unlike the present-day instrument of the same name.

Literature

The tragedies of Seneca (4 BCE–65 CE), the Stoic philosopher who had the misfortune to be Nero's tutor, are imitative of ancient Greek plays and often tell the same stories, as in the case of his *Oedipus*, reworked from Sophocles. The comedies of Terence (ca. 195–ca. 159 BCE), a former slave, are often based on Greek models as well and are known for their realism. Perhaps the greatest Roman comic writer, Plautus (254–184 BCE), also gives us a real picture of life in ancient Rome. Several of his plays are the source material for the hit musical *A Funny Thing Happened on the Way to the Forum*. Plautus is known for his slapstick comedy, complicated situations, and colloquial dialogue, as well as for his outspoken, sometimes raunchy sexual comedy. He adapted well-known Greek plays, since lost, but turned them into authentic Roman comedies.

Virgil's (70–19 BCE) *Aeneid*, translated any number of times (read the seventeenth-century version by Dryden and the contemporary one by Robert Fagles) continues the Homeric myths with the story of the ancestors of Rome's founders. Ovid's *Metamorphoses*, a book of mythology with stories about the transformations of Jupiter into various animal and avian forms for purposes of seducing mortals; Apuleius's (2nd c.) *The Golden Ass*; Horace's (65–68 BCE) philosophically-minded *Odes*; and Martial's (1st c.) twelve books of *Epigrams*—feisty, obscene, and hilarious—are among the other great Roman classics you should read. And peruse the speeches of Cicero for their contemporary politics as well as for their artistry.

For a look at how the Romans viewed their own history, read Suetonius's *The Twelve Caesars*—Robert Graves's modern translation is as brilliant as that of Philemon Holland—as well as the histories of Tacitus, among them the *Annals*; and Livy's (59 BCE–17 CE) multivolume *History of Rome*. Of the fourteen histories he wrote, five have survived the ravages of time, and they are indispensable for the study of living conditions and the history of the empire in general. Written in Greek, Plutarch's *Lives* of Greeks and Romans is also necessary reading. He recounts the lives of Alexander, Julius Caesar, Mark Anthony, Cleopatra, and Coriolanus, among many others. Shakespeare used stories from Sir Thomas North's widely read 1579 translation. Dryden's translation also became famous and replaced North's as the standard. For a firsthand account of the conquest of Gaul by the Romans—as well as general information about conditions in the Roman military and in Rome and ancient Gaul—read Julius Caesar's *The Gallic War*, available in a bilingual edition from the Loeb Classical Library, an indispensable series of Greek and Latin classics published by the Harvard University Press. All the books contain informative, erudite introductions. And read the Stoic philosophical *Meditations* of the emperor Marcus Aurelius, invaluable as a psychological character study.

Film and Television

The 2005 HBO series *Rome* and the 1976 PBS miniseries based on Robert Graves's *I, Claudius* present fascinating pictures of the period. Worth seeing too are the Hollywood epics *Ben Hur* (silent, 1925; talkie, 1959), with its famous chariot race, and *Spartacus* (1960), with its depiction of a slave rebellion and gladiatorial combat. Less accurate, but rewarding nonetheless, are the old film based on Edward George Bulwer-Lytton's novel *The Last Days of Pompeii* (1935) and the biblical epics *The Robe* (1953) and its sequel, *Demetrius and the Gladiators* (1954).

The 1946 film based on George Bernard Shaw's witty *Caesar and Cleopatra*; the panoramic 1934 film, *Cleopatra*, with Claudette Colbert in the title role; as well as the 1963 saga of the same name, with Elizabeth Taylor as the doomed Egyptian queen and Richard Burton as Mark Anthony are all splendid recreations of the period. There have been twenty-one film and television adaptations of Shakespeare's *Julius Caesar*, notably one in 1953 with Marlon Brando, James Mason, and John Gielgud, all outstanding as, respectively, Mark Antony, Brutus, and Cassius.

Federico Fellini's take on Petronius and on the decadence and eroticism of ancient Rome, *Satyricon* (1969), is erratic and bizarre—but then, so was Petronius. Richard Lester's film of the Broadway musical *A Funny Thing Happened on the Way to the Forum* (1966), while hardly authentically Roman, is highly amusing. Zero Mostel plays Pseudolus, a name that sounds invented but is the title of one of Plautus's comedies.

For More Information

Ancient Greece

Apollodorus. *The Library of Greek Mythology*. A new translation by Robin Hard. New York: Oxford University Press, 1997.

Athenaeus. *The Deipnosophists*. Translated by Charles Burton Gulick. 7 vols. Cambridge, MA: (Loeb Classical Library) Harvard University Press, 1929–41.

Bulfinch, Thomas. *Mythology: The Age of Fable; The Age of Chivalry; The Age of Charlemagne*. New York: The Modern Library, n.d.

Durant, Will and Ariel. *The Story of Civilization: Part II, The Life of Greece*. New York: Simon and Schuster, 1939.

Garland, Robert. *Daily Life of the Ancient Greeks*. Westport, CT: Greenwood Press, 1998.

Hamilton, Edith. *Mythology*. New York: Warner Books reissue, 1999.

Hesiod. *Cosmogony; Works and Days*. A new translation by M. L. West. New York: Oxford University Press, 1999.

Homer. *The Iliad*. Translated by Robert Fagles. New York: Penguin, 1998.

———*The Odyssey.* Translated by Robert Fagles. New York: Penguin, 2006.

MacDowell, Douglas M. *The Law in Classical Athens.* Ithaca, NY: Cornell University Press, 1978.

Renault, Mary. *The Last of the Wine.* New York: Pantheon Books, 1936.

Rider, Bertha Carr. *Ancient Greek Houses.* Chicago, IL: Argonaut, Inc., 1964.

Ringer, Mark. *Electra and the Empty Urn: Metatheater and Role Playing in Sophocles.* Chapel Hill, NC: University of North Carolina Press, 1998.

Schwab, Gustav. *Gods and Heroes of Ancient Greece.* New York: Pantheon Books, 1946.

Audio CD: *Music of the Ancient Greeks.* Pandourion Records, USA, 1997.

Ancient Rome

Aldrete, Gregory S. *Daily Life in the Roman City: Rome, Pompeii, and Ostia.* Westport, CT: The Greenwood Press, 2004.

Carcopino, Jérôme. *Daily Life in Ancient Rome: The People and the City at the Heart of the Empire.* Translated from the French by E. O. Lorimer. Edited with bibliography and notes by Henry T. Rowell. New York: Bantam Books, 1971.

Clarke, John R. *The Houses of Roman Italy, 100 B.C.—A.D. 250: Ritual, Space, and Decoration.* Berkeley, CA: University of California Press, 1991.

Durant, Will and Ariel. *The Story of Civilization: Part III, Caesar and Christ.* New York: Simon and Schuster, 1944.

Gibbon, Edward. *The Decline and Fall of the Roman Empire.* 3 vols. New York: The Modern Library, 2003.

Ovid. *Metamorphoses.* A new translation by E. J. Melville. New York: Oxford University Press, 1998.

Palmer, L. R. *The Latin Language.* Norman, OK: University of Oklahoma Press, 1988.

Petronius. *The Satyricon and The Fragments.* Translated with an introduction by J. P. Sullivan. New York: Penguin Books, 1969.

Slater, Niall W. *Plautus in Performance: The Theatre of the Mind.* Princeton, NJ: Princeton University Press, 1985.

Suetonius. *History of Twelve Caesars.* Translated by Philemon Holland. Edited by J. H. Freese, M.A. With an introduction and notes. New York: E. P. Dutton & Co., 1930.

Suetonius Tranquillus, Gaius. *The Twelve Caesars.* Translated by Robert Graves. New York: Penguin Books, 1965.

Tacitus. *The Annals*. Translated and with introduction and notes by A. J. Woodman. Indianapolis, IN: Hackett Publishing Company, Inc., 2004.

Valerius Maximus. *Memorable Doings and Sayings*. 2 vols. Edited and translated by D. R. Shackleton Bailey. Cambridge, MA: Harvard University Press, 2000.

Zimmerman, J. E. *Dictionary of Classical Mythology*. 18th printing. New York: Bantam Books, 1985.

CHAPTER FOUR

The Medieval Period: Chivalry and the Dark Ages

The Medieval European World

> Withoute bake mete was nevere his hous
> Of fisshe and flesshe, and that so plentevous
> It snowed in his hous of mete and drynke,
> Of all dantyes that men koude thynke...
> Ful many a fat partrich hadde he in muwe [mew: a pen for keeping poultry]
> And many a breem and many a luce [pike] in stuwe [fish-pond]

The wealthy *frankeleyene*, or franklin in modern spelling—a landowner, not of noble birth—is quite a sleek and contented hedonist. He is one of the many memorable characters in Geoffrey Chaucer's (1342/3–1400) *The Canterbury Tales*, a long, richly detailed narrative poem about a group of people traveling together on a pilgrimage to Canterbury and whiling away the tedium of their journey by telling each other stories. It is one of the best sources for what life was like and how people behaved in the late medieval era. We meet representatives of the various social classes, among them a knight who has traveled and fought widely and has the medieval virtue of loving chivalry, truth, and honesty, and his son, who serves him as a squire:

> Syngynge he was, or flotynge [playing the flute], al the day;
> He was as fresshe as is the month of May.
> Short was his gowne, with sleves longe and wyde.
> Wel koude he sitte on hors and fairly ryde,
> He koude songes make and wel indite [put words to his music]

They are accompanied by a servant "yeoman," "clad in cote and hood of grene." The others include a richly appareled merchant, "Upon his heed a Flaundryssh bever [Flemish beaver] hat"; a miller, a weaver, a dyer and an arras-maker; a prioress with her three priests; a monk; a nun; a manciple (the steward or officer who purchased supplies for a monastery or college); a clerk (student); a reeve (an official who represented the royal power in a district, much like the Sheriff—shire reeve—of Nottingham in the Robin Hood tales); and the wife of Bath, with her earthy love of life and laughter.

All the characters treat each other with the deference due to their different ranks and stations, but there is a sense of camaraderie and a feeling of nascent democracy and equality. These qualities are lacking, perhaps, in other medieval European cultures, with their emphasis on the sacrosanct nature of hierarchy, and on gallantry in arms and stories of courtly love, with knights in shining armor pining for unattainable, absent ladies and carrying a token given them by her in remembrance. This feeling of freedom is only natural in an England that was not ruled by absolute monarchy, although the king and the feudal barons, who had demanded of King John (1166–1216) that their rights be enshrined in the Magna Carta Libertatum (Great Paper of Liberties) in 1215, were extremely powerful.

Chaucer wrote *The Canterbury Tales* in Middle English, during the reign of Richard II (1367–1400), who ruled from 1377 to 1399. By the end of the following century, the population of England was divided no longer into the vanquished who spoke Anglo-Saxon and the conquering Normans who had taken over after 1066 and spoke their dialect of French: everyone spoke a dialect of English. But in Wales and Cornwall, Welsh and Cornish were spoken by the majority, just as Scottish Gaelic was in the highlands of Scotland. Latin, spoken by the clergy and used in education, legal documents, and the law courts, continued to be the lingua franca of Europe, and the upper classes in England continued to speak French—which, however, they now learned as a second language. Henry V (1387–1422) was the first king of England whose native language was English.

The medieval period lasts for a thousand years, from approximately 450–1450/1500. During all that time, much of Europe was ruled under the feudal system that divided social classes into nobles—who owed allegiance as vassals to a sovereign lord, duke, prince, or king, to whom they were bound to supply soldiers and arms—and peasants, who were bound as serfs to the land of the nobles. The clergy constituted a separate class, as did the citizens of the towns, who were merchants, artisans, and craftsmen. But almost needless to say, there are so many cultural and political changes over so long a span of time that there are many styles in manners, dress, and behavior to take account of.

There were many regional governments, including the dukedoms of Burgundy and Normandy; the kingdom of Navarre; the Moslem and Christian kingdoms of the Iberian peninsula; the baronetcies and dukedoms of Germany; the principalities and self-governing autocratic city-states of Italy; the French royal court, centered in Paris; and the monarchy of England, centered in London—the last two only gradually came to rule the united territories we associate with contemporary France and Britain.

In tenth-century Cordoba, a Moslem Spanish city, the sophisticated arts of music and poetry flourished, and the Jews there spoke and wrote in Arabic, or Judeo-Arabic. Like their Christian and Moslem neighbors, many of them from North Africa, they dressed in Arab garb. Ranging over every philosophical and amorous subject, the Hebrew poetry written in Spain for four centuries attests to the love the Jews had for their native land, despite the increasing discrimination they experienced. From before the tenth century until 1492, Christian, Moslem, and Jewish neighbors lived in relative harmony. But in that year, King Ferdinand (1452–1516) and Queen Isabella (1451–1504) completed the *Reconquista* (the Reconquest) making all of Spain officially Catholic; conquering the last Moslem stronghold, Granada; and expelling all those Jews who would not convert. They had established the Inquisition in 1478, much of its activity directed against converted Jews, many of whose lives became a nightmare.

From about the eighth to about the tenth century, the courts of the nobles of Provence in southern France were among the most cultivated in Europe. The language spoken there was Old Occitanian, also called Old Provençal, a Romance language related closely to Catalan and French. Provence itself was actually part of the Spanish kingdom of Aragon. The Provençal arts of song and dance were sophisticated and derived in part from the Greek and Roman inheritance of the region, for the Greeks had long before taken over Marseilles from the Phoenicians who founded it, and Rome had made Provence a province of the empire. Added to those traditions were the Moorish ones brought from North Africa by way of Spain. It is largely from the Provençal courts that the traditions of chivalry emanate, as the troubadours, who were known as great fighters as well as great poets, wrote and sang their famous poems dedicated to courtly love and erotic desire. Music from some of these poems, written in the same notation used for chants, has survived. In Germany, these traveling minstrels had their counterpart in the minnesingers, who also composed poems about courtly love that were set to music. Like the melodies of the troubadours, the songs of the minnesingers were often not noted down but were meant for oral transmission.

In the twelfth and thirteenth centuries, with the building of the Gothic cathedrals, after 1140, there was a short-lived Renaissance in France. And by the end of the fifteenth century, the feudal manorial system of serfdom was being modified. In England, for instance, *yeomen* (peasants freed of some, but not all feudal obligations) lived in villages where local justices of the peace, a new class of officials appointed to rule in the crown's name, held sway alongside the local feudal lords to whom the peasants still owed allegiance. The Black Death of 1348–49 would speed the process of change: so many of the peasants died, leaving the manorial lords short of manpower, that they had to yield to the demands of the recalcitrant survivors for more favorable conditions. Unless more rights were granted him, the serf, legally bound to the land, might risk fleeing to the town. There he could learn a craft, such as weaving or masonry, and earn a living as a laborer.

In the early medieval period, people were poorly educated, if at all, and illiteracy, even among the wealthier economic strata, was widespread. Boys of noble family might have private tutors at home, and they learned to wield the sword and the carving knife; but girls were rarely educated, except in such gentle arts as wielding the embroidery needle. Because of the system of primogeniture, the oldest sons of noble families inherited everything, and the younger sons had few prospects. In peacetime (rare enough) when their military services were not needed, the younger sons, if they did not wish to go into the legal profession or the church, would often be used as tutors, or apprenticed as squires or high servants to other noble families. Well trained in the arts of the table and courtly manners, they were the heads of the serving staffs in the castles where they were placed. If they were still quite young, the boys would first serve as henchmen—that is, cupbearers or chamberlains (valets). Unmarried younger daughters would also find positions as ladies in waiting.

Great universities were founded, among them Oxford in 1096, Cambridge in 1209, the Sorbonne in 1257, and the University of Heidelberg in 1386. Courses were taught in Latin to the eager university students, who were mostly from poor families, like the lean, impoverished Clerk in *The Canterbury Tales*. The university population was increasing by the later medieval period, and by the Renaissance, it would be considered proper for gentlemen to be educated; so they, too, flocked to the universities. But in medieval days, it was the poor students and monks, with their supreme art of illuminating manuscripts, who kept literacy alive, along with the Latin language. The monasteries of Ireland, for instance, were notable for the high level of their learning and culture from the fifth century on; for them, this was by no means the Dark Ages. All over Europe, there were also specially trained scribes who could write letters for the nobility. These lords and ladies would often have to have someone, usually a clergyman, read their correspondence. Among the Jews, men were expected to learn to read Hebrew and Aramaic in order to study the Torah and the Talmud (the vast compendium of commentaries on the Torah and religious law). In those days this was also civil law within the Jewish community itself, dealing with community affairs. Of course, the Jews also obeyed the civil laws of the places where they resided. The rate of literacy among Jewish men was very high.

Peasant boys were taught agricultural arts—and girls, domestic arts—by their parents. And in the later Middle Ages especially, when crafts and arts, weaving, engineering, architecture, masonry, and commerce were well developed, guilds for the various arts and professions were organized and established all over Europe, with systems of apprenticeship and master craftsmen for each area of endeavor. Much prestige was attached to membership in the guilds, which eventually controlled commerce and social life.

There was a great deal of international commerce, and many were the merchants and adventurers who wrote down their stories. These included Jewish voyagers, of whom one of the most famous is the linguist and geographer Rabbi Benjamin ben Jonah of Tudela (?–?) in Spanish Navarre, who left an account of his travels from 1165 to 1173. A hundred years before Marco Polo (1254–1324), he set out on a pilgrimage to the Holy Land, reached Baghdad and traveled through North Africa, and went to other places later described by the Italian traveler.

Life as it was lived by most people before technology made it easier was hard, rough, mean, cruel, and difficult. Europe was subject to intermittent epidemics of the plague and in the grip of endless warfare: the Hundred Years War, for instance, fought from 1337 to 1453 between England and France, was actually a series of dynastic wars. Among them were the Wars of the Roses, between the Houses of York and Lancaster, portrayed in Shakespeare's history plays. And there were at least eighteen brutally murderous Christian Crusades from 1095 on through the fifteenth century, fought to regain the Holy Land from the "infidel" Moslems or to convert the "heathen" or to stamp out so-called heresy on the continent of Europe itself.

It is a wonder that humankind survived at all in the frozen North of Scandinavia and the vast forests and inhospitable mountains of Europe. Everything had to be done from scratch: Food had to be grown, harvested, and cooked. Yarn had to be made, mostly by women who spun thread, and clothing sewn from cloth that had to be woven. Water had to be fetched from wells. Laundry had to be done (when it was done) at a stream or river. If you wanted soap or candles, you had to make them. In short, there was nothing convenient or easy in such a life. Freezing cold in winter, broiling in summer, serfs bound to the land of their masters in near slavery lived short, often miserable, and deprived lives. The peasants in their cramped hovels huddled near the smoky fire for warmth, the animals sharing the room with the family during the winter months. And we must picture the lord wrapped in furs and freezing nonetheless in his drafty castle, with its small window openings covered with translucent, oil-rubbed parchment. Life was also difficult in the growing towns and cities, with their unpaved streets and lack of sanitation and hygiene.

The Middle Ages in Europe was a world in which religion was paramount. The hierarchical order of the world was decreed by God and therefore sacrosanct. In 1486, a book authorized by Pope Innocent VIII (1432–1492) was published, which showed how deeply superstition had penetrated religion over the past few centuries and which was to prove influential for centuries more: the *Malleus Maleficarum* (The Hammer of Evildoers—meaning, in this case, witches). This was a very strange, lengthy, and convoluted text, giving the theological reasons for the existence of witches and the means of combating them. It was written by two terrified Dominican monks and inquisitors, Johann Sprenger (1436–1495) and Heinrich Kramer (1430?–1505). For them, witches and their compacts with Satan were real. They set out the procedures to be used at witchcraft trials: torture for extracting confessions was highly recommended. The book was accepted by the Catholic Church and Protestants as the authoritative, almost sacrosanct last word on the subject, and it went through twenty-eight editions. To reject its tenets was heresy, and people who denied its dogmatic pronouncements could be burned at the stake themselves.

Slavery, justified by the Bible and enforced by law, was part of the economic system throughout the medieval period. Slaves in Europe came from all over the known world and were owned by Christians, as well as by some Jews, when the local laws allowed them to do so. Conquered Slavs from eastern Europe were enslaved (hence the word "slave"); so were Moslems from the Middle East and North Africa and, later, Africans from farther south. The Islamic world, it must be said— so advanced at that time in mathematics, medicine, astronomy and the arts of living—returned the favor, and captured Christians were sold and enslaved in all the marketplaces where Islam prevailed.

In 1859 an English translation was published of *The Bondage and Travels of Johann Schiltberger, A Native of Bavaria, in Europe, Asia and Africa, 1396–1427*. It is a fascinating account. Schiltberger (1381–1440), born in Munich, was a kind of German Marco Polo, and his highly popular book went through several editions in the fifteenth and sixteenth centuries. He was apparently illiterate and dictated the memoirs of all he had done and seen to a scribe. Having followed his lord into battle against the Turks, he had been taken prisoner and enslaved, serving several different masters in succession. His travels with them took him as far as Siberia—which he describes in detail—and through the Arabian peninsula and Palestine, until he managed to escape from the Black Sea area in company with five of his fellow Europeans. The first European to have seen the holy places of Islam from the inside, he devotes eleven chapters to that religion. He wound up in Constantinople—it had not yet been captured by the Turks—before returning home to his native Bavaria and his deeply loved Catholic religion.

To reinforce the hold of religion, passion plays were done in churches all over Europe, providing easily accessible lessons accompanying the Mass: dramatizations of the life of Christ, especially his final Passion, and plays about other biblical subjects as well, all done within the precincts and under the auspices of the church. There were cycles of plays, some beginning with Genesis and going all the way through the Resurrection, and shorter cycles dealing only with the life of Christ. Along with the mystery plays—which were similar to what the Italians called a *sacra representazione* (holy or sacred performance) and the Spaniards an *auto sacramental* (sacred act), as well as miracle plays, largely about the lives of the saints—they were important means of teaching in an era when few except some members of the clergy and aristocracy could read. The Bible was therefore a mystery to most people, a sacred book and an object of veneration that some priest quoted in Sunday sermons. The priest, being the representative of God, was almost like a god himself. The passion plays and biblical cycles were also associated with particular towns, such as Chester in England and Oberammergau in Germany. Some complete cycles and fragments of others have survived. The style in which they were done was lively, not mannered or posed, and costumes depicted the characters in a standardized way.

Marketplaces and fairs became venues in which the players, groups of whom now strolled from place to place, could earn some money by entertaining the crowds. The devil was treated as a comic figure, playing practical jokes on unwary spectators, and religious episodes were sometimes done in a satiric way, eliciting laughter that even in the Middle Ages attests to the spread of impiety and anticlericalism. This form of mockery in an inflexible age became so popular that finally, in 1548, well into the Renaissance era, the Parlement of Paris felt obliged to prohibit all plays with biblical subjects or characters. But the way for secular farces and dramas had already been paved. The didactic morality play, which was a transitional drama between the church plays and the newer secular theater, dealt with situations in which a religious moral was taught but in a secular setting. The most famous is the fifteenth-century English play *Everyman*. But even as early as the tenth century we see the beginnings of that transition in the extant writings of Hrotsvitha of Gandersheim (935?–973), for instance. She was canoness of the Saxon Imperial Abbey of Gandersheim, and she wrote six plays meant to inculcate devoutness and discredit what she saw as the immorality of Terence's comedies—showing that knowledge of at least some ancient Roman literature was still alive even in the so-called Dark Ages. Her subjects include martyrdom (*Dulcitius*) and conversion (*Paphnutius*), and the plot of one play hinges on necrophilia (*Callimachus*).

The Stylistic Elements: Clothing, Accessories, Movement, Manners, and the Art of Living

Clothing, Accessories, and Movement in Costume: In Scandinavia, the Swiss Alps, and other high mountain areas, furs and animal skins were worn for protection against the cold, and they were sometimes cumbersome to move in. Helmets or cloth hats, gloves, tunics, undershirts, leg-hugging trousers, and high-laced boots completed men's clothing. Women's clothing was similar, but with the addition of gowns over the leggings.

In warmer climates, men wore tights or tight-fitting breeches. They wore gowns over tunics earlier in the period, or short jackets (doublets) over their hose later in the era. The loose or tight gowns (sometimes pleated), with no collar and with either great wide hanging sleeves or narrow ones, were fastened at the neck and belted around the waist. The long gown with a hood sewn onto it was common, and younger courtiers replaced it with colorful and even flashy jackets and hose that showed off their legs.

In Chaucer's England, the typical basic garment for both men and women was the *coathardie*, a tight-fitting sleeved tunic or gown closely fitted at the waist, which was of varying lengths for men—to the tops of the thighs or to the bottom of the knees—and usually close to floor length for women. The coathardie had a front slit, buttoned or laced from the neck to the waist. The sleeves, often embroidered or with strips of cloth sewn on for ornamentation, could also be slit and buttoned or laced part or all of the way up.

The Book of Keruynge (The Book of Carving), printed in 1508 by Wynken de Worde (d. 1535), is devoted largely to the arts of the table (see below) but also describes in detail how the chamberlain, who is enjoined to be "dyligent & clenly in his offyce," is to dress his lord. The book is based on earlier medieval sources, especially John Russell's (15th c.) *The Boke of Nurture*, written ("by me," says Russell) around 1430 and published in 1460. Russell served Humphrey, Duke of Gloucester (1391–1447), "a Prynce fulle royalle, with whom Vschere [Usher] in Chamber was Y, and Mershalle also in Halle [the dining hall]." Here is what the worthy Chamberlain must do of a morn, according to Wynken de Worde (I have modernized the spelling):

> See that he have a clean shirt breech [underpants] petticoat and dou-
> blet / then brush his hosen within and without and see his shoon and
> slippers be made clean / and at morn when your sovereign [lord]
> shall arise warm his shirt by the fire [Russell says to make sure the
> fire is not smoky] / and see he have a foot sheet made in this manner.
> First set a chair by the fire with a cushion an [sic] other under his feet.

Having thus prepared the dressing area near the fire and warmed the rest of the clothing, the chamberlain proceeds to dress the lord, who is now sitting in the prepared warm chair, having put on his breech, short petti-coat (underskirt), and shirt, which would be tucked between the thighs,

> & then put on his hosen and his shoon or slippers then strike up his
> hosen mannerly & tie them up [with laces, called points, passed
> through holes at the bottom of the doublet] then lace his doublet

hole by hole [up its front] and lay the cloth about his neck and comb his head / then look ye have a basin and an ewer with warm water and a towel and wash his hands / then kneel upon your knee and ask your sovereign what robe [gown] he will wear and bring him such as your sovereign commandeth and put it upon him then do his girdle [belt] about him and take your leave mannerly.

Russell adds the following details: Once his hose were on, the lord would put on ankle-high socks, called "vamps," and then his "shoon," "laced or bockelid." After the doublet, the lord would don a *stomacher*, a kind of jacket that could be richly embroidered and was also laced, before putting the gown over it; the top of the gown would be open to show off the stomacher. Russell tells the chamberlain that the stomacher, too, should be "welle y-chaffed"—that is, well warmed—before being put on. Lastly, the lord would don his hat.

At night, carpets would be laid near the fireplace and bed so that the lord would not have to walk on the cold stone floor after he was undressed by the chamberlain and had put on his nightcap and gown. In the morning, the bed sheets were taken off, shaken out, and brushed before being put back, or the bed was made with fresh sheets. The chamberlain also had to make sure, says Wynken de Worde, that "the house of easement be sweet and clean and the privy board covered with a green cloth and a cushion / then see there be blanket down or cotton [to serve as toilet paper] for your sovereign."

In the late twelfth and thirteenth centuries, there were a number of public baths in Paris, to which sick people were not admitted, but bathing was by and large still deemed dangerous to public health. Some town houses also had baths, but it is by no means clear whether these were steam baths or immersion pools.

Courtly, slow movement and few gestures were dictated by the voluminous nature of the clothing, especially when cloaks, sometimes floor length, were worn. When walking, one end of a cloak was sometimes draped over one arm. Or the cloak was held in both hands, either up off the floor and to the side or lifted and held in front, again with both hands. When standing, it was natural to place one hand on the waist and the other over the heart or hooked into the belt. If a sword was worn, it was natural to place one hand on it. Sometimes, both hands were held near the front collar, or if a cloak was worn, one hand was folded over it with the other at the side. But this was only the case when the sleeves were not the full, draped ones but fit close to the arm.

Jewelry was worn by both men and women. Daggers and swords were worn at the side. Hats could either be dispensed with altogether or were simple caps or elaborately cut and shaped bonnets, with snaking wide ribbons draped over the shoulder. In early fourteenth-century Florentine paintings, we see peaked hats with a brim that narrowed towards the front.

Women's clothing in the later period of the thirteenth to fifteenth centuries was voluminous and covered the body as much as possible, with gowns and overgowns quite common. The movement required by floor-length skirts and thin-soled shoes was slow and delicate. One simply could not move quickly in such clothing, which often tended to pull the body slightly backwards so that balancing could be awkward.

For women wearing more elaborate, multilayered gowns, it was natural to clasp the hands demurely in front of the upper waist or to rest them on the front of the gown. They sometimes wore high, elaborate headdresses—single or double horns, from which cloth was elaborately draped, for instance—which could also pull one backwards, so that the head had to be carefully poised, balanced, and held upright. Women's voluminous skirts were not always heavy, because they were often made of such light material as silk. They could be bunched into a ball and held in front of the waist or near the bosom in clasped hands as women walked, slowly gliding and comfortably bending the knees slightly. Or they could be draped over one arm and the hand held free, while the other hand dealt with keeping the gown off the floor.

Crossing the legs when sitting becomes impossible in this clothing, and people had to sit with uncrossed, slightly spread legs. For both men and women, any other positions would tend to be uncomfortable. Also, the draped, sometimes padded sleeves drooping over the wrists precluded extravagant gestures. To see these positions clearly, look at the religious paintings of the period, which show biblical figures in medieval clothing, sitting or standing in attitudes typical of the era when they were painted.

Medieval Jews were often obliged to wear distinctive articles of clothing, such as special hats; or badges marking them as Jews, such as the red circle sewn on Venetian Jewish clothing.

Greetings and Salutations: Depending on the rank of a superior, men made a full or half bow, sometimes low, sometimes with less of an inclination, from the waist, bending both knees slightly. Women curtsied low, sometimes all the way to the ground, with one leg held behind the other. In less formal situations, women would keep the knees and feet touching and bow slightly from the waist, bending the legs at the same time. These salutations were used both when entering and leaving the presence of a noble.

When paying homage to a lord or sovereign, men made a full genu- flection, bringing the left leg behind the right and kneeling on the left leg; and women curtsied, kneeling on both legs before rising as gracefully as possible. The body remained straight up while performing the man's bow, with no inclination but with the right hand held over the heart. It was customary to kiss the sometimes gloved hand of a monarch and the ring of a high clergyman, and for men to kiss women's hands. But note that the lips would not actually touch the hand but were merely held above it.

Written sometime in the mid-fifteenth century, *Urbanitatis*, an anonymous poem concerning manners and politesse, describes the pro- cedure to be followed when entering the presence of a nobleman (I have modernized the spelling):

> When thou comest before a lord
> In hall, in bower, or at the board [table],
> Hood or cap thou off do
> Ere thou come him all unto
> Twice or thrice withouten doubt
> To that lord thou must lowt [lower yourself; make obeisance]
> With the right knee let it be do
> Thy worship thou mayest save so
> Hold off thy cap & thy hood also
> Till thou be bidden it on to do

When a vassal paid homage to his lord and swore fealty or was granted a fief, or even in the ceremony conferring knighthood after having served other knights as a squire, he was obliged to enter the lord's presence in a state of purity, without any weapons or spurs, and to appear in a simple, beltless tunic, and bareheaded. He made a genu- flection—kneeling on the left knee and raising his arms, palms of the hands pressed together—to his liege, who then took both hands between his own while the vassal took an oath of perpetual loyalty. When con- ferring knighthood, the lord took his sword in both hands and tapped the squire lightly on first the left and then the right shoulder, saying as he did so, "I dub thee Sir ___."

The manners of the Vikings—hunters, sailors, and fishermen of the earlier medieval era—portrayed in the sagas and epics were rougher and readier than they were in the more refined southern lands, where the generally milder temperatures and living conditions gave more time for the development of elaborate systems of etiquette and precedence. Bows and curtsies were not for them, but hearty hand-clasps and hugs were.

Generally, the pieties of religion, publicly observed in the most obsequious and deferential manner, whatever one's private beliefs, were also supremely important: crossing oneself on every possible occasion, and always in church of course; kneeling on both knees before praying; and clasping the hands in the usual ritualized, prescribed manner were automatic habits. If you entered a room with an icon or a religious image in it, you automatically crossed yourself, just as you did in a church, while also bowing to the altar. Greek or Russian Orthodox crossed themselves from right shoulder to left, Roman Catholics from left to right.

Shaking or clasping right hands was a solemn custom used only at a ceremonial event to seal an agreement or treaty, and only between persons of equal rank, as Jean Froissart (ca. 1337–ca. 1405) tells us in his *Chronicles* was observed between King Richard II of England and King Charles VI of France (1368–1422) when they met in 1396 near Calais.

Living Spaces and Furniture: The clergy lived largely in convents and monasteries, the nobles in spacious castles. A more or less authentic look at such strongholds is provided by the ruins of the medieval fortified city of Carcassonne—largely a nineteenth-century restoration—in southern France. Altogether, the city is magnificent and impressive. But the rooms in such castles were poorly lit, and fireplace heating often left them smoky and unhealthy; they were drafty and badly heated in winter. Lighting at night was by torches, candles, and closed lanterns with candles in them. Decorated with ornate tapestries, rooms were often sparsely furnished with uncomfortable, flat wooden chairs and stools, and broad wooden tables for dining. The nobles had beds with mattresses and curtains, but they were not comfortable, although goose down was used for stuffing. Vast armoires and chests served for the storage of clothing and kitchenware. The chateau kitchens were huge and contained floor-to-ceiling fireplaces at which spit roasting was done; castle courtyards were also used for roasting huge carcasses. The animals often lived there side by side with the people.

People seldom washed either themselves or their clothing for fear of diseases carried in water, although of course they had no concept of germs or bacteria. But it is clear from John Russell's *The Boke of Nurture* that the nobility did sometimes desire to bathe. He gives the chamberlain detailed instructions for preparing "a bath or a stew, so called" (I have modernized the spelling):

> If your sovereign will to the bath, his body to wash clean,
> Hang sheets round about the roof [of the room]. . .
> Every sheet full of flowers and herbs sweet and green,
> And look ye have sponges.

The basin, or bathtub, is to be full of fresh herbs, the water nice and hot, and a great sponge is provided for him to sit on and another under his feet. After making sure the door is well shut, the chamberlain will give the lord a sponge bath. And as a final step, he will rinse the lord with rosewater before drying him off with a clean towel as he stands on a warm foot-sheet in front of the fire. The chamberlain will then help his lord to put on his nightclothes and lead him to bed, "his bales [cf. baleful] there to bete" (his troubles there to overcome), perhaps in sweet dreams.

The castle moats—into which chamber pots were emptied and holes leading down from the "house of easement" ran—were filled with raw sewage, which, of course, meant that the water would have been deadly to drink. The house of easement was sometimes located on the roof, affording the lords and ladies a pleasant view of their domains.

Most peasants lived in huts that had two rooms with dirt floors, if they were lucky, and those were shared with the animals, which also provided more heat in winter than a fireplace could, particularly when fuel was scarce. Like those of the aristocrats, these rooms were badly lit, and smoky from the fireplaces used for cooking as well as heating. There was usually no bedding, and people slept on straw, which had to be constantly replaced.

In the cities, there were separate small houses on their own land, with kitchen gardens, but increasingly there were also narrow, tall, cramped, uncomfortable houses with narrow staircases, so that even in medieval days, urban slums were developing. Poorer people often slept on floors and on straw, as in the countryside.

Food and Table Manners: The cliché of table manners that we see in films often shows the lords and ladies indulging in abysmal, vulgar, unhygienic, and coarse practices. People wipe their greasy mouths on their sleeves or the tablecloth, if there is one, and tear meat off roasts or pull poultry apart and fling bits to their dogs. It is true that such anonymous late medieval tomes as *The Boke of Curtasye*, dating from the mid-fifteenth century, contain so many strictures against such practices as spitting on the table ("thou shall be holden an uncourteous man"), blowing your nose into your hand ("if thy nose thou cleanse, as may befall / Look thy hand thou cleanse" by rubbing it on thy gown or wiping it on thy tippet—a scarf), or laughing with your mouth full, that we can deduce such behavior to have been common enough. Interestingly, one of the serious admonitions to gentlemen in *The Boke of Curtasye* is this (I have modernized the spelling):

> If thou sit by a right good man,
> This lesson look thou think upon:
> Under his thigh thy knee not put,
> Thou art full lewd if thou does it.

However, there are a number of books of manners and etiquette from the early thirteenth through the mid-fifteenth centuries that tell us that by this time refined manners were expected, and that there was decorousness in the way upper-class meals were served and consumed. In a specific manifestation of medieval piety, diners customarily made the sign of the cross over their mouths with their thumbs before beginning to eat. But nice manners were for the nobly born: servants sometimes sneezed, coughed, or spat when serving food, and they were severely reprimanded and usually beaten and kicked or had their ears boxed right then and there.

It is true that people often ate with their hands, but it would have been extremely vulgar and tasteless for a lord to tear meat off a roast or to dismember a fowl. The art of carving was quite refined, and specially trained servants were in charge of it; two knives were used, one to hold down the roast, the other to cut it up. Or one hand held the meat while the other was used to carve with the knife. The meat was then placed by the servant on the lord's and lady's trenchers. Only the thumb and first two fingers of the hand were used to grasp the food; the others were gracefully extended. Before drinking, people wiped their mouths. And it was considered boorish not to peel fruit before eating it. An anonymous twelfth-century French poem, "Regime pour tous serviteurs" (Regimen for All Servants), explains that to prepare for a meal, the tablecloth should be put on the table first, then, in the following order, salt, "knives, bread, wine and then meat." "Then bring whatever is requested; don't remove anything from the table without being ordered to."

The Prioress, "she was cleped madame Eglentyne" in Chaucer's *Canterbury Tales*, is known for her fastidious manners and the nicety of her conduct:

At mete [meat] wel ytaught was she with alle [withal]:
She leet no morsel from hir lippes falle,
Ne wette [dipped] hir fyngres in her sauce depe [deep] . . .
In curtesie was set ful muchel hir lest [on courtesy was set full much her desire]
Hir over-lippe wyped she so clene [clean]
That in hir coppe ther was no ferthyng sene [little bit seen].

Two of the most interesting books of manners and instructions to servants from the late medieval period are the previously mentioned *The Boke of Nurture* by John Russell and *The Book of Keruynge* (The Book of Carving) by Wynken de Worde. In both, we find not only descriptions of every kind of dish imaginable and detailed instructions on how to carve and serve everything, but also instructions for setting the dining tables. *The Book of Keruynge* tells us exactly how three tablecloths were put one on top of each other and elaborately folded. Five trenchers were set at the lord's place, four or three if he were of lower rank. It is clear from other sources that the top tablecloth was also sometimes used as a napkin. Salt was provided in open salt cellars, and bread was elaborately wrapped in cloth to keep it as fresh as possible.

The marshal of the banqueting hall led a procession of servants and waiters, carrying in the food on great platters. The sewer or sewers did their job of placing the dishes on the tables, ready for the carvers. *Sewer* derives from Old French *esculier*; the word *scullery*, where the dishes were kept, is form the same source. From the butler on down, servants wore long towels around their necks, just as waiters in French cafes today carry napkins over their arms. Here are John Russell's instructions to the butler, or whoever might be serving (I have modernized the spelling):

take a towel about thy neck / for that is courtesy,
lay that one side of the towel on thy left arm mannerly,
and on the same arm lay thy sovereign's napkin honestly;
then lay on that arm eight loaves of bread / with three or four trencher loaves; Then put the end of thy towel / in thy left hand, as the manner is,
and the salt cellar in the same hand, look that ye do this;
that other end of the towel / in right hand with spoons and knives y-wis.
Set your salt on the right side / where sits your sovereign,
on the left side set your trenchers one and twain,
on the left side of your trencher, lay your knife, singular and plain.

He would then distribute the bread and the other spoons and knives. Sometimes as a courtesy and an honor, the lord would serve out portions for his guests, and the butler would then hand them round. The diners usually sat on one side of the table, and servants approached the table from the side opposite them and served them from the front.

Typically, the first course consisted of soups and potages and great joints of meat, followed by a poultry course with more potages, all accompanied by little tarts and flans. Fish was served as well, and all kinds of game birds. Venison and mutton, with various sauces, were especially common, and such delicacies as beaver tail (classified by John Russell as fish) were regularly consumed. The conveniently cut-up food was eaten out of trenchers or off copper plates, and in some cases, everyone helped him- or herself with hand, spoon, and knife, digging into a common platter, once the lord and lady had been served. At the end of the meal, the table having been cleared and the *voiders* (dishes for garbage and leftovers) taken away to be emptied (possibly in the castle moat, or given as fodder to the animals), basins of water, ewers, and towels were placed on the table so people could wash their hands.

In an extraordinary compilation of documents from manuscripts in the British Museum, *A Chronicle of London from 1089 to 1483: Written in the Fifteenth Century*, edited by Nicholas H. Nicolas and Edward Tyrrell and published in 1827, we find the entire extensive guest list, seating arrangement, and menu for the coronation banquet of Catherine of Valois (1401–1437), "the kynges doughter of Fraunce." She and Henry V had just been married in June 1420 and went to England shortly afterwards. The famous Richard "Dick" Whittington (1358?–1423) was Lord Mayor of London, and he made sure the couple got the most sumptuous of royal welcomes. He and the aldermen had their own table "in the halle on the left hande of the Quene." There were three courses. The first course of various fish and shellfish preparations included as well a "furmente," a potage of creamed boiled wheat enriched with egg yolks and saffron, and "brawne," boned shoulder of boar stewed in red wine. The "sotelte" (subtlety), or centerpiece, must have created a sensation when it was ceremoniously paraded in: a pelican on her nest, surrounded by her young, with an "ymage" of Saint Catherine disputing with heathen priests and carrying a "Reason" on a printed placard. This read, in French, "Madame the Queen," while the pelican bore a placard that read, "Let her teach us!" The pelican was a Christian symbol of charity and of the passion of Jesus, because it was thought that the mother pelican would feed her chicks with her own blood. Each of the three elaborate courses betokening a groaning board had its own sotelte.

The coronation feast of their son—Henry VI (1421–1471), who became king at the age of one and was crowned when he was four—was just as elaborate. There were many meat dishes, including a furmente with venison instead of boar, stewed capon, and soups decorated with gold. Again there were three courses, each comprising many dishes; and soteltes, including the statue of a child holding a crown and kneeling to St. George.

Charlemagne (742–814) was perhaps the first great French gourmet, and the food at his court was sumptuous. Legend has it that upon returning from a journey in September 744, he and his knights stopped in a small village at nightfall in order to refresh themselves. They were offered the local cheese, whereupon the emperor, delighted, exclaimed, "I have just discovered in this cheese one of the most delectable foods imaginable!" And he ordered supplies of Brie delivered henceforward to his palace at Aix-la-Chapelle.

Ever since the days of the ancient Gauls, whom Caesar had conquered, food and long feasting had been important in what is now France. Roast reindeer, wild boar, and other game; freshly caught grilled fish; and boiled stews of game and fish together constituted the usual fare, and this continued to be the case in medieval days. Some of the more extravagant dishes served to Charlemagne included roast, flaming peacock and stuffed, spiced dormice with pepper, cumin, and ground nuts. Rose or violet wine was drunk, the wine having been steeped in rose petals or violets for at least a week, and melons were eaten with a sauce of honey, pepper, mint, wine, and vinegar. Coriander, rue, caraway, ginger, mustard, and lovage were also used often.

In 1326, the first French cookbook appeared, written by Guillaume Tirel (1314–ca. 1395), known as Taillevent. Duck with red wine sauce, gruels made from oats and other grains, and mutton hash were some of the dishes from this period. And the habit of serving everything at once on a groaning banquet table and of feasting for hours while jesters jested and dancers danced continued, as it had for centuries.

Joan of Arc (1412–1431) reportedly ate five soups at a time! She would pour some wine into a bowl, then pour the soup over that; the soup base was usually chicken broth with sieved chicken, eggs, and cream.

The Saxons ate with an all-purpose bronze or iron knife called the *scramasax*. Forks were unknown in western Europe until a Doge of Venice,

Domenico Selvo (d. 1087, ruled 1071–84), married a Greek princess who brought them with her, but they were considered a scandalous and even impious affectation, and they were not in general use until the fourteenth century in France. Germans generally used only spoons and knives in this period, and Italians, despite the eleventh-century scandal, used forks by the thirteenth century to spear solid food but drank soup directly from the bowl.

The diet of the peasants was largely wholesome and healthy in England, although on the Continent, bad harvests meant periodic famines and starvation. The eggs from the chickens English farmers kept, the peas and beans grown in the small gardens next to their houses, and the berries and other wild fruits they gathered were supplemented by small birds that were netted and rabbits or even deer that were poached, other game that ran wild on the moors and in the forests, and bacon and chops from pigs slaughtered in the villages and divided up among several families.

Medieval Time Keeping: The system of keeping time was adopted from the ancient Romans but was now geared to religious ritual. The hours of sext and none, for instance, were times for prayer. There was generally as little accuracy in keeping time as there had been in the days of the Roman Empire, but the addition of bells in churches began to change all that, and bells were rung every hour—and sometimes every quarter hour—to remind the people that they owed humble obeisance to the Lord. Since this could be done even at night, and did not depend on the light of the sun or the moon but on keeping a count based on the falling sands of an hourglass, the sense of what time meant began to change. The invention of the clock with gears at some point in the Middle Ages, and the use of public clocks also added to the consciousness of time.

Social Dancing: Since clothing in the period from about the eleventh to the thirteenth century—the era of the troubadours and minnesingers— was light in weight, dancing and merry making, which mostly took place out of doors or in the grand, open halls of castles, was easy and free. The social dances of the twelfth century include the *carole*, which was sung at the same time to words written by the troubadours. The dancers, who could be all men or all women or a mixture of the two, wore wreaths of flowers in their hair. In the *farandole*, which was one of two forms of the carole, the dancers held hands and danced in single file out of doors, the lead dancer taking the others either through the streets or around a public square or through a garden. The second form was called the *branle*, and it was a round dance, done in a circle holding hands, with the dancers swaying alternately to right and left. The branle, too, was done outside in public. But most dances then and in the next centuries were done in the great halls of castles, and they were more compact in form. For more information on these and other dances, consult Melusine Wood's *Historical Dances: 12th to 19th Century* (Dance Books, 1952), available in a recent paperback reprint.

Architecture and Painting

The great glory of the medieval world is its religious architecture: the immense, elaborately decorated gothic cathedrals of Notre Dame in Paris, Chartres, Reims, Cologne, and Strasbourg, among many others. Much, in fact most, medieval painting, as you might expect, is religious in nature—and rather flat before the discovery of perspective in the Renaissance. The same subjects, such as the Annunciation and the Crucifixion, are repeated over and over again, and since the paintings resemble each other, the effect can of course be rather monotonous if you are going through a room of them in a museum. Nevertheless, aside from the fact that they give you the atmosphere of the period, you will find it instructive to look at the costumes and how people held themselves in them, and in what positions or postures they stood or sat.

One of the most important of the many great Italian medieval artists was the Florentine Giotto (ca. 1276–ca. 1337), who was a friend of Dante. His masterpieces include the decoration of the Arena Chapel in Padua, and not only are the sense of color and form in his paintings magnificent, but he was also a genius as an architect, although the Giotto Campanile of the Duomo, of which he was appointed chief architect in 1334, was not actually completed according to his design.

In Flanders and in Holland, as in Germany and eastern Europe, painting was always in the service of religion in these centuries. As the nineteenth-century aesthete and art historian John Ruskin (1819–1900) writes in *The Stones of Venice*, "The early religious painting of the Flemings is as brilliant in hue as it is holy in thought." The secular portraits of Jan van Eyck (1370?–1440?) are exceptional in their subtle realism.

Music

As with fashion and manners, music in the medieval centuries cannot be easily or conveniently classified into simple categories. It developed and changed over the centuries. And it is an important component of the liturgy: Masses were often sung. At the various court events, there were concerts and background instrumental and vocal music, and graceful music to accompany dancing. This long period of time also saw the birth of popular music, narrative ballads, and folk song.

Medieval music is famous for the Gregorian chant, a form of liturgical plainsong that *The Harvard Dictionary of Music*, which goes into great detail, defines as basically "Monophonic Christian liturgical chant in free rhythm, as opposed to measured music." It was used for singing the Mass or the Psalms, and it could be sung with one note to a syllable or with a single syllable sung on two or more notes.

Among medieval instruments, we find the recorder, the flute, the horn, and the lute, which was apparently invented in the fourteenth century. The organ, a primitive form of which had been around since the days of the ancient Greeks, was reinvented and refined. Powered by bellows, it was used in churches throughout Europe beginning probably in about the eighth century. By the tenth century, organs were common.

Literature

Procopius's *Anecdota or Secret History* is a scathing, sometimes scatological view of the medieval Byzantine Empire. It recounts in lubricious detail the lives and loves of the Emperor Justinian I (483–565) and his scandalous Empress Theodora (508?–548), among other personalities, and tells the most incredible stories. Some of these people, like some of the ancient Roman emperors, stopped at nothing and felt entitled to fulfill any and every sexual desire. His eight books of *Histories* of the wars fought by the Byzantines against, successively, the Persians, the Vandals, and the Ostrogoths, in all of which Procopius participated, are the most important source we have for the events and personalities of the sixth century.

For early Anglo-Saxon history, the Venerable Bede's (672/73–735) *Ecclesiastical History of the English People*, written in Latin, is of supreme importance for the story of the Christianization of the English tribes; he begins his tale with the conquest of Britain by Julius Caesar.

Medieval piety is at the heart of his history, as it is, of course, in St. Augustine's (354–430) writings, especially his invaluable *Confessions*.

William Langland's *Piers the Plowman*, an allegorical religious poem written sometime between 1360 and 1399, reflects social and political conditions in the England of its day. Nothing is known about Langland, not even the dates of his birth or death, but his poem, which concerns the search for the best means of living a true Christian life, takes the reader through a satirical journey involving all social classes.

Another book that presents a slice of medieval life is Giovanni Boccaccio's (1313–1375) *The Decameron*, written in 1352. In order to escape the ravages of the Black Death, a group of Florentine nobles—seven men, three women, and their servants—leave the city and immure themselves within a castle in the countryside. While there, they pass the time in various amusements, including singing and dancing, but principally in telling stories. The book is rich in detail and presents a very real picture of life in Florence during the Black Death. Many of the stories are tragic and grisly, and many concern love, as well as the deterioration of civility during those terrible, dark, brutal times.

The almost unbearably tragic love story of Pierre Abélard (1079–1142) and Héloïse (1101–1164) is told in their *Letters*, and it attests to the barbarity of the age as well as to the immortal passion of this legendary pair. They were treated with great savagery. Héloïse's uncle, Canon Fulbert (?–?) of Notre Dame, had taken the unusual step of educating her, and she proved a brilliant student. Abélard, her tutor, was a well-known scholastic philosopher, accused more than once of heresy. They had a child, and he proposed they marry secretly. Her bitterly jealous, furious uncle would not hear of it. He and his confederates castrated Abélard. Héloïse entered a convent, and they never saw each other again.

The *Chronicles* of Jean Froissart are important for his account of the history of the first part of the Hundred Years War. He gathered material for his book partly through extensive travels in Great Britain, France, Flanders, and Spain, and partly through his connections with noble families, whom he served and was therefore able to observe at first hand. And he actually met Chaucer and Petrarch (1304–1374)—the nom de plume of the poet and humanist scholar Francesco Petrarcha, famous for his sonnets. Also important as both sociology and history is Jean, Sieur de Joinville's (1224–1317) *Histoire de Saint Louis*, the story of the King Louis IX (1214–1270) and the Seventh Crusade, which lasted from 1248 to 1254. Joinville was a participant in the events he describes, and his descriptions of Muslim life as he encountered it are also invaluable.

Equally valuable as an eyewitness account is Geffroi de Villehardouin's (1160–1213?) *Chronicle of the Fourth Crusade and the Conquest of Constantinople*. The Welsh clergyman and writer Geoffrey of Monmouth's (1100–1155) *Historia Regum Brittaniae* (The History of the Kings of Britain), finished in 1136, is largely mythological, despite its title. It includes the stories of King Lear and Cymbeline that inspired Shakespeare, and tales of Merlin and King Arthur and his Knights of the Round Table.

At the heart of medieval literature are the Icelandic sagas—which are full of blood, battle, revenge, and passion—and the Anglo-Saxon epic *Beowulf*. The story of the defeat of the Moslems by the Christians under Charlemagne in the Pyrenees is related in *The Song of Roland*, one of the *chansons de gestes* (songs of heroic deeds) devoted to the legends of Charlemagne. Among the most important stories of courtly love and romance are Gottfried von Strassburg's (late 12th c.) *Tristan* and the anonymous French epics *Tristan and Isolde* and *Aucassin et Nicolette*. Attesting to the overriding religiosity of the age are the stories of Percival and the Quest for the Holy Grail.

Among nonfiction books, *The Travels of Marco Polo* (1271), full of myth making though it may be, tells the story of the intrepid Italian traveler to Cathay, as China was then known. His epic journey along the silk and spice route between Europe and Asia through the fabled city of Samarkand, among other fabulous places, amazed all of Europe. Sir John Mandeville's *Travels*, published around 1357, although facetious and full of fantastically improbable tales, was widely accepted as true. But even the writer's name is a fiction: his identity remains uncertain.

Chief among the books you should read if you are doing a play set in the medieval era is Dante Alighieri's (1265–1321) *La divina commedia* (The Divine Comedy), divided into three parts: *Inferno* (Hell), *Purgatorio* (Purgatory, or Limbo), and *Paradiso* (Heaven). The Florentine Dante, who was forced into exile for political reasons and died in Ravenna, was famously in love with Beatrice Portinari (1266–1290), whom he had seen first from afar when he was a child and who hardly knew of his existence. His Christian epic is one of the towering achievements of European literature. Dante is guided through hell by the shade of the Roman poet Virgil, considered the most virtuous of the pagan ancients, and in the nine circles, each meant for a particular sin, he encounters the souls of the eternally unforgiven damned. The poet's journey takes him from the darkness of ignorance to the light of paradise and the revelation of true religion. When he arrives at the top of purgatory, where repentant sinners are preparing at last to be received into heaven, Virgil, who as a pagan cannot enter paradise, leaves the poet. He is guided through heaven by none other than Beatrice, and he experiences the grace that is conferred through divine favor.

Film and Television

Sergei M. Eisenstein (1898–1948) created the intense, melodramatic, riveting, surging medieval epics *Ivan the Terrible, Part One* (1948), *Ivan the Terrible, Part Two* (1955),and *Alexander Nevsky* (1938) that have become cinematic classics. The 1999 television miniseries based on the classic nineteenth-century novel by Henryk Sienkiewicz, *With Fire and Sword*, is breathtaking in its scope and period detail. Jerzy Hoffman's 1974 Polish television miniseries based on its sequel, *The Deluge*, is equally excellent, and medieval life in eastern Europe is astoundingly recreated.

Among films set in an idealized medieval Europe are *Ivanhoe* (1952), based on Sir Walter Scott's romantic novel, and that great classic *The Adventures of Robin Hood* (1938), starring Errol Flynn. There have been sixty-six films based on the legend of Robin Hood, as well as a television series in the 1950s and a miniseries for the BBC.

Tristan and Isolde (2006) has an authentic feeling of medievalism. So does *Royal Deceit* (1994), based on the Hamlet legend—which Shakespeare adapted to better purpose, but Christian Bale as Hamlet is superb; one would like to see him do Shakespeare's play.

There are several versions of the story of Joan of Arc. Among them are the 1948 film *Joan of Arc*, starring Ingrid Bergman, and Bernard Shaw's play *St. Joan*. She is also a character in Shakespeare's Henry VI plays, where she is treated as a witch.

At least 100 films and television programs have been based on the legend of King Arthur and the Knights of the Round Table, and the archetypal story of Sir Lancelot and his love for Arthur's Queen Guinevere. The 1949 film adaptation of Mark Twain's *A Connecticut Yankee in King Arthur's Court* stars Bing Crosby as the hapless Yankee who gets knocked on the head at the factory where he works and is transported back in time. Cedric Hardwicke plays a doddering, dithery King Arthur.

James Goldman's *The Lion in Winter* (1968)—with Katherine Hepburn as Eleanor of Aquitaine (1122–1204) and Peter O'Toole as Henry II (1133–89; King of England from 1154), parents of Richard

Lion-heart (Anthony Hopkins)—is worth seeing, despite its incredibly anachronistic dialogue. *Becket* (1964) tells the story of the murder of Saint Thomas à Becket (1118–1170) at the hands of Henry II's knights. One of the best films about the late medieval period is Daniel Vigne's *The Return of Martin Guerre* (1982), based on a late medieval fictional tale, with Gérard Depardieu in the title role, shot on location in the beautiful southwestern region of France. Aside from telling a suspense-filled and engrossing story, the film is a wonderful lesson in how such films should be done.

For More Information

Adler, Elkan Nathan, ed. *Jewish Travelers in the Middle Ages: 19 Firsthand Accounts*. Edited and with an introduction by Elkan Nathan Adler. New York: Dover Publications, Inc., 1987.

Bulfinch, Thomas. *Mythology: The Age of Fable; The Age of Chivalry; The Age of Charlemagne*. New York: The Modern Library, n.d.

Chaucer, Geoffrey. *The Works of Geoffrey Chaucer*. Edited by F. N. Robinson. 2nd ed. Boston: Houghton Mifflin Company, 1961.

Cole, Peter. *The Dream of the Poem: Hebrew Poetry from Muslim and Christian Spain 950–1492*. Translated, edited, and introduced by Peter Cole. Princeton, NJ: Princeton University Press, 2007.

Durant, Will and Ariel. *The Story of Civilization: Part IV, The Age of Faith*. New York: Simon and Schuster, 1950.

Furnivall, F. J., ed. *The Babees Book: Early English Meals and Manners (Early English Text Society Original Series)*. (Contains many medieval English, Latin, and French texts, including *Urbanitatis*, Wynken de Worde's *The Boke of Keruynge*, Hugh Rhodes' *The boke of Nurture, or the Schoole of good manners*, and John Russell's *The Boke of Nurture*.) London: Early English Text Society, 1868. Reprint, New York: Greenwood Press, 2002.

Geoffrey of Monmouth. *The History of the Kings of Britain*. Translated, with introduction and index, by Lewis Thorpe. New York: Penguin, 1966.

Kurlansky, Mark. *Salt: A World History*. New York: Penguin Books, 2002.

Maalouf, Amin. *The Crusades through Arab Eyes*. New York: Shocken, 1989.

Procopius. *The Anecdota or Secret History*. With an English translation by H. B. Dewing. Cambridge, MA: Harvard University Press, 1935; reprinted 2004.

Schiltberger, Johann. *The Bondage and Travels of Johann Schiltberger, A Native of Bavaria, in Europe, Asia and Africa, 1396–1427*. Translated from the Heidelberg MS. Edited in 1859 by Professor Karl Friedrich Neumann and

Commander J. Buchan Telfer, R.N., with notes by Professor P. Bruun. London: printed for the Hakluyt Society, 1859; Elibron Classics reprint, 2005.

Singman, Jeffrey L. and Will McLean. *Daily Life in Chaucer's England*. Westport, CT: Greenwood Press, 1995.

Singman, Jeffrey L. *Daily Life in Medieval Europe*. Westport, CT: Greenwood Press, 1999.

Summers, Montague, ed. *The Malleus Maleficarum of Heinrich Kramer and James Sprenger*. Translated, with an introduction, bibliography, and notes, by the Reverend Montague Summers. New York: Dover Publications, Inc., 1971.

Villehardouin and de Joinville. *Memoirs of the Crusades*. Translated, with an introduction, by Sir Frank T. Marzials. New York: E. P. Dutton & Co., Inc., 1958.

Worde, Wynken de. *The Boke of Keruynge (The Book of Carving)*. With an introduction, drawings, and glossary by Peter Brears. Lewes, UK: Southover Press, 2003.

Audio Recordings

A Feast of Songs: Holiday Music from the Middle Ages. Hallistic Music CD HMCD-001, 2006.

Music for a Medieval Banquet: The Newberry Consort. Classical Express CD HCX 3957038, 2001.

Music of the Crusades: The Early Music Consort of London. London CD 430 264-2, 1991.

Internet Resources

www.luminarium.org
   Provides the texts of and information about medieval plays.

CHAPTER FIVE

The Sixteenth Century:
The Renaissance and
William Shakespeare

Shakespeare's World

> The multitude (or whole body) of this populous Citie...bee natural
> Subjects, a part of the Commons of this Realme, and are by birth
> for the most part of all countries of the same, by bloud Gentlemen,
> Yeomen and of the basest sort, without distinction and by profes-
> sion busie Bees, and trauellers [workers; cf. French *travailleurs*] for
> their liuing in the hiue of this common wealth.

So writes John Stow (1525–1605) in *A Survey of London*, first published in 1598 and revised in 1603. Stow was a scholarly Elizabethan
whose book is richly detailed and all encompassing in its portrayal of
London: its history; the character of its various neighborhoods, architecture, "Towers and Castels," "Schooles and other houses of learning";
the people and their dress and customs.

The city was surrounded with abundant natural resources, its teeming harbor filled with ships of many nations. Water from lead cisterns
and wells was supplied to residents. Conduits had been built well before
the Elizabethan period, as Stow tells us: "The first Cesterne of leade
castellated with stone...was called the great Conduit...which was
begun to bee builded in the yeare 1285." And the waters of the Thames
were "conueyed into mens houses by pipes of leade." But the London of
the Tudors had no paved roads, only dirt streets, so that in foul weather,
even the wider thoroughfares turned into muddy sloughs; eventually,
cobblestones would be used. And there was no refuse collection: people
simply dumped garbage in the streets or threw it in "the towne Ditch
without the Wall of the citie," despite city ordinances prohibiting such
practices. Slops from chamber pots were also emptied into the streets, in

spite of the laws, largely unenforced. One had to be hearty and robust not to succumb to diseases, and the air was redolent of the smells of horse and dog manure, of decaying fish and rotting food. Carters carried rubbish to huge dumps outside London and other towns, but they were hardly efficient.

Nor were ideas of personal hygiene and cleanliness particularly advanced. Not to put too fine a point upon it, people stank and their teeth rotted. Laundry (underwear, shirts, sheets, table linen) was done at an area on the Thames; in the country it was washed at streams. Dresses or gowns, which were brushed but not cleaned otherwise, could be turned inside out and worn on the other side. But houses were kept clean and relatively free of odors, and industrious housewives and servants would sweep, clean, and wash the floors and strew them with reeds or straw, and polish the pewter and silver.

Although crowded, the walled metropolis, its gates shut at night, was small: it occupied approximately the area now called the City (the present financial district). There were inns aplenty to lodge the throngs of visitors, but William Harrison (1534–1593) tells us in *The Description of England* (1587) that they were the worst in the country. This may be Harrison's provincial prejudice against the capital: John Stow characterizes the many "innes" in London as "fair," meaning beautiful and excellent. Harrison's *Description* lives up to its name. He discusses everything exhaustively: food and diet, schools, universities, the state of the church, the laws, the punishment of criminals, clothing, houses and furniture, the navy, the gardens and parks, cities and towns, and so forth. And his parochial mentality is revealing: xenophobic, chauvinistic, and puritanical. He doesn't care much for the theater, for instance, on moral grounds.

More broadminded but still patriotic in his outlook, Fynes Moryson (1566–1630) gave the world *An itinerary vvritten by Fynes Moryson, gent. first in the Latine toungue, and then translated by him into English: containing his ten yeeres travell throvgh the tvvelve domjnions of Germany, Bohmerland, Sweitzerland, Netherland, Denmarke, Poland, Jtaly, Turky, France, England, Scotland, and Ireland* (1617). He penned the most amazingly detailed and complete geographical/sociocultural descriptions of every place he visited, especially considering that it was "a long time past since I viewed these Dominions"; he even provides conversion tables for money. Part of the book is a history of the bloody and tragic Irish Rebellion of 1594–1603, also known as Tyrone's Rebellion, which he helped suppress. He was secretary at the time to the merciless

Sir Charles Blount, Baron Mountjoy (1563–1606), Lord-Deputy, then Lord Lieutenant of Ireland.

Of English inns, Moryson has this to say:

> The World affoords not such Innes as England hath. . . . For as soone as a passenger comes to an Inne, the servants run to him, and one takes his Horse, and walkes him till he be cold, then rubs him and gives him meate [food], yet I must say that they are not much to be trusted in this last point, without the eye of the Master or his Servant to oversee them. Another servant gives the passenger his private chamber, and kindles his fire; the third puls of his bootes and makes them cleane. Then the Host or Hostesse visit him; and if he will eate with the Host or at a common Table with others, his meale will cost him sixe pence, or in some places but foure pence (yet this course is lesse honourable and not used by gentlemen): But if he will eate in his chamber, he commands what meate he will. . . . While he eates, if he have company especially, he shall be offred musicke.

Travelers who were not gentlemen could be roughly treated and were not comfortably lodged. And Moryson warns the traveler to be "warie not to shew any quantity of money about him, since Theeves have their spies commonly in all Innes, to enquire after the condition of passengers." And traveling conditions in other parts of the world could be extremely rough. On his trip through the Near East, the treks on camels and horses were arduous, to say the least. The difficult traveling in Syria was relieved when Moryson was able to stay as a guest with "a Christian who used to entertaine the French":

> And when I did see a bed made for me and my brother, with cleane sheetes, I could scarcely contain my selfe from going to bed before supper, because I had never lien in naked bed since I came from Venice to this day, having alwaies slept by sea and land in my doublet, with linnen breeches and stockings, upon a mattresse, and betweene coverlets or quilts, with my breeches under my head.

(Fynes's brother, Henry Moryson, died shortly afterwards, in 1596 at the age of twenty-seven, of the "Flux," probably amebic dysentery.)

At the city's eastern edge was the Tower of London, that vast, walled fortress prison and sometime royal residence. Newgate and Ludgate prisons were on the western perimeter, and Westminster, then a separate town, was a mile or so away. There was one huge bridge with twenty arches, spanning the Thames with its teeming boat traffic. One could hear the boatmen's cries of "Westward, ho!" or "Eastward, ho!" as they warned people on the other side of the bridge that the boats were going under the narrow arches in either direction. London Bridge had a covered walkway and was lined on either side with shops, and "on both sides be houses builded," some of them quite impressive.

It cost a penny to walk to the other side, Southwark, where the public theaters and bear-baiting rings, the taverns, and the "stews," or brothels, were located. John Stow tells us that "these allowed stewhouses had signs on their frontes, towards the Thames, not hanged out, but painted on the walles, as a Boares head, the Cross keyes, the Gunne... there was a plot of ground, called the single womans churchyeard, appointed for them, far from the parish church." Henry VIII (1491–1547) had tried unsuccessfully to close "this row of Stewes" down—"no more to be priueleged, and vsed as a common Brothel." In Southwark, there was also "the Clinke, a Gayle or prison for the trespassers of those parts." The "Inne of the Tabarde," made famous by Chaucer's *Canterbury Tales*, was, as Stow informs us, still very popular.

Actors as a class were looked down upon as not quite respectable. Still, the theaters of such prestigious companies as the Lord Chamberlain's Men, of which William Shakespeare (1564–1616) and Richard Burbage were the mainstays, and the Admiral's Men, for whom Christopher Marlowe (1564–1593) wrote plays, were flourishing commercial enterprises, well attended by all social classes. Also popular were two boys' companies attached to choir schools: the Children of the Chapel and the Children of St. Paul's. Ben Jonson (1573?–1637) and others wrote plays especially for them. The lucky students at those schools had two meals a day (lunch and supper), unlike many other people. They were up at five and busy from six a.m. until nine at night. The day began with church and continued with hours of music, French, Latin, and Greek lessons. There was free time for games and other pastimes from eight until bedtime.

A primary source of information about aspects of Elizabethan theater is the *Diary* covering the years 1593–1603 of the producer Philip Henslowe (1550–1615), a wealthy entrepreneur with many business interests. The diary indicates that as many as six productions a week were done of plays in repertory, and it details his production expenses: "Layd owt for the companye, the 16 of maye, 1602, for to bye a dubblet and a payer of venesyons [*Venetians:* breeches with ballooning oval-shaped legs, tied at the knees with ribbons] of clothe of sylver wraght with read sylke, the some of fower pound and ten shellynges, I saye." That was a lot of money in those days, and there are constant similar entries. Costumes could be elaborate and expensive, because servants, who were given their noble employers' cast-off clothing, sold it to producers. Henslowe paid Marlowe and other famous Elizabethan dramatists for their plays, and he bought the actors wine when they had first readings of plays at a local tavern. Shakespeare—who, like the other dramatists, did not write his plays for publication or as literature, but as working scripts for actors, to be emended or altered as necessary during the rehearsal process—is not mentioned in the diary, but the names of many of his plays and some details of production expenses do appear.

The "groundlings" stood for a penny in the center of the unroofed oval auditorium, while the upper classes—who paid two pennies, or three if they wanted a cushioned seat—sat in the covered balconies surrounding it. Food and drink could be purchased from vendors, who made the rounds during the performance. The "tiring [dressing] rooms" and the stage, with its extended apron open to the air and its trapdoor(s), were on one side of the auditorium of such theaters as the Globe. At the back of the stage was a covered balcony with an entrance underneath it—hence the stage direction "enter above," onto the balcony—and there were stage left and right entrances. Although there may have been flying pieces, there was apparently little or no scenery, except for an occasional set piece suggesting a tree, or a tent in a military encampment, or chairs and tables. Rather than lying in a cumbersome, heavy bed, characters who were supposed to be ill were usually in a "sick-chair," as published stage directions indicate; it could be easily lifted and carried. The famous stage direction "alarums and excursions" indicates that military music was played during battle scenes; excursions means the staged movement of soldiers. Given the scanty evidence, we have no very real idea of how the plays were presented or what rehearsal or performance practices were, but we do know from eyewitness accounts that the plays were performed at two in the afternoon, since there was no stage lighting.

There were several private theaters in the city itself, including the Blackfriars, where the Children of the Chapel performed, and there were taverns and ale houses and inns. The mansions of the upper classes lined the Strand, on the river, and there were districts associated with various industries and professions. Paul's Yard, for instance, near St. Paul's—which had a vast precinct that, like the church itself, was a popular tourist attraction and recreation ground—was the center of the publishing trade, where booksellers hawked their wares. And Fleet Street was where furniture and carpentry shops were located; the manufactories must have created quite a din.

In 1436–37, Johannes Gutenberg (1400?–1468) invented the printing press in Mainz, Germany. William Caxton (1415? or 1422?–1492) imported the first printing press into England in 1476. Caxton's foreman was Wynken de Worde from Alsace, and Caxton taught him the trade, including how to cut his own type out of lead or tin. Caxton was also a bookseller, and he had his printing house and bookshop in Westminster. He published a number of books of etiquette, some of them translated from French sources, as well as editions of Chaucer's *Canterbury Tales.*

In 1453, the fall of Constantinople to the Turks sent Christian refugees flooding into Europe; they brought the Greek and Roman classics with them. The Aldine Press, founded by Aldus Manutius (1450–1515) in Venice, began printing Aristotle's works in 1495–98.

All those developments represent the beginning of the European Renaissance and the dawn of humanism, when the ancient worlds of Greece and Rome and their wisdom and rationality were rediscovered in the West, and the Church Scholastics tried to reconcile them with scripture. The period also saw the beginning of the Protestant Reformation, with Martin Luther's (1483–1546) challenge to the authority of the pope in 1517, and Henry VIII's establishment of the Anglican Church in 1531.

From the splendid Italian princely courts, the books—and the ideas, knowledge, and philosophical, aesthetic, and ethical points of view expounded in them—spread quickly throughout Europe and across the channel to the British Isles. The doyen of Elizabethan translators was the linguist, medical doctor, and grammar school teacher Philemon Holland (1552–1637), celebrated for his Pliny, Plutarch, Suetonius, and Xenophon. The English Renaissance was well underway by the time of the ascension to the throne of Elizabeth I (1533–1603) in 1558, ushering in a flowering of the literary and dramatic arts.

Moryson's observations of other European cities show us that life in the Elizabethan age was very much the same there as in London, despite the differences in food, customs, and culture. In France, for instance, at the inns, "as soone as passengers lighted from their horses, the Hoast gave them water to wash, and bread and wine"; this was not the case in other countries. People everywhere ate well, they worked hard, and commerce thrived:

The French have many commodities by which they draw forraigne Coynes to them, but foure especially, Wine, Salt, Linnen course cloth, and Corne, which in that respect some call the loade-stones of France. Neither is it a matter of small moment, that they have many Rivers, giving commodity to the mutuall trafficke of their Cities. They have plenty of Flaxe and Hempe, whereof they make canvas, sayles, ropes, and cables: Neither want they wooll, whereof they make cloth, little inferiour to the English cloth, but not in quantity to be exported. Bourdeaux is a famous City for exportation of Wines, as Rochell and the neighbour Ports are no lesse for Salt.... The English bring into France great quantity of woollen cloaths, called Kersies and Cottons, Leade, Tynne, English Vitriall, or Shooemakers blacke, sheepe skinnes, and by stealth other Hides, forbidden to be exported [smuggling was rampant], great quantity of Hearrings, and new found land [Newfoundland] Fish dried, of wooll (though forbidden to be exported), Oyle, Soape tunned, Soape ashes, old worne cloakes, and (I know not to what use) very old shooes, with other native and forraigne Commodities.

So this was the widening and nationalistic world into which William Shakespeare was born and in which he grew up. It was the age of exploration and the conquering of the New World. Political and religious lines were clear: to the Protestant English, the enemies, even though they traded with them, were the Catholic French—who persecuted the Protestant Huguenots—and the fanatically religious Spaniards (as the English saw them), with their growing New World empire and their infamous Inquisition. The attempted invasion of England by the Spanish Armada in 1588, defeated by the celebrated admiral, navigator, explorer, and privateer Sir Francis Drake (ca. 1540–1596), was proof enough of the hatred Spain harbored for Protestant England. As for the Jews, not officially permitted to live in England since medieval days— they would be readmitted by Oliver Cromwell in the seventeenth century—some of their story is told by John Stow, who provides an account of the foul and shockingly brutal persecution of medieval English Jews. Small numbers of converted Portuguese and Spanish Jews escaping the Inquisition did live in Elizabethan England, but there were none who dared, or indeed could, practice Judaism openly. The medieval and Elizabethan attitude was that Jews who did not accept Christ as their savior deserved their harsh fate, ordained by God as punishment for their sin.

Learning, science, exploration, and the arts may have been in flower, but the great cities of London, Paris, and Rome were also places that housed an impoverished underworld, and the streets were thick with prostitutes, cutpurses, pickpockets, beggars, and thieves. Crime was rampant, and there was no regular police force anywhere in Europe. This is one reason why men wore swords and daggers, and they were quick to use them, even in tavern brawls. Almost every crime was a capital offense, and public executions were popular entertainments, but they did little to deter thieves or confidence tricksters. The streets were not generally lit, and they were unsafe at night, although they were patrolled by town criers, or bellmen, who carried lanterns and cried out the hour.

Dealing with Shakespearean Verse and Grammar

In act 3, scene 2 of *The Winter's Tale*, Hermione says, "You speak a language that I understand not." That is doubtless the reaction of many an actor approaching an Elizabethan play. But Shakespeare's Early Modern English is so close to our own that it presents no great difficulty for the actor, who can easily assimilate its grammar and archaic vocabulary. Laurence Olivier asks in his introduction to Michel Saint-Denis's *Theatre: The Rediscovery of Style* (Theatre Arts Books, 1960) what an actor playing Coriolanus would "do if required to speak, 'The Moon of Rome, chaste as the icicle that's curded by the frost from purest snow and hangs on Dian's Temple; dear Valeria'—in character!" Do you adopt an old-fashioned approach, making the language even more important than the character you are playing? You can hear that approach on recordings of nineteenth- and early twentieth-century Shakespearean actors, and it strikes us today as pompous and bombastic—with some notable exceptions, such as Edwin Booth.

Iambic pentameter, a meter that takes account of the natural rhythm of the English language, is the primary but not the only verse form in which Shakespeare wrote. It consists of five feet, each of which is in two syllables: the first unstressed, the second stressed. These two syllables are known as an *iamb*, or *iambic foot*: "Thou *canst* not *speak* of *that* thou *dost* not *feel*" (*Romeo and Juliet*, act 3, scene 3). The lines sometimes include an extra weak (unstressed) syllable at the end: "To *be* or *not* to *be*: that *is* the *question*." Shakespeare occasionally uses the *hemistich*, which is half a line that ends in a *caesura* (a break or pause in the middle of a line of verse) and continues in the next line of dialogue, as in this exchange from act 4, scene 4 in *Richard III:*

K. RICH.: Now, by the world—

Q. ELIZ.:   'Tis full of thy foul wrongs.

K. RICH: My father's death—

Q. ELIZ.:   Thy life hath that dishonor'd.

Obviously, although you cannot emphasize the rhythm or the rhymes, you have to take them into account. And of course, you have to speak real thoughts with real psychological motivation and intentions. However you read rhymed lines, the audience will hear the rhyme inescapably; but the lines should be the character's organic expression, arising spontaneously in the moment, as in Hamlet's expression of frustration and misery in his exit line, "Oh, cursed spite / That ever I was born to put it right!"

Thee and Thou: Still heard in some rare dialects, the words *thee* and *thou*, meaning "you," are immediately comprehensible. The possessive adjectives are *thy:* "Nymph, in thy orisons be all my sins remembered" (Hamlet to Ophelia) or *thine:* "thine eyes." There is also the pronoun *thyself.* The second-person singular pronoun *thou* was the familiar form that we still find in French, Italian, Spanish, Russian, German, and many other languages. It was used with children and intimates, but not with persons of superior rank or strangers. The word *thee* is the objective form, occurring both as an object—"I will touch thee"—and after a preposition: "I have done nothing but in care of thee" (Prospero to Miranda in *The Tempest.*) In the conjugation of the irregular verbs "to be" and "to have," the forms of the present tense are "thou art" and "thou hast." In regular verbs, such as "to ask" and "to answer" an -*est* ending is added for the second-person singular: "thou askest"; "thou answerest." Some verbs had multiple forms: you would hear "thou doest" or "thou dost." In irregular verbs, the -*st* ending was also used: "thou canst"; "thou couldst." The past tenses of "to be" and "to have" are "thou wert" and "thou hadst." The future tense is formed with *wilt* or *shallt:* "thou wilt be (or have)"; "thou shallt be (or have)." The second-person singular of the verb "to love" is conjugated as follows: "thou lovest"; "thou dost love"; "thou didst love"; "thou lovedst"; "thou wilt love."

The Third Person of Verbs: The third person of "to have" is *hath:* "he hath"; "she hath"; "it hath." The ending -*eth* is used for the third person singular, sometimes shortened to *th:* "he cometh," "she asketh," "he writeth," "she doth [does]," "he hath [has]." The form "he doeth" was just as common as "he doth." The final *s* is found alongside the *-eth* ending and gradually takes over, as it has in today's usage: "he comes," "she asks," and so forth.

The Subjunctive: Much more widely used then than today, the subjunctive strikes us as poetic, but it was simply natural speech: "if it be true," and "hold, as 'twere, the mirror up to nature" (*Hamlet*); "I think he be transformed into a beast" (*As You Like It*).

Miscellaneous Archaisms: There are certain other archaic usages to which you must accustom yourself. These include the use of *but* to mean "except": "I have done nothing but in care of thee" (Prospero to Miranda in *The Tempest*); contractions such as *'tis* or *'twas*; and such constructions as placing a possessive adjective after another adjective: "good my lord."

Some verb forms that Shakespeare uses we no longer consider correct, but there is no problem in understanding when he uses *mistook* where we would use *mistaken*, *wrote* where we use *written*, or *digged* where we use *dug*.

The *-ed* ending was pronounced in such words as walked, arrived, and believed, and an apostrophe in Shakespeare indicates that it is dropped—*walk'd, arriv'd, believ'd*—a habit much deplored by Elizabethan grammarians, who also hated the fact that people no longer pronounced the *b* in *lamb*. The word *beloved* is pronounced with the final *-ed* or not, as the speaker wishes or the rhythm of a line dictates.

There is an archaic dative construction that Shakespeare uses, as in this line of Petruchio's from *The Taming of the Shrew:* "Villain, I say, knock me at this gate / and rap me well." The word *me* is in the dative case—that is, it implies the use of the preposition *for.* (The dative can also imply the preposition *to.*) The phrase allows Grumio to say grumpily that he should knock *him* first, before he knocks at the gate.

Theatrical Conventions: The Aside, the Soliloquy, and the Eavesdropping Scene

From the days of Roman comedy onwards, and up through the nineteenth century, the aside was a theatrical convention that playwrights found useful and audiences accepted. The *aside* is a speech that is part of the dialogue and is not meant to be heard by any of the other characters. It is spoken for the character's own benefit and tells the audience his or her real feelings, ideas, or opinions. When an aside is delivered, usually quickly and in a parenthetical way—that is, in a dropped or lower tone of voice—the action freezes for a moment. The character turns away briefly from the other character or from the scene, and delivers the aside either as a direct expression to the audience of feelings, questions, or ideas, or else as a remark spoken aloud by the character to him- or herself. The aside may even be simply a knowing look, nod, or wink directed at the audience, with no words spoken. Usually, the actor will stand in place and turn his or her head towards the audience to deliver the aside, but the director may ask the actor to move away, usually downstage, and then return to place, while the action freezes.

The *soliloquy* is a monologue spoken by a character to him- or herself when alone. The character always states the truth as he or she sees it. Again, the character may address the audience, viewed as complicit, or the character may be speaking only to him- or herself, overheard by the audience. When a character is driven to talk to him- or herself, it is usually to work on or solve an overwhelming problem.

In *eavesdropping scenes*, one or more characters observe one or more other characters, who do not know they are being observed. The eavesdropping scene is usually not problematic for actors in performance, but it does require a director's orchestration for tempo and rhythm—an object lesson in why Stanislavsky thought actors had to develop a sense of tempo in each scene. Timing, as in comedy, is all. In act 2, scene 5 in *Twelfth Night*, where Malvolio finds the letter planted for him by Sir Toby, Sir Andrew, Fabian, and Maria, they watch him and listen to his reactions, and comment to each other throughout the scene—all unheard by Malvolio, in a convention accepted by the audience.

The Stylistic Elements: Clothing, Accessories, Movement, Manners, and the Art of Living

Much of what follows applies not only to Elizabethan England but to the rest of Renaissance Europe as well: Whether you lived in London, Paris, Amsterdam, Brussels, Madrid, Rome, Berlin, Prague, Warsaw, or Vienna, clothing (although fashions varied from country to country), the houses of the rich and the poor, and the development of urban life all followed similar patterns. Each city had its individual architectural style. And some cities, such as Paris, had many paved streets and even street lighting in the form of streetlamps with candles. Food developed differently in the different countries, but otherwise living conditions were quite similar, as were class divisions and the monarchical system of government—although in England, exceptionally, the monarchy was not absolute.

All over Europe, for both the aristocratic and middle classes, elementary education was in public, or in private with tutors. Elizabethan ideas on education—particularly the teaching of Latin, but also general theories on how best to teach—are embodied in an invaluable book by Princess (later Queen) Elizabeth's tutor, the brilliant linguist and classics scholar Roger Ascham (1515–1568): *The Scholemaster*, written in 1563. He advises teachers to be compassionate and understanding as well as thorough. There were town grammar schools, such as the one Shakespeare attended in Stratford or the school in Coventry where Philemon Holland taught, and so-called public schools, where the sons of the wealthy were sent. They were called "public" because the boys were not tutored individually at home but in classes with the other boys. And in this period of the revival of classical learning, the universities flourished, and new ones were founded. Needless to say, given the male chauvinism of the period, women were not given education, although many learned to read and write. In fact, literacy was increasing among the population in general.

Clothing and Movement: Clothing was often uncomfortable and sticky, and it could be difficult to move in because it was so elaborate, with collars and cuffs, sometimes made of lace, and ruffs being all the fashion. Men and women wore a long-sleeved shirt that fitted over the head as an undergarment—silk for the rich, linen for the poor. Men's shirts were often thigh length. Later in the period, they were ornamented with embroidery or even lace. Some came with ruffs attached. It was unusual for men to appear in shirtsleeves unless they were doing hard labor of some kind, such as chopping wood; or playing some sport, such as indoor tennis.

Over their shirts or smocks, women wore either a *kirtle*, a kind of floor-length fitted gown, or else an upper garment called a *bodice* and a *petticoat* (skirt). The bodice, which was like a combination of a bra and a vest, came together in a point at the front bottom and was either laced or fastened with hooks and eyes; it could be sleeveless or sleeved, and had a flattening effect on the bosom. And they wore ruffs around their necks. To achieve a fashionable, bell-like shape below the waist, women wore *farthingales*, which could be beautifully embroidered and ornately decorated. The farthingale was a skirt that was ribbed with hoops to make it flare out; originally, it was an underskirt. Gowns were sometimes made even more voluminous by the use of a *roll* tied around the waist underneath the skirt; the roll was a stuffed, padded cylinder, something like a little pillow. Farthingales with rolls, called *wheel farthingales*, stuck straight out from the waist and then fell gracefully in a cylindrical shape to the floor.

Men sported long cloaks or short capes, sometimes with sleeves, and doublets and hose (tights); and they too often wore ruffs, or elaborate collars. The *doublet*, a close-fitting jacket with buttons down the front, was actually worn by women as well as men; women wore theirs over a sleeveless bodice. The doublet was fastened to the hose with lace ties, called *points*. Men also wore codpieces of various kinds, to conceal—or reveal—the male equipment. Some were simply fastened with laces to the hose at the top two corners and provided an opening for various necessities. Some were stuffed, presumably to be attractive and to indicate prowess and potency. Both men and women's clothing was sometimes edged with tabs, called *pickadills*.

In portraits of King Henry VIII and other men of the period, you can see codpieces just below the outer jacket—which had slashed puffy sleeves through which the sleeves of the jerkin worn underneath it could be seen—and a long fur collar, wide at the top, that extends down the front sides. The jacket was worn open to reveal the front of the jerkin, with diagonal or straight slashes through which the lining or shirt was pulled to make little puffs.

In the early Renaissance, clothing was made of velvet and furs without much ornamentation: Albrecht Dürer (1471–1528), in a 1498 self-portrait, wears a loosely draped cloth hat over his long, curled tresses and a loosely fitted shirt-jacket with a low-cut neckline, fastened across the top by a braided rope. The sleeves are slightly puffy at the top and narrow at the elbows, and are decorated with sleeve-length vertical stripes.

Women wore *coifs*, which were tight linen caps, and men wore various kinds of hats, among the most popular being a tight flat cap with a floppy surrounding brim. Fynes Moryson tells us that the French customarily had a jewel at the base of the feather on their caps. And John Stow has an amusing description of how fashions set by the king were followed by all:

Henry the eight (towards his latter raigne) wore a round flat cap of
scarlet or of veluet, with a bruch or Jewell, and a feather, diuers
Gentlemen, Courtiers and other did the like. The youthful Citizens
also tooke them to the new fashion of flatte caps, knit of woolen
yearne black, but so light that they were forced to tye them vnder
their chins, for else the wind would be maister ouer them.

Movement for men in a short cloak, doublet, and hose was usually
free and easy, fairly athletic, and much as it is today. But if your costume has padded sleeves, they preclude relaxing the arms at the sides,
so standing with the arm bent and the right or left hand on the waist
while the other holds the hilt of the ubiquitous sword is a common position. Without padded sleeves, men stood with one hand on the hip and
the other on the sword, or with one hand over the heart and the other
on the sword. The heavier the velvets, embroidered silks, and furs, and
the more elaborate the costume, the more men wanted to feel evenly
balanced. So they stood with one foot slightly behind the other and with
the legs fairly far apart and slightly turned out, as in some full-length
portraits of Henry VIII. In any kind of formal situation, men did not
cross the legs when sitting, but sat with one foot slightly in front of the
other. Both men and women sat with straight backs, dictated by the
clothing, whose stiffness prevented them from sitting in any other way.
Women's gowns were draped as gracefully as possible around the seats.

Clergymen and older men often wore long gowns, sometimes with
long sleeves with openings near the top through which their sleeved
arms fitted; when standing, hands were clasped in front, as in portraits
of Elizabeth's venerable ministers of state.

Theatrical costumes of the period were often quite elaborate, not
only in the English theater, but also in French and Italian court presentations, and even in boy's colleges (secondary schools). For instance,
shepherds and peasants were usually dressed in variegated satin outfits.
In Honoré d'Urfé's (1568–1625) *Épithalame pudique* (Epithlamium on
Modesty, 1583), the playwright wants the god Apollo's costume to consist of "a great robe of crimson-orange taffeta decorated with silver, a
silver cape," and a large wig.

Accessories: Belts were worn by both men and women of all classes.
They were called "girdles," as in medieval days, and worn not for the
purpose of keeping trousers or skirts in place but for carrying things,
from the sheath in which a sword hung to the usual *pocket* (drawstring
purse) to bunches of keys or anything else that could be hung from

them—for instance, little mirrors, called *looking-glasses*, or tobacco pouches.

Wigs were sometimes worn, or at least hairpieces to fill out the head. Mary, Queen of Scots (1542–1587) wore false hair, and Queen Elizabeth I had eighty hairpieces, or "attires." Both men and women wore perfumes, and used makeup to make themselves as pale as possible. The cosmetic was toxic because it was usually lead based. In portraits of Queen Elizabeth, you can see the deathly pallor the makeup gave to her face. Combs were used by the wealthy, and comb cases carried on the girdle.

The personal watch had been invented and was much in vogue. It was attached to a fob and carried in the pocket, or hung on a ribbon around the neck or from the girdle. Watches could be ornate, just as they are today, and were often little jeweled works of art. In fact, keeping time was becoming more accurate in general. Not only were church bells rung, but there were mechanical public clocks. There were also the less accurate hourglasses and minute glasses, filled with sand that dripped slowly from a top globe to the one below. These were much used by navigators. Their shape was admired, and it was considered pleasing to have an "hourglass figure"—easily seen in both men and women's portraits, where, for men, the doublet and cloak provided the top half and the pumpkin-like overhose and tights, with codpiece attached, provided the attractive lower half.

Women all over Europe, in Renaissance Italy, and in England, from Queen Elizabeth on down, carried fans, but they were usually not the bladed folding fans we know today. Rather, they were whisks, or bouquets of plumes attached together at the bottom like a feather duster; or flag-fans, consisting of a square or rectangle of leather or stiff cloth, ornately decorated, attached to a long staff. They were originally used as fly whisks, but their use for cooling became fashionable. Queen Elizabeth was quite enamored of fans and had an enormous collection, partly because she received many as presents. The *pomander*, a dried orange studded with cloves, was carried by members of the upper classes against the stench when they were outdoors in crowds. It was held up to the nose and was otherwise carried in its own pouch, which hung from the girdle.

Greetings and Salutations: For the Elizabethan man's bow that is the at origin of the expression "break a leg"—used for curtain calls, at court, or in any formal situation—put the left foot forward and the right foot back, while gracefully bending the right knee (breaking the leg, or "making a leg") and simultaneously bowing from the waist and placing the right hand over the heart, all in a single elegantly executed movement.

Women curtsied in a similar fashion by placing the right leg almost directly behind the left, lifting the skirts delicately at the sides with both hands, and taking the body down without bowing forward, while nodding the head very slightly.

In New England, the Puritans were less attached to rigid forms of showing deference to those who were more highly placed socially, because they paid lip service, at least, to the idea that we are all equal in the sight of the God they worshipped. Hierarchies did exist, of course, based on the models the colonists knew in Europe, but since there was no king, there was no need in either the English or French colonies for a system of etiquette that demanded bowing and scraping. Although prerogatives and forms of deference were prevalent, as they were in an even more severe way in the Spanish Americas, they were often confined to simple salutes or nods of the head and not to full bows, since the Puritans believed man should bow only to their God. On the other hand, the relationship of servants or employees to masters was more formal, and female servants gave a slight curtsey on entering a room to speak to their employers.

Manners and Style According to Castiglione: The manners of a courtier and proper etiquette are described in minute detail in Baldassare Castiglione's (1478–1529) *The Book of the Courtier*, first translated into English in 1561. In particular, the art of elegance and good deportment require *sprezzatura*, which means concealing artifice so that it appears natural. It takes great refinement of manner and endless practice to appear absolutely nonchalant and graceful in one's deportment.

The book, which is written as a series of dialogues, was also translated into French, German and Spanish, and it became the standard work of manners and good conduct and deportment throughout Europe. Between 1528 and 1616, it went through 108 editions!

The true, elegant courtier should be graceful of countenance and pleasing in appearance, and above all, he should be the epitome of the well-bred, widely knowledgeable Renaissance man. First and foremost, he should be a brilliant soldier: brave and full of prowess on the battlefield, vigorous, bold, and, withal, modest about his successes. By no means should he brag or bluster about any of this; that would be most unseemly and unmannerly. But it would not be too unseemly to indulge in modest, humble self-praise. Castiglione also thought that an ability in wrestling was very important, because hand-to-hand combat in battle might require it. And of course, the courtier must be an expert in the use of all different kinds of weapons.

And he must be the scrupulous embodiment of virtue: knowledgeable in all the arts, and as easily able to draw and paint as to sing and play musical instruments. He should also be as adept in the use of the carving knife as of the sword. In peace, he should be able to ride, hunt, fence, and play manly sports—especially tennis, which teaches dexterity, and vaulting for nimbleness. And he should be at home in the company of scholars, with whom he should be able to discourse eloquently and without the least touch of pedantry on philosophy and every other scholarly subject. To courtly ladies, he will display exquisite politeness and courtesy, because his manners are perfect. The true courtier avoids affectation and is prudent and thoughtful. If he knows how to write prose and compose poetry as well, and if his handwriting is perfect and his spoken diction excellent, he will be a truly worthy gentleman indeed. He will be fit for life at the most sophisticated Renaissance court, such as that of Urbino, where *Il libro del Cortegiano* was written and which it holds up as a model. This at least is the ideal for which one must strive, while remembering that nobody is perfect. Polonius's well-known advice to Laertes in act 1, scene 3 of *Hamlet* is along the same lines, and harmonizes well with Castiglione's ideas on the principles gentlemen should follow.

Manners and Style According to Giovanni della Casa, Archbishop of Benevento:

In 1576, Robert Peterson of Lincoln's Inn, about whom very little is known, published his translation into English of della Casa's *Galateo, ovvero dei Costumi* as *Galateo, Of Manners and Behavior in Familiar Conversation*. The word *galateo* comes from the name of a courteous Neapolitan doctor who wrote a book on education and whose tone della Casa adopted, as he himself tells us, when writing his own book, which became so famous that the word passed into the Italian language with the meaning of "a book of etiquette, good manners and breeding." By the end of the sixteenth century, it had been translated into almost every European language and was held in great esteem.

The good archbishop (1503–1556)—who had a distinguished if sometimes precarious career in Vatican diplomacy, and retired from church politics to devote himself to literature—was a much-admired writer in his day. Della Casa thought good manners and politeness the highest of virtues, and appalled by the uncouth behavior he saw all around him, he penned his corrective treatise, which was destined for a middle-class audience of citizens and burghers, and is therefore more mundane than Castiglione's book. Peterson must have thought it also spoke to the Elizabethan town dwellers, with their similar lack of good behavior. The book provides actors with a sense of how people actually behaved (I have modernized the spelling):

> And therefore, it is an ill-favored fashion, that some men use openly to thrust their hands in what part of their body they list.
>
> Likewise, I like it as ill to see a gentleman settle himself, to do the deeds of nature, in presence of men: And after he hath done, to truss himself again before them.
>
> And when thou hast blown thy nose, use not to open thy handkerchief, to glare upon thy snot, as if thou hadst pearls and rubies fallen from thy brains.
>
> ...they are much more to be blamed, that pull out their knives or their scissors and but pare their nails, as if they made no account at all of the company...
>
> Besides, let not a man so sit that he turn his tail to him that sitteth next to him: nor lie tottering about with one leg so high above the other, that a man may see all bare that his clothes would cover. For such parts be never [dis]played, but amongst those to whom a man need use no reverence. It is very true that if a gentleman should use these fashions before his servants, or in the presence of some friends of meaner condition than himself: it would betoken no pride, but a love and familiarity.
>
> Let a man stand upright of himself, and not lean or loll upon another man's shoulder: and when he talketh, let him not punch his fellow with his elbow, (as many are wont to do) at every word they speak...
>
> ...it is a rude fashion for a man to claw or scratch himself when he sitteth at the table. And a man should at such a time have a very great care that he spit not at all. But if need enforce him, then let him do it, after an honest sort.... We must also beware that we eat not so greedily that we get the hicket [hiccups] or belch withal.... Likewise, you must not rub your teeth with your napkin, and much less with your fingers. For these be tricks for a sloven. Neither must you openly rinse your mouth with the wine, and then spit it forth.

And to wear a toothpick, about your neck: of all fashions, that is the worst.

[Some people eat and] never lift up their heads nor look up, and much less keep their hands from the meat and with both their cheeks blown (as if they should sound the trumpet or blow the fire) not eat but raven: who, besmearing their hands, almost up to their elbows, so bedaub the napkins ... And ... be not ashamed, many times with these filthy napkins, to wipe away the sweat that trickleth and falleth down their brows, their face and their neck (they be such greedy guts in their feeding) and otherwhile to, (when it comes upon them) spare not to snot their sniveled nose upon them.

Also inadvisable are loud, slurping noises when you eat, coughing or sneezing in somebody else's face, and standing too close to someone and breathing on them when talking. And we should "show reverence, meekness and respect to the company, in which we fellowship ourselves." And stop railing at and beating your servants! In fact, in general "if thou be angry, show it not." Be circumspect and not boastful in conversation, and don't show off by wearing too much jewelry, which it was very fashionable for men to do, with necklaces, chains, and earrings. Wherever you travel, learn and observe the customs of the country and the manner of greeting and addressing people that prevails there, so that you can treat everyone you meet with proper respect and address people by their proper titles. Della Casa goes on to give a great deal of sage advice and counsels moderation in all things.

Living Spaces and Furniture: Although aristocratic men and women both dressed in extravagantly embroidered clothing and could be extremely elegant, their surroundings were often uncomfortable. Even wealthy Elizabethan tradesmen's houses were often incommodious and badly lit (except for the usual tallow and beeswax candles for those who could afford them), although they were kept clean by sweeping them out with brooms and washing the wooden floors. Living conditions for the poor were crude, and they were not that much better for the rich in some ways. In the country, farmers and their families often lived in two-room hovels, with their animals in one room for warmth in winter. Cesspits were built for the disposal of human waste, which was then collected and used for fertilizer by the farmers.

There were great manor houses as well, and in the cities, with their expanding populations, vast streets were built up. On the street side, the ground floor of a city house usually contained a tradesman's shop, and private commerce flourished.

Heating was by means of wood fires, and in many of the country huts the hearth was in the middle of the floor and the smoke was supposed to escape through the roof, but as you may imagine, much of it stayed right there in the room. Great fireplaces at the sides of rooms with chimneys were the rule, however, in all the great houses, and in monasteries and convents as well.

The manor houses built for the local gentry followed a pattern of a great central hall reached from an outside courtyard that set off the house. Off the hall on one side was the kitchen section, with pantries and larders, leading at the back to kitchen gardens and stables, and on the other side was a great dining hall. Bedrooms were on the second story, and cramped servants' quarters either outside near the barn, or in it, or on a third story of the main house. There was heavy furniture, such as chests and armoires and great wooden dining tables, and the wooden chairs with backs, which were more rarely used than benches and stools, could be hard and uncomfortable until the invention of upholstery. Chairs had arms, but when the fashion of women's clothing began to include voluminous hooped farthingales, chairs had to be built without arms because women could not sit in them. Tapestries and heavy rugs were used to add to warmth. Conditions had scarcely improved much since medieval days, but there were now extensive glass windows and casements for the well-to-do, and torches and lanterns for light. And there were all kinds of other technological advances as well, among them the improvement of paper and parchment and the use of the quill pen with a nib, or point, carved into it; it usually consisted of the feather's central shaft with the plumage shaved clean off, although by the eighteenth century nobody was bothering to do that any more, and the quill as we usually see it was in use.

The most famous style of building was the half-timbered, in the interstices of which was daubed a mixture of clay and straw. This was seen all over gothic northern Europe and in England and France as well.

Food and Table Manners: For table manners during this period, the excerpts from della Casa's *Galateo* above tell you just about all you need to know on the subject. Hugh Rhodes's (?–?) *The boke of Nurture, or Schoole of good manners,* published in 1577 and written partly in prose and partly in verse, repeats much of what had been previously published in the Middle Ages. It also gives instructions on the serving of meals and for servants' general behavior. The wary diner must apparently keep an eye on his personal spoon, "and take heede who takes it vp, for feare it be conuayed"—conveyed, that is, stolen. He is also instructed, "Rend not thy meate asunder, for that swarues [swerves] from curtesy." And "Belche thou neare to no mans face, with a corrupt fumosytye [fumosity; fumes of bad breath; "fumous" meant indigestible]." Don't pick your teeth with your knife or fingers, but "take a stick, or some cleane thing." As a general rule, "Eate softly, and drink mannerly."

In Renaissance England and on the Continent, food was quite sophisticated. Poultry was stuffed with chestnuts and liver, then braised, and served with a sauce of reduced stock and truffles. Fish, vegetables, and salads were eaten as well as pies and tarts of all kinds, sweet and savory. A spectacular dish was spit-roasted swan or cygnet (baby swan): after cooking, its feathers were rearranged over it and sometimes gilded; it was then ceremoniously presented to the banqueters in all its splendor. In the late medieval era, swan was served with a sauce called *chawdron*, made from the swan's giblets and liver, wine, ginger, cloves, salt, and pepper, and thickened with bread.

In Venice during the High Renaissance, there were food booths all around the Rialto Bridge where one could snack on international specialties, as one still can. The cooking of France and Italy was especially renowned, and England was famous for its roast meats of all kinds, especially the celebrated roast beef and leg of mutton, but all over Europe, gargantuan feasts continued to be the order of the day. In fact, the word *gargantuan* comes from the name of the famous gluttonous giant Gargantua in Rabelais' hilarious, bawdy classic—which in Rabelaisian extravagant manner is actually five novels, under the title *Gargantua and Pantagruel* (Gargantua's son), an almost pagan tribute to the joys of sex and food. But François Rabelais (the pen name of Alcofribas Nasier, 1494–1553) was a Franciscan monk before he became a Benedictine. A true Renaissance man, he studied law and also became a doctor. In his books, he satirized the pedantry and Scholasticism of the church and its rigid educational system, which he wanted to reform in the direction of humanism, in support of the liberal religious ideas of King François I (1494–1597).

The diet of the English people was generally hearty and healthy, although it did not include many vegetables. Fynes Moryson discusses it at length: a great deal of poultry was consumed, as well as rabbit and hare, and country people loved "barley and rye brown bread" more than the white bread the nobility preferred. Venison was one of the principle meats:

> In the seasons of the yeere the English eate Fallow deare plentifully, as Bucks in summer and Does in winter, which they bake in Pasties, and this Venison Pasty is a dainty rarely found in any other Kingdome.... English Cookes, in comparison with other Nations, are most commended for roasted meates.

The French, he informs us,

> sup with roasted meates, each having his severall sawce: but their Feasts are more sumptuous then ours, and consist for the most part of made fantasticall meates and sallets, and sumptuous compositions, rather then of flesh or birds. And the cookes are most esteemed, who have best invention in new made and compounded meats.

When French travelers stay at inns

> at times of eating, they call the Cookes dwelling neere the Innes, who bring the best meates they have, and when the guests have chosen their meate, and agreed for the price, they carry it backe to dresse it, and so send it warme with sawces. In generall, through the Cities of France, passengers seldome dine at their Innes, but with some companions goe to the Tavernes or Cookes shops.

Social Dancing: There were often dances at the feasts of the nobility, as well as other forms of entertainment: jugglers, jesters, and acrobatic displays. Elizabethans were robust dancers, much given to leaps and bounds. Court and country dances were developed during this period, and they were used in stage entertainment and court *masques* (pantomimes) as well. The masques, performed by masked actors, were elaborate allegories in verse, performed in ornate costumes with spectacular scenery. National dances emerged also, such as the slow, restrained and stately Spanish pavane, and the French galliard, adopted by the Elizabethans, but the French style of dancing had been popular as well in the court of the queen's father, Henry VIII. All over Europe there were dancing schools, even in English villages. Dancing had many advantages "necessary to good society," as Thoinot Arbeau (1520–1595) tells us in his important book of instruction, *Orchésographie* (Orchesography) published in 1589:

Dancing is practiced in order to know if the lovers are healthy and sound of limb, and at the end of a dance it is permitted them to kiss their mistresses, so that they may respectively touch, and smell each other's odors, to see if they are shapely, and if they smell of the malodorous smell named "shoulder of mutton."

Queen Elizabeth—who played the lute, as we can see in a portrait of her, and who enjoyed dancing and watching her courtiers dance—liked the graceful, energetic galliard, which showed off men's legs and athleticism. A ball at her court might begin with a solemn pavane, but the atmosphere would be sure to change quickly as the younger courtiers danced the galliard. An accomplished courtier was expected to be able to play an instrument and, most especially, to be a good dancer.

The galliard begins with a *révérence*, which is done on a slow count of eight: four down, four up. Here is how Thoinot Arbeau describes it in "Movements of the Galliard":

At the beginning of the Galliard, it is to be presumed that the dancer holds the demoiselle by the hand and makes the reverence while the instrument players begin to sound; the reverence done, he assumes a handsome and decent expression. To make the reverence, you hold the left foot firmly on the ground, and, bending the shank of the right leg, carry the point of the shoe of the right foot behind the said left foot: taking off your bonnet or hat and saluting your demoiselle and the company.... After the reverence is thus made, straightening up your body and covering your head again, you will draw forth your right foot, and you will put and place the two feet [so that they are] joined, in what we understand to be a decent position. When the two feet are thus arranged, with one beside the other... the points of the shoes are in a straight line, and equally support the dancer's body.

Then the dancer springs energetically up on the left foot and crosses the right in front of it. He then leaps up on the right foot, crossing the left in front of that one. This pattern is repeated three times, and on the last time the right foot, which is on the floor, is pointed to the front. Once again, the pattern is repeated. This is known as the *pieds croisés* (crossed feet). And it is the first of several patterns that are repeated, and that include various hops and leaps and special passes for the ladies in front of the gentlemen.

An Italian variation on the theme of the *révérence* and how to begin the dance is to be found in Fabritio Caroso's (1526 or 35–1605 or 20) books, the *Nobiltá di Dame* (1600, The Nobility of Ladies) and *Il Bal-larino* (1581, The Dancer). In the former book, there is a dialogue between a disciple and his master, who explains that before beginning the dance, you must doff your hat with your right hand, straighten the arm and hold the hat with the inside against the right thigh, then switch the hat immediately to the left hand and "pretend to kiss the right hand (but without bringing it into contact with your mouth), while she does the same." The dancer then takes the lady's left hand with his right and makes the *réverénce* as described above. In *Il Ballarino*, he specifies that the dancer is to move the left foot and bow down on a count of four, and to rise on the following count of four, in time to the music that will already have begun.

Painting

The glory of the Italian Renaissance is its painting and sculpture, and I scarcely need to remind the reader of the masterpieces of Leonardo da Vinci (1452–1519) and Michelangelo (1475–1564). The artist Giorgio Vasari (1511–1574), who studied with him, wrote his amazing *Lives of the Most Excellent Painters, Sculptors and Architects* (usually known as *Lives of the Artists*), published in 1568 and dealing mostly with Florentine artists, for whom it provides superb source material.

Much Renaissance painting is devoted to religious subjects—those of Veronese (1528–1588), for instance—or to mythology, as in the series of paintings by Correggio (1494–1534) based on the myths in Ovid's *Metamorphoses*. But the depiction of landscapes and cities and of daily life; portraits of wealthy sitters; and group pictures showing government meetings, banquets, receptions, and ceremonial events abound. And the art of drawing and painting with a sense of three-dimensional perspective amounts to an artistic revolution. As Wylie Sypher puts it in *Four Stages of Renaissance Style* (Doubleday, 1955), "As the Renaissance fine arts mastered the third dimension, the tendency was to create 'in depth,' in cubical space, in sculptural volume, or to shatter, perforate and complicate the plane."

For the purposes of actors who want to absorb the atmosphere of the Renaissance in visual images, not to be missed are the gorgeous work of the Italians Correggio, Raphael (1483–1520), Tintoretto (1518–1594), and Botticelli (1444?–1510), who was much given to delicate fantasy; the German portraits and etchings by Albrecht Dürer and Albrecht Altdorfer

(1480?–1538) and portraits by Lucas Cranach the Elder (1472–1553); and the work of the Bruegel family in Flanders—including the realistic paintings of peasant life by Pieter Bruegel the Elder (1525–1569), founder of the dynasty. Other noted Flemish painters include Hieronymus Bosch (1450?–1516), whose bizarre works of fantasy are intense and almost surrealistic.

In Venice, Titian's (1477–1576) sometimes austere and magnificent portraits give us a sense of the seriousness with which the wealthy men of the city took themselves. The dramatic Spanish landscapes and portraits of El Greco (1541–1614)—who was born in Crete, which at that time belonged to the Republic of Venice, and died in Toledo, Spain—show something more about what life was like in the era of the conquistadors. His individual style and sense of color, and the elongated faces in all his portraits that almost seem to prefigure those of the twentieth-century Italian artist Amedeo Modigliani (1884–1920), lend a strange aspect to his portraits that is uniquely his. In fact, in his day he was misunderstood, and his painting would not really be appreciated until the twentieth century, when his mannerism and expressionism was seen as precursive of modern art.

The exquisite miniatures by the English portraitist Nicholas Hilliard (1537–1619) of such highly placed Elizabethans as Sir Walter Raleigh (1552?–1618) and the queen herself show you the fashions of the time, as worn by wealthy dandies and members of the court. Hans Holbein the Younger's (1497?–1543) splendid portraits of Kings Henry VII (1457–1509) and VIII, as well as of other notables, are exceptional in their nuanced portrayal of the sitters' personalities. Renaissance painting is almost a completely new art, with the addition of perspective going well beyond the medieval flatness. However, in early paintings of the period, the perspective is lacking, and medieval models seem to be followed in such works as the paintings of English banquets, concerts, and royal council meetings by unknown artists.

The Renaissance is also the era when oil painting begins in earnest, popularized in earlier days by Jan van Eyck. Before he started using it as a medium, it had been thought suitable only for painting the exteriors of houses. Water-based paint—such as tempera, made with egg washes to fix or bind it—had been the preferred medium, used for example in illuminated manuscripts; and tempera and watercolor painting would, of course, continue to be popular through the centuries. But oil painting now became the favorite medium, with its promise of permanence. Mixing pigments they ground from various sources in oils they extracted from linseed and such products as walnuts and poppy seeds took up major amounts of time in the artist's working life. The process could be extremely dangerous, since it created vast amounts of dust and since some substances contained lead or other harmful chemicals. Two popular yellow pigments, orpiment and realgar, for instance, were made from arsenic. Emerald green, manufactured by heating copper and arsenic together, was also highly poisonous. These paints obviously had to be handled with extreme care, and gloves were worn when using them.

Stretching canvases and mounting them on frames also took a great deal of the artist's time, or that of his apprentices and students. The canvasses then had to be primed with coats of gray or brown paint, or whatever other color the artist chose, often mixed with a binding agent such as mastic, before the oil paints themselves could be used. When the paintings were finished and dry, coats of varnish were applied to them. And artists became known for their recognizable palette of colors, which was a hallmark of their styles, along with the individual, distinctive way in which they built up their paintings in layers, from the darkest to the lightest colors. Techniques for painting everything from beards to leaves on trees, metals, and cloth were further developed in detail during the Renaissance, refined during the seventeenth century, and carried through succeeding epochs. Anyone wanting to do realistic painting today still uses techniques invented during the Renaissance.

Music

Richard, Duke of Gloucester—the future Richard III (1452–1485), whose reign lasted only for the last two years of his life—can never "caper nimbly in a lady's chamber to the lascivious pleasing of a lute" in the manner of a galliard dancer. Shylock warns Jessica to avoid "the squealing of the wry-necked fife." And there are innumerable other references to music and musical instruments throughout Shakespeare's plays, many of which have songs that were sung with or without accompaniment.

It was presumably Henry VIII who gave the world that immortal and touching tune about the sadness of lost love, "Greensleeves." Thomas Tallis (1510?–1585) was the major composer of his reign. And many another ballad and love song from Elizabethan days has come down to us. Music was undergoing a vast sea change in this era, with the invention and perfection of viols, lutes, and other stringed instruments, but not much composed music has survived. Chamber music as well as individual solo pieces were being composed by lutists John Dowland (1563?–1626) and his son Robert (1585?–1641) in England; and earlier by Johannes Ockeghem (1430–1495), Guillaume Dufay (1400?–1474), and Josquin Desprez (1450?–1521) in the Netherlands, where each headed his own school of music. They also composed Masses, madrigals, and motets and, aside from using the old modes, developed the scales we still use.

Folk and dance music in the developing national styles was being composed. The Renaissance also saw the rise of through-composed secular dramas. Giulio Caccini (1551–1618) and his colleagues of the Florentine Camerata, critical of the overuse of polyphony, had invented *recitative*, a vocal solo that was a form of song imitative of natural speech. This monody was accompanied by nonpolyphonic (simple) harmony, and with its pathos and evocation of emotion, it became the basis of opera—such as those, based on classical myths and history, of the prolific Claudio Monteverdi (1567–1643).

Literature

The rationality and occasional acerbity of the somewhat pessimistic Elizabethan philosopher Sir Francis Bacon's (1521–1626) *Essays*, and the brilliant, deeply personal *Essays*, first published in 1580, of Michel de Montaigne—who also left valuable accounts of his travels in Italy— present to us a real portrait of two men of those times. And they attest to the growing hold of reason and thoughtfulness, as well as the development of conscious compassion, in a Europe that was heading slowly towards the Enlightenment.

A lawyer and a classicist by training, Michel de Montaigne (1533–1592), former courtier of Charles IX (1550–1574), planned to spend his retirement after 1571 writing his essays. But he interrupted his leisure to accept the post of Lord Mayor of Bordeaux, and to mediate, as a moderate Roman Catholic, for the Huguenot Henri de Bourbon of Navarre (the future King Henri IV, 1553–1610) with the royal party in Paris. He was known as an advocate of toleration towards the Protestant Huguenots, his attitude arising perhaps from his background, since his mother was a Jewish convert.

Considered a master Latin prose stylist, the Dutch humanist scholar Desiderius Erasmus (1466–1536), an ordained priest who never practiced his profession, was an independently minded but faithful Roman Catholic.

He was the author of diverse and varied works, among them the satirical *The Praise of Folly*. Folly, who praises madness and self-deception, is supposed to be one of the gods, a son of Pluto, and is nursed by Ignorance and Inebriation. He also wrote *On Civility for Boys*, a book of etiquette which inculcates principles of courtesy and cleanliness similar to those in the medieval and Renaissance works already discussed. And he tried to reconcile scriptures with the ancient Roman philosophers. He was great friends with the Lord Chancellor of England, Sir Thomas More (1478–1535), whose tragic refusal to disavow his Catholicism cost him his life when he opposed Henry VIII's founding of the Anglican Church. In 1535, More was canonized as a saint by the Catholic Church. He was the author of *Utopia*, which compares the ideal sociopolitical and economic arrangements on the fictional island of Utopia with the bitter strife and warfare of More's Europe.

Edmund Spenser's (ca.1552–1599) *The Faerie Queen*, published in 1590, an epic about Elizabeth that is almost too adulatory, is incredibly long but also incredibly gorgeous in its use of the English language. To this era, and the religiosity of King James I (1566–1625), we also owe the exquisite translation of the Bible from Hebrew and Greek into English. It may have the reputation of being inaccurate, but it is unsurpassed in the beauty of its language to this day.

The Jacobean revenge tragedy, with its strain of bloodthirstiness, includes *The Duchess of Malfi* by John Webster (1580–1625) and the plays of Philip Massinger (1583–1639/40), Thomas Middleton (1570–1627), and Cyril Tourneur (1575–1626), among others. They tell you a great deal about the taste of the times, as do the varied dramas of the most celebrated Spanish playwright of the Golden Age, Lope de Vega (1562–1635), whose major theme is honor and whose melodramas are known for their complicated intrigues. He also wrote historical plays, as well as plays set in rural Spain. One of the greatest Spanish classics is the long, immensely complex, pessimistic *La Celestina*, almost a novel rather than a tragicomedy, in twenty-one acts. The early acts are of anonymous authorship; it was completed by Fernando de Rojas (d. 1541).

Machiavelli's (1469–1527) *Il Principe* (The Prince), published in 1513—a cynical, worldly book that gives sage advice on how to rule cleverly as a tyrant by using lies, prevarication, hypocrisy, manipulation, and playing people off against each other—is one of the great classics of the Italian Renaissance. Its unscrupulous techniques are still employed today, even by people who have never heard of Machiavelli.

Worth delving into are the *Chronicles* of Raphael Holinshed (d. ca. 1580), on which Shakespeare drew so much for his histories and such tragedies as *Macbeth*. Also prime source material for the period is Benvenuto Cellini's (1500–1571) outspoken, vivid *Autobiography*, published in 1545. In an age of brilliant artists, Cellini vied with the best as a master craftsman, an exquisite sculptor, and an astounding goldsmith, whose creations in the ornate High Renaissance mannerist style were much sought after by popes and princes such as the Medici and King François I. He was also an adventurer, roisterer, roustabout, swordsman, and murderer—about all of which he is very frank, and even boastful, in his writing.

Miguel de Cervantes (1547–1616) published the two volumes of *Don Quixote de la Mancha* ten years apart, the first in 1605, the second in 1615. Although written in the seventeenth century, the novel harks back to Renaissance Spain and evokes the medieval romances, with their code of knightly honor and courtly love. The wealth of detail about daily life—manners, customs, and behavior—is unparalleled.

The noted antiquarian William Camden (1551–1623) wrote the first history of Elizabethan England, in Latin, the first part of which was published in 1615, the second posthumously in 1625. The book was translated into English as *The History of the Most Renowned and Victorious Princess Elizabeth Late Queen of England*, and it is an invaluable source for how he and his contemporaries viewed their own times. His greatest work was *Brittania*, which includes geography and topography, as well as history. It too was written in Latin, and translated into English in 1610 by Philemon Holland.

Primary source material for the age of exploration and colonization in North and South America abounds. Among the most important memoirs is the account by Bernal Diaz de Castillo (1492 or 93–1584), *The True History of the Conquest of New Spain*, concerning the conquest of Mexico. The papers and logbooks of Christopher Columbus (1451–1506) detailing his explorations are fascinating. For conditions in the English colonies, read the writings of the Puritans, such as Governor John Winthrop (1587 or 88–1649), first governor of the Massachusetts Bay Colony. He was a religious Puritan who preached fiery sermons and was not averse to slaughtering the Pequot nation and selling the survivors into slavery. And read as well the account by Sir Walter Raleigh, founder of the failed colony of Roanoke in Virginia, of his exploration and discovery of Guiana. Typical of accounts of the times and quite wonderful reading still is Sir Richard Hawkins's (1562?–1622) *The*

Observations of Sir Richard Hawkins, Knt. In His Voyage into the South Sea in the Year 1593.

Among the most interesting pieces in the abundant primary-source material on the early experiences and history of the British colonization of North America are two accounts by William Strachey (1572–1621). The first is *The History of Travaile into Virginia Britannia*, which contains detailed accounts of Native American life as well as descriptions of everything connected with the colony. The second is *A True Reportory of the Wracke and Redemption of Sir Thomas Gates, Knight, upon and from the Islands of the Bermudas: His Coming to Virginia and the Estate of that Colony Then and After, under the Government of the Lord La Warr, July 15, 1610*, the true tale of the shipwreck he survived in 1609 when making the voyage to Virginia on the *Sea Venture*, the Virginia Company of London's flagship. The extensive description of the Bermudas and the life they led there after the shipwreck is spellbinding. The manuscript, which was in the possession of Shakespeare's patron, Henry Wriothesley, third Earl of Southampton (1523–1674), is said to have been read by the playwright, who used it for *The Tempest*. Sir Thomas Gates (1585–1621) was Governor of Virginia. Lord La Warr is Thomas West, third Baron de la Warr (1577–1618), for whom the state of Delaware is named. Here is some of Strachey's almost Shakespearian description:

> A dreadful storm and hideous began to blow from out the northeast, which swelling and roaring it were by fits, some hours with more violence than others, at length did beat all light from Heaven; which, like an hell of darkness, turned black upon us, so much the more fuller of horror, as in such cases horror and fear use to overrun the troubled and overmastered senses of all, which taken up with amazement, the ears lay so sensible to the terrible cries and murmurs of the winds and distraction of our company, as who was most armed and best prepared was not a little shaken.

Film and Television

The life of King Henry VIII has been filmed and made into television series more than fifty times. These include *The Private Life of Henry VIII* (1933) and *Young Bess* (1953), both with Charles Laughton as the merry monarch; Walt Disney's *The Sword and the Rose* (1953) with James Robertson Justice; the 1970 miniseries *The Six Wives of Henry*

VIII with Keith Michell; the 2007 Showtime miniseries, *The Tudors*, with Jonathan Rhys Meyers; and *A Man for All Seasons* (1966), adapted by Robert Bolt from his play, with Robert Shaw as the unforgiving king and Paul Scofield as the intransigent Thomas More. In *Anne of the Thousand Days* (1969), Richard Burton played Henry, and Geneviève Bujold played Anne Boleyn.

More than fifty films have been made about the life of Queen Elizabeth I. She has been played by Sarah Bernhardt in a 1912 silent film; Bette Davis in *The Private Lives of Elizabeth and Essex* (1939) and *The Virgin Queen* (1955); Cate Blanchett, in *Elizabeth* (1998) and *Elizabeth: The Golden Age* (2007); Judi Dench in *Shakespeare in Love* (1998); Florence Eldridge in *Mary of Scotland* (1936), with Katherine Hepburn as Mary, Queen of Scots; Flora Robson in *Fire Over England* (1937), *The Lion Has Wings* (1938), and *The Sea Hawk* (1940), with Errol Flynn in the title role; Jean Simmons in *Young Bess*; Judith Anderson in a 1968 television film, *Elizabeth the Queen*; Glenda Jackson in a six-part miniseries, *Elizabeth R* and in the film *Mary, Queen of Scots*, both made in the same year, with Vanessa Redgrave in the role of Mary; and Helen Mirren in a two-part miniseries in 2005, *Elizabeth I*. Another two-part miniseries, *The Virgin Queen*, had just been shown the same year, with Anne-Marie Duff in the title role. Miranda Richardson played a dotty Queen Elizabeth in Rowan Atkinson's zany *Blackadder II* television satire in 1986. The part has even been played in drag by Quentin Crisp in the 1992 film adaptation of Virginia Woolf's androgynous novel *Orlando*.

Aside from the BBC television versions of Shakespeare (all currently available on DVD), there are many old and newer films of various plays, including *Gamlet* (Hamlet, 1963), a brilliant Soviet film, and *Olivier's Shakespeare: Henry V, Hamlet, Richard III* on a Criterion Collection DVD, 2006.

Films set in the Renaissance in Italy include *Affairs of Cellini* (1934), with Fredric March in the title role; Orson Welles's *Prince of Foxes* (1949), in which Welles plays Duke Cesare Borgia, ruler of Ferrara; and *The Agony and the Ecstasy* (1965), based on Irving Stone's novel about Michelangelo (Charlton Heston) painting the Sistine Chapel. In 2004, PBS showed a two-part documentary/docudrama called *Medici: Godfathers of the Renaissance*, about the ruling house of Florence, available on DVD.

Based on Alexandre Dumas' novel, *La reine Margot* (1994) tells the story of Henri de Navarre, who became King Henri IV by converting to

Catholicism. In the infamous St. Bartholomew's Day massacre of August 24, 1572, hundreds of Huguenot Protestants had been killed, and religious wars raged throughout France. To resolve the conflict, Henri married Margaret of Valois (1553–1615), called Margot—sister of the Catholic King Charles IX, whom he would succeed on the throne—and in 1598 promulgated the Edict of Nantes, giving Protestants the right to practice their religion.

Films about the colonies established in the New World in the early seventeenth century include the 1934 and 1995 versions of *The Scarlet Letter*, based on Nathaniel Hawthorne's novel. Nicholas Hytner's 1996 film adaptation of Arthur Miller's *The Crucible* shows details of the Salem witchcraft trials accurately, although Miller's language is often very contemporary. The story of Jamestown and of Pocahontas and her trip to England are the subjects of Terrence Malick's *The New World* (2005), somewhat ahistorical despite claims to the contrary, but with many excellent period details.

For More Information

Arbeau, Thoinot. *Orchesography*. New York: Dover Publications, Inc., 1967.

Ascham, Roger. *The Scholemaster*. Edited by Edward Arber. Boston: Willard Small, 1888.

Barber, Charles. *Early Modern English*. Edinburgh: Edinburgh University Press, 1997.

Bloom, Harold. *Shakespeare: The Invention of the Human*. New York: River-head Books, 1998.

Caroso, Fabritio. *Courtly Dance of the Renaissance: A New Translation and Edition of the "Nobiltá di Dame" (1600)*. Translated and edited by Julia Sutton. New York: Dover Publications, Inc., 1995.

Cohen, Elizabeth S. and Thomas V. Cohen. *Daily Life in Renaissance Italy*. Westport, CT: Greenwood Press, 2001.

Columbus, Christopher. *The Four Voyages: Being His Own Logbooks, Letters and Dispatches with Connecting Narratives*. Translated by J. M. Cohen. New York: Penguin, 1992.

Cowell, Stephanie. *Nicholas Cooke: Actor, Soldier, Physician, Priest, A Novel*. New York: W. W. Norton & Co., 1993.

———*The Physician of London: A Novel*. New York: W. W. Norton & Co., 1995.

———*The Players: A Novel of the Young Shakespeare*. New York: W. W. Norton & Co., 1997.

Cummins, John. *Francis Drake: Lives of a Hero*. New York: Macmillan, 1997.

Del Castillo, Bernal Diaz. *The Conquest of New Spain*. New York: Penguin, 1963.

Dessen, Alan C. *Recovering Shakespeare's Theatrical Vocabulary*. New York: Cambridge University Press, 1995.

Durant, Will and Ariel. *The Story of Civilization: Part V, The Renaissance*. New York: Simon and Schuster, 1953.

———*The Story of Civilization: Part VI, The Reformation*. New York: Simon and Schuster, 1957.

———*The Story of Civilization: Part VII, The Age of Reason Begins*. New York: Simon and Schuster, 1961.

Erasmus, Desiderius. *The Praise of Folly and Other Writings*. Selected, translated and edited by Robert M. Adams. New York: W. W. Norton & Company, 1989.

Fraser, Antonia. *Mary Queen of Scots*. New York: Delta, 1993.

———*The Gunpowder Plot*. New York: Phoenix Press, 2002.

———*King James VI of Scotland, I of England*. New York: Random House, 1975.

Harrison, William. *The Description of England: The Classic Contemporary Account of Tudor Life*. Edited by Georges Edelen. New York: Dover Publications, Inc., 1994.

Hawkins, Sir Richard. *The Observations of Sir Richard Hawkins, Knt. In His Voyage into the South Sea in the Year 1593*. Edited with an introduction by C. R. Drinkwater Bethune. Internet: Elibron Classics, Adamant Media Corporation, 2005.

Henslowe, Philip. *The Diary of Philip Henslowe*. Internet: Elibron Classics reprint of the 1845 edition, Adamant Media Corporation, 2005.

Hibbert, Christopher. *The Virgin Queen: Elizabeth I, Genius of the Golden Age*. New York: Addison Wesley Publishing Co., 1992.

Jones, Ernest. *Hamlet and Oedipus*. New York: Doubleday & Co., 1949.

Joseph, B. L. *Elizabethan Acting*. 2nd ed. London: Oxford University Press, 1964.

Linklater, Kristin. *Freeing Shakespeare's Voice: The Actor's Guide to Talking the Text*. New York: Theatre Communications Group, 1992.

Mann, Charles C. *1491: New Revelations of the Americas before Columbus*. New York: Alfred A. Knopf. 2005.

Monroe, Paul, Ph.D. *Thomas Platter and the Educational Renaissance of the Sixteenth Century*. New York: D. Appleton and Company, 1904.

Morrison, Samuel Eliot. *Admiral of the Ocean Sea: A Life of Christopher Columbus*. Boston: Little, Brown & Co., 1991.

Neale, John E. *Queen Elizabeth the First: A Biography*. New York: Doubleday, 1957.

Partridge, Eric. *Shakespeare's Bawdy: A Literary and Psychological Essay and a Comprehensive Glossary*. New York: E. P. Dutton, 1960.

Rowse, Alfred Leslie. *The Elizabethan Renaissance: The Life of a Society*. New York: Ivan R. Dee, 2000.

Salgàdo, Gàmini. *The Elizabethan Underworld*. London: J. M. Dent & Sons, Ltd., 1977.

Singman, Jeffrey. *Daily Life in Elizabethan England*. Westport, CT: Greenwood Press, 1995.

Stow, John. *A Survey of London*. Reprinted from the text of 1603. With introduction and notes by Charles Lethbridge Kingsford. Internet: Elibron Classics, Adamant Media Corporation, 2005.

Thomas, Hugh. *The Conquest of Mexico: Montezuma, Cortés and the Fall of Old Mexico*. New York: Simon and Schuster, 1993.

————*Rivers of Gold: The Rise of the Spanish Empire, from Columbus to Magellan*. New York: Random House, 2003.

Recordings

Elizabethan Consort Music 1558–603. Alia Vox CD AV 9804, 1998.

Great Shakespeareans. (Edwin Booth, Herbert Beerbohm Tree, Arthur Bourchier, Lewis Waller, Ben Greet, John Barrymore, Sir Johnston Forbes-Robertson, Sir John Gielgud, Henry Ainley, Maurice Evans.) Pearl: Gemm CD 9465, 1990.

Paraísos Perdidos: Christophorus Columbus: Lights and Shadows in the Age of Columbus: History and Poetry in dialogue with Arabo-Andalusian, Jewish and Christian music of Ancient Hesperia until the discovery of the New World. Illustrated book and 2 CDs. Alia Vox: AVSA9850A+B, 2006.

Shakespeare's Women. (Claire Bloom; Sarah Bernhardt in a silent film excerpt of *Hamlet*.) First Run Features DVD, 1998.

Internet Resources

www.graner.net/nicholas/arbeau
   The complete French text of Arbeau's *Orchésographie*.
www.luminarium.org
   Information on Shakespeare, and on many of his contemporaries and their works.

www.pbm.com/~lindahl/Caroso/
> The complete Italian text of Caroso's Il *Ballarino*.

www.virtualjamestown.org
> Very informative site; also contains the complete text of William Strachey's *A True Reportory of the Wracke*.

www.william-shakespeare.info/site-map.htm
> An exhaustively informative site.

CHAPTER SIX

The Seventeenth Century: The Conflict of Absolutism and Liberty

The Puritan Interregnum and the Restoration of the English Monarchy

Despite the freezing winds blowing down the streets on that raw day, a crowd had gathered in Whitehall to await the execution of King Charles I, born with the century in 1600. The Civil War that had begun in 1642 was over, and with it his troubled twenty-four year reign. He stepped through the window onto the hastily erected scaffold outside the Banqueting House. To the bishop who attended him he had said, "I go from a corruptible crown to an incorruptible crown, where no disturbance can be, no disturbance in the world." Some in the shocked throng, watching silently and shivering in the cold, groaned when the axe fell. It was the 30th of January, 1649.

The self-righteous, unctuous Puritans, led by the unforgivable Oliver Cromwell (1599–1658)—the Lord Protector would sack Drogheda and Wexford and massacre thousands of the Irish in September 1649—now ruled a self-proclaimed commonwealth in which the promise of civil liberties went unfulfilled: the moribund tyranny of the monarch had been replaced by the theocratic dictatorship of obtuse sabbatarian fanatics.

In 1642, in an outrageous onslaught on culture that King Charles was powerless to stop, Parliament had banned the playhouses, a prohibition they were obliged to renew in 1647. Eventually they would outlaw "fute-ball and golfe," dancing, and of course, blasphemy. (Tennis, anyone? No! Lest your immortal soul be imperiled!)

In order to get round the parliamentary decrees, Shakespeare's godson, the daring Sir William Davenant (1606–1668), turned one of the rooms in his home, Rutland House, into a private theater. *The First*

Day's Entertainment at Rutland House was a musical evening of tributes to Oliver Cromwell, who loved music if he loved little else. Operas followed, chauvinistic and Puritan in theme, and then, when Sir William thought it was safe, plays, some of which were deemed seditious.

He had been convicted of high treason for his support of Charles I. The only thing that had saved his neck was that he had been out of the country during Cromwell's takeover, serving as Lieutenant Governor of Maryland. Taken back to England, he had spent 1651 in the Tower, from which he was released to await a pardon, awarded at last in 1654. In 1659 he was arrested again because of his theatrical activities, but he was released shortly afterwards. Such was the uncertain atmosphere of those ill-tempered, humorless times. Which way would the wind blow next? It blew him straight to exile in France.

The Puritan regime came crashing down, and the beheaded monarch's son was invited to ascend the throne in 1660. The tolerant King Charles II (1630–1685) promised the English freedom of religion and reopened the theaters. As if to make up for time lost and fun repressed, the almost irrepressible orgasmic dam burst, and while libertinage reigned in the wings, outrageous comedies of sexual intrigue flooded the stage. Since theaters had to put on the old plays until new ones could be written, King Charles issued licenses for the rights to perform Jacobean and Elizabethan plays, dividing them between the two new theater troupes to which he had given royal patents. These were the King's Servants, commonly called the King's Company, under the management of the Caroline playwright, Thomas Killigrew (1612–1683), who had been with Charles in his exile; and The Duke of York's Servants, known as the Duke's Company, under the direction of Sir William Davenant, now safely home again.

The technologically up-to-date indoor theaters for both companies, in Drury Lane and Dorset Gardens, were equipped with movable scenery and machinery for creating storms, and were designed by the renowned architect Christopher Wren (1632–1723). The lights in theaters—which served to illuminate the stage as well as the auditorium—were not dimmed during performances, so actors saw the audience very clearly, and audience members saw each other. Going to the theater was as much a social event as an artistic one: one went to see and be seen, and to enjoy flirtations and amours.

One of the Duke's Company's trump cards was its star, Thomas Betterton (1635–1710), hailed as the greatest actor of the Restoration stage. Samuel Pepys (1633–1703), the celebrated diarist, was an enthusiastic admirer: "And so to the Duke's House; and there saw 'Hamlett' done, giving us fresh reason never to think enough of Betterton." *Hamlet* was the only Shakespearean play allowed to the Duke's Company.

In his 1740 autobiography, *An Apology for the Life of Mr. Colley Cibber*, dramatist and actor Colley Cibber (1671–1757) describes Betterton's acting in act 1, scene 4 of *Hamlet*, where he sees the ghost for the first time:

> [Betterton] open'd with a Pause of mute Amazement! then rising slowly to a solemn, trembling Voice, he made the Ghost equally terrible to the Spectator as to himself! and in the descriptive Part of the natural Emotions which the ghastly Vision gave him, the boldness of his Expostulation was still govern'd by Decency, manly, but not braving; his Voice never rising into that seeming Outrage or wild Defiance of what he naturally rever'd. But alas! to preserve this medium, between mouthing and meaning too little, to keep the Attention more pleasingly awake by a temper'd Spirit than by meer Vehemence of Voice, is of all the Master-strokes of an Actor the most difficult to reach. In this none yet have equall'd *Betterton*.

The History of the English Stage—published in 1741 as a work written by Betterton, but probably actually penned by its publisher, the bookseller and writer Edmund Curll (1675–1747)—contains interesting disquisitions on the art and the period's style of acting. The author counsels against posing and using extravagant gestures on stage, and he has this to say about the playing of emotions:

> Thus when a man speaks in anger, his imagination is inflamed, and kindles a sort of fire in his eyes, which sparkles from them in such a manner, that a stranger, who understood not a word of the language, or a deaf man, who could not hear the loudest tone of his voice, would not fail of perceiving his fury and indignation...
>
> The looks and just expressions of all the other passions has the same effect, as this we have mentioned of anger. For if the *grief* of another touches you with a real compassion, tears will flow from your eyes, whether you will or not.

The Duke's Company raked in so much of the profits as a result of Betterton's popularity that the King's Company found itself unable to compete. The two companies joined forces in 1682, becoming the monopolistic United Company. Betterton and others would eventually withdraw from it after years of abusive treatment by the management and form their own troupe under royal license: the Players' Company.

As Simon Callow points out in his excellent book *Acting in Restoration Comedy* (Applause, 1991), the spelling in the language of certain characters is a great clue as to who they are. He cites Lord Foppington's "curious vowels" in John Vanbrugh's (1664–1726) popular 1697 comedy *The Relapse, or Virtue in Danger:* Foppington substitutes *a* for *o*, so *shot* is pronounced "shat" for obvious comic effect; and *aw* for the usual *ow*, in such words as *town*, which he pronounces "tawn" and *house*, which he utters as "haws," to rhyme with the English pronunciation of *horse*, dropping the postvocalic *r*. Vanbrugh took his cue for Foppington's extravagant, affected, simpering pronunciation from Colley Cibber's performance as Sir Novelty Fashion in Cibber's wildly successful play, *Love's Last Shift, or Virtue Rewarded* (1696), to which *The Relapse* was the sequel. Cibber repeated his triumph, Sir Novelty having become Lord Foppington, who likes to look at prettily bound books but not to read them, and pays more attention to his wig and lace ruffles and general appearance than he does to people.

Samuel Pepys and John Evelyn

John Evelyn (1620–1706) and Samuel Pepys were great friends, and kept up a voluminous and notable correspondence. Evelyn was a founding member of the Royal Society and an expert on various subjects, from trees and forestry to architecture and cooking, on all of which he wrote books. Like his friend Pepys, Evelyn was a supporter of the Stuart cause and kept a lifelong, very frank diary, beginning in 1641. The diaries of these two famous contemporaries present an unsurpassed, vivid account of the era—its events, attitudes, manners, and the personalities that navigated its heady waters.

An able naval administrator with aristocratic connections, and well placed to know everybody who was anybody in Restoration England, Samuel Pepys observed everyone and everything with an objective, if sometimes jaundiced and cynical, eye. He witnessed the coronation of the Merry Monarch, Charles II; saw the plague devastate England; and lived though the Great Fire that destroyed London on September 2, 1666, of which he gives the most extraordinary description: one can feel viscerally the chaos, desperation, and pandemonium throughout the city. John Evelyn too paints a vivid picture of the Great Fire, with "the whole Citty in dreadful flames.... The Fire having continued all this night (if I may call that night, which was as light as day for 10 miles round about after a dreadful manner)." "The burning still rages," he wrote on September 4, "the Lead melting downe the streetes in a streame, & the very pavements of them glowing with fiery reddenesse."

Pepys was a constant and inveterate theatergoer. And he had his opinions. He thought *Romeo and Juliet* "the worst [play] that ever I heard in my life." *Macbeth*, on the other hand, was "one of the best plays for a stage, and variety of dancing and music, that ever I saw." On January 3, 1661, he went to see a revival of *Beggars' Bush*—written in 1622 by Francis Beaumont, Philip Massinger, and (possibly) John Fletcher—and had a startling experience: "Here the first time that ever I saw women come upon the stage."

Why, such a thing had never been heard of, not in England! But, yes, there they were, playing women's roles, alongside men who were known for their female characters, such as the celebrated Edward (Ned) Kynaston (ca. 1640–1706), whom Pepys much admired, as he makes clear in his diary entry for January 7, 1661:

> Tom [probably his brother, Thomas Pepys (1634–1664)] and I and my wife to the Theatre, and there saw "The Silent Woman" [written in 1609 by Ben Jonson]. The first time that ever I did see it, and it is an excellent play. Among other things here, Kinaston [sic], the boy had the good turn to appear in three shapes: first, as a poor woman in ordinary clothes, to please Morose [characterized by Jonson as "a Gentleman that loves no noise"]; then in fine clothes, as a gallant, and in them was clearly the prettiest woman in the whole house, and lastly, as a man; and then likewise did appear the handsomest man in the house.

Pepys did not hesitate to note stories he had heard regarding the new actresses. He has rumors and tales to tell, for instance, of the buxom, talented, vivacious Eleanor (Nell) Gwyn (1650–1687), the nonchalant Good King Charles's favorite mistress, whom Pepys enjoyed seeing on stage:

> After dinner, with my wife, to the King's house to see "The Mayden Queene," a new play of Dryden's, mightily commended for the regularity of it, and the strain and wit; and, the truth is, there is a comical part done by Nell, which is Florimell, that I never can hope ever to see the like done again, by man or woman. The King and Duke of York [the future King James II (1633–1701)] were at the play. But so

great performance of a comical part was never, I believe, in the world before as Nell do this, both as a mad girle, then most and best of all when she comes in like a young gallant; and hath the notions and carriage of a spark the most that ever I saw any man have. It makes me, I confess, admire her.

This was on March 2, 1667, and *Secret Love, or The Maiden Queen*, a blank verse tragicomedy full of witty repartee by the admired poet, dramatist, scholar, translator, and literary critic John Dryden (1631–1700)—who was so famous that the literary period in which he lived and wrote is often called the Age of Dryden—was one of the hits of the first season when the theaters were reopened after the Great Fire.

Nell, as Pepys calls her familiarly, and the new class of actresses generally, were little better than common prostitutes in the eyes of many—such as John Evelyn, who, though a Royalist, could be quite puritanical in his attitudes. But we must allow Colley Cibber the last word on the subject:

The additional Objects then of real, beautiful Women, could not but draw a proportion of new Admirers to the Theatre. We may imagine too, that these Actresses were not ill chosen, when it is well known, that more than one of them had Charms sufficient at their leisure Hours, to charm and mollify the Cares of Empire.

Life in the France of the Sun King, Louis XIV

In 1649, the year his uncle was executed in England, eleven-year-old Louis XIV (1638–1715) had been badly frightened by the Fronde—one of a series of revolts by the nobles challenging the powerful Prime Minister, Cardinal Mazarin (1602–1661), and Anne of Austria (1601–66), Louis' mother and official regent for her son. The Fronde would finally fritter out in 1653, leaving royal authority bruised but intact. But Louis had learned his lesson. To avoid anything of the sort ever occurring again, the king decided that the nobility should be separated from the rest of the population and attached to the royal court, on which it would henceforth depend. He had the immense baroque palace of Versailles constructed with room for thousands, beginning in 1662, for just that purpose, and moved there from Paris in 1682. Henceforth, to be exiled from the court and out of the king's favor would be a dreaded punishment.

John Evelyn, who had fled across the channel with many other Royalists to join the exiled Charles II (Evelyn soon returned to England), was deeply impressed on September 7, 1651, by the splendid spectacle of the parade mounted when Louis attained his majority as a boy of thirteen and announced to the Parlement that he was ready to take the reins of power. The Parlements were regional governing councils and courts of appeal, quite unlike the English Parliament. The most important and powerful was the Paris Parlement, which registered and enforced the king's legislation.

There were, so Evelyn tells us, "4 Trumpets habited in black velvet, full of Lace," and another "4 Trumpets in blew velvet embrodred with gold," and hundreds of brightly uniformed guardsmen and soldiers preceding and following the king, clattering through streets "pav'd with a kind of freestone of neere a foote square which renders it more easy to walk on than our pibbles of London." The boy king was greeted by the populace with great acclaim. Even at that age, Louis knew how to play his part. All his life, everywhere he went, events of which he was the center and the focus were staged, not only to impress, but also to dazzle the beholder with a sense of majesty, splendor, and divine grace. But for all the acclaim he received there, Paris, with its endless traffic and crowds, failed to give the king a sense of ease and safety.

In his charming, erudite book *A Journey to Paris in the Year 1698*, the cultivated, knowledgeable Englishman, Dr. Martin Lister (1638–1712), describes every aspect of the city of Paris—"one of the most Beautiful and Magnificent in Europe"—often comparing it to London, so that the reader learns something about both. As for the general environment of Paris—quite different from the present city—"it must needs be said, the Streets are very narrow, and the Passengers a-foot no ways secur'd from the hurry and danger of Coaches, which always passing the streets with an Air of haste, and a full trot upon broad flat Stones, betwixt high and large resounding Houses, makes a lot of Musick." In other words, Paris was a very noisy place. Lister tells us that it was easier to keep the streets clean in winter than in summer; in hot weather and with a strong breeze, the pervasive stenches in both Paris and London were "very troublesome, if not intolerable." Evelyn, who describes Paris extensively, also remarks on the smells: "some places very durty, and makes it smell as if sulphure were mingled with the mudd." Both cities were also lit up at night. Lister reports:

> The Streets are lighted alike all the Winter long, as well when the Moon shines, as at other times of the Month; which I remember the rather, because of the impertinent usage of our people at *London*, to

take away the lights for half of the Month, as though the Moon was certain to shine and light the Streets, and that there could be no cloudy weather in Winter. The Lanthorns [with four candles in each one] here hang down the very middle of all the Streets.

A natural scientist, Lister gives the reader information on the plants and animals of the Paris region, and exhaustively details specialists' collections of minerals, flora, and fauna that he was personally shown, all of which is a great lesson in the state of science at the time. He describes as well the exterior and interior appearances of houses, and the custom, manners, modes of transportation, and habits of the people: "As for their *Recreations and Walks*, there are no People more fond of coming together to see and to be seen. This Conversation *without-doors* takes up a great part of their time." And the poverty, contrasted with the immense wealth of the rich in their gilded coaches, going through the *portes-cochères* (wide portals with double doors that allowed coaches to pass into the courtyards of their mansions), is striking: "The great multitude of *poor* Wretches in all parts of the City is such, that a man in a Coach, a-foot, in the Shop, is not able to do any business for the number and importunities of beggars."

The court of the king—to whom John Evelyn had the pleasure of being presented, and who became the arbiter of fashion and reigned as supreme monarch until his death in 1715 at the age of nearly seventy-seven—was notable for its absolutism (unlike the English court), its rigid etiquette, its intrigues and sexual affairs, its extravagant banquets, its theater pieces, and the king's ballet performances, at which attendance was de rigeur. Evelyn saw him one evening: "The *French King* in person daunc'd five enteries." Louis was quite the robust balletomane! He had made his debut at the age of twelve and found that he adored dancing. But in 1670, twelve years before he moved to Versailles, he decided that the time for such pursuits was past, and he gave up the ballet in order to devote himself to his mistresses, his building projects, his disastrous wars, and the governance of his realm.

Life at the court of Versailles is described vividly in the *Memoirs* of Louis de Rouvroy, duc de Saint-Simon (1675–1755). These begin in the year 1691, when the almost unvarying daily routines were already well established. Filled with *morgue*—overweening haughty arrogance— Saint-Simon is an amazing mixture of brilliant observer and deeply involved participant in all that he knows to be futile, trivial, banal, and even stupid, as he writes in detail of ephemeral strivings after status and vain, shallow honors that can really interest nobody. He paints an unforgettable picture of the king, the courtiers, and the numerous royal progeny, both legitimate and illegitimate, with their endless quarrels and disputes about precedence. Louis XIV ennobled all his illegitimate sons and daughters. And because of the parlous state of government finances, in 1695 he also ennobled 500 wealthy bourgeois citizens, who were obliged to purchase their titles at great cost.

The courtiers' presence was absolutely required at various points throughout the day, and Saint-Simon was sure to be there as much as possible. The official day began at eight-thirty a.m. with the king's *Petit Lever*, (levee; small rising), when an officer roused the king with the words "Sire, voilà l'heure" (Sire, now is the hour). The king's doctors, some favorites, and members of the royal family would often be ushered in for successive private audiences—these were the people permitted the *Grande Entrée*, meaning that they had access to the king almost for the asking, once the grand chamberlain had informed the king that they wished to see him. He was shaved every other day and put on thick layers of make-up. Then the *Grand Lever* (great rising) commenced, at which the king received the highest courtiers, those who were allowed the simple *Entrée* to the king's presence. The honor and privilege of handing him the various items of clothing, once he was ready to dress, was jealously guarded. Allowed in only to witness the event were those courtiers with the lesser privilege of the *Entrée de la Chambre* (entry to the bedroom). During the levee, the king would also order his meals for the day, and these were prepared by a staff of thirty-five cooks who worked for him alone. Orange-flower water or rosewater was poured over his hands after he was dressed, and then wiped off. He would breakfast on a bowl of bouillon before proceeding to Mass.

Everyone went in splendid array to the Royal Chapel through the Hall of Mirrors, where those members of the public who had been admitted could hand written petitions to officers to be given to the king. Mass was at ten o'clock, but only the king was allowed actually to observe the ceremony; the rest of the courtiers had their backs to the altar out of respect for His Majesty. Then, returning to his private apartments at eleven, the king held his council of state. Attended by various members of the royal family and selected courtiers, who stood and watched him, he would then have his lunch, called the *Petit Couvert* (little cover; the term comes from the fact that all the dishes presented to the king were covered, in an attempt to keep them warm, since they were brought from the kitchens that were very far away).

After lunch, at about two, the court went for a promenade, to see and be seen, in the sumptuous grounds of Versailles, or else for a hunt or a picnic in the nearby forests. Upon the return of the king and the court, there was the ceremony of the removal of the king's boots, the *Débotter* (disbooting), at which, once again, attendance was required, possibly with scented handkerchiefs discreetly held before the courtier's noses, since nobody ever washed much, not even the king. The fetid reek of the unwashed, perfumed noble lords and ladies and their army of unbathed, unperfumed servants and attendants pervaded the splendid and polished gilt corridors of Versailles.

But then, as Dr. Lister informs us, bathing was considered unhealthy, although he counsels that putting on a clean linen shirt every day would be a very good, hygienic idea. In George Etherege's (1635–1692) English Restoration comedy *The Man of Mode*, written in 1697, Sir Fopling Flutter—the part was created to great acclaim by Cibber with all the affected mannerisms he could muster—makes a great point of going off to take a bath, which must have elicited roars of laughter from an audience to whom such an undertaking seemed the height of pretension and extravagance.

By around six p.m., the king would have returned to his private apartments, where he would go over documents and sign letters prepared by his secretaries before proceeding in later years to visit the ultra-religious, mordantly jealous Madame de Maintenon (1635–1719), the trusted mistress whom he married secretly and with whom he would discuss public policy. There would then be a festivity of some kind, whether a grand ball, with buffets of refreshments and side tables for gambling and card games; a play by Racine or Molière in the theater; or the presentation of an ambassador at a court reception.

Having been informed by *le grand chambellan* (the grand chamberlain) or, in his absence, by one of the lesser chamberlains that it was time to dine, Louis XIV would proceed to the table in the *Antichambre du Grand Couvert* for a very public, rigidly formal dinner, the *Grand Couvert*, always served at ten o'clock. The king and, sometimes, specially invited members of the royal family would eat while the other members of the royal court watched. The chief royal doctor was always stationed directly behind the king's crimson velvet chair. Everything was so well orchestrated that the elaborate, impressive repast usually lasted only about three-quarters of an hour.

On most nights, the king proceeded after the *Grand Couvert* to his bedroom, accompanied by royal princesses and perhaps some others for the *Bonsoir aux Dames* (good night to the ladies). This was followed by the final elaborate, drawn-out ceremony of the day, the king's *Grand Coucher*, at which the reverse of the leaden morning rites were observed as the king disrobed and donned his sleeping garments before lying down in his extravagantly huge bed by about eleven-thirty every night.

By design, there was no room for independence in this wearisome, boring, stifling life. Louis was the most tyrannical of autocrats. He was cold and unforgiving, and he insisted absolutely on always having his way. Saint-Simon describes the following incident: The king was about to go to Marly, to which he sometimes escaped in order to get away from the rigid etiquette of Versailles that ultimately exhausted him, and he insisted that his pregnant granddaughter, the Duchesse de Bourgogne, accompany him. Her doctors advised her against it, and several women of her intimate circle thought the trip impossibly risky. She therefore excused herself from following the king's orders.

Louis was livid with rage and walked by himself in the park of Versailles, with Saint-Simon and the other courtiers keeping a safe distance, while awaiting the duchess's response to his order to change her mind. The duchess's lady in waiting approached and said something to the king that made him even angrier. Addressing the courtiers, he said in the most sarcastic, contemptuous tone he could muster, "La duchesse de Bourgogne est blessée" (the Duchesse de Bourgogne is hurt). And he added even more coldly:

> Even if that should be the case, what difference does it make to me? Doesn't she have a son already? And if he were to die, isn't the duc de Berry [one of the royal grandsons] of an age to marry and have more? What do I care which of them has children? Aren't they all my grandchildren?... She is feeling hurt because she wanted to feel hurt! And I will not stand to have my plans crossed for any trip I wish to make or for anything else I want to do because of the representations of doctors and the reasoning of old women.

And he turned disdainfully on his heel and strode off, leaving even the most cynical of his courtiers in shock at his heartlessness.

It was a coarse, vulgar, and brutal age. Severe corporal punishment and other forms of physical and sexual child abuse were usual. The brutality extended to behavior at public events. Even so refined and sensitive a noble lady as the Marquise de Sévigné (1626–1696)—who divided her time between Paris and her estates in Brittany, and whose letters to her daughter in Provence are an excellent source for the life of the period—enjoyed public hangings. So did the vast crowds who went to gawk at them and who loved to see those convicted of witchcraft burned at the stake—there were hundreds of such horrors, for example, in Bamberg and Würzburg, Germany—as if these grisly events were good occasions for feasting and laughter.

Meanwhile, the performing arts flourished under Louis XIV, and French culture, fashion, art, and literature reigned supreme as though it were religious gospel in much of continental Europe. This included all the German-speaking lands except Bavaria and its dependencies, which were influenced by Italian culture, and Vienna, which was still under the influence of Spain's ultrareligiosity. The court, and indeed the whole of France, had grown lax in its observance of Roman Catholicism, except for the obligatory attendance at daily Mass. Louis XIV and his regime remained nevertheless deeply intolerant of any dissension, whether Protestant or within the church itself. Louis even committed the appalling, stupid error of revoking the Edict of Nantes.

Women—talented, courted, and admired—were on the stage in France long before they were allowed to be in England. This afforded immense opportunity to dramatists, who did not have to limit the female parts they could write or worry whether a boy's voice would change in the middle of rehearsals. The three greatest dramatists of the age were Jean Racine (1639–1699), whose florid, passionate verse tragedies—*Phèdre*, for example—would later prove irresistible to such great stars as Sarah Bernhardt, and Rachel before her; Pierre Corneille (1606–1684), whose more austere patriotic plays, such as *Le Cid*, are no less lacking in passion than Racine's; and the inimitable Jean-Baptiste Poquelin, known as Molière (1622–1673), whose ability to amuse and to satirize the court and the wealthy bourgeoisie—in other words, to bite the very hands that fed him—would prove his eventual undoing, as malicious tongues whispered rumors of his disloyalty to the king, with whom he fell into disfavor.

In most of the baroque plays of both Racine and Corneille, the neo-classical unities were observed, which meant that the plays dealt with one principle event and unfolded in one place and usually within the space of one day. The world of the play was supposed to be depicted in real terms, despite the artificiality of the poetry, which followed strict rules: the standard form was the twelve-syllable alexandrine verse line in which all three playwrights wrote. As Michel Saint-Denis tells us in *Theatre: The Rediscovery of Style*, the innovative director Jacques Copeau (1879–1949) thought "that such plays . . . should be performed in a small auditorium made of wood, where the sound of the text would have the quality of chamber music.... Racine requires extreme immobility; the whole of the action being an inner one, it has to be expressed outwardly with the utmost sensitivity." Racine's tragedies, set in the ancient classical world, were costumed in the grandest court attire, which the playwright himself thought ridiculous and inappropriate, but although he tried, he could do nothing to change the situation.

The influence on Molière's plays of the Italian improvisational commedia troupes that performed in Paris was enormous. For a time, Molière's company shared the stage space of the Palais Royal with the Comédie-Italienne, granted a royal license in 1680. The commedia form began at country fairs in Italy in the middle of the sixteenth century, and developed further through groups of strolling players. They performed brief or long improvisational plays based on standard situations involving stock characters.

When the commedia form was adopted in France, the characters' names were changed to French ones, and many of these were also used in English. The characters represent not only psychological types and characters of various ages, but also social classes. They influenced theatrical writing for centuries. The commedia itself was performed with a certain style of movement and mask or half mask for each character, and each character had a particular kind of voice that the audience expected to hear. Among the well-known stock characters are Arlecchino (Harlequin), Pantalone (the pantaloon), Columbina (Columbine), Pierrot and Pierrette, Pulcinella (Polichinelle in France, Punch or Punchinello in England, where he is married to Judy), the Capitano (or braggart warrior), and the Young Lovers, who have various names.

Manners, Clothing, and Social Customs in the English Colonies

The first English settlers were largely from the middle and poorer classes, and they did not, therefore, have a background in gentility and politesse. But they came, of course, from a monarchist background, which conditioned their deferential behavior to those above them in the social scale.

In the New England colonies founded by the Puritans, one obeyed those in authority, and woe betide the refractory or especially the dissenter or nonconformist. Still, the Puritans believed that all were equal

in the sight of God. As a logical consequence, one of the Puritans' valuable, far-reaching, and equitable reforms was the legal elimination of
primogeniture in favor of a more equal distribution of inheritances.

In the South, too, once the colonies were established on a permanent
basis—Jamestown, Virginia was settled in 1607—the social classes
would be divided much as they had been in the old country. In 1619, a
representative assembly, the House of Burgesses, was established in
Jamestown, and that same year the first African slaves arrived there,
traded by a Dutch slave trader for food. Tobacco was already a substantial cash crop, and the Africans were forced to work on the plantations.

Sir John Pory (1558–1635?), Virginia's "Secretary of Estate," wrote
reports back to England on conditions in the colonies, including the
abundance of natural resources in Virginia and Plymouth, which he
visited. On September 30, 1619, he wrote a letter to the noted diplomat
Sir Dudley Carleton (1573–1632), in which he reported that there had
been "great sickness and mortality" that summer among "both those of
our nation and the Indians." The economic situation was somewhat
perilous, but the colonists were doing well enough:

> Now that your lordship may know, that we are not the veriest beg-
> gars in the world, our cowekeeper here of James citty on Sundays
> goes accoutred all in ffreshe fflaminge silke, and a wife of one that
> had in England professed the blacke arte not of a Scholler but of a
> Collier of Croyden weares her rough bever hatt with a faire perle
> hatband, and a silken suit there to correspondent.

Dress for the upper class was nearly as extravagant as it was in England, ornamented with feathers, jewelry, laces, and ribbons. But in
1660, the importation of lace, silk, and ribbons with gold or silver
thread was forbidden to Virginians. The law was neither obeyed nor
enforced.

By the 1680s slavery was a legal institution, but the plantation owners
euphemistically referred to their slaves as "servants" until the end of the
Civil War. By the end of the seventeenth century, the wealthy had
assumed the manners and mores of their aristocratic counterparts across
the ocean: the masters went hunting and riding to hounds and held fancy
balls at which genteel etiquette was the rule. The Southern plantation
houses and the governor's mansions were the center of social activity.

In the cities of the Northern colonies, taverns and coffeehouses
became popular gathering places: the first coffeehouse opened in Boston
in 1689; New York's followed in 1696. A well-established city, New

York—so named by the English—had been seized in 1664 from the Dutch, who had founded the city as New Amsterdam thirty-eight years before. In Philadelphia, taverns were popular. Less puritanical than the early New Englanders, the Quaker William Penn (1644–1718) had thought about banning them, but he decided to allow them.

The somber Calvinist Puritan religion that the persecuted Mayflower colonists had brought with them from their exile in Leyden, Holland to Plymouth in 1620—and that was preached by the ninety members of the clergy who made the Great Migration to New England during the next decade or so, and formed the colony's leadership elite—laid great stress on asceticism, austerity, and self-denial. In common with their fellow Europeans, nobody washed much either. But they burned herbs and fragrant leaves, bayberry, pine, and cedar on their household fires to help cover the unpleasant body odors.

Puritan men were enjoined to dress as plainly as possible, and women were at all times to dress with modesty. The most common "sad" colors were various shades of ßbrown—"phillymort" (*feuille morte*: dead leaf), russet, ginger, and fawn. Black was also worn, especially by many in the upper class and by the clergy. Brown, gray, blue, or drab green cloaks and broad-brimmed steeple hats of black wool felt were worn by both genders; women also wore white winged caps. In 1633, John Winthrop, first Governor of the Massachusetts Bay Colony, who sported black velvet suits, was obliged to import a consignment of scarlet coats instead of black from Bridgwater, the leading textile manufacturing town in England. His contact there wrote to him:

> I could not find any Bridgwater cloth but Red; so all the coats sent are red lined with blew, and lace suitable; which red is the choise color of all.

Beaver steeple hats, considered extravagant, were banned in 1634 by the Massachusetts General Court. Also forbidden that year was "wollen silke or lynnen with any lace on it, Silver, golde, silke or thread." And in 1636, short sleeves "whereby the nakedness of the arm may be discovered" were prohibited. In 1651, a more sweeping law was passed, and "great boots" as well as "gold or silver lace, or gold or silver buttons or any bone lace above 2 shillings per yard," silk scarves for women, and more were outlawed for all whose income was less than £200. Bone lace was so called because it was manufactured using bone bobbins. A fine of £200 could be imposed on anyone judged "to exceed their ranks and abilities in the costliness or fashion of their apparel in any respect." The court declared itself grieved at the "intolerable excess . . . especially among people of mean condition, to the dishonor of God," and to the court's "utter detestation and dislike." Great slashed Cavalier-style sleeves were also forbidden: Puritans could have no more than one slash to a sleeve, and even that was frowned upon.

These sumptuary laws were constantly disobeyed, and members of town boards were indicted for not enforcing them. The wealthy dressed as they pleased. When Colonel Thomas Richbell's (d. 1682) fashion-plate wardrobe was inventoried for the probate court of Boston, it included five suits, two rapiers "with silver hilts," a silver-headed cane, "3 small Perriwiggs," and two outfits: "1 Sattin coat with Gold Flowers & blew breeches" and "1 Scarlet coat & breeches with Silver Buttons." His wardrobe had been willed to his heirs. In both Europe and the American colonies, it was a common custom for clothing, which was expensive, to be worn for generations, as long as it lasted.

Aside from cloak and/or coat, and hat, the usual New England men's outfit, made for warmth and durability, consisted of underbreeches; a suit of doublet and hose or, later in the century, a waistcoat and wide breeches or pantaloons; a linen or cotton shirt; low shoes—either plain slip-ons; or brogues, which had one lace at the top; or "batts" with shoelaces—and stockings held up with garters. Bands—white, stiff collars, usually made of linen or cambric—were simple or had falling front folds, and were fastened on by laces or cords. Those of lower estate could only afford canvas, from which breeches were made, or kersey, an inexpensive twilled woolen cloth mixed with cotton, for their suits. In the winter, snowshoes resembling tennis rackets were in general use.

Women wore underbreeches, stockings and garters, a chemise, and a bodice and petticoat; or a long one-piece dress instead of a bodice and petticoat. A broad white collar and blue, green, or white aprons completed the indoor clothing. Cosmetics, considered sinful, were not used.

The wearing of wigs was inveighed against from the pulpit and denounced in the legislature, but there was no stemming the tide of fashion. Even that revered and upright divine Cotton Mather (1663–1728), born and bred in Boston, wore a wig.

Most colonies had sumptuary rules and laws, meant not only to inculcate modesty and seemliness in dress but also to enshrine snobbish class distinctions; not all were quite as strict as those in Massachusetts. Only Maryland had no sumptuary laws. In Pennsylvania, founded by Quakers in 1677, men and women were encouraged to dress in plain clothing with no ornament, and men did not usually wear wigs unless they were bald. Women wore aprons and tied kerchiefs around their necks with the ends covering the bodice. Plain, broad-brimmed hats or hoods were the only style encouraged. New York City had been known for its fashionable dress ever since the old Dutch days, and wealthy New Yorkers wore velvets, furs, laces, and jewelry without any restrictions. Dutch women wore an ornamental girdle, often of gold or silver—these were forbidden in Massachusetts by the 1634 law, although leather girdles were allowed. The girdle was a wide belt, from which hung keys, a small purse, and an *etui*, a case containing such articles as a toothpick case, a small knife, thimble, scissors, and so forth.

The sermons the Puritan congregations listened to every Sunday were delivered in a passionate but restrained manner, befitting those who preached restraint. They were not the hellfire rants and dramatic perorations we associate with some present-day preachers. The Puritans were sure they had found the key to eternal salvation and that this justified their cruel persecution of those who disagreed with them. The road to heaven was a thorny one, beset with doubt and difficulty. This vale of tears is all we deserve, for we are all sinners, and we need to cleanse ourselves of sin. This is not an easy thing to do. "If a cloth be foully stained," preached Cotton Mather, "it is not a little rinsing in cold water that will get it out, but it will take much rubbing, batting and scouring."

Breaches of decorum and manners were punished in public with the pillory, the stocks, or the ducking-stool. As in Puritan England, blasphemy, profanity, cursing, scandal-mongering, lying, and even flirting were criminalized. These were also misdemeanors in other colonies, but Connecticut, with its famous Blue Laws, had the strictest prohibitions against violating the Sabbath. Certain kinds of sexual activity were criminalized as well. In New England, the death penalty could be imposed for adultery; sodomy (criminalized in most colonies); and, in New Haven, for masturbation. Contraception, while not illegal, was strictly forbidden on religious grounds.

In primary and then secondary schools, Latin and religious studies were taught in all the English colonies. Ignorance was one of the lures Satan laid for mankind, so the Puritans were all for learning, which would reinforce adherence to a scriptural life: Harvard College was founded in 1636, leading to the establishment of Harvard University in 1639. Yet the superstition, intolerance, and downright religious insanity that existed alongside the quest for knowledge led to the horrendous Salem witchcraft trials in the summer of 1692, in which Cotton Mather played such a disgusting part.

The Stylistic Elements: Clothing, Accessories, Movement, Manners, and the Art of Living

Clothing and Movement: Aristocratic clothing in the seventeenth century was voluminous, and the human form was enveloped, adorned, and ornamented with ribbons and laces at the same time as it was concealed. The body's titillations were not to be shown but hinted at; hence the use women made of fans and men of their knowing smiles and raised eyebrows. Physical contact in public could be considered scandalous, and this is an important element of this period's style. When promenading or going in to dinner or to dance at a ball, a man would offer a woman his arm, and she would place her gloved hand on his gloved hand, resting it there lightly before proceeding, and that was supposed to be the extent of public physicality in this publicly straitlaced age.

At the beginning of the century, stiff, starched ruffs of various sizes, or high, stiff lace collars that rose in back of the head, were worn by both men and women. In Spain, the tight clothing of which was fashionable throughout Europe in the early 1600s, they remained popular for a long time, as portraits of the period attest. Indeed, they grew so large and had so many layers, and stretched so stiffly out in all directions, that nobody could move their heads very far in any direction or eat with ordinary implements for fear of spilling food all over them, so long-handled spoons became the fashion!

Women continued to wear the ruff longer than men did, since they were not required to be soldiers. With it they wore starched bodices and barrel-shaped skirts, with hip pads fastened around the waist inside the skirt to make them even larger, all of which was most unwieldy to move about in. Eventually, looser, more comfortable clothing—still voluminous—became the fashion. Bodices, worn over undergarments, were no longer starched; hip pads were eliminated. By the 1660s, low-cut necklines became fashionable, with lace collars attached to them. They showed off not only jewels but also a good deal of flesh, and they were considered scandalous in religious circles. Molière makes fun of this attitude when he has Tartuffe, the worldly hypocrite parading his piety, tell the servant girl Dorine to cover her breasts as he ostentatiously hands her a handkerchief.

Fashions became so extravagant and so much money was spent on expensive textiles that sumptuary laws were passed in many places proscribing certain modes and limiting the amount of various types of cloth that could be worn. But nobody paid any attention, despite the imposition of heavy fines. In Nuremberg, for instance, Christoph Endter (1632–1672), a printer whose family firm was known for publishing beautiful editions of Luther's translation of the Bible, was fined numerous times for buying clothing for his wife that was considered far too magnificent for one of her class.

The devastating Thirty Years War (1618–1648) between Catholic and Protestant powers, fought mostly on German and east European soil, also had an effect on fashion and style. It virtually put an end to the ruff and to tight-fitting clothing, in which it was impossible to move more than slowly, because soldier's uniforms simply had to have a more relaxed fit. For men, the ruff was replaced by the long square collar that we see draping down almost to the shoulders in many portraits. And men were able to grow their hair longer, since it was not limited by the ruff, which made long hair uncomfortable. This fashion took hold, and the Cavaliers in the England of Charles I wore long hair, in contrast to the severe short cut of the Roundheads, as the Puritans were known.

As the century wore on, men's clothing generally became wider and looser, with open coats—beribboned and ornamented, and sometimes with slashed sleeves—long vests, and loose trousers fitted into low or high shoes or boots. Cavalier boots in the days of Charles I were high and had flaring tops. Footwear later in the century consisted of either riding boots or, with the advent of wide knee-length trousers, shoes that were elaborately ornamented with buckles or lace roses, and stockings of various colors that could also be quite ornamental. For a number of decades, it was fashionable for men to wear a sort of short, ornamental skirt, consisting of several broad flaps; these were fastened at the waist over the doublet, which was retained from the Renaissance era for the first few decades of the century. By the end of the century, the doublet was gone, replaced by the waistcoat or vest worn over a shirt—with the coat, often elaborately embroidered and with rows of buttons, worn over the waistcoat. Plumed hats were worn, even over wigs. Capes and cloaks, short or long, were also fashionable.

The Wig, the Fan, and Other Accessories: Wealthy men, both aristocrats and merchants, wore huge, shoulder-length wigs of varying styles and degrees of ostentation. The wearing of hairpieces that covered the head completely began in earnest in the France of Louis XIII (1601–1643), who discovered one day that he was going bald. Embarrassed, he took to wearing a wig, and the courtiers followed suit. By the middle of Louis

XIV's reign, the wearing of wigs was de rigueur, and the fashion had spread throughout Europe and to England.

When Cromwell ruled England, the wig, of course, was out. But it was very much in vogue once Charles II was restored to the throne. Under Queen Anne (1665–1714, reigned from 1702), last of the Stuarts, the effort was made to wear curly wigs that looked natural and were lighter in weight. But only a few years before her reign began, Colley Cibber as Lord Foppington in Vanbrugh's *The Relapse* (1697) had his huge, extravagant powdered wig carried on stage every night in a sedan chair. He donned it with elaborate ceremony amidst the jubilation of the wildly cheering audience, whose mirth was redoubled because the wig that made such a hilarious entrance was almost as big as the small-framed, squeaky-voiced actor.

Women used fans gracefully and elegantly. The fans were often doused with perfume, so that when fanning herself, a woman also smelled a pleasant scent, which, like perfumed handkerchiefs, helped dispel the unpleasant odors of the environment.

Fans were used for far more than cooling off in hot weather. They were also a means of communication and coquetry. Fast fluttering could express indignation or anger, while slow languid fanning, accompanied by a languorous look, could be very sexy and flirtatious. The fan could be used as an extension of the arm, and it could be used held against the cheek, with the head cocked—in conjunction, once again, with a telling look—to indicate an amorous interest in someone. It could be snapped shut to make a point, such as "This conversation is at an end," or snapped open to convey "Please continue; I am interested in what you have to say." In Colley Cibber's *Love's Last Shift*, for instance, Young Worthy tells Narcissa that he has observed "the genteel flirt of your fan;—the designed accident in your letting it fall, and your agreeable manner of receiving it from him that takes it up."

In Etherege's *The Man of Mode*, Young Bellair is in love with Emilia, but his father, Old Bellair, wants him to marry the beautiful heiress Harriet, or he will cut him out of his will. Harriet is in love with Dorimant, a notorious rake and a lady's man; the part was created by Betterton. In act 3, scene 1, Young Bellair gives Harriet lessons in how to feign love for him, using her fan, so that they can deceive those who would prevent them from pursuing their own amorous interests:

> YOUNG BELLAIR: At one motion play your Fan, roll your Eyes, and then settle a kind look upon me.

HARRIET: So.
YOUNG BELLAIR: Now spread your Fan, look down upon it, and tell [count] the Sticks with a Finger.
HARRIET: Very modish.

. . . . . .

HARRIET: 'Twill not be amiss now to seem a little pleasant.
YOUNG BELLAIR: Clap your Fan then in both your hands, snatch it to your Mouth, smile, and with a lively motion fling your Body a little forwards. So—Now spread it; fall back on the sudden, Cover your Face with it, and break out into a loud Laughter—take up! [Stop!] Look grave, and fall a-fanning of yourself.

Men carried walking sticks and wore watches, usually with fobs. They had a snuffbox in a vest pocket, and tucked elaborate handkerchiefs into their sleeves or hung them out of their low-slung pockets, which were sometimes as low as the calf. Both genders wore gloves, and men were expected to doff the elaborate plumed hats they wore over their wigs when a lady entered the room. See de Courtin's rules about hats, below.

When taking *snuff* (powdered tobacco), a man would remove his left glove, grip the snuffbox in his left hand, hold the glove in that same hand between the middle and fourth fingers, and place the snuffbox between his thumb and index finger. He would then tap the box to settle the snuff, flick open the lid, and decorously take a pinch of snuff with the right thumb and forefinger, lift it to the nostril and inhale the snuff. He would do the same for the other nostril. He would then close the snuffbox and return it to his waistcoat pocket, flick any remaining snuff away with the handkerchief he would have pulled from his sleeve, and sneeze as decorously as possible into it, although sneezing after taking snuff was not considered good manners. There is an oil portrait of Colley Cibber as Lord Foppington taking snuff: in his left hand, Cibber holds the snuffbox decorously with the thumb and forefinger, and both his gloves between the middle and fourth fingers. His right hand, raised, holds the invisible pinch of snuff.

Eyeglasses are seen in period portraits, but whether they were efficacious in improving sight is open to question. The magnification was like that of reading glasses available in pharmacies today. Eyeglasses are useful for certain parts, such as some of the doctors in Molière or any pedant, lawyer, or professor.

When attending a ball or going to the theater, which was still not considered quite respectable in the early days of the Restoration, aristocratic ladies wore masks, or *vizards*, to conceal their easily guessed identities. On June 12, 1663, Pepys was at the theater with his wife: "When the House began to fill she put on her vizard, and so kept it on all the play; which of late is become a great fashion among the ladies, which hides their whole face." However, loose women took to wearing them in public too, so the high-born ladies eventually stopped doing so.

Men, particularly noblemen, wore swords as a regular part of their dress. *The Memoirs of Sir John Reresby* (1634–1689)—a Yorkshire nobleman and government official, who left England for France in 1654 and returned when the monarchy was restored—tell endless tales of sword fights, duels, and violent quarrels; brawling in the streets; and drunken, obstreperous, wealthy youthful scions of English aristocratic families attacking coaches and sedan chairs (carried on poles by servants before and behind) for a lark. But the story was the same everywhere in Europe. In Germany, for example, university students were known to be rough, and ready with the sword.

Here is just one of the many fights and contretemps Reresby describes in his lively, refreshing, and very unliterary manner, from his entry for July 1663:

> He demanded satisfaction, either by my denying I had meant any injury to him by the saying of the words, and asking his pardon, or by fighting with him. I denied the first, and so being challenged was obliged to fight him that afternoon in Hyde Park, which I did, an Irish gentlemen that he met by the way being his second.... At the first pass I hurt him slightly on the sword hand, and at the same time he closeing with me we both fell to the ground (he haveing hould of my sword and I of his). Sir Henry [Reresby's second] and his man were fighting at the same time close by, and Sir Henry had gott the better, wounded the other in the belly and disarmed him, and was comming in as we were both risen and I had gott sword out of his hand, which I took home with me, but sent it to him the next day.

Soldiers' accessories included the bandolier, a leather-covered wool or metal case containing shot and powder, and hung on a belt worn over one shoulder and draped diagonally down towards the hip. They wore cloth spatterdashes, also called boot-hose, which covered their long boots and trousers and protected them from mud; the word spats is the shortened form of spatterdashes.

The New Treatise on Civility as Practiced in France among Decent People *by Antoine de Courtin:* In 1671, Antoine de Courtin (1622–1685) published his *Nouveau Traité de la Civilité qui se pratique en France parmi les honnêtes gens.* The English translation, which also appeared in 1671, was called *The Rules of Civility; or Certain Ways of Deportment Observed in France; amongst All Persons of Quality, upon Several Occasions,* and it was extremely popular in Restoration England—not surprising when you remember that Charles II spent so many years in exile at the court of his cousin, Louis XIV. The book's invaluable advice on the politeness, niceties of conduct, etiquette, and manners of the period, as they should ideally be practiced and no doubt usually were, therefore applies to England as well as France. It is also full of details on the use of various accessories, such as hats and gloves, and advice on everything from what to talk about in public to how to pay compliments and write letters. The treatise was so popular that de Courtin constantly published revised editions. It would continue to be published into the 1760s.

Its principle idea, which lends itself to Molièresque satire, is that rank matters more than anything and that inferiors owe deference to "people of quality," their superiors, whereas it is *bienséant* (fitting, suitable) for superiors to treat their inferiors with familiarity. Kindness and respect, however, are owed to everyone. One must always do what is fitting, and one must always remain "in countenance"—that is, never lose one's composure and calm placid attitude. One must never make a display of feelings. And one must always remember that modesty, humility, civility, and politeness are pleasing to the soul. Pride, self-love, and false confidence are the enemies of civility.

Among his behavioral precepts for the outward marks of respect for others is advice not to indulge in certain habits once allowable, but now considered unseemly:

> Formerly, for example, spitting on the ground in the presence of people of quality was permitted, and it sufficed to cover the spot with one's foot; at present, this is an indecency.

And by all means, remember that when you are in conference with a person of quality, you must never pull him by the buttons, the sleeve, or the hand, and most of all, you must not punch him on the stomach. De Courtin points out that this would be rude and ridiculous.

Hats were de rigeur. Men had to take them off indoors, and they were always to be removed in the presence of a superior. It is extremely rude to suggest to a superior that he "cover himself," so that you may put your hat on in his presence, if he allows you to do so at all. But you may tell a person of inferior rank to cover himself, in which case you are being extremely polite. And you should never suggest that anyone put on his hat by using the phrase "cover yourself" directly, but rather "employ such circumlocutions as 'It's cold in here,' etc. or you might say, for example, 'Would you care to follow my lead? Let us leave off these fashions, and cover ourselves.'" But if you are greatly superior in rank, do not hasten to allow an inferior to put on his hat, "lest you enforce a dereliction of his duty."

On the other hand, Saint-Simon informs us, everyone was always to keep his hat on in the presence of the king. The sovereign alone had the right to remain uncovered. But when you spoke to the king, you removed your hat as you bowed, and put it back on when the conversation was over and you were bowing yourself away. These usages also obtained in conversation with the king's brother—Philippe, duc d'Orléans, called Monsieur (1640–1701)—and the Dauphin. But in converse with princes of the blood it was enough merely to touch one's hand to the hat in salute.

Men and women waiting in the king's antechamber, or that of a superior noble, are enjoined by de Courtin not to mill about and not to lean on the backs of chairs, which would be extremely impolite. Maintain dignity and reserve. He especially advises against whistling to pass the time—whistling is unsuitable anywhere, he adds. Always walk softly, and be careful that the heels of your shoes make no noise, especially important in an era when men as well as women wore high-heeled shoes.

If you are allowed to sit in the presence of someone of superior rank, always take a chair or a stool lower than that person's. And be sure to turn yourself so that the other person sees your profile, perhaps in three quarters, so that you are not directly facing the other person. Do not yawn or laugh loudly or make extravagant gestures, and do not take snuff, unless the person of quality offers you some; if you find it disgusting, you must at least pretend to take it anyway. And in leaving the company assembled in the august presence of a "grand seigneur," you must back unobtrusively out of the room, not looking behind you. If you are noticed, you must acknowledge that with a bow. And of course you must allow persons of superior rank to precede you.

He also counsels everyone to dress always according to the latest fashions but not to overdo anything—advice which no doubt was never heeded—and to remember that the fashions emanate from the highest echelons of the royal court. It would be most uncivil therefore to pay them no mind. In fact, you would have been in disgrace with the king, who was purposefully the supreme arbiter of fashion—another way of controlling the nobility, who were expected to spend their money on clothing that was up to date.

Greetings and Salutations, Bows and Curtsies: When greeting people, men might simply incline the head slightly if the person were of equal rank, or they might return a nod from someone of lesser rank, or ignore it and simply look at the other person as a sign that they had seen him or her. They would bow to someone of superior rank, and women would curtsey and perhaps use their fans to hide their faces. Aristocrats simply touched the brim of their hats to persons of equal rank, or doffed them with a flourish to show off the plumes that adorned them. As several sources inform us, three bows when entering and leaving the royal presence were de rigueur, in England as well as in France.

As de Courtin warns, men must be sure always to remove their gloves and kiss a proffered hand, while bowing low. Remove the glove also when handing something to someone, and kiss their hand after you have given whatever it is to the other person. "And when we speak here of the hand, we mean that it should be the right hand." And do not actually touch your lips to the hand, but make a show of doing so.

The manner of men's bowing in Restoration England and in France is as follows: Stand with the right foot slightly forward and turned out slightly to the right; nod forward from the head, right hand on heart. Bow from the waist—higher or lower, depending on the status of the character being thus saluted, and without breaking the leg as in an Elizabethan bow. De Courtin tells us that the higher a person's rank, the lower the bow. If you meet someone in the street of higher rank, it is only polite, so he informs us, to remove your left glove and, holding it in your gloved right hand with the palm facing the person you wish to salute, touch the glove almost to the ground as you bow low. You might doff your hat as well with the left hand, while making obeisance with the glove.

A woman's curtsey is done while decorously holding both sides of the gown up slightly and then going as low as possible, one foot behind the other for balance. De Courtin tells us that indoors women must remove the masks they wear to disguise themselves out of doors, and also take off their coifs, or head coverings. And they must make sure their dresses are well in order and, when they enter a room, make a slow and stately reverence to the assemblage, curtseying low to the floor.

In France, certain ceremonial reverential displays of affection carried great weight: Saint-Simon tells us that when he was presented by his father to the king, Louis XIV kissed the future duke's father three times—that is, he placed his face from left to right to left, without actually touching the other's cheeks. This was considered the greatest honor, and his father was duly conscious of it and deeply grateful to the monarch. Physical contact in public in this period was kept at a minimum, as I have said, and kissing the monarch's or somebody else's hand or someone's cheek meant making a ceremonious show of doing so; but as de Courtin prescribes, lips never actually brushed against the hand or face, nor was a kissing sound ever heard.

In this period, a flourish of the hand, beginning palm downward and circling upward to a higher or lower position, may be used to illustrate a point. A similar flourish is also used when addressing someone: if the person addressed is of a superior rank, incline the head slightly while gesturing with the right hand, beginning palm downward, and turning the palm up gracefully in a semicircular movement, as when first addressing a superior with the words "My Lord" or "Milady."

Living Spaces and Furniture: The Palace of Versailles is truly awe inspiring, and the royal apartments are extravagantly furnished with comfortable, ornate upholstered chairs with gilt legs and embroidered seats and backs. Only the king sat in an armchair, framed in gilt and backed in red velvet, or on his throne. Everyone else was obliged to stand in the royal presence—except for those members of the royal family, such as the king's brother, Monsieur, who sat on portable folding seats with black morocco leather backs, or those who were invited by the monarch to sit on a low stool or hassock, called a *tabouret*. Those not invited were inordinately jealous of those who had been accorded this coveted privilege.

With the improvement of glass manufacturing, vast, airy, light windows with elaborate floor-to-ceiling curtains gave a very different feeling in baroque palaces and homes all over Europe than the cramped quarters and ill-lit rooms of the Renaissance.

Among the most magnificent seventeenth-century baroque chateaux is Vaux-le-Vicomte, designed by the chief architect of Versailles, Louis Le Vau (1612–1670); decorated by Charles Le Brun (1619–1690), one of the most important artists of the period; and with gardens by the celebrated André Le Nôtre (1613–1700), who also designed the gardens and grounds at Versailles, as well as St. James's Park in London. This masterpiece was built for Louis' finance minister, the handsome and dashing Nicolas Fouquet (1615–1680), Marquis de Belle-Isle, Vicomte de Melun et Vaux. He was a patron of the arts, and of such writers as Molière and Jean La Fontaine (1621–1695), the poet and fabulist. His chef was the celebrated Franz (François) Vatel (1631–1671) from Switzerland, who later ran himself on his sword at the charming baroque chateau of Chantilly, rather than risk disgrace when an order of fish failed to arrive from the coast for the king's banquet. Ironically, as he was expiring, the cart from Brittany arrived.

Vaux-le-Vicomte almost rivaled Versailles, and when it was finished, Fouquet invited the king and court to an incredible inaugural feast, on August 17, 1661. The king had already been warned by Jean-Baptiste Colbert (1619–1683), his chief adviser and a man with a reputation for incorruptible integrity, to be wary of Fouquet's extravagance. Colbert asserted that the chateau had been constructed using misappropriated funds, and Louis, who marveled at what he saw, had Fouquet arrested shortly after the festivities, never to enjoy again the vast rooms and delightful vistas of his home.

The rural and urban poor continued to live much as they had for centuries, in uncomfortable huts in the countryside and ramshackle apartment houses in the city. Because of the widespread poverty, filth, and disease, despair and crime were rampant, and people were executed or sent to the galleys for life for the most trivial offenses.

Food and Table Manners: Upper-class seventeenth-century table manners were supposed to be formal and elaborate, but they were often quite coarse. De Courtin has an extensive list of dos and don'ts, quite aside from the deference due to people of rank with whom one may be dining. First of all, keep your hat, coat, and sword on. It would be rude to take them off before sitting down at table! Among his admonitions is that you should not take food with your hands, but only with your fork, although "you must remember also to take olives not with your fork, but with your spoon." Wipe your spoon before using it to take something from a serving dish. You should not eat too avidly or be obstreperous in any way, nor should you spit or belch. Don't remove inedible morsels from your mouth and throw them on the floor. Also,

> If by some misfortune you burn yourself, you must put up with it, or, if you cannot, surreptitiously, before anyone notices, bring your plate right up to your mouth with one hand, and, covering your

movement with the other, remove the offending food from your mouth and put it on your plate, and give it quickly to the nearest footman behind you. Civility demands that one be polite, but that does not mean you have to kill yourself.

And don't wipe your hands on your bread as if it were a napkin. You should accept everything offered to you, but you need not eat what disgusts you, and it is extremely impolite to ask for anything. Do not clean your teeth at the table at any time during the meal: this is "indecent and disgusting." And, for goodness' sake, don't take fruit or rolls off the table and put them in your pocket for later! Haven't you had enough to eat, you glutton? The fact that de Courtin has to make a point of all these things shows that the behavior he proscribes must have been widespread.

In some places, good table manners had to be carefully imposed by regulation, because even the highest of aristocrats at the court of Vienna, for example, would arrive for a meal sloppily attired and drunk. And they thought nothing of using the tablecloth as a napkin and a handkerchief, into which they would blow their noses, or of noisily licking their fingers or spitting into their dishes—all of which unseemly, foul behavior was banned by decree in 1624. It probably did no good.

In general, people used their fingers and knives to eat with, ignoring the forks and using spoons to dip into soup tureens as they wished, without regard to hygiene. Gentlemen were expected to as be as expert at wielding their knives to carve roasts of all kinds as they were at using the sword.

Table manners may have been rather coarse, but the food in France, for instance, with newly invented dishes and an attention to detail and gastronomic finesse, was beginning to be very much what we know today as French haute cuisine. Fine wines were produced all over France, and the art of winemaking was improved. During this period, coffee became popular. Louis XIV drank it first in 1644, and in 1672 the first Paris coffee shop was opened. Such establishments soon spread all over the capital. Tea from China and chocolate, imported by the Spaniards from their American empire, were also popular beverages. Bread, the main food of the poor, was becoming a staple food among the middle and upper classes as well, and bakeries opened all over Europe.

The king's meals were served with elaborate ceremony, especially the daily public ten o'clock dinner, superbly recreated in Roberto Rosselini's 1966 television film *La Prise du pouvoir par Louis XIV* (The Assumption of Power by Louis XIV). At the *Grand Couvert*, the king's silverware was placed on a silver platter, and his salt and pepper were in a locked coffer to prevent their being poisoned. It was unlocked ceremoniously in the king's presence. Everything he did was announced with rigid formality: When the king said "J'ai soif," (I am thirsty), an *échanson*, or gentleman cupbearer, would shout out "A boire pour le roi!" (Drink for the king!), bow as low as he could, and go to a sideboard. There, the *grand échanson* (chief cupbearer) would hand him a gold tray with two crystal decanters on it, one of water and one of wine, and a fine crystal glass covered with a napkin. The chief cupbearer, the cupbearer, and an assistant cupbearer (noblemen all) would hasten back to the table, and after bowing low once again, the assistant would pour from both decanters into silver goblets; then the *grand échanson* and the *échanson* would proceed to test the drinks. If they did not expire from having been poisoned (nobody seems to have done so), the *échanson* would bow, take the napkin from His Majesty's glass, and holding out the tray, allow the king to make his own customary mixture of wine and water. Bowing low, the cupbearers retired to the sideboard with their paraphernalia. If the king were drinking champagne, which was all he drank after 1693—the year the Benedictine monk Dom Pierre Pérignon (1638–1715) invented it—he always doffed his hat in salute to that august beverage, so Saint-Simon tells us.

After the stentorian announcement, "Les viandes du roi!" (The king's meats [food]!), fifteen waiters who served the king alone processed formally in with His Majesty's first courses, or "services," of soups and various other dishes. The waiters were preceded by a parade of two guards, who accompanied no fewer than nine court officials—including the major-domo, who led the procession, and an official keeper of the royal porcelain. Another procession accompanied the roasts and salads, and a last parade followed with courses of various puddings, cheeses, and desserts.

Louis XIV was quite gluttonous and ate without really understanding food, unlike many of his courtiers, whose tastes were rather refined. He, like many noblemen and noblewomen, ate huge quantities and, so Saint-Simon informs us, consumed at one meal "two boars with their accompanying side dishes, quantities of sole, and excellent crabs and oysters to keep them company." And the king's difficult sister-in-law— Charlotte Elizabeth, the Princess Palatine (1652–1722), whose outspoken, complaining letters make amusing reading—says that he ingested at another meal "four full plates of different soups, a whole pheasant, a partridge, a plate of salad, two great slices of ham, mutton au jus with garlic, and a plate of pastries." Later in life, he lost his teeth and could only eat purees and moistened bread crumbs.

Aside from the thirty-five cooks whose job it was to prepare the king's food, more than 600 kitchen staff would prepare the meals for up to 5,000 courtiers who dined every day at Versailles after the king, and were all seated at long tables according to rank.

It had been usual for middle-class people to eat in their bedrooms or in the hallway, holding their plates when there were no tables set, but the custom of having a separate dining room now became ubiquitous in bourgeois households. Also at this time, the mistress of a middle-class household began to be in charge of overseeing the cooking, and by the end of the century, quite a few cookbooks and books on entertaining had been published. Dr. Lister informs us that "the [usual staple] diet of the *Parisians* consists chiefly of *Bread* and *Herbs*." And even so long ago, the French used gray sea salt—"incomparably better and more wholsom than our White salt." He goes on to tell us that "in *Lent* the common People feed much on White *Kidney Beans*, and White or Pale *Lentils*." Soups made from mild-flavored turnips, cooked carrots and baby cabbages, and stews of mutton are also among the people's fare, but "The *Potato* are scarce to be found in their Markets, which are so great a relief to the People of *England*, and very nourishing and wholsome Roots; but there are store of *Jerusalem Artichokes*." In the south of France, onions and leeks were popular, and among the other foods he mentions as being abundantly available are lettuce, white beets, asparagus, sorrel, and mushrooms, as well as a great variety of fruit, fish, and poultry. In short, the average diet appears to have had plenty of variety, and the culture of food to be already very well developed. And then there were the wines...in great profusion and of excellent quality, according to Dr. Lister, who sampled everything.

Ballet, Movement, Posture, and Social Dancing: The French school of ballet represented the flowering of the art, along with the other two important schools: the Italian and the later Russian. In fact, all the terms for ballet movements are French. It would be a good idea for anyone doing one of the plays of this period to study ballet and learn the elegant arm movements and different positions. They are very useful in giving the movement in costume a style that is very much in period, and in pointing up a phrase in a particularly elegant manner.

Here are some suggestions for the sort of arm movements, gestures, and positions that you should find of service. They should eventually feel natural and organic, although they may seem precious and pretentious at first. If you are playing a servant, there should be no such elaborate movements; simple bows and curtseys will suffice:

1. To emphasize a point with a gesture or to indicate something, the right arm may be held out forward slightly in a line from the shoulder: elbow slightly bent, hand held palm upwards, forefinger forward, and other fingers partly folded towards the palm; left hand over heart for men or women or on hip for men.

2. To point, lead with the elbow, then the wrist, then the finger, in a single, smooth, seamless gesture that is graceful, elegant, and curved. The hand may be palm up or palm down when the pointing is finished.

3. To emphasize something, extend both arms slightly and not to their full extent, with palms down or up, facing the person addressed or facing upward toward the ceiling. One arm may be slightly higher than the other.

4. As in the first position of the arms in ballet, the arms may be slightly curved and held at the sides—near the thighs, costume permitting—and resting on women's skirts or on men's coats.

When standing, men should keep the legs one slightly behind the other, the front foot turned out from the hip, the back foot on a line, as in ballet—the graceful carriage of the leg is stressed in period manuals of deportment. One hand may be on the hip, holding the sword if one is worn, and the other in the middle of the lapel or across the heart. Or one hand may be behind the back. The position in which aristocratic men stand when in repose is typically a variation of the first or fourth classical position of the feet in ballet:

1. In classical first position, the feet are turned out and in a line, heels touching. In this variation of first position, however, when standing during a play, the heels are not touching but as far apart as is convenient for comfort and repose. They are balanced by the cane or walking stick held elegantly out to the side slightly and touching the floor.

2. In this variation of the fourth position—the most elegant for Restoration comedy or for Molière—the feet are behind one another, the back foot extended to left or right, with the front foot pointing forward, its heel in the direction of the middle of

the back foot (similar to third position, in which, however, the heel of the front foot touches the middle of the back foot; in classical third and fourth positions, both feet are pointed out to their natural right and left). Again, the position is balanced by the cane or walking stick.

Men's canes, sometimes quite long and elaborate, helped maintain balance in the voluminous clothing and high-heeled shoes (which not all men wore; boots and low-heeled shoes were also worn). One should hold a cane with the tip outward and the bottom near the leg; the other hand is over the heart or on the hip, or it may hold a handkerchief between the thumb and forefinger, with the hand palm upward. When using a cane while walking, an elegant, slightly flourishing movement forward and back is required. This has to be practiced so that it simply becomes habit.

When sitting, men's and women's costumes preclude crossing the legs. If you are a man, when you wish to sit, approach the seat with the back of the right leg; grasp the back of the seat, if it has one, with the right hand; then, guiding yourself down, sit gracefully down without turning to look at the seat. Women would approach a chair similarly, gliding down into it without touching the back of the chair, and were often obliged to sit on the edge, almost off the chair, with their bodies slightly sideways. To balance themselves, they would arch their backs and lean forward a bit, while keeping one arm stretched full length along the back of the chair and the other holding one of the chair's arms.

Dances of the period are usually quite decorous. As you might expect, the movement is limited by the clothing, except for country dances, which are freer in movement partly because the clothing is looser. Here is Samuel Pepys's description of the royal New Year's ball on December 31, 1661:

> Into the room where the ball was to be, crammed with fine ladies, the greatest of the Court. By and by comes the King and Queen, the Duke and Duchess, and all the great ones: and after seating themselves, the King takes out the Duchess of York; and the Duke, the Duchess of Buckingham; the Duke of Monmouth, my Lady Castlemaine; and so other lords other ladies: and they danced the Bransle [branle; a round dance with people holding hands]. After that, the King led a lady a single Coranto [a swift and lively dance with running steps] and then the rest of the lords, one after another, other ladies very noble it was, and great pleasure to see. Then to country

dances; the King leading the first, which he called for; which was, says he, "Cuckolds all awry," the old dance of England. . . . The manner was, when the King dances, all the ladies in the room, and the Queen herself, stand up: and indeed he dances rarely, and much better than the Duke of York.

Painting

The seventeenth century saw the development of the baroque, a dramatic kind of art and architecture that emphasized balance and harmony, exemplified in the Italian churches designed by Francesco Borromini (1599–1667); they would inspire the rococo school of art and design in the next century. Ancient classical forms and motifs were used as sculptural ornaments, and the baroque gloried in making heavy architectural materials seem light. Its soaring lines and huge rounded arches suggested flowing movement, elevation, and height. The ornamentation could be elaborate, with ceilings painted as spectacles of heaven: cherubs and the Lord of Hosts, Christ and angels, or ancient heroes in chariots drawn by horses are surrounded by billowing clouds.

The versatile Peter Paul Rubens (1577–1640)—the Flemish artist known for his paintings of buxom women and his magnificent portraits, landscapes, and altarpieces—was commissioned in 1621 by Queen Marie de Médicis (1573–1642), widow of Henri IV and mother of Louis XIII, to paint a notable series of huge canvases, now in the Louvre, depicting her life. They are the epitome of the baroque style at its most grandiose and impressive.

The chiaroscuro of Rembrandt van Rijn (1606–1669), the luminescence of Jan Vermeer (1632–1675), and the dark landscapes and tufted trees of Jacob van Ruysdael (1628?–1682) are all products of the gorgeous seventeenth-century Dutch school of painting, which flourished in the era when Holland was one of the greatest commercial powers in Europe.

Another great Flemish master, Anthony van Dyck (1599–1641), is remembered largely as the court painter of Charles I, whose portrait he painted numerous times. He also gave his name to the typical Caroline beard—worn by the king, as well as the artist and many Cavaliers—the *Vandyke* in its anglicized spelling. He captured his sitters' personalities with great intimacy, and he painted their ornate clothing in exquisite detail.

In the days of these Old Masters of painting, artists had to prepare their own canvases and stretch them on frames, and they had to prepare the paints as well by grinding pigment powders and mixing them with linseed oil. Before they could paint, they had to make the surface of the canvas ready by priming it. They then did an underpainting, which could be an outline sketch done with paint thinned with medium—turpentine, for instance—before filling the outline in and laying the details over it.

Rembrandt sized his canvases with animal glue so that the paint would not be absorbed. He primed the canvas by painting it with a medium brown or reddish-brown ground that he had prepared by mixing ochre with resin and more animal glue, and when it was dry, he began to compose the painting according to his own unique vision. Working from dark to light, he built the picture up layer by layer, doing a monochrome underpainting of the broad areas of light and shade before proceeding first to fill in the general areas of color and then, by using glaze after glaze, to shape the contours of the figures and objects in the picture, with its layers of thick impasto. Then he laid in the lighter washes and glazes, heightening his chiaroscuro effects and letting the background show through as necessary, eventually adding the finishing touches and details that would give the painting richness, concreteness, and reality. The portraits painted by Rembrandt show the austerity of the wealthy upper-middle-class Dutch merchants and their wives, and their clothing is complete with the ruffs mentioned above or with square-cut collars and lace.

Vermeer's basic ground was grayish brown, made from mixing umber, charcoal, and lead white. It is presumed that in order to lay in the preliminary outline drawing, he used a *camera obscura*, an invention consisting of a box with mirrors and lenses inside it that could project a reduced image of what he wished to paint onto the canvas. He then laid in broad areas of color and built up his painting layer by layer, putting in the fine details last: the pearl necklace, the lines on a map, the highlights on a piece of cloth. The interiors painted by Vermeer in loving detail are very informative as to the environment in which people lived in Holland—for instance, it was common for ornate Persian rugs to be used on tables, as well as on floors, to retain the heat.

Traditional ways of painting still lifes were developed. Landscapes were supposed to contain a tree or house or large rock or some other important feature in the foreground, warmly colored details in the middle ground, and mountains or whatever was on the horizon in graduated blue tones that grew paler as they receded into the distance. In France, Nicolas Poussin (1594–1665) was known for his severe baroque classicism, defining painting as the imitation of an action (exactly as Aristotle defined the drama), and accepting the idea that a picture must appear in a frame and therefore be a closed work of art. This attitude reflects the aesthetic and psychologically repressive values of an authoritarian aristocratic culture.

The influential landscape artist Claude Lorrain (1600–1682) painted the countryside around Rome, altering it to give it a mythological cast. He built up his paintings in true Old Master fashion in layers from dark to light, using a simple palette of graduated shades of color, and paid special attention to the composition of his canvasses and their perfect perspective. He arrived at his tonal gradations through the use of a "Lorrain glass," which he is said to have invented and which became very popular with artists. It consisted of a black convex mirror in which a landscape was reflected. The colors were tinged with black by the reflective ground of the mirror, enabling him to see their gradations.

In Spain, the dark, brooding, and sometimes strange portraits of royal sitters by Diego Velazquez (1599–1650) are memorable for the merciless light they shed on Spanish royalty and its rigid pretensions. The portraits of King Philip IV (1605–1665) repay study, as do the luminescent religious paintings of Bartolomé Murillo (1617–1682).

Music

In music, the period known as baroque began about 1590 and ended around 1750, overlapping with the beginning of classical music. Listening to mid-seventeenth-century baroque music, with its coruscation of ornaments and sometimes complicated harmonies, gives you an incomparable feeling for the emotional atmosphere and ceremonial aspects of the period. There are many wonderful baroque composers (Tommaso Albinoni, Aracangelo Corelli, Antonio Vivaldi, Johann Pachelbel, Henry Purcell, and Alessandro Scarlatti, among others), but the most justifiably famous is Johann Sebastian Bach (1685–1750), many of whose children became musicians as well known as their illustrious father.

A dancer as well as a composer and instrumentalist, the brilliant, sensitive, naturalized Frenchman Jean-Baptiste Lully (1632–1687), born

Giovanni Battista Lulli in Florence, himself danced the role of the Mufti in the ballet he composed for *Le Bourgeois Gentilhomme*. Discovered as a page at Versailles, his talent was quickly recognized, and he soon rose to prominence as he encouraged the king to practice the art of the ballet. Lully's music, along with that of his successor, the other famous French baroque composer, Jean-Philippe Rameau (1683–1764), is very typical of the period.

Although each of these composers has an individual, distinctive style, they still have certain characteristics in common: they observe fairly stringent forms, such as the fugue, in their compositions; and they follow the scale, the rules of harmony, and the strict key relationships that had been developing in an innovative way since the inception of baroque music around the end of the sixteenth century. The basic characteristic of this music is a melodic line sung or played above a harmonic accompaniment. Baroque church music, for instance, is characterized by the *basso continuo* (continual bass), meaning that the melody sung by the soloist or chorus is constantly accompanied by harmony below it, played on the organ or other instruments.

Among the popular baroque musical forms was the dance suite, which generally included a prelude, followed by an allemande, courante, sarabande, an optional dance, and a gigue. Each dance in the suite was a separate composition that could actually be played separately, and the usual pattern of the suite was susceptible of variations.

The *sonata form* began to develop in this period. The term refers to the structure of an individual movement, rather than to the larger composition. This is simply a "sonata," one form of which was ternary—in three movements: fast–slow–fast. The sonata form is also used in other chamber music works, as well as in symphonic movements and in concertos. Each movement is binary: the first part opens expositionally on a tonic key and expands on a theme; then modulates to a related key, thus beginning the second part; then it may modulate to other related keys, returning to the tonic as the movement ends. In other words, a theme is developed and then recapitulated. Schematized, it might look like this: ABA.

Antonio Stradivarius (1644–1737) of Cremona was the most famous violin maker of this or any other age. Over 600 of his instruments still exist. Period instruments include the *spinet*, an ancestor of the harpsichord and then the piano; the flute; the horn; and the recorder. Other string instruments and early reed instruments were also developed around this time.

Literature

For a certain strain of mysticism and religion, read the poetry of John Donne (1572–1631), the courtly Andrew Marvell (1621–1678), and the other mystics. Donne's poetry, gorgeous in its pessimistic lyricism, is a descent into the depths of despair and somber, apocalyptic religiosity, mixed with cautious optimism. And for a typical pious view of the Anglican religion, read the beautifully written *Religio Medici* of Sir Thomas Browne (1605–1682), who, although a Royalist and no Puritan, was deeply devout.

The war against Satan was paramount in the minds of the Puritans, as John Milton (1608–1674) made clear in his gorgeous epic poem *Paradise Lost*. In its rich sensuality, it is uncharacteristic of Puritans to say the least—but then Milton has been said to be the last of the Renaissance Christian humanists. His views were not orthodox, although he worked as a secretary in Cromwell's government, handling diplomatic correspondence. He wholeheartedly supported the England he now saw as the standard bearer of the religious and civil liberty preached, but not practiced—he must have known that—by the new rulers. The Restoration destroyed his hopes, but the Puritans had never fulfilled them. Still, *Paradise Lost*, published in 1667, is on one level a passionate sermon raging against the restoration of the monarchy that had taken place in 1660. Says Satan, having been cast out of heaven and down into "the fiery gulf":

> To bow and sue for grace
> With suppliant knee, and deify his power
> Who from the terror of this arm so late
> Doubted his empire, that were low indeed,
> That were an ignominy and shame

Jammersminde (Memories of Woe), the memoirs of Countess Leonora Christina Christiansdatter af Slesvig og Holsten (1621–1698), which were not published until 1869, is another wonderful source for numerous period details. The book tells a well-nigh incredible story of faithful love and suffering, of woe and redemption. The countess describes her ordeal and the complicated machinations and intrigues of court life, as well as the conditions in the vermin-infested dungeon where she was incarcerated. The history of the Danish royal family in the seventeenth century is more complicated, more filled with fierce jealousy and intrigue and the desire for vengeance, than *Hamlet*.

Her husband, the arrogant, highly placed, and cordially disliked Count Corfits Ulfeldt (1606–1664), was accused of high treason: of conspiring with one of his mistresses to poison the royal family. The accusation was false, but he fled the kingdom with his wife and children and spent the rest of his life in exile. The countess went to London to beg King Charles II to pay back the money Ulfeldt had lent him to help in restoring him to the English throne, and Charles did so, but as she was about to embark on a ship for the continent, he had her arrested and turned over to the Danish authorities.

Under interrogation, she refused steadfastly to denounce her husband or accuse him of any crimes, and she was imprisoned without trial in the infamous Blue Tower, a hellish prison that was actually one of the buildings attached to the royal palace in Copenhagen. There she languished for twenty-one years, until a change of regime and the death of the Queen Dowager—Sophia Amalia von Braunschweig-Lüneburg (1570–1664), her implacable enemy—finally brought about her release. Her husband had died, and she never saw him again.

The middle to end of the seventeenth century saw the beginning of the scourge of piracy in the New World that would last well into the eighteenth. A fascinating account was published in 1678 in Dutch, *De Americaensche Zee-Roovers* (The American Pirates) by A. O. Exquemelin (1645?–1707?), a Frenchman who emigrated to Holland, and who had been to Tortuga in the West Indies and actually served as a barber-surgeon on a buccaneer ship for three years before returning to Europe. He recounts the history of one of the most famous pirates of the times, Sir Henry Morgan (1635–1688).

In France, the novel begins its journey towards modernity with *The Princess of Cleves*, published in 1678 by Madame de Lafayette (1653–1683). It is one of the first examples of a psychological novel concerning the emotions of romantic love, which is endlessly and fascinatingly analyzed in French literature.

In Spain, the dramas of Pedro Calderón de la Barca (1600–1681) are a mixture of psychological complexity and mystical religiosity. In England, among the many wonderful Restoration plays is William Congreve's (1670–1729) exquisite comedy of manners, *The Way of the World*, in which Betterton created the part of Fainall; it premiered in 1700 at the theater that Congreve managed at Lincoln's Inn Fields. As is so often the case with plays in this period, the character's names tell us much about them: Lady Wishfort and Mrs. Fainall (the only married woman in the play), her daughter; Sir Wilful Witwoud, the country aristocrat; young

Millamant (she of 1,000 would-be lovers; *mille amants* means "1,000 lovers" in French), our leading lady; the aspiring rake, Witwoud, and the young scamp Petulant; and Lady Wishfort's maidservant, Foible. The male protagonist, in love with Milamant, is named Mirabell: handsome to look at. His patient servant is named Waitwell.

The plot of this play is extremely complicated, and it is considered one of the wittiest plays in an age of witty comedy. The expository opening scene takes place in a "chocolate house" just as a card game is ending. Gambling was an extremely popular pastime, as was smoking tobacco in long-handled clay pipes at coffeehouses and taverns.

Film and Television

The story of Charles I and Cromwell is ably told in *Cromwell* (1970), with Richard Harris as the ruthless Puritan dictator and Alec Guinness particularly moving as the unfortunate misguided monarch, a part that seemed tailor made for him. He had the king's slight stammer and a diffident but regal manner that accords well with the descriptions eyewitness have left of him.

The life of the French composer Marin Marais (1656–1728), recounted in the film *Tous les matins du monde* (All the Mornings of the World, 2000), shows the rigor and discipline demanded of baroque composers and their austere devotion to their art. Ahistorical but fascinating nonetheless, *Le Roi danse* (The King Dances, 2001; zone 2 format only) is about the relationship between Louis XIV and Lully, as well as both their relationships with Molière. Gorgeously photographed with sumptuous decors, it shows the development of ballet and the elaborate performances at Versailles, with Louis himself dancing. And there have been any number of film and television versions of Alexandre Dumas' nineteenth-century novels about seventeenth-century France: *The Three Musketeers*, including those of 1939, 1948, 1974, and 1993; and *The Man in the Iron Mask* (1939, 1976, and 1998), all good for observing period style. The opening scenes of Douglas Fairbanks's last silent swashbuckler, *The Iron Mask* (1929), are reminiscent of John Evelyn's descriptions of the parade of Louis XIV to the Parlement. The expert technical advisers assured the accuracy of period details and behavior.

The attempt to recreate the presumed style of acting and presentation of the period falls flat in the 2005 French film of Molière's *Le Bourgeois*

Gentilhomme, although it is fascinating to hear seventeenth-century pronunciation. The actors in the film seem terribly self-conscious and ill at ease with the putative style of the era. This obscures the comedy, which emerges as tendentious and preachy, and is eminently not funny. On the other hand, the supremely comic 1958 Comédie Française film, with the brilliant Louis Seigner (1903–1991) as the would-be gentleman, could scarcely be bettered.

Billy Crudup plays Ned Kynaston beautifully in the film *Stage Beauty* (2004), which is about that transitional time when women were being allowed on the stage alongside men. Set in rural England in 1692, Peter Greenaway's *The Draughtsman's Contract* (1982) is scrupulously accurate in every period detail, from the extravagant wigs and huge cuffs on shirtsleeves to manners and mores. *The Girl with the Pearl Earring* (2004), based on Tracy Chevalier's novel, is about Vermeer and the young lady who was the subject of one of his most exquisite paintings. It is fascinating to see the artist preparing his paints, and naturally, many of the decors and costumes resemble Vermeer paintings. The 1936 film *Rembrandt*, with Charles Laughton at his best in the title role, is an excellent depiction of the period. *Vatel* (2000) tells the story of the banquet at which he committed suicide; the details of the food and period etiquette are first rate.

For More Information

Bédoyère, Guy de la, ed. *Particular Friends: The Correspondence of Samuel Pepys and John Evelyn*. Rochester, NY: The Boydell Press, 1997.

Callow, Simon. *Acting in Restoration Comedy*. New York: Applause Theatre Book Publishers, 1991.

Congreve, William. *The Comedies of William Congreve*. Edited by Anthony G. Henderson. New York: Cambridge University Press, 1982.

Durant, Will and Ariel. *The Story of Civilization: Part VIII, The Age of Louis XIV*. New York: Simon and Schuster, 1963.

Earle, Alice Morse. *Costume of Colonial Times*. New York: Charles Scribner's Sons, 1894.

Evelyn, John. *The Diary of John Evelyn*. Edited by E. S. de Beer. Selected and introduced by Roy Strong. New York: Everyman's Library, 2006.

Exquemelin, A. O. *The Buccaneers of America*. Translated from the Dutch by Alexis Brown. With an introduction by Jack Beeching. New York: Penguin Books, 1969.

Fischer, David Hackett. *Albion's Seed: Four British Folkways in America*. New York: Oxford University Press, 1989.

Fraser, Antonia. *Charles II*. New York: Orion Publishing Co., 2002.

———*Cromwell*. New York: Grove Press, 2001.

Lister, Martin. *A Journey to Paris in the Year 1698*. Edited, with annotations, a life of Lister, and a Lister bibliography, by Raymond Phineas Stearns. Urbana, IL: University of Illinois Press, 1967.

Miller, Perry. *The New England Mind: The Seventeenth Century*. Boston: Beacon Press, 1961.

Pepys, Samuel. *The Diary of Samuel Pepys*. Richard Le Gallienne, ed. Introduction by Robert Louis Stevenson. New York: Modern Library, 2001.

Pevitt, Christine. *Philippe, duc d'Orléans: Regent of France*. New York: Atlantic Monthly Press, 1997.

Mitford, Nancy. *The Sun King*. New York: Penguin, 1995.

Reresby, Sir John. *Memoirs of Sir John Reresby*. The complete text and a selection from his letters, edited with an introduction and notes by Andrew Browning. 2nd ed. with a new preface and notes by Mary K. Oetter and W. A. Speck. London: Offices of the Royal Historical Society, 1991.

Rudlin, John. *Commedia dell'Arte: An Actor's Handbook*. New York: Routledge, 1994.

Saint-Simon, Louis de Rouvroy, duc de. *Memoirs*. Edited by Lucy Norton. New York: Prion, 2000.

Sévigné, Madame de. *Selected Letters*. Introduced and translated by Leonard Tancock. New York: Penguin Classics, 1982.

Styan, J. L. *Restoration Comedy in Performance*. New York: Cambridge University Press, 1986.

Sypher, Wylie. *Four Stages of Renaissance Style: Transformations in Art and Literature 1400–1700*. Garden City, NY: Doubleday & Company, Inc., 1955.

Ulfeldt, Countess Leonora Christina. *Memoirs of Leonora Christina, Daughter of Christian IV of Denmark*. Written during her imprisonment in the Blue Tower of Copenhagen, 1663–1685. Translated by F. E. Bunnett. New York: E. P. Dutton & Company, Inc., 1929.

Womersley, David, ed. *Restoration Drama: An Anthology*. Oxford, UK: Blackwell Publishers, 2000.

Zumthor, Paul. *Daily Life in Rembrandt's Holland*. Translated from the French by Simon Watson Taylor. Stanford, CA: Stanford University Press, 1994.

CHAPTER SEVEN

The Eighteenth and Early Nineteenth Centuries: The Enlightenment and Regency Periods

The Age of the Rococo, Reason, and Revolutions

The upper classes in eighteenth-century Europe might as well have been French: whatever their national origin, all the European monarchs and the members of their courts—from Austria and Prussia to Russia and Naples—thought, spoke, wrote, and no doubt dreamed in French. The French model of art, interior design, costume and furniture; French food and wine; French style, gallantry, and manners were all the rage, even in England. French was the language of diplomacy, and French culture was considered the height of sophistication. French fashion in clothing held a supreme place, and dolls decked in the latest Paris modes were sent across the channel for the admiration of the ladies at the Court of St. James, who could then place their orders with Paris couturiers for the newest gowns and accessories.

Seventeenth-century French neoclassicism and the grandiose architecture of the baroque gave way to eighteenth-century French rococo: dynamic, ornate, sensuous. Italian, French, and German artists luxuriated in ornamental garlands, arabesques, and curlicues, twining their gilt-filigreed tendrils over walls, furniture, and clothing. On numerous ceilings, demure cherubs and chaste angels frolicked amidst billowing clouds. On painted canvases and walls, dewy-eyed, pink-cheeked lovers—innocently pastoral and lighthearted, but hardly naïve—trysted in leafy bowers, sheltered from storm and strife.

But the storm and strife hovered nonetheless. And the clouds would pour forth the rains of revolution in two hemispheres.

It was the Age of Enlightenment. But not everyone was interested in being enlightened. Formal education among the reactionary upper classes was generally considered mere undesirable pedantry. King George II (1683–1760) of England—who spoke English poorly and with a heavy German accent, preferring on many occasions to speak French—set the tone. Lord Hervey (1696–1743), Vice-Chamberlain to the royal household, informs us in his inimitable, sometimes hilarious *Memoirs:*

> The King used often to brag of the contempt he had for books and letters; to say how much he hated all that stuff from his infancy; and that he remembered when he was a child he did not hate reading and learning merely as other children do on account of the confinement, but because he despised it and felt as if he was doing something mean and below him.

Queen Caroline (1683–1737), on the other hand, loved to read, and he often "rebuked her for dabbling in all that lettered nonsense (as he termed it), called her a pedant." Learning to use the sword—duels were frequent—and to hunt were more important than studying academic subjects, except perhaps for Latin and Greek, and even that was merely for show. "Upon the whole, remember that learning (I mean Greek and Roman learning) is a most necessary and useful ornament," says Philip Dormer Stanhope, fourth Earl of Chesterfield (1694–1773) in a letter of February 22, 1748, to his son, Philip (1732–1768): "Wear your learning, like your watch, in a private pocket: and do not pull it out and strike it; merely to show that you have one." And in Benjamin Franklin's (1706–1790) very funny, satirical *Silence Dogood* letters of 1722, written in the character of a young widow, "she" writes in "No. 2": "I intend now and then to beautify my Writings with a Sentence or two in the learned Languages, which will not only be fashionable, and pleasing to those who do not understand it, but will likewise be very ornamental."

An English gentleman's education consisted of traveling through Europe on the Grand Tour: Holland, Germany, Italy, especially Rome, and after the discovery of Pompeii in 1748, Naples and the south. Lord Chesterfield enjoined his son in a letter of October 2, 1749, to make Rome his headquarters for six months at least: "More things are to be seen and learned there, than in any other town in Europe." And of course France, especially Paris and Versailles, was most important on any gentleman's itinerary.

On the continent, where they traveled with their servants or hired temporary servants on the spot, they visited museums, went to the opera and the theater, and experienced all kinds of pleasures, from those of carousing at sophisticated banquets and balls to those of the bawdy-house and the gaming table. And they learned about all the arts. "Form a taste of painting, sculpture, and architecture, if you please, by a careful examination of the best ancient and modern artists; those are liberal arts, and real taste and knowledge become a man of fashion very well," Lord Chesterfield advised Philip, in a letter of September 27, 1749. And he warned his son enigmatically: "But beyond certain bounds, the man of taste ends and the frivolous Virtuoso begins."

George II had his own taste in painting. When Lord Hervey, at the queen's request, had replaced some of the paintings in the king's gallery, he was outraged and demanded that "the picture with the dirty frame over the door, and the three nasty little children" be taken away. He added, "I like my fat Venus better than anything you have given me instead of her." The Rubens was restored to its previous place, and van Dyck's portrait of Charles I's children removed.

Traveling was quite unsafe: street lighting, even in the large cities, was very poor or virtually nonexistent; the roads were bad; coaches were clumsy and uncomfortable and prone to accidents; and the countryside was infested with highwaymen, romanticized in such theater pieces as John Gay's (1685–1732) popular, satirical *The Beggar's Opera* (1728), with its swaggering, amorous, two-timing hero, Captain Macheath. Robberies in broad daylight were not unknown even in the streets of London, and piracy was rife on the seas in this age of pirates and buccaneers. And at inns or hotels in the larger cities, the beds were filled with lice and bedbugs as often as not. In any case, once the French Revolution broke out, the days of the Grand Tour were over.

Liberty and Despotism seethed and roiled in the Caldron of Discontent. It was no accident that most of the great Enlightenment intellectuals who called for freedom of thought and speech came from the middle classes. For them, learning was a key to advancement, and they were proud to work for a living. They were despised for it by many European aristocrats, for whom pedigree was everything and work was decidedly déclassé. But the increasing economic power of the bourgeoisie would change even deportment, manners, and styles of behaving within 100 years, inspired by the American and French Revolutions, Jean-Jacques Rousseau's (1712–1778) advocacy of liberty and equality, and the laissez-faire capitalist theories of the Scottish economist Adam Smith (1723–1790). Still, as the century began, class divisions all over Europe seemed sacrosanct, immutable, and eternal.

In all the courts of Europe, there were endless petty disputes about titles and precedence. And there were rigid, stagnant local hierarchies: the sovereign city-state of Wolfgang Amadeus Mozart's (1756–1791) birth, Salzburg, had been governed for centuries by its archbishops, who reigned for life as nonhereditary, elected absolute monarchs. They were also, ex officio, princes of the largely mythical and mystical Holy Roman Empire, whose titular heads in the eighteenth century were the Hapsburg Emperors of Austria. The Salzburg aristocracy consisted of the canons of the cathedral's consistory, who elected the archbishop from among its members, many of whom were his relatives. Essentially a kind of private club, the consistory controlled its own membership rules and usually admitted only the scions of the local Bavarian and Austrian gentry. Of lesser status were the "paper nobles"—diligent, perfervid civil servants, rewarded by the prince-archbishop with patents of nobility. Intrigue, sycophancy, greed, and venality predominated at the stodgy and increasingly irrelevant archiepiscopal court.

It was the Age of Reason. In most cases religion no longer ruled the state; the state ruled religion. The secular power had become paramount in much of Europe by the end of the seventeenth century, and it seemed that religion, the rightness of which had been taken for granted in the preceding ages of faith and unquestioning belief—and still was by many—was going to have to prove the validity of its ideas. In 1695, John Locke (1632–1704) had written *A Vindication of the Reasonableness of Christianity*; the very title was startling. It was now possible, but perhaps still inadvisable, to proclaim one's skepticism; skeptics would continue to be ridiculed and looked on with suspicion.

The era was not known for its health or hygiene, any more than were preceding centuries. Squire Bramble's opening lines in his letter to his doctor in Tobias Smollett's (1721–1771) epistolary novel, *The Expedition of Humphrey Clinker* (1771), could serve as a motto for the whole period, medically speaking: "The pills are good for nothing. I might as well swallow snowballs." Medicine was still in its infancy and slow to mature, and the old saying that the cure is worse than the disease was often the literal truth. Bleeding was a common medical practice of the day, and doctors let blood using unsterilized instruments. Blood poisoning or infectious disease were frequent results of their well-meaning but misguided ministrations. And medical theory still relied on the four humors of Aristotle, Hippocrates, and Galen.

Still, there was some progress: in 1796, the smallpox vaccine, experimented on in Europe since the early part of the century, was at last acceptable to the superstitious fearful public at large, thanks to the efforts of Dr. Edward Jenner (1749–1823). In fact, inoculation was an ancient African procedure: a slave, Onesimus, had told Cotton Mather all about it in Boston during the smallpox epidemic of 1721. But inoculation there and in Europe had aroused passionate controversy, for some feared it spread the disease, until Jenner was finally able to convince people otherwise.

Habits of cleanliness were beginning to be viewed as necessary to health. Lord Chesterfield, who counsels his son against too much bathing (it exacerbates rheumatism!) nevertheless advises him (in his letter of November 12, 1750) to "be accurately clean; and your teeth, hands, and nails should be superlatively so; a dirty mouth has real ill consequences to the owner. . . . I insist, therefore, that you wash your teeth the first thing you do every morning, with a soft sponge and warm water, for four or five minutes."

The gutters of major European cities ran with rotting garbage and raw sewage. The stink must have been overwhelming almost everywhere, even in the aristocratic neighborhoods. In the age of the horse and carriage, there was endless horse manure that piled up in the mostly unpaved streets and on the paved ones, and it had to be swept away. Jonathan Swift's (1667–1745) highly popular poem "A Description of a City Shower," written in 1710, elicited roars of rueful, complicit laughter from his contemporaries, but little had been done even by 1799 to change conditions very much:

> Filth of all Hues and Odours seem to tell
> What Street they sail'd from, by their Sight and Smell . . .
> Sweepings from Butchers Stalls, Dung, Guts, and Blood,
> Drown'd Puppies, stinking Sprats, all drench'd in Mud,
> Dead Cats and Turnip-Tops come tumbling down the Flood.

David Garrick and His Theatrical Revolution

The century also saw the beginning of realism in the English theater, with new stage technology that you can still see demonstrated at the court theater at Drottingholm, Sweden. Realism in acting began particularly with the arrival on the stage of David Garrick (1717–1779). Growing up in Lichfield, he and Samuel Johnson (1709–1784), one of the great intellects of the age, were close friends from boyhood on. As a result, Johnson tended to treat him with a sometimes jealous proprietary interest and could be quite critical, as indeed he was of everybody. But the bearish lexicographer, literary critic, and prose stylist admired his friend's acting: "True conception of character and natural expression of it, were his distinguished excellencies." James Boswell (1740–1795) says of him in one of the greatest biographies ever written, *Life of Samuel Johnson*, that "Garrick . . . could imitate Johnson very exactly; for that great actor, with his distinguished powers of expression which were so universally admired, possessed also an admirable talent of mimickry."

Among those who saw him in London was Georg Christoph Lichtenberg (1742–1799), a German intellectual, scientist, and writer from Göttingen, and a friend of Goethe and Kant. He describes Garrick's acting in detail in his *Briefe aus England* (Letters from England). The theater was darkened—the stage lit with candles—and the audience sat in silence and rapt attention when, on December 12, 1775, he saw Garrick as Hamlet. In act 1, scene 4,

> Waiting for the Ghost, he paces up and down. Horatio says, "Look, my lord, it comes." Hamlet moves back, his hat falls to the ground. He is supported by Horatio and Marcellus, to whom the apparition is not new, and there he stands with trembling knees . . . almost as if hypnotized. His open left hand is raised somewhat higher than his face, the fingers spread open, arms outstretched; and there he stays for a moment, his face so impressed with terror that every spectator is equally terrified, and then he says, "Angels and ministers of grace defend us."

Lichtenberg penned other descriptions of this same scene, and Garrick performed it somewhat differently each time. In another performance, for instance, he fell to his knees. It is quite clear that he left room for spontaneous, organic, real reactions while remaining within the parameters that had been set up in rehearsal.

A friend of King George III (1738–1820) and Queen Charlotte (1744–1818), the novelist Frances (Fanny) Burney, Madame d'Arblay (1752–1840), kept diaries that give an invaluable account of life among the middle classes and at court, wrote innumerable letters, and was witness to events in France where she lived with her husband for ten years, from 1802 to 1812. She was also an acquaintance and admirer of Garrick, "the most entertaining of mortals." On May 29, 1772, she saw him as Richard III:

> Garrick was sublimely horrible!—how he made me shudder whenever he appeared! it is inconceivable how terribly great he is in this Character! I will never see him so disfigured again—he seemed so truly the monster he performed, that I felt myself glow with indignation every time I saw him.

As the exemplar of the overdone, the vainglorious, loveable Colley Cibber, whom we met in the last chapter, was the antithesis of Garrick's new way of thinking about acting and the theater. Where Garrick was acclaimed for his realistic performance of Richard III, Cibber had been roundly excoriated in the same role for his "shrugs and grimaces." "He looks like a pickpocket," wrote an anonymous correspondent—"Somebody"—to the Grub Street Journal in 1734.

Cibber emerged unscathed from the attacks of his critics and detractors, among them the viper-tongued Alexander Pope (1688–1744), satiric poet and mordant observer of humanity's foibles, who, his pen dipped in poison, made Cibber the hero of the revised version of his 1728 mock-heroic epic *The Dunciad* and railed against Cibber's unmerited appointment as poet laureate in 1730. Cibber, who thought his own talent supreme, rewrote Shakespeare to his satisfaction, feeling that he had vastly improved the Bard's style and expression and made his plays at last fit for acting. So famous did some of his lines become that many thought Shakespeare himself had written them. Actually, there was already a long tradition of adapting Shakespeare. Garrick himself adapted *Hamlet*, leaving out the "Gravediggers" scene (Lichtenberg found that unaccountable); and he used Cibber's version of *Richard III*.

Cibber's autobiography, *Apology for the Life of Colley Cibber*, is invaluable reading, both for the amusement and instruction it provides and the inimitable picture of the actors—whom he is generous in praising—and the theater of his day. Ensconced in an extravagant coruscation of verbiage and enthroned upon the lofty dais of self-righteousness, he informs us that the theater is in drastic need of reform, but that the actors should not be blamed if the public, with its "deprav'd taste," allows "Vice and Farcical Folly" to be profitable. Cibber himself, often accused of hypocrisy, had no interest in attempting to reform the theater from which he reaped such financial benefit.

That would remain for Garrick to do. And he had much to contend with. Aaron Hill writes in number 62 of his periodical *The Prompter* on June 13, 1735:

> [The actors] relax themselves as soon as any speech in their own part is over, into an absent unattentiveness to whatever is replied by another, looking around and examining the company of spectators with an ear only watchful of the cue, at which, like soldiers upon the word of command, they start suddenly back to their postures.

And on November 7, 1735, in number 104, he castigates actors who deliver soliloquies using "the ridiculous practice of approaching the pit with an arch leer of familiarity and communicating to their friends." Some actors would even break character to say hello to their acquaintances or flirt with a likely prospect in the audience during other actors' speeches. Popular actors entered grandly and strutted around the stage to applause from their adoring public, one arm raised high in an elegant pose meant to be noble. The bows and hand waving over, they would begin to recite their lines, using extravagant gestures to illustrate them. And when they exited it was with a grand flourish, arm held high once again, head thrown back, waving kisses to the audience.

Garrick changed all that. Many actors agreed with him and would never indulge in such behavior but were always in character—among them, the respectable and even somewhat prudish Mrs. Sarah Siddons (1755–1831), who was considered the greatest tragic actress of the English stage. She appeared briefly at the Drury Lane under Garrick in 1775, but she was not successful. She acted in the provinces and did not act again on the London stage until 1782. After that, however, she had no rivals, and every character in plays set in this period would have known her name, just as they would know Garrick's. William Hazlitt (1778–1830), the essayist and critic, wrote of her that "Power was seated on her brow; passion emanated from her breast as from a shrine. She was tragedy personified.... To have seen Mrs. Siddons was an event in everyone's life."

No doubt audiences found all the carrying on a hugely enjoyable part of the evening's entertainment, just as amusing as the pheasant under glass and champagne they were devouring in their expensive private boxes when they were not indulging in their amours—lace jabots thrown aside, breeches torn open and bodices ripped. Few but the wealthy could afford to go to the theater, in fact, although there were cheaper seats for the hoi polloi, where they could perch and munch and talk and shout at the actors on the stage and at the occupants of the more expensive places.

Theater audiences had to be trained. But at least even the aristocrats paid for their tickets, whereas in the early days of the Restoration, many of the "sparks" insisted on entering for free and would threaten to beat the ticket takers if they were not allowed to do so. In Garrick's day—an age of licentiousness without any consistent police force to maintain law and order—drunken louts, aristocrats though they might be, thought nothing of interrupting a performance with jeers and gibes. There were expensive seats on the stage that these boors sat in. There was no tacit consent to remain as quiet as possible and attend to the performance, and talking was common. But such public ill manners were increasingly found revolting and would no longer be tolerated when Garrick performed. And he decided that audience members should not be on the stage. But the profits! Hang the profits! At the same time, he continued the distracting custom of the prompter's bell and whistle: the whistle, audible to the audience, signaled to the stagehands that the scenery was to be moved; the bell told the orchestra that it was time to begin playing music, whether during the play or at the start of the interval.

Unfortunately, Garrick left no written record of his methods and techniques of working on a role, but he did advise a young protégé of his to read everything, not only plays, and to read Shakespeare continually. His satirical 1744 "An Essay on Acting" is a self-mocking diatribe, and much of it is not meant to be taken seriously.

Theater, which had been confined to London and a few large cities, proved so popular that playhouses were opened all over the country. There were traveling companies and strolling players. Although their acting was often well appreciated, many "strollers" were considered scamps and untrustworthy vagabonds pursuing a profession that was still not thought quite respectable, despite Garrick and Mrs. Siddons.

Manners, Social Customs, and Political Ideas in America

The School of Good Manners. Composed for the Help of Parents in Teaching Their Children How to Behave During Their Minority, a book attributed to the Boston schoolteacher Eleazar Moody (?–?), was published in 1715. A guide to politeness and civility for generations of Americans, it went through many editions, up to around 1846. Some of its rules would be sacrosanct through the nineteenth and early twentieth centuries: "Never speak to thy parents without some title of respect, as, *sir, madam,* &c." "If thy superior be relating a story, say not, 'I have heard it before'...If he tell it not right, snigger not," is still sage advice.

The first chapter of this religiously oriented book is devoted to pithy instructions that enshrine class consciousness, such as "Submit to thy superiors.—Despise not thy inferiors.—Be courteous to thy equals." Later chapters contain admonitions obviously meant for the postpubescent: in "Of Behavior at the Meeting-House," the young person is instructed, "Decently walk to thy seat or pew; run not, nor go wantonly." Moody covers behavior in every situation one could think of, whether the child is at home, at table, at school, in conversation with "superiors" or other children, or "abroad"—the usual eighteenth-century expression for "away from home." The child is told not to come to the dinner table without having first washed hands and face and combed the hair. Nor must the child sit down until "bidden" to do so by parents or superiors. Particular attention must be paid to the saying of grace. And in order, I presume, to teach hypocrisy as well as gratitude, the child is admonished, "Find no fault with anything that is given thee." Reminiscent of all the other books on the subject of manners on which Moody's book is based is, "Spit not forth anything that is not convenient to swallow, as the stones of plums, cherries or such like; but with thy left hand neatly move them to the side of thy plate." And "Foul not the tablecloth.—Foul not the napkin all over, but at one corner."

As a young man, George Washington (1732–1799) copied out 110 "Rules of Civility" from a book called *Youth's Behavior, or Decency in Conversation amongst Men,* translated from the French in 1640 by one Francis Hawkins. Among the rules that Washington was sure would make him into a courteous, well-spoken gentleman, we find as the very first one: "Every Action done in Company, ought to be with Some Sign of Respect, to those that are present." From that, all else follows: no coughing, sneezing or spitting; no singing or humming or drumming your feet and fingers; and (rule 2) "When in company, put not your Hands to any Part of the Body, not usually Discovered." Important for the style of the period is the tenth rule: "When you Sit down, Keep your Feet firm and Even, without putting one on the other or Crossing them." Rule 15: "Keep your Nails clean and Short, also your Hands and Teeth clean, yet without Shewing any great Concern for them." Rule 20: "The Gestures of the Body must be Suited to the discourse you are upon." There are rules for removing your hat and bowing to persons of quality and distinction, whom you are enjoined to let pass through doorways before you. Be modest in your apparel, and always make sure your clothes are clean, and brushed at least once a day. Rule 100: "Cleanse not your teeth with the Table Cloth Napkin Fork or Knife but if Others do it let it be done w' a Pick Tooth." And "talk not with Meat in your Mouth" (rule 107). Avoid frivolity and loud laughter, don't pontificate, don't be tedious, and above all, always be dignified and modest, and, rule 110: "Labour to keep alive in your Breast that Little Spark of Celestial fire Called Conscience."

The influence of Native American culture on the ideas of democracy that were to take root in an imperfect form—with slavery still in force as the law of the land, once the United States won its independence—was a strong one, and the amazing example of how the Native Americans conducted their sophisticated political life was not lost on the colonists, although we seem to have more or less forgotten it now. But the Native American population was destined to be decimated, murdered, and dispossessed, treated as if they and not the Europeans were the interlopers.

Religion played a major role in colonial life, and many of the founding fathers, including Thomas Jefferson (1743–1826) and Washington, were deists—that is, they espoused the philosophy, based on reason and the observation of nature, that a supreme being, God, had created the world but no longer intervened in humanity's affairs. They did not believe in divine revelation or in the divinity of Christ, whom they nevertheless regarded as the greatest and most morally superior man who ever lived.

Etiquette was less rigid in America than in Europe, except in exclusive upper-class circles. There was not so much bowing and scraping. Men doffed their tricorn hats in the street, and bowed to each other and to women, who curtsied. And servants nodded or curtsied slightly when entering their employers' presence.

In the sophisticated households of Boston, Philadelphia, and New York, tea parties were very popular. Cakes and toast were served by the hostess with some formality, using elaborate china and silver tea services laid out decorously on round tea tables set up especially for the parties, but the new tax on tea and the Boston Tea Party of 1773 put an end to all that until after the American Revolution. Protesting patriots, disguised as Indians, dumped three shiploads of chests of tea into the harbor, and coffee now became the American drink of choice. Attesting to the new patriotism, in 1774, a charming, anonymous bit of doggerel entitled "A Lady's Adieu to Her Tea-Table" was printed in several newspapers. It begins:

FAREWELL the tea-board with your gaudy attire,
Ye cups and ye saucers that I did admire;
To my cream-pot and tongs I now bid adieu;
That pleasure's all fled that I once found in you...

The village grammar school was well attended and an important community center. Great American universities were founded, among them Yale (1701); Princeton (in 1746; the College of New Jersey moved to Princeton in 1756); Columbia, first called King's College, in 1754; and Rutgers, founded as Queen's College in 1766. In 1819, Thomas Jefferson founded the University of Virginia in Charlottesville, near his home, Monticello, and designed the campus himself.

J. Hector St. John de Crèvecoeur's (1735–1813) *Letters from an American Farmer* and *Sketches of Eighteenth-Century America* are invaluable but idealized accounts of life in the colonies before the American Revolution. De Crèvecoeur was a French aristocrat, born Michel Guillaume Jean de Crèvecoeur in Caen, Normandy; he changed his name when he headed south from Canada to the British colonies, becoming a naturalized citizen of New York Province. He was later French Consul to the new United States. Among his many friends, he counted Benjamin Franklin, Thomas Jefferson, and George Washington. His book, which he wrote in English, was immediately famous when he published it in 1782. It shows very clearly the mental world and views of people who fought to found a new country. Although obviously ethnocentric in his outlook, his basic principle was "Men are the same in all ages and in all countries. A few prejudices and customs excepted, the same passions lurk in our hearts at all times."

The book covers many aspects of colonial domestic life. He even tells us something about American fashions:

> You'd be surprised to see what beautiful colors some families will have in their garments, which commonly are streaked gowns, skirts and petticoats of the same stuff. This we have borrowed from the Dutch, as well as the art of producing so many colors from the roots and barks of our woods, aided with indigo and alum, the only foreign ingredients we use. I have often, while among the Indians, wished, but in vain, to find out how they dye their porcupine quills with that bright red and yellow which you must remember to have seen on the moccasins I gave you. Nor is the art of their squaws to be despised when you consider it as it is displayed in the embroidery of their belts, shoes, and pouches, knife cases, etc.

He hated violence and war and, although he owned some slaves, deplored slavery and thought it should end, as did a number of delegates who refused to sign the final draft of the Constitution at the Philadelphia Convention of 1787 because it did not do away with slavery— slaves were 20 percent of the population. During the revolution, Alexander Hamilton (1755–1804), less prejudiced than many, wrote on March 14, 1779, to his friend and fellow New Yorker, the President of the Continental Congress, John Jay (1745–1829), future Chief Justice of the Supreme Court, suggesting that slaves be recruited into the army, that plantation owners be required to supply contingents, and that "an essential part of the plan is to give them their freedom with their muskets." "I foresee," he wrote, "that this project will have to combat much opposition from prejudice and self-interest." There were slaves who fought for the British, having been promised their freedom. And there were also those who fought with the rebels.

Equally engrossing and invaluable are the posthumously published diaries of the travels in America by the devoted Polish patriot, student of history, poet, and playwright Julian Ursyn Niemcewicz (1757–1841)— a friend of Tadeusz Kościuszko (1746–1817), who played such a gallant part in the American Revolution and was the construction engineer for the fortifications of West Point. Both men were instrumental in the abortive Polish uprising of 1794. They were captured and imprisoned for two years by the Russians, and Poland was partitioned for the third time in 1795, its territory divided among Austria, Prussia, and Russia.

Niemcewicz served his sentence in solitary confinement and later went to the United States with Kościuszko, paying a visit to George Washington at Mount Vernon. His diaries were published under the title *Under Their Vine and Fig Tree: Travels through America in 1797–1799, 1805* (The Grassmann Publishing Company, Inc., 1965). He traveled extensively, and he describes life in Niagara Falls; New Brunswick, NJ; Princeton; Philadelphia; Boston; Albany; and New York City.

The French Revolution

The ancien régime and its rigid class system were not the only things to fall victim to the violently egalitarian uprising that gave birth to the Declaration of the Rights of Man: politeness and elaborate civility, which the revolutionaries considered inherently aristocratic, also disappeared, creating a public atmosphere of familiarity between persons that closed the distance between them and changed the style and sense of entitlement with which people related to each other. A law was passed banning absolutely the titles of Monsieur and Madame, which originally meant "my lord" and "my lady," and replacing them with *Citoyen* and *Citoyenne*: Citizen and Citizeness. Anyone who even accidentally uttered the old terms, or used the formal *vous* (you) instead of the informal *tu* (thou) when addressing someone, was politically suspect. In one incident, an elderly waiter at Le Procope (the restaurant, one of the oldest in Paris, is still there) forgot himself and addressed two customers as "Messieurs." Not wanting to appear suspect themselves, they began to berate him, and he was in danger of being denounced and arrested when the management intervened and calmed everybody down.

Authorized by the Convention and published in year 3 of the Republic (1794), the *Véritable Civilité Républicaine A l'usage des jeunes citoyens des deux sexes* (True Republican Civility for the Use of Young Citizens of Both Sexes) by "le citoyen Prévost" (?–?), was one of many such books and pamphlets advocating equality of treatment among all classes, ages, and genders; its popularity is attested to by the fact that it went through a number of editions. Prévost advocates natural politeness without servility as being necessary to the proper functioning of society, and he advises young people to honor and love their parents; to keep clean, but not unduly so; to wear their hair simply; and to wear plain, clean clothes—nothing ornate or affected: "It was this sort of magic that our tyrants used to impose themselves on us and to dazzle us." But do be sure to buy clothing, since it is necessary to the economy. Do not use extravagant gestures, and study the dance so you can move gracefully, but don't devote a lot of time to it, because "the particular study of that same dance is unworthy of a Republican." And, in order to inculcate a proper sense of equality, the young person should be sure to treat servants well:

> The domestic who serves you is similar to you; need, perhaps some adversity, has forced him to sell you his services; have for him the same care that you would wish to have given you in the same circumstances; perhaps one day you will find yourself in his place.

And Prévost concludes his book with a selection of "Republican" maxims from the writings of the ancient Roman Emperor Marcus Aurelius! Also suspect was anyone who continued to celebrate January 1 as New Year's Day, with its customary visits and greetings: a new revolutionary calendar (used until 1806) was promulgated; it went into effect in September 1793. The month of *vendémiaire* (derived from the word *vendanges*, meaning "wine harvest") lasted from September 22 to October 22, in year 2 of the republic. The names of the twelve thirty-day months (with five "complementary" days left over) were changed to reflect natural phenomena: *pluviôse* (rainy), *ventôse* (windy). The English made great fun of the new names with such fake translations as Slippy, Nippy, and Drippy; Freezy, Wheezy, and Sneezy.

Within less than twenty years, these innovations would disappear, and the antiquated code of politesse would have a revival in France, first with the empire of Napoleon I (1769–1821) in 1804—who reinstituted court etiquette, placing his large family in positions of power and ennobling his marshals—and then with the Restoration of the Bourbon monarchy in 1815. But the revolution had done its work: civility and manners would never be quite the same. The women's equality movement and the abolition of slavery in France and the French colonies—the former slaves had been granted absolutely equal French citizenship—also helped to change attitudes, manners, and ways of relating. (In one of the most infamous crimes against humanity ever committed, Napoleon attempted to reinstitute slavery in 1802.) One small sign of the general change is that bows and curtseys were no longer as deep as they had been, nor did those offering reverence prolong the show of deference.

Almost nothing had been deemed more important in upper-class circles than what was considered suitable conduct. One evening in 1773 at a royal card party, the Marquis de Chauvelin (b. 1716), member of an old aristocratic family, had the temerity to suffer a stroke, which killed him on the spot. Someone dared to cry out, "M. de Chauvelin is ill!" Hardly glancing at the body, Louis XV (1710–1774) said, "Ill? He is dead; take him away; spades are trumps, messieurs." He would be dead himself of smallpox a year later.

The masses loathed Louis the Well-Loved, but what did he care? "This will last my time," he said, "after me, the deluge." After him, starvation. The winters were unusually severe, crops failed, harvests were meager, and famine visited the country. The indigent flocked to Paris in the thousands, and there they found...nothing. No food. No jobs. Beggars clogged the city, with its sprawling slums and narrow, infected streets that spread contagion even between the wings of the Louvre.

At Versailles, 10,000 candles a day were burned: the price of one candle amounted to the weekly wage of a worker. Marie Antoinette (1755–1793) never said, "Ils n'ont pas de pain? Qu'ils mangent de la brioche!" (They have no bread? Let them eat cake!) But it was the prevalent attitude of the upper classes. And while the real shepherds might be starving, she would escape the palace very often and go to her Petit Hameau (Little Hamlet), which was an elaborate tiny farm village in the park where everything was in miniature, and play at being a shepherdess while wearing impractical clothing like that of a porcelain figurine. But her favorite clothing was the informal *gaulle*, a comfortable white muslin shift without corset or stays, often tied round the waist with a broad blue sash.

Before the revolution, it had been almost impossible to rise above the social class one was born into, and even in the aristocracy there were classes: those of more ancient lineage, the *noblesse de l'épée* (nobility of the sword), some of whom traced their ancestry to the Crusaders; and the *noblesse de la robe* (nobility of the robe), whose ancestors, having purchased their offices with money earned in commerce, had served the crown in a ministerial or legal capacity and had been granted titles (which they had to purchase). These two noble classes, who constituted what was called the "first estate" in the national assembly called the States General, treated each other with cruel snobbery. The "second estate" was the clergy; the "third estate" was the property-owning, wealthy middle class; and people began to talk of a "fourth estate": the poor urban working class and the impoverished rural peasantry, still bound by a semi-feudal system of near serfdom that the revolution would abolish.

Every office in the kingdom was sold by the king, from usher to court judge to admiral to general to tax collector. This resulted in a system rife with offenses, as those who bought their offices, paid for annually, tried to make their money back. There was a totally arbitrary and inconsistent system of justice and taxation. The first and second estates were virtually exempt. It was the third estate who paid, and the poor.

On the eve of the revolution, while the States General convened by Louis XVI to deal with the crisis looming over his government was meeting in Versailles (for the first time since 1614), there was a heady atmosphere of political ferment in Paris. In a letter dated April 26, 1789, to his wife in Saumur, Charles-Élie, Marquis de Ferrières (1741–1804), the elected first estate deputy for Poitou, described his experiences:

> This evening at the Palais Royal...I went into five or six cafes, and
> no Molière comedy can rival the scenes I saw: Here a man is redrafting and reforming the Constitution; another is reading a pamphlet

aloud; at another table, someone has put the ministers on trial; everybody is talking; each person has his audience that listens very attentively to him. I spent about ten hours there; if I wasn't staying so far away, I would go every evening. On the paths, crowds of girls and young people are promenading. The bookshops are packed with people who browse, read, and don't buy. Go to the cafes and you just suffocate.

Once the revolution had started, panic and paranoia prevailed on all sides. In August, 1789, just a few weeks after the storming of the Bastille, the marquis wrote to his wife:

> You do well to write, my dearest friend; I am very worried if I have received no news from you; not that I believe in the supposed brigands who, they say, are marauding through the countryside pillaging and laying waste; everyone is talking about them, and nobody has seen them; but in this general state of fermentation, the people, manipulated and egged on by those who are ill-intentioned, might become the blind instrument of private vengeance.

As a character study, the correspondence of the marquis for the years 1789–91 is invaluable. Albert Mathiez (1874–1932), the Marxist historian of the revolution, points out in his preface to the correspondence that it "teaches us about the feelings of a country gentleman, who no doubt shares the prejudices of his class, its wary attitude towards the court, its hatred of financiers, its jealousy of the high clergy," but who was also gifted with a certain intelligence that prevented him from being intransigent and allowed him to sympathize with the liberal ideas of the third estate. He condemned those of his class who chose to emigrate, and he thought they should stay to do the necessary work of reform.

Especially after the king had been tried and executed in January, 1793, thousands of the nobility fled the country—most bound for England, some for Brussels, where they felt they would be safe. As the *Memoirs* of Comte Joseph Élizabeth Roger de Damas d'Antigny (1765–1823), aide de camp to the Comte d'Artois (the future Charles X), inform us, in Brussels they lived with an astonishing indifference to events unfolding in Paris and as much as possible as they had in the old days. They gave balls and dinner parties and read the daily newspapers with the list of the latest victims of the Terror, among whom were invariably to be found the names of friends and relatives.

The brief but shocking bloodbath known as the Reign of Terror, which began in September 1793 and saw the execution of Marie Antoinette in October, lasted for about eleven months. It was instituted to quell the very real, frightening dangers of internal dissension, counterrevolution, and the threat of invasion by the surrounding monarchist powers. Throughout the country, between 30,000 and 40,000 people lost their lives, about 9 percent of them aristocrats and 7 percent clergy. The rest were bourgeois, peasants, or workers, guilty (or not, in many cases) of various counterrevolutionary activities.

Some were acquitted. Jean-Louis Fargeon (1748–1806), perfumer to Marie Antoinette, amassed a fortune during his years at Versailles, but he was able to prove at his trial, with the help of witnesses who took the dangerous step of appearing on his behalf, that he had used it in the service of the people, that he was very much for the revolution, and that he always treated his servants and those who worked for him with egalitarian consideration. He survived, but the ordeal of his imprisonment and trial hastened his premature death at the age of fifty-eight.

There were tragic miscarriages of justice. Antoine Laurent Lavoisier (1743–1794), the father of modern chemistry, discovered oxygen and formulated the law of the conservation of matter. But the money for his laboratory equipment had come from his percentage of the revenues he made as a *Fermier Général* (farmer general), a tax collector. Although he had tried to mitigate the lot of the middle class and the poor by tax reform, he was guillotined. "The Republic does not need geniuses," interrupted the judge, as Lavoisier pleaded for his life. The administration apologized to his widow in 1796 for his wrongful conviction.

The Terror came to an end with the downfall and guillotining of those who had sponsored it: the National Convention's Committee of Public Safety, of which the brilliant Maximilien de Robespierre "the Incorruptible" (1758–1794), was chairman. He had wanted to abolish capital punishment, as he forcibly stated in his speech to the convention on May 30, 1791:

> The news having been carried to Athens that some citizens had been condemned to death in the city of Argos, they ran to the temples, and implored the gods to turn them away from such cruel and baleful thoughts. I come to pray not to the gods but to you, the legislators...the death penalty is essentially unjust.

But by December 17, 1793, as the Terror was steamrolling ahead, he addressed them in the following terms:

Representatives of the French people, know your strength and your dignity! You may conceive a legitimate pride: Applaud yourselves not only for having annihilated royalty and punished kings, striking down the guilty idols before whom the world prostrated itself, but especially for... letting fall the blade of justice on the guilty who had held their heads high among you.

The Terror over, people celebrated with parties and dances. There were "Victim's Balls," and to gain admittance, you had to be a relative of someone who had been guillotined and prove it by showing the requisite papers to the doorman. It was the fashion at these soirées for women to wind a very thin red ribbon tight around their necks and to wear their hair swept up so that the backs of their necks were bare. This grisly style was called *la toilette du condamné* (the toilette of the condemned).

The National Convention was replaced first by the Directory and Council of Five Hundred, and then by the Consulate, in imitation of ancient Rome. Napoleon was made first consul for life. But that wasn't good enough: he wanted to be emperor.

The Bourbon Restoration and the Age of Jane Austen and the Regency

In England, extravagance, luxury, profligacy, and gentility characterized the Regency of George, Prince of Wales (1762–1830), the future King George IV, who reveled more than he ruled. For all the decorousness of manners Jane Austen (1775–1817) portrays as being de rigeur in the English middle- and upper-middle-class milieu with which she was familiar, and for all the proprietary protectionist attitude towards women, the privileged elite often indulged their most decadent libertine whims.

While George enjoyed himself, his mad, blind father, George III—suffering from the rare disease of porphyria—roamed the halls of Buckingham Palace, and the allied armies fought Napoleon, whom they finally defeated in 1815 at Waterloo. The Restoration of the Bourbons in France was engineered at the Congress of Vienna by the wily Austrian diplomat Prince Metternich (1773–1859) and the even craftier French ambassador Prince Charles-Maurice de Talleyrand-Périgord (1754–1838), the ex-bishop, wit, and gastronome who had managed to survive and prosper under every regime. He knew there would eventually be a revolution against the Bourbon Restoration, but at the moment of Napoleon's defeat, "legitimacy" was the only way to secure peace and the briefest possible occupation of France by allied troops. Louis XVI's younger brother, the Comte de Provence, became Louis XVIII (1755–1824). On his demise, the youngest brother of the three, the ultrareactionary Comte d'Artois, became King Charles X (1757–1836). He was overthrown in the July Revolution of 1830, bringing his cousin, the "Citizen King" Louis-Philippe of the House of Orléans, to the throne. In 1832, there would be an abortive uprising against the rule of Louis-Philippe—the one depicted in Victor Hugo's (1802–1885) Les Misérables and vividly recreated in Raymond Bernard's (1891–1977) 1934 must-see version of that novel, available on a Criterion DVD.

For several years immediately after the Restoration, confusion and chaos reigned, allied troops occupied Paris, and crookedness and crime were rampant in all levels of society. There were even impostors at the royal court who were able to pass themselves off as aristocrats of ancient lineage. Several of them were unmasked by one of the great personalities of the era, an ex-convict named Eugène-François Vidocq (1775–1857), a real-life Sherlock Holmes who had abjured a life of crime and become an internationally famous police inspector and chief of the Sûreté, serving through many changes of government. His Memoirs were an instant bestseller, and the autobiographical one-person show he gave in London was a huge success. He was a master of disguise, and it was said he would have made a wonderful actor. A friend of Balzac, Alexandre Dumas, and Victor Hugo, who all used him as a model for characters, Vidocq was the basis for both Jean Valjean—the reformed ex-convict who makes good—and Inspector Javert in Les Misérables. But he was not implacable like Hugo's relentless, obsessive policeman. In fact, he campaigned for prison reform and believed in rehabilitation, which Javert does not.

By the end of the eighteenth century, education had improved, and the upper classes were prolific letter writers, diarists, and authors of lengthy memoirs, to which we owe so much information about the period. Among the most useful sources on attitudes and living conditions during the age of Jane Austen are the writings of Lady Bessborough, who had a notorious relationship with the playwright and MP Richard Brinsley Sheridan (1761–1816)—quite displeasing to her husband, who started a law suit against them, which he saw fit in the end to give up in order to avoid further scandal. Related to many of the great English aristocratic families, Henrietta Frances (Harriet) Spencer,

Countess of Bessborough (1761–1821), traveled extensively in Europe and was the author of journals and a voluminous correspondence, of which her great-grandson published excerpts in *Lady Bessborough and Her Family Circle* (John Murray, 1940).

Her daughter was Caroline Lamb (1785–1828). "Caro," as the family called her, adored her husband, William, but their marriage was a disaster, and they fought constantly. Lady Caroline, who was in some ways the bane of her appalled mother's existence and was always making scenes, is best known for her tempestuous love affair with George Gordon, Lord Byron (1788–1824). In 1812, Caro caused a great scandal the day after she met Byron, by having herself carried into dinner at her maternal aunt Georgiana, the Duchess of Devonshire's house, naked on a silver platter. As Samuel Rogers tells us, "She was mad; and her family allowed her to do whatever she chose."

Samuel Rogers (1763–1855)—the poet, banker, art collector, patron of the arts, and charming, gossipy host and entertaining dinner guest who knew everybody—was born early in the reign of George III and lived well into the Victorian era. He has left us a wonderful record of the period in *Recollections of the Table-Talk of Samuel Rogers*, published in 1856 by his friend, the editor and Shakespeare scholar Alexander Dyce (1798–1869), who had acted in a Boswellian capacity, taking down everything Rogers said. Among other things, Rogers decries changes in the pronunciation of English:

> It is curious how fashion changes pronunciation. In my youth everybody said "Lonnon," not "London"...The now fashionable pronunciation of several words is to me at least very offensive: "cóntemplate" is bad enough; but "balcŏny" makes me sick.

Through the late eighteenth century and beyond, the stress in "contemplate" used to be on the second syllable. And the second syllable of "balcony" was fully pronounced.

The future George IV was quite a clothes horse. Venetia Murray, who has gone through the Royal Archives at Windsor, wonders in *An Elegant Madness: High Society in Regency England* (Penguin, 1998) whether he actually used such accessories as "a large sea otter muff" or "six fencing masks lined with blue silk and nine fencing gloves bound with blue silk," which the Royal Archives files inform us he purchased. But then, he "ordered at least eight full-dress field-marshal's uniforms." And he did sport "rich Muscovy sable muffs," along with endless new shirts and coats, "prime doe pantaloons," and "superfine scarlet flannel

230 DOING PERIOD STYLES

underwaistcoats lined with fine calico." His underdrawers were made of black silk, and he had scores of shirts.

In his magisterial two-volume history *The Beaux of the Regency* (Hutchinson, 1908), Lewis Melville describes many of the prince's outfits. Among the most extravagant was one he wore at in the House of Lords, consisting of "a black velvet suit, richly embroidered with gold, and pink spangles, and lined with pink satin, and shoes with pink heels... while, to give an appropriate finish to his costume, his hair was pressed much at the side and very full frizzed with two small curls at the bottom." Led on by the influential dandy and arbiter of fashion, his sometime friend Beau Brummel (1778–1840), George cut an ornamental figure indoors and out. At a ball in Brighton, his costume was so fantastically elaborate and so decorated with a profusion of knightly orders attached with sprigs of diamonds that "even the imagination of the heir-apparent could go no further, and he rested, content, the most over-dressed man of his day!"

The age of Jane Austen was truly the period when clothes made the man, at least in aristocratic and upper bourgeois circles. And fashions were still largely French, even during the Napoleonic wars, when English ladies could not do without their French-style gowns. After peace was declared, on the other hand, French women, who admired English riding dress, went to London to purchase them from the renowned, ultrafashionable tailors in Bond Street. Not only were modes, food, and wine in England French, but so was the preferred language of conversation among the upper classes—at least through the Regency era, in spite of the revolution and the drawn-out Napoleonic wars. Venetia Murray cites the astonished American ambassador, Richard Rush (1745–1813?), who wrote, "The foreigners spoke English: nevertheless, the conversation was nearly all in French. This was not only the case when the English addressed the foreigners, but in speaking to each other."

The papers of Thomas Creevey (1768–1838), a conformist Whig MP, tell us much about the politics of the era and about how the liberal opposition reacted to the Tories who seemed to be perpetually in power. He knew everyone and was a friend of the Prince of Wales, who boasted for a time that he was a Whig, and would pull Creevey aside to ask his opinions on various personalities and questions. Creevey was, of course, suitably dazzled, and then as shocked as the other Whigs when "Prinny" turned into a reactionary Tory immediately upon assuming the Regency in 1811. *The Creevey Papers*, a one-volume edition of his diaries and correspondence published by John Murray in 1905, reveal Prinny's personality in all its petulance, pomposity, and grandeur, and tell us not a little of his peccadilloes. Mrs. Creevey, who was a guest of the prince's at the Pavillion in Brighton, where she went essentially to advance the Whig cause of electoral and political reform, was an appalled witness to his carryings on. On one night, for instance, the prince had been royally drunk and used an air gun to shoot up the place, insisting that all the ladies take turns popping shots too.

The sexual mores of the era were free and easy, and marital fidelity, in an age when marriages were really business arrangements made for money and not love, was all but ignored by just about every member of the upper classes, who also indulged in the pleasures of horse racing and the gambling table. But behavior was gradually growing more staid, and marriage for love was becoming important, at least in the middle classes, as we can see, for instance, in the attitudes of the characters in Jane Austen's novels.

Hunting was another great passion. In *The Greville Memoirs* (see also pages 296–298), Charles C. F. Greville (1794–1865) describes a "chasse" he went to at the end of December 1820 at Woburn in Bedfordshire, seat of the Dukes of Bedford and site of a famous ruined abbey. The guests included Napoleon's nemesis, the Duke of Wellington (1769–1852), and a great many other notables: "The chasse was brilliant; in five days we killed 835 pheasants, 645 hares, 59 rabbits, 10 partridges, and 5 woodcocks." Two weeks later, he is back for more: "We shot the whole week and killed an immense quantity of game," and then, "On Sunday last arrived the news of the king's death [on January 29, 1820]." What a shame, but at least they could dress for his funeral, and that of the Regency, since the Prince of Wales would now be king! "Thus we trifled life away," writes Greville.

Naturally, these people could not exist without armies of servants, whose duties were laid out in a popular book (there were several others on the same subject) published in 1825, *The Complete Servant* by Samuel and Sarah Adams. This was already late into the era, and the Prince Regent had succeeded to the throne, but the authors inform us that they are setting out for the first time the usual practices and the duties of every servant in a concise handbook, so that there should be no confusion. Whether you play a servant or a master, this book is invaluable. Details of income, and how many servants one can afford on a specific income, are included. And there are recipes and useful hints for the cook, as well as a chapter with recipes for tooth powder (among its ingredients: snuff and tobacco ashes), and scents for clothing and gloves, and so forth. People still did not bathe very much, although they washed in the morning using a basin and ewer and cleaned their teeth with the tooth powder—also using a mixture of water, lemon juice, salt and alum "with a small bit of sponge tied to a stick, once a week"—so that the scent they used for clothes covered, but did not eliminate, body odors.

The book even provides details that would be useful for the offstage life of a servant character. The lady's maid, for instance, after making the fire in the morning, preparing her lady's dressing room, bringing in hot water so her lady can wash, and awakening her lady, goes to have breakfast with the other servants. When summoned, she then helps her lady dress, combs her hair, and tidies up the dressing room, putting away the night clothes. She is always to be at the ready in case her lady should summon her, and while she waits, "She then retires to her work-room . . . and employs herself in making dresses, millinery, &c." The valet's duties are quite similar: he also has to clean and polish his master's boots and shoes, and keep hairbrushes and toothbrushes clean; and he has to make sure the housemaid has lighted the fire in the morning in his master's rooms. Altogether, the duties of thirty-seven servants are detailed, including those of the gardeners; the land steward, who supervises the treatment of livestock and everything else on country estates; and the stable staff; as well as those of governesses, nurses, and all the household servants in town and country. In wealthy establishments especially, the household servants dressed according to rank and duties—as they had for centuries and still do. Some footmen and other servants wore specially designed, often very ornate livery, identifiable as their master's.

The hierarchy of seating arrangements by rank is as rigid at the dining table in the servants' hall is it is in the master's dining room: the housekeeper sits at the head of the table, the butler at the lower end, the cook to the housekeeper's right, the lady's maid to her left; the under butler sits to the butler's right and the coachman to his left; and all the other servants sit at places in between, according to rank, with the men servants always at the lower end of the table:

> The dinner is set on the table by the cook, the beer is drawn by the under butler. . . . In well regulated families, the servants' hall is distinguished by decorum, good order, and even good manners.

Servants are enjoined not to be coarse or vulgar and not to use profanity, and they are not to be extravagant and wasteful. I suppose they could leave that to their masters!

This is all quite a contrast with Jonathan Swift's hilarious, sometimes vicious, unfinished *Directions to Servants*, published in 1731 and written with the accumulated wisdom of many years of observing and dealing with domestics. The book begins with "Directions to All Servants in General," and Swift's sage advice includes the following:

> Never come till you have been called three or four times, for none but dogs will come at the first whistle; and when the master calls, 'Who's there?' no servant is bound to come, for *Who's there* is nobody's name.

> When your lady sends for you up to her chamber to give you any orders, be sure to stand at the door and keep it open, fiddling with the lock all the while she is talking to you, and keep the button in your hand for fear you should forget to shut the door after you.

His "Directions to the Butler" include:

> When you cut bread for a toast, do not stand idly watching it, but lay it on the coals and mind your other business; then come back, and if you find it toasted quite through, scrape off the burnt side and serve it up.

> When you are to get water on for tea after dinner (which in many families is part of your office), to save firing and to make more haste, pour it into the tea-kettle from the pot where cabbage or fish have been boiling, which will make it much wholesomer by curing the acid, corrosive quality of the tea.

And here is a piece of rather surrealistic advice from "Directions to the Cook":

> Never send up a leg of fowl at supper while there is a cat or a dog in the house that can be accused of running off with it. But if there happen to be neither, you must lay it upon the rats or a strange greyhound.

The Stylistic Elements: Clothing, Accessories, Movement, Manners, and the Art of Living

Clothing and Movement in Costume: European court costumes were extremely elaborate, particularly for women, as we can see in the gorgeous colored prints of costumes that were published sporadically between

1778 and 1787 in seventy portfolios called the *Galerie des Modes*. In France during the revolution, however, wearing anything other than plain, simple garb was deemed counterrevolutionary: the splendid clothing and the gorgeous, extravagant jewelry worn by the aristocratic class had cost millions while people were starving.

Movement in the simpler, less ornate American clothing of the period was a bit easier than it was in Europe. But in royal governor's mansions, with their genteel regal courts and politesse, the upper classes deliberately dressed as their English counterparts did. In all classes, men wore powdered wigs and jabots attached to neck-cloths that were fastened at the back with laces or ties. The *stock*, or *neck-stock*, was a readymade neck-cloth or cravat with a metal spring sewn into it to keep it in place. Plain cravats, wrapped around the neck in several folds, were also worn. In the South, in the 1730s and '40s, many men only wore a wig when going out in public, and not always then. At home they were woolen or cotton caps, or nightcaps. But everyone of whatever social class wore wigs, and there was a brisk trade in second-hand wigs.

Women wore long gowns, petticoats, and tightly laced corsets that limited their movement, but nothing as extravagant as the incredible headdresses so popular at European courts was seen in America. From 1750 to about 1790, they wore *buffonts*, a kind of puffy, wide collar covering the throat and upper bosom and tucked into the bodice. They were plain or with lace ruffles at the neck, as was the similar *partlet*, a sort of half shirt also worn tucked into the bodice.

Wide hoopskirts imported from England became fashionable. In 1722, Benjamin Franklin, writing as Silence Dogood, made fun of the new mode in "No. 6" as "this monstrous garb": "I would at least desire them to lessen the Circumference of their Hoops, and leave it to them to consider, Whether they, who pay no Rates or Taxes, ought to take up more Room in the King's High-Way, than the Men, who yearly contribute to the support of the Government." But the fashion remained popular in Europe and America through to the Napoleonic era.

Madame Jeanne Louise Henriette Campan (1752–1822) was first lady-in-waiting to the queen, from whom she was forcibly separated in 1792 when the Tuileries Palace was sacked. She noted in her *Memoirs of the Court of Marie Antoinette, Queen of France*, published posthumously in 1823, that Franklin, accustomed to plain, practical Philadelphia clothing, appeared at the French court "in the dress of an American agriculturalist. His straight unpowdered hair, his round hat, his brown cloth coat, formed a contrast with the laced and embroidered coats, and the powdered and perfumed heads of the courtiers at Versailles."

But the American upper classes could be quite as fastidious and fashion conscious as the Europeans. George Washington gave detailed instructions to his tailor in 1747, when he was only fifteen, about how to make his new frock coat with lapels: he wanted "The Lapel to contain on each side six Button Holes & to be about 5 or 6 inches wide all the way equal...to have it made very long Waisted and in Length to come down to or below the bent of the knee." He was later very conscientious about his stepchildren's wardrobe, and he ordered clothing and accessories very carefully for them and for his wife.

In Virginia there was a class distinction readily apparent in people's dress. Red was a popular color for upper-class women, who wore mantles or cloaks of scarlet *camlet*, a fabric of camel's hair woven with silk, which women of the middle and lower classes could not afford. Upper-class men, carrying fur muffs and sporting the occasional earring (early in the century), wore coats with gold buttons, embroidered buttonholes, and detachable or sewn-on lace ruffles at the sleeves; tricorn hats, which could be richly ornamented with gold trim; silk stockings; and pumps or red-heeled shoes with silver buckles. By contrast, working men wore short jackets or jerkins, caps, cotton stockings, and shoes with low, black heels and no buckles. Sailors and fishermen wore short jackets and sturdy knee-length or full-length wide-bottomed trousers. Until after the revolution, when the custom died out, Virginia aristocrats would not leave home without their swords, carried in ornate sword belts. In Northern colonies, it was unusual to see men wearing swords, but similar class distinctions in dress there and in Europe were the norm.

European and American women wore *chemises* (undershirts, usually called shifts) under their stayed corsets, into which they had to be laced by servants; stockings or tights under wide underpants (linen was the most usual material); and bodices (laced up the front) or blouses—which could have long, ruffled sleeves—over the corsets. Fastened around the waist, often, underneath the hoop skirt, were two *paniers* (baskets), which widened the hooped petticoats that were sometimes lined with silk. The petticoats usually had five rings, or hoops, broader at the bottom than at the waist. An overskirt covered the petticoat, and could be a one-piece garment; or, alternatively, the petticoat could be covered with a waist-high overskirt and a separate top. Upper- and middle-class women sometimes wore bustles under their overskirts and petticoats. The hoops were heavy and made of iron or wood, and later of lighter whalebone. The hoopskirts were sometimes so wide that women could only go through doors sideways, and when they sat, which they could only do with great difficulty on the edge of a chair, they took up an immense amount of room.

The gorgeously ornate overskirts that covered the hooped petticoat were embroidered with gold and silver thread, and with rococo sprays of flowers and endless lace and ruffles and bows of ribbons. They ended in long trains—the longer the better. This made movement even more difficult, and the train had either to be held from behind by a servant or held with one hand so it could be swirled decorously around to facilitate moving. Matters were settled by royal decrees about the length of trains in the different ranks of nobility—the lower you were on the scale, the shorter your train—so as to avoid undue competition. On the other hand, shoes with six-inch heels and higher were worn underneath the gowns, so that it became difficult to get around even with a short train.

Outerwear included long hooded cloaks, called *capuchins*, which could be worn over the entire outfit, and hats could be worn as well. Or *pelerines*, short capes with long front ends, were worn to cover the bare neck and upper bosom. When riding, an outer petticoat called a *safe-guard*, *foot-mantle*, or *weather-skirt*, known since at least Elizabethan times, protected the intrepid horsewoman against splashes of mud.

Movement was generally easier for middle-class and poor women, whose dresses were not that long and were sometimes the length of modern skirts. Here, for instance, is Frances Burney's description of fisherwomen she saw working "with amazing strength" at the seashore near Teignmouth, a port from which boats set off for the fisheries off Newfoundland. While the men sailed, the women stayed home, and went every day to spread the broad seines, or fishing nets, and to empty them of their catch:

> They are all robust and well made, and have remarkably beautiful Teeth:... their Dress is barbarous: they have stays half Laced, and some thing by way of Handkerchiefs about their Necks, they wear a single colored Flannel, or stuff petticoat;—no shoes or stockings; notwithstanding the hard Pebbles and stones all along the beach:— and their Coat [petticoat] is Pin'd up in the shape of a pair of trousers, leaving them wholly Naked to the knee.

Depending on their station, European men wore embroidered or plain frock coats. The coats of the wealthy sported great cuffs, often but not always ornamented with lace ruffles hanging out of them; vests or longer waistcoats; and lace jabots. The middle class wore jabots of plain linen, or long cravats or ties wound several times around the neck and knotted at the throat. Sometimes, in an effort to appear casual or non-chalant, the cravats were simply wound once or twice around the neck and the ends pushed through buttonholes instead of being knotted. During the reign of Louis XV, a broad black ribbon called a *solitaire* was worn to protect the cravat or jabot and the top of the coat from the wig powder. Sometimes the solitaire was wound around the tail of the wig, and the ends of the ribbon were tucked into the shirt ruffle. Later in the century, cravats with a large, floppy white bow were a popular style. Coats, sometimes flared at the bottom, made of stiffer material than in the previous century so that they would drape well, were generally worn open, despite the numerous lines of buttons that were there more for adornment than practicality. Knee breeches were the fashion, and the rich wore them with silk stockings and silver-buckled shoes. Men also wore capes and cloaks, such as the *abbé*, which had three caped layers of graduated length and was worn over a long-sleeved coat; or the *artois*, worn by coachmen, with the cape layers reaching to the waist.

Both men and women slept in nightgowns and wore nightcaps. But in the eighteenth century, the word *night-gown* meant not a sleeping garment but a bathrobe or dressing gown. They could be beautifully embroidered, with matching caps, and were worn informally all day at home and even sometimes when receiving guests. What we now call a nightgown was usually called a *night rail*.

Women did not cross their legs when sitting: their voluminous gowns precluded that position. Men usually did not cross their legs when seated except in very informal situations, although there are a number of portraits from the period that show them doing so. Those portraits are of men alone in their libraries, looking rather studious. In company, and particularly in very formal situations, they would usually not cross their legs, but sit with one leg gracefully and slightly behind the other.

Some upper-class men, particularly if they were dandified, wore corsets over their long undershirts. The position in which men sat, almost on the edge of the chair, allowed them to be more comfortable. Crossed legs were almost impossible if one wore a corset, which already tended to cut off circulation. To sit, men backed one leg, usually the right one, against the chair and, without looking round, sat down, placing the left leg forward slightly, then changing the position of the legs so that the right leg was forward and the left leg behind and slightly under the chair. Joseph Schildkraut playing the Duke of Orléans, the king's cousin, provides a perfect example of this movement and sitting position in *Marie Antoinette* (1938). The feet were slightly turned out in balletic fashion. During these movements, the sword was held up slightly with the left hand and allowed to relax once its wearer was seated. As the man was just about seated, the sword was released and guided to the floor, and the two front sides of the coat were lightly flicked out, so that they would not be sat upon but would drape elegantly down.

During the French Revolution, blue, white, and red became the fashionable colors, and the red Phrygian bonnet with a tricolor cockade was popular, as was the *coiffure à la nation*, with bunches of tricolor ribbons tied in the hair. Actors on stage wore the tricolor cockade anachronistically, no matter the era in which the play was set or the character they played, so that you could see Oedipus or Brutus sporting the blue, white, and red.

Catherine Hyde (1749–1844), Marquise de Gouvion Broglie Scolari, "in the Confidential Service of the Unfortunate Princess" Lamballe, lady-in-waiting to Marie Antoinette, tells the following anecdote concerning herself in chapter 16 of *Secret Memoirs of Princess Lamballe: Her Confidential Relations with Marie Antoinette*, which she edited. She had returned from a trip to England and went to the opera in Paris (this is the unaccredited 1901 translation):

> The fashion then in England was a black dress, Spanish hat [a kind of puffy turban-like beret, often of black velvet], and yellow satin lining, with three ostrich feathers forming the Prince of Wales's crest, and bearing the inscription "*Ich dien*, I serve" [the Prince of Wales's motto, dating from medieval days]. I also brought with me a white satin cloak, trimmed with white fur.

She was immediately and roundly booed by the audience and told that if she did not remove the hat and cloak, she would have to leave the theater. Unwittingly, she had offended the audience by wearing royalist garb and by not wearing the three requisite revolutionary colors.

In France, the style of the revolution, the Directory, and the Napoleonic Empire, with its pseudo-Greco-Roman revival in dress and furniture, meant that people were able to be much freer in their movement than before the revolution.

In her *Memoirs*, published in eighteen volumes from 1831–34, Laure Junot, Duchesse d'Abrantès (1784–1838)—a friend of the Bonaparte family from childhood on—describes the fascinating, statuesque salon hostess, Mme. Thérèse Tallien (1773–1835), wife of Jean-Lambert Tallien (1767–1820). The latter, although he had presided over the Terror in Bordeaux, was one of the men instrumental in Robespierre's downfall. Madame Tallien was known for her many lovers, for taking baths in which kilos of strawberries were crushed to make her skin silky, and for her extravagance in costume, but at a ball in 1797 she dressed with simple elegance (this is the unaccredited 1895 translation):

> Her dress . . . consisted of a plain robe of India muslin, with folds in the antique style, and fastened by a cameo on each shoulder; a gold belt encircled her waist, and was likewise fastened by a cameo; a broad gold bracelet confined her sleeve considerably above the elbow; her hair, of a glossy black, was short and curled all round her head, in the fashion then called *à la Titus* [after the Roman emperor Titus]; over her fair and finely turned shoulders was thrown a superb red cashmere shawl, an article at that time very rare and in great request. She disposed it around her in a manner at once graceful and picturesque.

Women's Empire-style dresses attempted to imitate the graceful draping of classical antiquity, and furniture designers made Greco-Roman canapés on which great beauties such as Madame Récamier (1777–1849) could display their charms; she was famously painted reclining on hers by Jacques-Louis David (1748–1825) in 1800. Women wore revealing diaphanous gowns tied under the bosom, and bare arms, sometimes covered on formal occasions with long gloves that reached at least to the elbow. Since the hair was natural, it could be longer or shorter, and it was often tied up with a ribbon. But the light sandals that women often wore, particularly at formal balls and parties, precluded fast walking or large steps, and slow movement with small steps was the only way to get around, creating a necessity to be graceful and even dainty. The usually lubricious Napoleon, however, was uncomfortable with women's immodesty, so he decreed that the diaphanous material be replaced by less transparent silk and velvet. Still, high-waisted, gowns were now less form fitting and had puffy high sleeves.

Men began the nineteenth century by wearing slimming, revealing long trousers, which replaced knee-length breeches except on formal occasions; trousers had buttoned flies later in the century. Both full and cutaway coats were in fashion.

In the Directory period of the late 1790s that succeeded the Terror in France, the *Muscadins* (popinjays, coxcombs; derived from the word *muscade*, nutmeg) wore revealing, pale nutmeg-colored breeches. They were ardent royalist "legitimists," and their coats were lined with black as a sign of mourning for Louis XVI. The Republican *Incroyables* (Incredibles) of the same period were known for their sloppy oversize coats with huge leg-of-mutton sleeves; their extravagant, huge, half moon–shaped hats, with tassels hanging off both corners; and such ornaments as oversized gold-framed spectacles, jeweled watch fobs, and kid gloves, as well as their form-fitting, revealing trousers. Lace jabots were superseded by enormous white or dark-colored ties that were wound several times around the throat with large knots and concealed the chin, and they wore their hair in long, hanging locks resembling spaniels' ears and sloppily covering their foreheads. The *Incroyables* were frequently accompanied by their feminine counterparts, the *Merveilleuses* (Marvelouses), with their exceedingly revealing tulle or gauze gowns, open down the sides and with the décolleté leaving nothing to the imagination; and their long, flamboyant tresses, multiplicity of wigs—some of them green or blue—trailing scarves, feathered hats, and jewelry. It was even the fashion to drop as many consonants as possible, so that the *Incroyables* became the "Incoyab"; their speech was said to be nearly incomprehensible, except to themselves.

Accessories: Short light *periwigs*—often with sausage curls at the sides, just as one still sees them in barrister's wigs in English law courts— became the fashion in the eighteenth century, although as late as the 1730s and '40s, the older style of long wig was seen. The wigs had to be powdered daily, and there was even a garment called a *powdering jacket*, donned for the purpose of having a servant powder the wig already on the head of its wearer. The morning dressing ritual usually included shaving as well; beards are rare among the upper classes during this period. During powdering, a long tapered horn with a breathing hole at the small end was held over the face to prevent the powder from being breathed in. The wigs were stored on blocks or wig stands.

   Wigs came in a great variety of styles, and they had many names, among them the "campaign wig," which was a full wig with curled sides and forehead used by travelers and military men; the "scratch" wig, which was short, could be unkempt, and covered only part of the head; and the "feathertop," with a puffy top. There were long-tailed, bob-tailed, and fox-tailed wigs, and they even came in various colors. The "bag wig" had its tail encased in a black bag that was tied with a bow at the top.

In his *Dictionary*, published in 1755, Samuel Johnson defined *periwig* ("wig" is simply a shortening of the word) as "adscititious hair." The word *adscititious* means, he writes, "that which is taken in to complete something else, though originally extrinsick; supplemental; additional." The celebrated dictionary is worth reading for its own sake. It can be hilarious, as well as highly instructive, and it "provides a record of a fascinating age" as well as being a "a great work of literature," as Jack Lynch's introduction to the 2004 Levenger Press edition of excerpts informs us.

Frances Burney tells us in her diary entry for March 26, 1775, that David Garrick showed up for a visit to her family while her father was being attended to by the "Hair Dresser." Garrick had on

> a most odious scratch Wig, which Nobody but himself could dare be seen in: He put on a look ... of *envy* and sadness as he examined the Hair Dresser's progress;—and when he had done, he turned to him with a dejected Face, and said '—pray Sir,—could you touch up *This* a little?' taking hold of his frightful scratch. The man only Grinned, and left the Room.

Some wore no wig at all. There are portraits of squires and other country gentlemen sporting their own hair. And the eccentric, excessively pale General James Wolfe (b. 1727), who was to die on the Plains of Abraham after winning the Battle of Quebec for the British in 1759, was proud to display his long, loose, bright red locks, and disdained to wear a military wig under his tricorn hat.

Men's wigs may have been simpler than those of the previous century, but women's hairdos, particularly among the upper classes, were sometimes amazing works of art. As Samuel Rogers tells us:

> The head-dresses of the ladies, during my youth, were of a truly preposterous size. I have gone to Ranelagh in a coach with a lady who was obliged to sit upon a stool placed in the bottom of the coach, the height of her head-dress not allowing her to occupy the regular seat.
>
>   Their tight lacing was equally absurd. Lady Crewe told me, that, on returning home from Ranelagh, she has rushed up to her bedroom, and desired her maid to cut her laces without a moment's delay, for fear she should faint.

Lady Crewe was the wealthy Frances Anne (Greville), Baroness Crewe (1748–1818), whose portrait by Sir Thomas Lawrence (1769–1830) is in the National Portrait Gallery in London. Ranelagh and Vauxhall were privately owned enclosed pleasure gardens to which people repaired for refreshment, dancing, and intrigue, sometimes wearing masks and *dominos* (floor-length, hooded cloaks) to disguise themselves. Samuel Rogers informs us that

> St. James's Street used to be crowded with the carriages of the ladies and gentlemen who were walking in the Mall,—the ladies with their heads in full dress, and the gentlemen carrying their hats under their arms. The proprietors of Ranelagh and Vauxhall used to send decoy-ducks among them, that is, persons attired in the height of fashion, who every now and then would exclaim in an audible tone, "What charming weather for Ranelagh" or "for Vauxhall!"
>
> Ranelagh was a very pleasing place of amusement. There persons of inferior rank mingled with the highest nobility of Britain. All was so orderly and still that you could hear the *whishing* sound of the ladies' trains, as the immense assembly walked round and round the room. If you chose, you might have tea, which was served up in the neatest equipage possible. The price of admission was half-a-crown. People generally went to Ranelagh between nine and ten o'clock.

The "decoy-ducks" were also called *puffers*, and they were hired by theater managers to publicize plays in coffeehouses and taverns.

The incredibly elaborate headdresses, which were supported by metal ribs and an elaborate contraption called a *fontange*—named for Marie Angélique de Scorailles de Rousille, Duchess of Fontanges (1661–1681; a mistress of Louis XIV), who invented it—took a great deal of getting used to. A fontange consists of a base of linen cylindrical rolls two feet high or more that are attached together, and around which hair could be wound; it was securely fastened to the real hair. Many women wore their long hair simply piled up on the head. But particularly at the French court and sometimes in England and elsewhere too, around the middle of the century until the French Revolutionary era, there were whole ships or pageants, as well as mountainous displays of vegetables and fruits and birds on top of the head. These had to be held high and demanded slow and stately movement and, sometimes, a servant following behind to support them with a stick. The slow movement not only showed off the extravagant, unwieldy hairdo but also prevented it from falling apart, or its wearer from toppling over out of sheer top-heaviness.

Marie Antoinette was thrilled with what was called the "pouf" fashion, which was not only ornamented as just described, but often portrayed current events. Her trusted fashion consultant, milliner, and designer, the modist Rose Bertin (1747–1813), practically invented the pouf, which she created with the royal hairdresser Léonard Alexis Autier (1751–1820), whose *Memoirs* make fascinating reading. He interwove Marie Antoinette's real hair with false tresses, arranging it on a wool-padded wire fontange. He then stiffened the hair with pomade before powdering it. On this foundation, as on an artist's primed canvas, he would proceed to construct his elaborate works of art. One of his most famous conversation pieces was "The Inoculation," which she wore to celebrate Louis' smallpox vaccination. It displayed a serpent, the symbol of Aesculapius, the Greek god of medicine, wound around an olive tree, representing wisdom, and behind it was a golden rising sun, symbolizing the Sun King, common ancestor of the king and queen.

During the French Revolution, wigs continued to be worn even by some of the revolutionaries, most of whom switched to their own hair. After the revolution, natural hair for both men and women of all classes became the norm. Many men had short hair, meant originally to accommodate their wigs.

Among other unhygienic practices, hair was not usually washed or even combed, sometimes for months at a time, so that it was full of dust, lint, and dirt. And it was often infested with lice and other vermin, even at court. Women carried ornate, long-handled ivory or gold head-scratchers that they were obliged to use frequently. They also wore elaborate makeup, as did some men, and it stayed on, layer after layer, until it cracked or peeled off and had to be replaced. Sometimes, however, it was scraped and replaced daily. Since the chemicals used in its manufacture were usually toxic, all kinds of horrible skin and eye diseases resulted, which necessitated more makeup to hide the scars and pockmarks—also true of those who survived smallpox. Beauty patches in a number of shapes were also the fashion and were applied in strategic places—to set off a bright blue eye or a pert nose—after the rest of the makeup.

Both men and women wore fobbed, bejeweled pocket watches, women often wearing them on a ribbon around the neck or hanging from the waist. They also wore gloves, and it was the custom for a man to remove a glove when shaking hands. Women sometimes wore *mitts*, which were mittens with the tops of the fingers cut off; they could be of lace or plain material. Men wore plumed tricorn hats over their powdered wigs both indoors and out and raised them slightly to women or to a man of superior rank when they entered or left a room, or lifted them with a flourish and bowed, as circumstances demanded. Fur muffs were carried; in the Regency period, men as well as women used them.

Both men and women doused themselves with scent and carried handkerchiefs in their sleeves. They were obliged to hold the delicate lace and cambric, or linen, handkerchiefs, soaked with perfume, to their noses because of the noxious odors that surrounded them. In fact the use of the handkerchief is another hallmark of the style of this period: it could be twirled and flicked and flourished, and often was, to make a point. When removed from the sleeve, it was held between the second and third fingers, steadied by the thumb.

Both genders took snuff—those "pungent grains of titillating dust," as Alexander Pope called it in *The Rape of the Lock* (canto 5). One method was to place a pinch of snuff on the wrist or glove of the hand holding the snuffbox, then inhale it after raising the hand to the nostrils. When the snuffbox had been replaced in its pocket, any remaining snuff was flicked away with a handkerchief.

As a matter of fashion, the prince regent took snuff, but since he detested it, he only pretended to inhale it; he let it fall through his fingers and did not sneeze. If a gentleman offered the snuffbox to a woman, who would not be expected to carry one, she would flick open the lid, if this had not already been done, and take a pinch of snuff for each nostril, sneezing afterwards into a handkerchief. Samuel Rogers tells us about the artist Sir Joshua Reynolds (1723–1792): "What a quantity of snuff Sir Joshua took! I once saw him at an Academy-dinner, when his waistcoat was absolutely powdered with it."

In colonial North America, men carried snuffboxes and canes, and sometimes wore swords, although mostly on ceremonial occasions. Both genders wore hats and gloves when in public. Women also wore bonnets or *calashes*, which were hoodlike sunshades tied around the throat with ribbons; they could have a cape extending down the back of the neck. Older women wore linen or cotton caps indoors, but young, unmarried women did not. The fan was used for cooling purposes, and occasionally, no doubt, for coquettish ones, particularly at balls and dances.

In Europe, men carried elaborate jewel-headed canes, and in town they wore swords, but in England it was unusual for casual pedestrians to wear them: they were reserved for ceremonial occasions. Coats were slashed on the left side to allow the sword to pass through. It would be lifted slightly with the left hand when a man bowed, so as not to scrape against the floor. Men bowed from the waist, right hand held over the heart, left hand holding the sword. The fashion for dueling with swords, or pistols, on the slightest pretexts, was rife throughout the century. There were even dueling clubs in German universities, and it was considered an honor to have a scar on the cheek. But, finally, in 1792, the students of the University of Jena appealed for the abolition of dueling, and it was at about this time that, as a general rule, men stopped wearing swords.

In Europe, women's folding fans were sometimes doused with perfume as handkerchiefs usually were, and were often very ornately painted in the rococo fashion.

Known for his satirical publication *The Tatler*, Joseph Addison (1672–1719) was the English essayist who, along with that other redoubtable gossip and social critic, his close friend from boyhood on, Sir Richard Steele (1672–1729), founded the popular satirical journal *The Spectator* (published from 1711 to 1714). He wrote an essay in 1711 in *Spectator* number 102 called "Academy for the Instruction in the Use of the Fan"; as a supplement to his byline, he lists himself as "Author of 'Passions of the Fan.'" He tells us:

> Not to be tedious, if I only see the fan of a disciplined lady, I know very well whether she laughs, frowns, or blushes. I have seen a fan so very angry that it would have been dangerous for the absent lover who provoked it to come within the wind of it; and at other times so very languishing that I have been glad for the lady's sake the lover was at a sufficient distance from it.

Louis-Antoine, Marquis de Carracioli (1719–1803), author of *Le livre à la mode* (1759, The Fashionable Book), called the first chapter of *Le livre de quatre couleurs* (1757, The Book of Four Colors) "On the Different Ways of Using the Fan," and it is replete with irony. His extensive and facetious advice to young ladies includes the following, for occasions when "some important question" is raised:

> The fan is opened very negligently; and after having turned and turned it again, unfolded, back and forth between both hands, one fixes one's eyes upon it as if it were a book, and appears really to read what is said therein. Many ladies, by this stratagem alone, have appeared to be women of great sense and much reflection.

Should a young lady be approached by a young man with obviously seductive intentions, she must rap him "like lightning" soundly on the knuckles, the fan being folded. When an anecdote is being recounted, the fan must be used "like a pigeon's wing" and be constantly agitated, folding with a loud noise at the end of every sentence. And "all passions are painted" by using the fan correctly: To indicate jealousy, apply the lips to the tip of the fan, "holding it up like a candle, and not uttering a word." If you wish to show that you are bored, scratch the bottom of your ear with the fan and yawn. And you may easily spy on people through the interstices between the fan's blades.

Men and women carried toothpicks, which women kept in the tiny, ornate *reticules* (purses) many hung on their wrists. They would use the toothpicks behind their fans, as men would behind their handkerchiefs—if they were well mannered. Dentistry, except for pulling teeth, was in its infancy, and people had terrible, often highly discolored teeth, which were not brushed every day if they were ever brushed at all. By the end of the century, however, toothbrushes were in fashion, and a tooth powder made of sassafras and various dried, pulverized herbs was used.

Another common accessory was the *equipage*, also called an *etui*. Hooked onto the left side of a belt or at the waist, it was a small decorated case that could be quite ornamental, containing such necessaries as a toothpick case, scissors, tweezers, a pencil, a small knife, and a nail cleaner. Also hooked on were *pockets*, which were capacious drawstring bags, often embroidered.

Women sometimes carried parasols, and by the late 1780s, umbrellas were in use as well. In America, they had been used since the 1750s. Samuel Rogers tells us:

> During my youth umbrellas were far from common. At that time every gentleman's family had *one* umbrella,—a huge thing, made of coarse cotton,—which used to be taken out with the carriage, and which, if there was rain, the footman held over the ladies' heads, as they entered, or alighted from, the carriage.

In "A Description of a City Shower," Swift had written, back in 1710:

> The tuck'd up sempstress walks with hasty strides
> While streams run down her oil'd umbrella's sides

But since those days, the umbrella had fallen into disuse. Jonas Hanway (1712–1786), a philanthropist who agitated for the humane treatment of children and was instrumental in starting the Foundling Hospital, had been roundly mocked as an eccentric by passers-by, sedan chairmen, and cab drivers waiting for their fares during thundershowers, for carrying an umbrella when nobody else did. But finally, his efforts to reintroduce it were rewarded when everybody started using them.

Manners, Greetings and Salutations, Bows and Curtsies: Manners and politesse were high arts in an era when formality and elegant deportment reigned—taught by dancing masters hired to tutor young ladies and gentlemen and prepare them for their entrances into high society. Bows and curtsies were endlessly practiced, including the curtsey given to someone by inclining the body slightly to the right or left as one walked past.

The movement of the arms was freer than it had been in seventeenth-century coats, because the cuffs and lace ruffles, when worn, were not as huge. "Take particular care that the motions of your hands and arms be particularly graceful; for the genteelness of a man consists more in them than in anything else," Lord Chesterfield counsels his son in a missive dated May 2, 1751.

Men touched the front corner of their tricorn hats when passing each other in the streets and when greeting women, or raised them slightly. To persons of greater rank, men bowed by removing the tricorn hat with their left hand holding the front of the hat, lowering it elegantly and gracefully and turning the hat so that it faced outward, while bringing the right hand over the heart and bending slightly from the waist. After entering a house, if the hat were not taken by a servant, a man would hold it under his left arm, pressed to his side. Gloves would be removed and held as well. Men bowed twice: once on entering a room and, after taking one or two steps, again, to salute the assemblage. At a ball or reception, when moving through the room, men bowed or inclined the head slightly from side to side as a greeting. When leaving a room, two bows while moving backwards were customary, three if departing from the royal presence: Step to the right, and bring the left foot slightly forward, then bow from the waist, without bending the legs. Move the arm with the hat in it very slightly outwards from the body; the other hand touched the heart or not, as the person wished. Then take several steps backwards, and bow again. These movements should all be graceful, elegant, and small—nothing extravagant. Early in the nineteenth century, during the Regency, it was customary for men to bow slightly from the waist while holding both hands over the heart.

Women curtsied by grasping both sides of their gowns, putting one foot behind the other, and on very formal occasions, lowering themselves to the floor, while keeping the torso upright. They then also inclined their heads slightly before rising, again, keeping the torso in an upright position. But the usual gentle, graceful curtsey was a very slight one, using the same position of the legs just described and bending the knees as little as possible. As they passed through a room at a ball or reception, women might incline their heads almost impeceptibly to either side as a greeting to those they wished to acknowledge.

Court etiquette decreed absolute fastidiousness of manners and silent attention to the sovereigns. And as Frances Burney informs us, one dared not even cough: "If you find a cough tickling in your throat, you must arrest it from making any sound; if you find yourself choking with the forbearance, you must choke—but not cough." Nor, she says, must you sneeze, move, or spit, although you may bite the inside of your cheek or lip to relieve any agony you may be feeling, provided nobody realizes you are doing so.

Servants curtsied slightly or bowed, inclining the head, on entering a room and on addressing their masters. In act 1 of Oliver Goldsmith's (1728–1774) *She Stoops to Conquer*, the provincial country Squire Hardcastle is expecting sophisticated guests from London. He desperately wants to impress them, but he feels he needs more servants in order to do so, so he attempts to train some peasant boys, dressed in their work clothes, to be domestics. This hilarious scene is full of slapstick farce reminiscent of its commedia dell'arte roots. The satire of sophisticated town manners versus those of boorish if well-meaning country bumpkins is very much part of the class and social prejudices of the day. It is obvious from the dialogue that the classes fraternize with each other in the country as they did not do in town, and that nevertheless Hardcastle is clearly the master, entitled to give orders and accustomed to being obeyed. And the squire is scarcely more cultivated than the peasant boys he wishes to train, which is also part of the humor: his pose as a sophisticate rings false, but amusingly so, much like Molière's well-meaning, insecure, bourgeois would-be gentleman.

Loud laughter, loud talking, gesticulation, and boisterous, raucous manners, all associated with the lower classes, had been generally warned against since medieval days. Lord Chesterfield tells Philip, in a letter dated March 9, 1748:

> True wit, or sense, never yet made anybody laugh; they are above it: they please the mind and give a cheerfulness to the countenance...how low and unbecoming a thing laughter is: not to mention the disagreeable noise that it makes, and the shocking distortion of the face that it occasions.

Living Spaces and Furniture: There is little change in living spaces to be noted for the eighteenth and early nineteenth centuries from what preceded them in the seventeenth, except that the newer houses tended to be roomier. Middle-class houses in the town, more cramped and less comfortable than those in the country and with smaller rooms, were usually well lit and well furnished, with comfortable, upholstered chairs that had slender, gracefully curved legs. Beds were usually curtained. Clothing was stored in chests and armoires. Furniture was lighter in its lines and imitated Greco-Roman models during the Napoleonic period, superseding the ornate rococo Louis XV and Louis XVI styles.

In London, where the teeming river traffic on the Thames continued to play a central role in the life of the city, there were more than twenty landing places for passenger boats, and new squares and larger houses were built as the city expanded. A typical one-family English city house had a cellar; a kitchen on the ground floor, together with pantries; and perhaps some servants' rooms. The dining room, sitting room, and perhaps a library or office was on the second floor; the family bedrooms, with washstands and, in larger houses, dressing rooms, on a third floor; and the servants' quarters on the fourth, with attics above. In larger establishments and in the country, the stable boys might sleep in the stable and the grooms over the stables. The butler's and head housekeeper's rooms were a bit roomier than those of the other servants, but still quite sparsely furnished, with a single bed, a table and chair, and a washstand. Their clothing was stored in a trunk.

In America, many houses in smaller towns had two stories, with bedrooms on the second floor. But in the larger cities, they could be as elaborate as those in Britain or France, where the townhouses of the wealthy could have three wings with sprawling apartments on several floors. The house and gardens were enclosed by a high wall pierced only by a carriage gate leading into the courtyard in front of the house.

There was little indoor plumbing, and we have already seen what hygiene and waste disposal were like. Toilet chairs with chamber pots in them were used indoors, as were chamber pots all by themselves, usually kept under a bed and covered with a cloth. Slops were emptied out the window into city streets, as they had been for centuries.

Food and Table Manners: Eighteenth-century meals and banquets in all the courts of Europe were just as elaborate, formal, and lavish for the upper classes as they had been under Louis XIV. But in Britain, the monarchs dined in private; George II had tried to institute public banquets in the French manner, but this quickly grew wearisome—particularly as the monarchy was a constitutional one—and the custom was abandoned. George III and Queen Charlotte, known for their frugality, always dined in private.

But in France the custom of the *Grand Couvert* continued, with the modification that Louis XVI and Marie Antoinette dined in public at nine o'clock, with the same elaborate ceremony, but once a week. The public was now invited on Sundays, and there were tiered seats for them to sit in, as if they were at a theater. Marie Antoinette disliked being stared at, so she only pretended she was eating, and her real meal came later in her own private rooms. In his diary, the future second president of the United States—John Adams (1735–1826), who was at Versailles many times—relates that he watched the king and queen at the *Grand Couvert* on Sunday, June 7, 1778, where he "had a fine seat and situation close by the royal family, and had a distinct and full view of the royal pair":

> The King was the royal carver for himself and all his family. His Majesty ate like a king, and made a royal supper of solid beef, and other things in proportion. The Queen took a large spoonful of soup, and displayed her fine person and graceful manners, in alternately looking at the company in various parts of the hall, and ordering several kinds of seasoning to be brought to her, by which she fitted her supper to her taste.

Table manners had taken a turn for the better, and people now used their forks instead of their hands to spear what they wished to eat from the great serving platters. They might still sometimes use the tablecloth as a napkin, but they were more fastidious in their conduct, more decorous in how they ate. Chocolate, tea, and coffee for afternoon parties in middle-class and aristocratic households were brought in on trays in ornate rococo pots and served with cream and sugar—a cup handed to each individual guest, along with such refreshments as brioches or other pastries, in a ritual that would graduate to become the Victorian tea party.

And in France it was an age of great gourmets, as the aristocrats themselves took to cooking as a hobby. All kinds of sauces were invented, including mayonnaise. And the potato became popular at this time, due to the good offices of the pharmacist Antoine-Augustin Parmentier (1737–1813), who, in a bit of historical irony, considering the devastating potato famine that was so catastrophic for Ireland in the mid-nineteenth century, extolled its virtues as a replacement for grain in times of famine. Beef was the most prized meat, usually available only to the rich.

The art of viticulture was really coming into its own, with the great wines of Bordeaux and Burgundy dominating the scene, along with champagne, sherry, port, and Madeira. Dishes were given the names of illustrious patrons: filet of sole Pompadour, for instance, named for Louis XV's mistress, was stuffed with mushrooms and truffles, then lightly poached in champagne and served garnished with shelled crayfish.

Louis XV preferred intimate little suppers with his mistresses to the *Grand Couvert*, and these soon became all the rage among the courtiers. Tables were set on the floor below the king's dining room, and then the table was raised on a trapdoor elevator through an opening in the floor. When the dish was finished, the table was lowered again and set with the next course. This style of dining would be repeated by King Ludwig II (1843–1886) of Bavaria, who had such elevators installed in his palace of Herrenchiemsee, an imitation of Versailles. He usually had more than one place set, since he fancied he was dining with such august figures as Louis XIV, who had been dead for more than 100 years but apparently retained his hearty appetite.

Unlike his grandfather, Louis XVI did not have a discriminating palate, but he loved to eat. And he was famously obese, like his brother Louis XVIII, who was so fat that he had to resort to a wheelchair to get around. Louis XVIII was a great gourmet, as well as a glutton and an amateur cook. As Alexandre Dumas informs us in his *Grand Dictionary of Cuisine*, the king invented such extravagant dishes as this version of charcoal-grilled lamb chops: three thick chops were tied together and grilled, then the two outer chops were discarded, and only the one in the center was eaten. Napoleon was his exact opposite: although the food at his court was sumptuous, he didn't care about it, and according to several memoirs by people who knew him intimately, he seldom spent more than twenty minutes at table and even then grew impatient.

In aristocratic and royal circles, dinner service was of gold and silver and ornately decorated porcelain plates and platters. In the kitchens of the Prince of Wales, Marie-Antoine Carême (1784–1833), the great French chef who served him at his ornate toy house, the Pavillion at Brighton (now a delightful museum), invented various sauces, refined French haute cuisine, and engineered mountains of shellfish and poultry into sculptures. But the middle classes and the poor had no such luxuries, of course, and ate from pewter or wooden plates using iron or steel cutlery.

Whether in the palace or the town or country house, kitchen fireplaces were used for cooking: meat was roasted on spits, and kettles were placed on trivets over hot coals arranged on the broad hearths to cook stews, pan fry meat or potatoes, or boil vegetables. Everything, of course, had to be done from scratch, as in previous centuries.

Eighteenth-Century English Rural Life as Seen by Parson James Woodforde (1740–1803): Reverend James Woodforde's *The Diary of a Country Parson* is full of rich stories of his days at Oxford, of his occasional travels by coach and stays at inns, and of homely details about the life and inhabitants of the village of Weston Longeville, Norfolk, where he was rector and kept a farm of eight acres. The un-self-conscious but worldly Woodforde was lacking in vanity, and he wrote his diary without any intention of having it published. The phrase with which he begins so many entries is a kind of signature, like Pepys's constant ending, "And so to bed": "We breakfasted, dined, &c. again at home." When we read the diary of this charitable and gently placid man—who led the kind of life so many people lived, as the seasons for seeding, growing and harvesting succeeded each other year after year— we are transported back in time to a tranquil island of peace in the midst of a world that in all his days knew only endless war. But even that small village was, of course, deeply affected by events elsewhere, as well as by the local heartaches and tragedies of illness, death, and accident. On January 25, 1783, the parson is able to rejoice at a rare event: "This Evening the Ipswich News brought us the joyful news of peace being signed at Versailles," ending the American War of Independence.

Even people of modest means could afford servants. The entry for December 2, 1766 reads:

> Luke Barnard came to live with me as a servant this day. I am to give him per annum three pounds, a coat and waistcoat and hat besides victuals and drink, washing and lodging.

By way of comparison, the parson had been offered a curacy at £40 per annum; a new wig cost him £1, and a new suit £4.

On Christmas day in 1773, Woodforde dined at the Hall at New College, Oxford, of which he was subwarden; one of his jobs was to order the meals:

> We had for dinner, two fine Codds boiled with fryed Souls round them and oyster sauce, a fine sirloin of Beef roasted, some peas soup and an orange Pudding for the first course, for the second, we had a lease of Wild Ducks roasted, a fore Qu: of lamb and sallad and mince Pies. . . . After the second course there was a fine Plumb cake.

They also drank each others' health in a "grace cup" that was passed around, and wished each other "a merry Xmas." They could certainly put food and drink away in those days! Throughout the diary's pages, meals are described, and uncountable bottles of wine and port are imbibed by all and sundry, including the good parson.

A kindly man, who describes with compassion the conditions in the local poorhouses, Woodforde lived in an age that could mete out brutal justice—there were 222 capital offences on the books. On July 22, 1777, he "would not contribute one Farthing" to help defray costs for the hangman (it was usual practice to take up a collection to pay that official) to whip "Robert Biggen, for stealing potatoes...through the streets of Cary [in Somerset]...at the end of a cart."

On April 15, 1778, the parson "Brewed a vessell of strong Beer today":

> My two large Piggs, by drinking some Beer grounds taking out of one of my Barrels today, got so amazingly drunk by it, that they were not able to stand and appeared like dead things almost, and so remained all night from dinner time today. I never saw Piggs so drunk in my life.

> April 16: My 2 Piggs are still unable to walk yet, but they are better than they were yesterday. They tumble about the yard and can by no means stand at all steady yet. In the afternoon my 2 Piggs were tolerably sober.

On August 4, 1789—"Dies Memorabilis"—he, members of his family, and friends made a special trip in a small procession of carriages and phaetons to Sherborne, a nearby town, especially to gawk at the "Royal Family":

> After they had taken some refreshment, they all walked upon the Terrace before the Crowd. We were all very near indeed to them, the King [George III] looked very red and is very tall and erect, The Queen and Princesses rather short but very pleasing Countenances and fair.... The King was in his Windsor Uniform, blue coat with red Cape and Cuffs to the Sleeves, with a plain round Hat with a black Ribband round it, The Queen was in a purple Silk, and white Bonnett, the Princesses all in Pink Silk, and white Bonnetts.

Thomas Turner (1729–1793), Pillar of the Community: Thomas Turner was a very busy shopkeeper in East Hoathly, Sussex. At his general store, he sold everything from tools, cloth, needles, clothing, gloves, and hats to flour, salt, and other foodstuffs; and he worked as a schoolteacher, occasional barber, highway surveyor, informal banker, and undertaker. He sold insurance, for the Sun Fire Insurance Company, and he sold goods wholesale as well as retail: sheep fleeces in quantity, rags to a paper factory. He was present, too, on February 14, 1756, at the auction by candle of a house: a candle was lit, and people placed bids; the last person to bid when the flame went out was the buyer.

Turner's *Diary*, which he kept from 1754 to 1765 (only about a third of it has ever been published), brings the village and its inhabitants, their concerns, relationships, quarrels, celebrations, and carryings-on vividly to life. Turner describes what he did every day and tells us about his daily expenditures, the books he read, the food he ate, the many people with whom he came into contact, his relationships with his family (not always good), his quarrels with his wife (about which he gets very emotional), the tragic death of his infant son, and the medical treatments he underwent.

For over a week, starting on Wednesday, September 10, 1755, he suffered from a terribly painful inflammation of the eye. On Monday, September 22, one of his doctors paid a house call and "ordered a poultice of conserve of roses, and about 6 gr. of champhire [camphor] in each poultice, to be laid to my eye, with purging twice a week with sal. glabuler [Glauber's salt, a laxative: sodium sulfate decahydrate; named for the seventeenth-century chemist who discovered it] and manna." This was quite aside from several bleedings he was subjected to. Such remedies were hardly more effective than the cure-all nostrums sold at country fairs by mountebanks, whom Turner derides and his wife patronizes.

Turner was a great observer of life and an avid reader of newspapers and periodicals, and he made frequent business trips, of which he provides many details. In addition, we have a very real psychological picture of a kindly, pessimistic, sensitive, touchy, insecure man who suffered from bouts of depression and attempted to control his drinking, for which he often seriously reproached himself—"I do think I am prodigiously silly and apish when I am in liquor."

Well read himself, he had a great respect for the learning of others, and he was much impressed on August 22, 1755, to meet a young man whom he considered a great scholar, who spoke Greek and Latin fluently and was able to quote famous contemporary authors from memory. The young man also wrote beautifully in different styles of calligraphy and knew shorthand, which had been devised in the seventeenth century by

Jeremiah Rich (d. 1667?), who wrote two books on the subject. In 1727 James Weston's (1688–1751) *Stenography Compleated* set out a system of shorthand that also proved very popular. Both Weston's and Rich's systems were in current use.

A member of his parish council, Turner attended vestry meetings and participated on March 24, 1763, in the debate over arranging the poor rate—a quota (percentage) of the members' rents (income), determined every year by each parish on its own (there was no general social security) and earmarked for the care of the community's poor:

> We stayed till near 1 o'clock quarreling and bickering about nothing and in the end hardly did any business. . . . I blush to say what artifice and deceit, cunning and knavery there was used by some (who would think it cruel and unjust to be called dishonest) to conceal their rents, and who yet would pretend the justice of an equal taxation was their desire.

On April 6, he arranged a delicate matter on behalf of the parish: a friend of Turner's, Edward Hope (d. 1766)—a farmer in his seventies, a widower, and like Turner, an active member of the church—agreed to exempt the parish from all expenses for the child he had fathered on his young servant girl, Catherine Jenner. Like another gentleman Turner describes, Mr. Hope had had an "insurrection of an unruly member, which might prompt him to make his advances to her." So-called illegitimacy was a terrible stigma, even though kings recognized and ennobled their "illegitimate" children. Despite his brilliance and amazing achievements, Alexander Hamilton, for example, born out of wedlock and orphaned at an early age, suffered all his life from the handicap of his status as a "bastard."

Dorothy Wordsworth (1771–1855): Dorothy was the sister of the poet William Wordsworth (1770–1850) and as much a romantic as he. They rented Alfoxden, a mansion in Somerset, for a year, from July 1797 to June 1798, in order to be near William's friend, the poet Samuel Taylor Coleridge (1772–1834); and Dorothy kept a journal at their home in Grasmere from 1800 to 1803.

The Grasmere and Alfoxden Journals are notable for their descriptions of nature, couched in beautiful, poetic prose, and for Dorothy's deep sensitivity. Her portraits of people, the rhythms of her daily life, and the depiction of her brother writing his poetry are all evocative of an era when people could be with each other without the distractions of the telephone or television. It took a long time to get anywhere, and communication with people far away was difficult, particularly in rough weather, even if they lived only a mile or two down the road. Reading these diaries, we can feel what it was like to live back then, in a techno-logically more primitive age, when it was hard to get warm on a freez-ing winter's day even with the help of a roaring fire and a hot cup of tea—and also experience how wonderfully close people could feel to each other.

On May 15, 1800, she, William, and their brother John set off on a long walk. John Wordsworth (1772–1805) was a sea captain, who drowned along with most of his crew when his ship, the *Earl of Aber-gavenny*, was driven in a storm onto the treacherous Shambles Bank, off Portland Bill near Portsmouth, on the eve of his departure on another voyage. He had made the arduous sea trip to Bengal and China in the 1790s and entertained Chinese royalty on board. He visited his brother and sister whenever he could. They saw him for the last time in London in September 1802. On that May day in 1800, the brothers were going to visit friends on a farm farther along, and Dorothy walked the five miles back home by herself, as she had planned to do:

> Wm & John set off into Yorkshire after dinner at ½ past 2 o'clock—cold pork in their pockets. I left them at the turning of the Low-wood bay under the trees. My heart was so full that I could hardly speak to W when I gave him a farewell kiss. I sate a long time on a stone at the margin of the lake, & after a flood of tears my heart was easier. The lake looked to me I knew not why dull and melancholy, the wel-tering of the shores seemed a heavy sound. I walked as long as I could among the stones of the shore. The wood rich in flowers.

Social Dancing: Fancy dress balls were very popular in all classes, and the wearing of masks was a deliberately intriguing custom at such gath-erings. The graceful minuet was one of the principle dances. It was very formal: the top half of the body was held steady, while only the legs and feet moved. Its principle step consisted of bending both knees slightly and moving forward, first on the right foot and then on the left, while rising on the toes, the legs being brought together and the heels dropped simultaneously.

You can see an excellent example of another important dance of the period, the gavotte, in the elaborate court ball scene in the 1938 film *Marie Antoinette* and in the engagement ball of the Dauphin and the Dauphine in the 2006 *Marie Antoinette*.

Samuel Rogers relates the following anecdote about Richard Nash (1674–1772), called Beau Nash, a well-known dandy and arbiter of fashion. He was responsible for introducing less formal manners at the balls and spas of Bath, where he wanted all social classes to enjoy themselves, and which, thanks to him, became the most fashionable resort in the eighteenth and early nineteenth centuries, as the novels of Jane Austen attest:

> Beau Nash was once dancing a minuet at Bath with a Miss Lunn. She was so long of giving him *both her hands* (the figure by which the lady, when she thinks proper, brings the performance to a close), that he lost all patience, and, suiting the words to the tune (which was *Marshall Saxe's minuet*), he sung out, as she passed him,—
>
> > "Miss Lunn, Miss Lunn,
> > Will you never have done?"

The minuet followed by a contredanse was a common sequence in middle-class dance halls. The *contredanse* was a country dance usually performed with the partners facing each other in two long lines, but the term is general enough to admit of any number of different dances. This includes movements still done in American square dancing, such as the do-si-do, in which partners circle around with their backs to each other. A *ländler* (country dance) is a slow contredanse that includes spinning the partner around and rhythmic clapping. The *cotillion* was popular in the colonies: it is a kind of square dance, and partners changed often as the dancers went round.

Painting

The genre paintings of Jean-Baptiste Greuze (1725–1805), while vigorous and fresh, can be rather melodramatic. On the other hand, the genre paintings of Jean-Baptiste Siméon Chardin (1699–1779), one of the very greatest eighteenth-century artists and quite opposed to the rococo school, are realistic and not sentimental. The flowery rococo fantasies of Jean Antoine Watteau (1684–1721), Jean Honoré Fragonard (1732–1806), and François Boucher (1703–1770) give a highly romanticized picture of the age and were anathema to Chardin. Antonio Canaletto's (1697–1768) detailed, crisply painted cityscapes of Venice and London show what the environment was like, although they are considerably cleaned up. And the splendid, gorgeously painted portraits by Thomas Gainsborough (1727–88) and Sir Joshua Reynolds in England, and by John Trumbull (1756–1843) and Gilbert Stuart (1755–1828)—as well as the engravings of Paul Revere (1735–1818) and the paintings of Benjamin West (1738–1820) in America—tell us not only about how clothing looked, draped, and felt but also about the attitudes of the sitters and how they wished to be seen. Reynolds's portraits of the Prince of Wales, General Burgoyne, Boswell, Samuel Johnson, Sarah Siddons, and Garrick are superb studies and full of character.

In France, the classical paintings—among them *The Oath of the Horatii* and *The Death of Socrates*—of Jacques-Louis David (1748–1825), who spans the Revolutionary, Napoleonic, and Bourbon Restoration periods, show us that the Republicans wished to be seen as people of austere principle reviving the ancient republics of Athens and Rome. David's dramatic paintings of contemporary scenes, from the "Tennis Court Oath" that saw the birth of the French Revolution to the crowning of Napoleon, are as invaluable as a photographic record would have been.

For both satire and realism, look at the works of William Hogarth (1697–1764) and the engravings of the caricaturists Thomas Rowlandson (1756–1827) and James Gillray (1757–1815).

Music

The period of classical music lasts from around 1740 through the early part of the nineteenth century, overlapping with and replacing the baroque. It is characterized by harmonic complexity and set forms that nevertheless allowed for expansive thematic and melodic development.

Georg Friedrich Handel (1685–1759), born in Germany, emigrated to England during the reign of Queen Anne, and on the accession of his former sovereign the Elector of Hanover to the British throne as King George I (1660–1727), he was granted an annual pension of £600. In the course of his amazingly long career, he composed innumerable operas in the late baroque style, but he is perhaps best known as the composer of the dramatic oratorio the *Messiah* (1741) and the *Water Music* (ca. 1717), meant to accompany the royal procession of barges on the Thames. In the *Messiah* are typical examples of the baroque and early classical stylistic conventions that Handel brought to perfection, such as the use of trumpets and drums together to symbolize power, victory, and triumph. And the accompaniment to the famous bass aria, "Why do the people so furiously rage," is in the *stile concitato* (agitated style), which is a series of oscillating sixteenth notes representing passion and seething unrest—in this case, with brilliant, throbbing violins. The Austrian Franz Josef Haydn, (1732–1809)—known as "Papa" Haydn to many, including Mozart, to whom he was a great friend and mentor—was one of the most prolific composers, with symphonies, masses, concertos, and chamber music to his credit. The Italian Luigi Boccherini (1743–1805) composed very charming lyrical music. He is best known for his Minuet in A, used to great effect in the hilarious Alec Guinness comedy *The Ladykillers* (1955).

But of all the eighteenth-century composers, the preeminent and most loved is, of course, Wolfgang Amadeus Mozart. There is no more sprightly or more serious composer, nor one more loving and generous of heart (even if he could sometimes be a difficult person), and if you want to awaken a real feeling for the eighteenth century, listen to his endlessly evocative music. For a romantic interpretation, you might enjoy the later symphonies conducted, with the lush orchestral textures brought out, by Bruno Walter; for a leaner, sparer, more classical approach, try Otto Klemperer's recordings. And listen especially to his operas, particularly *Don Giovanni* and *The Marriage of Figaro*, which show the moral and sexual attitudes of the age, with rising disapproval of libertinage. The libretti were written by the Venetian Jewish convert to Catholicism Lorenzo da Ponte (1749–1838), who ended his life in New York as a professor of Italian at Columbia University. His memoirs, like Casanova's, make fascinating reading.

In the book of essays that Mark A. Radice edited, *Opera in Context* (Amadeus Press, 1998), there is an essay by Malcolm S. Cole entitled "Mozart and Two Theaters," in which Cole describes Wye J. Allanbrook's analysis of Figaro's aria "Se vuol ballare" (If You Want to Dance): the rhythmic choices Mozart ingeniously made in composing it reflect the dance-hall sequence of the minuet followed by a contredanse, which would have been familiar to his audiences, although it is lost on most of us today.

The infamous "droit du seigneur" (the right of the lord to sleep with the bride of one of his peasants or servants on the wedding night, before the groom sleeps with her) is at the heart of Pierre Caron de Beaumarchais' (1732–1799) revolutionary play *The Marriage of Figaro*, as it is of da Ponte's adaptation. Beaumarchais' two plays about Figaro, *The Barber of Seville* and *The Marriage of Figaro*, provide a very real picture of the period and represent a literary protest against the prevailing class system. He was persona non grata among the aristocracy.

Perhaps the greatest composer of the early romantic age was Ludwig van Beethoven (1770–1827), with his nine symphonies, five piano concertos, one violin concerto, string trios, and quartets. His only opera is *Fidelio*, but it is one of the greatest and most moving ever written. Like his symphonies, it tells of his passionate yearning for freedom. The tempestuous, temperamental composer—who was suffering from increasing deafness by the time he composed his Sixth Symphony, known as the "Pastoral"—was an emotional supporter of the ideals of the French Revolution and a great admirer of Napoleon as the embodiment and exporter of those ideals. He composed his Third Symphony, called the "Eroica," in Napoleon's honor, but he excoriated him and cursed his name when the Corsican adventurer crowned himself emperor, revealing his true nature and his arrogant, overweening desire for power at the expense of those ideals.

Literature

A growing humanitarianism and sense of humaneness was characteristic of the eighteenth century. We see it in the diarists Woodforde, Turner, and Dorothy Wordsworth, for example, and it is reflected in the century's literature in such characters as Squire Allworthy in Henry Fielding's (1707–1754) *Tom Jones*, written in 1749. Fielding's novels depict the life of the era extensively and with a broad range that no other English novelist of the period has. He was also known as a humane magistrate, and he helped run an effective private London police force—Fielding's "runners"—in an era when there was still no regular police.

In chapter 155 of *Tom Jones*, the eponymous hero of the novel—together with his landlady, Mrs. Miller, and his friend, the pedagogue Partridge—go to see Garrick in *Hamlet*. But for Partridge, "the little man" Garrick's acting in *Hamlet* is not wonderful, because it is so lifelike:

> Jones asked him, "Which of the players he had liked best?" To this he answered, with some appearance of indignation at the question, "The king, without doubt." "Indeed, Mr. Partridge," says Mrs. Miller, "you are not of the same opinion with the town; for they are all agreed, that Hamlet is acted by the best player who ever was on the stage." "He the best player!" cries Partridge, with a contemptuous sneer, "why, I could act as well as he myself. I am sure, if I had seen a ghost, I should have looked in the very same manner, and

done just as he did. And then, to be sure, in that scene, as you called it, between him and his mother, where you told me he acted so fine, why, Lord help me, any man, that is, any good man, that had such a mother, would have done exactly the same. I know you are only joking with me; but indeed, madam, though I was never at a play in London, yet I have seen acting before in the country; and the king for my money; he speaks all his words distinctly, half as loud again as the other. Anybody may see he is an actor."

Of great literary and historical importance are the novels of Samuel Richardson (1689–1761, *Pamela*); that unique book *Tristram Shandy* by Laurence Sterne (1713–1768); the novels of Daniel Defoe (1639?–1731; *Robinson Crusoe*, *Moll Flanders*); and the satirical poetry and prose of Jonathan Swift, who condemned pretension, indifference, and obtuseness with trenchant sarcasm and scornful animosity. His masterpiece, *Gulliver's Travels*, is anything but the mild piece of children's literature for which it is often taken. The Scottish writer Tobias Smollett's novel, *The Expedition of Humphrey Clinker*, affords a unique look at the life of the period, as Squire Bramble and his family journey around England, meeting Humphrey on the way. He is of lowly origin, as they would have said back then, and attaches himself to the travelers as a servant. The Penguin Classics edition is well annotated.

For the notorious libertine side of the age, read the books of the Marquis de Sade (1740–1814), among them *Justine*. Having renounced his titles and privileges during the French Revolution, he survived because he had been one of the prisoners in the Bastille when it was taken on July 14, 1789. Imprisoned again anyway during the Reign of Terror, he was saved from execution only by Robespierre's timely demise. The revolution over, he was no longer plain Citizen Sade but once again the Marquis, and he insisted on his noble prerogatives.

And do read Voltaire's (1694–1778) most famous book, *Candide*, even more famous perhaps to modern audiences as Bernstein's musical comedy of the same name. Voltaire was an enigma and full of contradictions: brilliant, yet filled with the most vile prejudices, especially anti-Semitism, despite the outspoken stand in favor of human liberty that made him a favorite symbol of Enlightenment in France during the revolution he never lived to see. He had an odd sort of symbiotic relationship with Frederick the Great, King of Prussia (b. 1712)—the largest and most powerful of more than two hundred German states, dukedoms, and principalities—ensconced in Potsdam from 1740 until his death in 1786 at his misnamed palace, Sans Souci (Without a Care). As Bruscambille (1610–1634), a well-known Parisian farceur and mountebank, remarked, for the poor, life could be "une vie sans soucis et quelquefois sans six sous" (a life without care and sometimes without six cents). Persona non grata in France, Voltaire, the dry, acerbic anti-monarchist, stayed there for many years, bored and resentful but determined to take full advantage of the situation.

Very influential in terms of his impact on the revolutionists' thought was Jean-Jacques Rousseau, who died in the same year as Voltaire. Born in Geneva, he spent most of his life in Paris. He wrote the articles on music and political economy for Diderot's *Encyclopedia*, but he is chiefly remembered for his *Confessions*; his romantic novels, such as *Emile, or A Treatise on Education*; and especially for *The Social Contract*, the last two of which were published in 1762. In *The Social Contract*, he maintained that political power resides in the people, and he famously wrote, "L'homme naît libre, mais il vit avec des menottes" (literally: Man is born free, but he lives with handcuffs; usually translated "everywhere he is in chains.") And in his *Discourse on the Sciences and the Arts* (1750), he wrote, "Man is naturally good and happy; it is society that corrupts him and makes him unhappy." The Paris Parlement condemned *Emile* for its ideas on religious dogma, and he was forced to flee, but he was eventually able to return to Paris, where he died after finishing his *Confessions*.

The plays of Oliver Goldsmith and Richard Brinsley Sheridan's *The Rivals* and *The School for Scandal* are important, not only as pictures of the period's manners and mores, but also for the natural, conversational tone of their dialogue. They are also full of those theatrical conventions the aside, the soliloquy, and the eavesdropping scene, such as the one where characters hide behind a screen in *The School for Scandal*.

Among the books you should read if you are doing a play set in this period are the previously mentioned *Life of Samuel Johnson* by James Boswell, published in 1791, and most especially, Boswell's diaries, which give a brilliant, detailed picture of the era.

Lord Chesterfield's *Letters to His Son*, quoted throughout this chapter—meant to educate him in the ways of the world and to teach him how to conduct himself to greatest advantage—are also a goldmine of information on the attitudes, etiquette, and manners of the period, in part because his advice is so conventional. But Samuel Johnson, who had applied unsuccessfully for Chesterfield's patronage, held the letters in the deepest contempt, as teaching "the morals of a whore and the manners of a dancing-master." After Johnson's famous dictionary was published, Chesterfield, who had refused to help finance it, wrote two public letters recommending it. But it was a case of too little, too late, and the embittered Johnson, who always bore grudges, wrote a scathing letter telling him so. Among his other detractors was the acerbic fourth Earl of Oxford, Horace Walpole (1717–1797), who seldom had a good word to say about anybody; he loathed Samuel Johnson. He liked and admired Colley Cibber though, and he deplored Pope's attacks on him. Walpole thought Chesterfield arrogant, ungallant, and not witty, despite the reputation for cleverness of which Chesterfield boasted. Walpole's correspondence, prime source material for this period, fills forty-two volumes, and he was the author of the Gothic horror novel *The Castle of Otranto*, among many other works.

The sprightly, romantic comedies of Pierre Carlet de Chamblain de Marivaux (1688–1763)—who made no attempt to examine, let alone criticize, the class system—were much in vogue, with their lighthearted, commedia dell'arte approach to love and the airy persiflage of their dialogue. In fact, so popular were they that they gave rise to a word especially describing them, *marivaudage*. Marivaux's plays were as well known to the French-speaking theater public as Sheridan's and Goldsmith's were to the English.

Be sure to read Joseph Addison's essays from *The Tatler*, and the work of those boon companions and writing partners Addison and Richard Steele's *The Spectator*, in which they created the character of the naïve, pompous country squire Sir Roger de Coverly, through whose eyes we see the world. The essays in *The Spectator* are an invaluable source for the behavior, hierarchy, manners, customs, and style of the early eighteenth century.

If you need to know about the arts and crafts of the period, look in Diderot's *Encyclopedia*, which is copiously illustrated. The Dover Pictorial Archive series has published a particularly useful selection in two volumes under the title *A Diderot Encyclopedia of Trades and Industry* (Dover Publications; reprint edition, 1993), with 485 illustrations. They cover everything from agriculture and the art of war to fashion, paper making, and miscellaneous trades. There is also a volume of *The Architectural Plates from the Encyclopédie* (Dover Publications, 1995).

The epistolary psychological novel *Dangerous Liaisons* by Pierre Choderlos de Laclos (1741–1803), published in 1782, portrays the sorts of manners and sexual intrigues prevalent in the French aristocracy, in an age when emotional professions of love, fainting fits, and sobbing marathons were the rule for both genders. Copious tears were considered the mark of true affection, heralding the rise of the romantics in the next century—as did the phenomenally popular sentimental outpourings of the medieval Irish poet-warrior Ossian, whose newly rediscovered poems were a hoax perpetrated by one James Macpherson (1736–1796).

Three psychologically astute, superbly plotted nineteenth-century novels about the French Revolution are eminently worth reading: Victor Hugo's *Ninety-Three*, about the counterinsurrection in the Vendée; Anatole France's *The Gods Are A-thirst*, about the Reign of Terror; and Balzac's first novel, *Les Chouans*, written in 1829, also about the counterrevolution and its aftermath (the Chouans are the counterrevolutionaries).

For life in the United States and the ferment of political ideas, look into the journals, papers, letters, and other works of the founding fathers: Washington, Franklin—especially his well known *Autobiography*—Jefferson, and John Adams, as well as those of James Madison (1751–1836) and Alexander Hamilton. Of primary importance for the mentality of the period are the pamphlets and papers of the ardent revolutionary Thomas Paine (1737–1809).

The German Enlightenment saw the dramas and philosophical works of Gotthold Ephraim Lessing (1729–1781). A great humanist and rationalist, Lessing was also an important aesthetician. The humanitarian writer Johann Wolfgang von Goethe (1749–1832) was producing his masterpieces, among them the long narrative dramatic poem *Faust*. Goethe was a genius, a kind of Renaissance man who studied science and philosophy and was a rationalist critic as well as a romantic poet and storyteller. And Friedrich Schiller (1759–1805) was penning his emotionally searing verse dramas, such as *William Tell* and *Don Carlos*, both of which speak of the longing for freedom and democracy. His poems were almost instantly famous, and one of them, "An der Friede" (Ode to Peace), changed by the censors to "An der Freude" (Ode to Joy), was set to music by Beethoven in the finale to his Ninth Symphony.

Precursive of romanticism was Goethe's 1772 novel *The Sorrows of Young Werther*, in which the sensitive, artistic young hero, disappointed in love, commits suicide—almost on the model of the English "gothic" revivalist poet, Thomas Chatterton (1752–1770), who claimed to have discovered fifteenth-century poetry that he had actually written himself and who ended his own life by swallowing arsenic. There is a famous painting by Joseph Severn (1793–1879) of a rather androgynous Chatterton stretched out on his deathbed. Incidentally, it was thanks to Goethe,

Schiller, and other great German authors that it became respectable to write in German.

In the beautiful city of Weimar, a great cultural center, Goethe directed plays at the Weimar Court Theater and wrote an essay, "Rules for Actors," based largely on his observations of the people he worked with or saw in performance; he published it in 1808. The rules mostly concern pronunciation, recitation, and declamation; posture and movement; as well as rehearsal procedures. They are revealing of the performance practice of some actors of the era, but they are not exactly helpful to modern actors wanting to create a role. For one thing, he opposed realism in the theater and preferred the declamatory style for poetic verse drama.

The age of romanticism begins in the age of classicism, with, among other literary productions, Scottish poet James Thomson's (1700–1748) *The Seasons*, and even with Thomas Gray's (1716–1771) "Elegy in a Country Churchyard," which General Wolfe recited while standing in the prow of the boat that was taking him up the St. Lawrence river to his doom on the Plains of Abraham outside Quebec: "The paths of glory / Lead but to the grave." One could hardly imagine a more romantic gesture. And then there is the extravagant and wonderful Regency-era poet, George Gordon (Lord Byron), and the other great romantic poets. These include William Wordsworth, known for his naturalistic but romantic lyrics and simple, deceptively straightforward style; his great friend Samuel Taylor Coleridge, one of whose masterpieces is *The Rime of the Ancient Mariner*; and the mystical artist-poet William Blake (1757–1827); the lyric and sensual John Keats (1725–1821); and the passionate and political Percy Bysshe Shelley (1792–1822), Byron's friend, who married Mary Wollstonecraft and drowned during a raging storm off the coast of Italy.

Immanuel Kant's (1724–1804) influential *Critique of Pure Reason* tries in its own way to dispel the darkness that inhabits our minds when it comes to answering questions about the nature of intuition and perception, and whether or not the mind can transcend itself. The book, which is a key to the philosophy of the Enlightenment, is difficult to understand or summarize, but it does represent one of the most important departures from the simplistic, faith-based theological thinking that had dominated Europe for centuries.

Frances Burney's novels, especially her huge hit *Evelina*, were much admired, and she influenced Jane Austen, one of the greatest writers of English prose. Austen began writing what proved to be her most enduringly popular novel, *Pride and Prejudice*, in 1796, under the title

First Impressions. Her father, a rector, offered it to a publisher, who refused even to read it. She put it aside, and in 1811, encouraged by the success of *Sense and Sensibility*, she picked it up and started working on it again. In 1813, seventeen years after she had first begun it, she finally published this polished, witty, psychologically astute, charming book, originally in three volumes. She lived long enough to enjoy the great success of her books, although all of them were published anonymously, and it was only after her death that her brother Henry revealed their authorship. In a letter dated January 29, 1813, to her sister, Cassandra Elizabeth, Jane Austen calls *Pride and Prejudice* "my own darling child," and with regard to the character of Elizabeth Bennett, the novel's heroine, she continues: "I must confess that I think her as delightful a creature as ever appeared in print, and how I shall be able to tolerate those who do not like *her* at least, I do not know."

Film and Television

Films set in the eighteenth century include *Monsieur Beaucaire* (1924), starring Rudolph Valentino—Stanislavsky, invited to see the filming when he was on tour with the Moscow Art Theatre, was particularly outraged by the inability of the actors to do the style of the period. Then there are the largely ahistorical *Marie Antoinette* (1938); the swashbuckler, *Scaramouche* (1952); Tony Richardson's delightful *Tom Jones* (1963); and Stanley Kubrick's *Barry Lyndon* (1975), based on William Makepeace Thackeray's nineteenth-century novel. Milos Forman's film of *Amadeus* (1984), with some beautiful period details, is based on Peter Shaffer's egregiously ahistorical, silly hit stage play. *Dangerous Liaisons* (1988), based on Choderlos de Laclos' novel, is a perfect example of what not to do: despite gorgeous costumes and decors, the film is just too contemporary in feeling and too American, with little or no sense of the period. *Valmont* (1989) is a slightly better version of the same story. *Ridicule* (1996) is very authentic in feeling, but the abysmally bad *The Affair of the Necklace* (2001), based on a scandal at the court of Louis XVI, is even worse than the egregiously ahistorical, exceptionally silly 2006 *Marie Antoinette* (with gorgeous costumes that won a well deserved Academy Award, and some superb period details of theatrical performances). And do avoid the film adapted from Patrick Suskind's unusual, compelling novel *Perfume: The Story of a Murderer* (2006); read the book instead.

It seems very difficult to escape one's own period when interpreting another. All the films mentioned have the stamp of their decade in the look they give the eighteenth century. This is not the case where the furniture and decors are concerned, because they are actually often the real thing. But with the makeup and hair of the characters, and sometimes with the costumes, we have styles typical of a decade. In any case, it is usually the acting and the writing that take us out of the period.

For a perfectly hilarious example of eighteenth-century acting as it must have been at its worst, see the episode "Sense and Senility" in *Blackadder III*, with Rowan Atkinson as the Prince's clever, cynical valet and Hugh Laurie as the dimwitted Prince, who hires two hammy actors to teach him elocution. In a much more real vein and eminently worth seeing is Nicholas Hytner's film of Alan Bennett's play (he wrote the screenplay as well) *The Madness of King George* (1994), with the late Nigel Hawthorne as the mad monarch. Among other things, it shows the state of medicine in that period, very much as recounted in her journals by Frances Burney, who was a witness to all that transpired. *Jefferson in Paris* (1995) also recreates the period beautifully, and has an interesting story to tell of the enforced relationship between Jefferson and Sally Hemmings (1773–1835), the slave who was the mother of several of Jefferson's children.

The Fabulous Fraud (1948) and *Mesmer* (1994), with Alan Rickman in the title role in the latter, both tell the story of Dr. Franz Anton Mesmer (1734–1815), the inventor of mesmerism, who maintained that he was possessed of a mystic power. The court of Vienna and the city of Paris were spellbound by his theory of animal magnetism, as he hypnotized patients and used magnets to cure them. Louis XVI appointed a committee to examine his claims; among its members was Lavoisier. They concluded that none of his ideas had any validity and that he was a rank charlatan.

The notorious womanizer Giacomo Casanova (1725–1798) has been a character in over a hundred films, including the 2005 *Casanova*, with Heath Ledger in the title role, and Fellini's bizarre fantasy *Il Casanova di Federico Fellini* (1976), with Donald Sutherland as the aging roué. Both are worth seeing for the decors and costumes.

Andrzej Wajda's *Danton* (1982), about the conflict between Robespierre and Danton at the time of the Reign of Terror, is very authentic in feeling, right down to the dirt and poverty. Less wonderful but still interesting is Sax Rohmer's stylized film, full of painted backgrounds instead of real sets, *L'Anglaise et le duc* (The Lady and the Duke) (2002), based on Grace Dalrymple Elliott's *Journal of My Life During the French Revolution* (first published in 1859). The film and television adaptations of Charles Dickens's *A Tale of Two Cities*, especially the 1936 version with Ronald Colman as Sydney Carton, are also worth looking at, as are the many swashbuckling films about pirates.

Of the many adaptations of Robert Louis Stevenson's *Treasure Island*, the best is Walt Disney's 1950 version, with a delightful Robert Newton as Long John Silver, who also hammed it up as *Blackbeard the Pirate* in 1952. In 1942, Tyrone Power made a great swashbuckler about the pirate Henry Morgan: *The Black Swan*. Errol Flynn had made an even better one in 1935: *Captain Blood*, based on Rafael Sabatini's novel, full of epic battles at sea, stormy love affairs, and exciting duels. A swashbuckling hero of a different sort, the rebellious Scottish Highlander Rob Roy McGregor, a man of principles and integrity, is superbly played by Liam Neeson in the splendid film *Rob Roy* (1995), worth seeing for its magnificent scenery and period details. James Fenimore Cooper's fictitious Native American hero, Hawkeye, is ably played by Daniel Day-Lewis in the 1992 film of *The Last of the Mohicans*, set during the latter part of the French and Indian Wars (1689–1763), which was actually a series of intermittent wars, skirmishes, and conflicts.

There are several versions of the mutiny led by Fletcher Christian against the tyrannical rule of Captain Bligh on the H.M.S. Bounty in 1789—all worth seeing, especially the 1935 Academy Award winner for Best Picture, *Mutiny on the Bounty*, with Charles Laughton in a classic performance as Bligh and Clark Gable as Christian. The political overtones of the 1930s, when dictators ruled in Italy and Germany, are quite clear in both the depiction of the characters and the situation that gives rise to the mutiny.

Adapted for the screen several times, Robert Louis Stevenson's *Kidnapped* is based loosely on sensational historical events that took place in the aftermath of the 1745 uprising led by Charles Edward Stuart, called Bonnie Prince Charlie (1720–1788)—the Stuarts, ruled by law out of the succession to the crown, attempted twice to regain the throne of their ancestors, in 1715 and 1745. The 1971 film with Michael Caine as Alan Breck Stewart incorporates plot elements from its sequel, *Catriona*, including the trial of James Stewart of the Glen, Alan's relative, falsely accused and convicted of ambushing and murdering the king's factor (tax collector)—Colin Roy Campbell of Glenure—as he passed through Appin in May 1752. Stewart was hanged in November of that year at Ballachuilish, near the scene of the "Appin Murder," but the crime remains unsolved to this day. Alan Breck was suspected of the assassination, but he had presumably escaped to France, so of course he could not be tried. *The Master of Ballantrae*—one of Stevenson's best and most interesting psychological novels, again about the abortive 1745 and its aftermath—was also adapted for the screen, in a not overly faithful version, in 1953, with Errol Flynn in the title role; the 1984 television version with Michael York has a better script.

The moving television docudrama *Culloden* (1968), available on DVD, realistically recreates the final battle of the quixotic uprising, as if it were being filmed with television cameras by a news crew. We also follow its horrible aftermath, in which the Highlands were mercilessly subdued, the Highlanders massacred or driven from their homes, and Scottish culture suppressed and forced underground. It would only be truly revived when it was popularized by the prolific novels and stirring epic poetry of Sir Walter Scott (1771–1832) and by the beloved poems of Robert Burns (1759–1796), many of them set to music, after the terrible events had receded into history, as far as most people south of the Scottish border were concerned.

The BBC has made television adaptations of every one of Jane Austen's novels, and many are available on DVD. *Pride and Prejudice* has been adapted nine times for the large and small screen, most recently in 2005, in a film that is notable mainly for its recreation of the period; both the 1980 and 1995 television miniseries are better versions. The 1940 Hollywood film is notable for the performances of Greer Garson and Laurence Olivier. William Makepiece Thackeray's (1811–1863) *Vanity Fair*, set in the Jane Austen era, was adapted for film a number of times. The 1931 film, updated to the 1920s, for which it is a perfect object lesson, with Myrna Loy as Becky Sharp, and the 1935 version (the first Technicolor film feature, designed by Robert Edmond Jones) with Miriam Hopkins in the same role, are better both at telling the story and at period effects than the 2004 version with Reese Witherspoon, colorful as it is. One of those typical, lavish 1950s Hollywood costume dramas full of excellent period detail, *Beau Brummell* (1954), with Stewart Grainger in the title role and Elizabeth Taylor as Lady Patricia Belham, is a delightful romance, completely fictionalized. Peter Ustinov is superb as the Prince of Wales, and Robert Morley is equally memorable in his brief appearance as the mad King George III, while Rosemary Harris is stunningly beautiful as the Prince of Wales's mistress, Mrs. Fitzherbert. As of this writing, the film is only available in VHS format.

That Hamilton Woman (1941), with Laurence Olivier as Lord Admiral Horatio Nelson and Vivien Leigh as his lover, Lady Emma Hamilton, is also well worth a viewing; Winston Churchill is said to have loved it. I wonder what he would have thought of *Young Winston* (1972), the very good biopic starring Simon Ward as Churchill and the excellent Ann Bancroft as his mother, the American-born Lady Randolph Churchill.

Gothic (1986) is a dark film about Mary Shelley and the genesis of that arch-romantic horror classic *Frankenstein*. Byron and Percy Shelley are also portrayed, and the film is a mélange of drug-induced dreams, game playing, and near madness—very romantic.

Films about George Sand include *Les enfants du siècle* (1999) and *Impromptu* (1991); both are, once again, admirable for the period costumes and decors but less so for the acting and scripts.

And do see Vincent Price's hilarious films of Edgar Allan Poe's stories and poems, which are, of course, required reading for anyone doing a project set in the romantic era: thrills, chills, and shudders galore, and all quite delightful.

Marcel Carné's classic, *Les enfants du paradis* (1945), with a wealth of details about early nineteenth-century theater, is required viewing. The word *paradis* (paradise) refers to the theater seats known in England as "the gods": the highest balcony, where the poorer economic classes sat. The film's period style is perfectly done. *Lacenaire* (2005), starring Daniel Auteuil as the nineteenth-century thief and con man who wrote his memoirs while in prison awaiting execution, is rich in period details and fascinating as a story; Lacenaire (1800–1836) is also a character in *Les enfants du paradis*.

Desiree (1954) stars Marlon Brando as the young Napoleon and Audrey Hepburn as his first love, Desiree Clary, before he met Josephine de Beauharnais; period details are well observed. Serge Bondarchuk's Soviet film of Tolstoy's *War and Peace* (1968) is important for early nineteenth-century study because it is so superbly done in every way, and the 1956 Hollywood version is also excellent for the period recreation. And don't miss Abel Gance's great silent epic *Napoleon* (1927), an extraordinary recreation of the era, including the Reign of Terror and the horrible battles of the Napoleonic wars.

On the other hand, *Captain Horatio Hornblower* (1951), also set during the Napoleonic wars, is a perfect example of how not to make a period film, despite the nice costumes, authentic ships, and exciting battles. There is, however, a truly excellent, exciting Emmy Award–winning

British 1998–2001 television miniseries based on the C. S. Forester novels—*Horatio Hornblower*, starring Ioan Grufudd—that is eminently worth watching and very authentic in feeling.

Based on Herman Melville's novel, *Billy Budd* (1962) shows conditions in the navy in 1797 in a graphic, very moving story. Also excellent is *Damn the Defiant* (1962), starring Alec Guinness as the humane captain of a man o' war in 1797 and Dirk Bogarde as his nemesis. The film is based loosely around the true incident of a successful mutiny through the entire British fleet; the object of the strike was to secure better conditions for the sailors, many of whom had been forcibly made to serve by the infamous press gangs who had the legal right to abduct them wherever they found them.

Set during the Napoleonic wars, *Master and Commander: The Far Side of the World* (2003), based on the first novel in the popular series by Patrick O'Brian, stars Russell Crowe as Captain Jack Aubrey. It is remarkably convincing in the recreation of shipboard life; it also provides a fascinating glimpse at the science of the period.

For More Information

d'Abrantès, Laure Junot, Duchesse. *At the Court of Napoleon: Memoirs of the Duchesse d'Abrantès*. (Excerpts.) Introduction by Olivier Bernier. Foreword by Katell Le Bourhis. New York: Doubleday, 1989.

Adams, John. *The Adams Papers: Diary and Autobiography of John Adams*. L. H. Butterfield, ed. 4 vols. Cambridge, MA: Harvard University Press, 1961–64.

Adams, Samuel and Sarah. *The Complete Servant*. Orig. pub. 1825. Edited by Ann Haly. With an introduction by Pamela Horn. Lewes, UK: Southover Press, 1989.

Alder, Ken. *The Measure of All Things: The Seven-Year Odyssey of the Hidden Error That Transformed the World*. New York: The Free Press, 2002.

The American Revolution: Writings from the War of Independence. New York: The Library of America, 2001.

Benedetti, Jean. *David Garrick and the Birth of Modern Theatre*. London: Methuen, 2001.

Bessborough, the Earl of, G.C.M.G., ed. in collaboration with A. Aspinall, Ph.D. *Lady Bessborough and Her Family Circle*. London: John Murray, 1940.

Blum, Stella, ed. *Eighteenth-Century Fashions in Full Color: 64 Engravings from the "Galerie des Modes", 1778–1787*. New York: Dover Publications, Inc., 1982.

Boswell, James. *The Journals of James Boswell: 1762–1795*. New Haven, CT: Yale University Press, 1994.

——*The Life of Samuel Johnson*. New York: Oxford University Press, 1998.

Bourienne, Louis Antoine Fauvelet de. *Memoirs of Napoleon Bonaparte: Amplified from the Works of Las Cases, Rovigo, Constant, Gourgaud, Rapp, and Other Celebrated French Writers*. London: S. Andrus, 1856.

Burney, Fanny. *Journals and Letters*. New York: Penguin, 2001.

Campan, Madame Jeanne-Louise Henriette. *The Private Life of Marie Antoinette: A Confidante's Account*. New York: 1500 Books, LLC, 2006.

Carlyle, Thomas. *The French Revolution*. Introduction by John D. Rosenberg. New York: Modern Library Classics, 2002.

Casanova, Giacomo. *The Story of My Life*. New York: Penguin, 2001.

Chernow, Ron. *Alexander Hamilton*. New York: Penguin, 2004.

Chesterfield, Lord. *Lord Chesterfield's Letters to His Son*. Edited and with an introduction by Oliver H. Leigh. New York: Tudor Publishing Co., n.d.

Cibber, Colley. *An Apology for the Life of Colley Cibber*. New York: Dover Publications, 2000.

Cowell, Stephanie. *Marrying Mozart*. New York: Viking, 2004.

de Crèvecoeur, Hector St. John. *Letters from an American Farmer* and *Sketches of Eighteenth-Century America*. Edited with an introduction by Albert E. Stone. New York: Penguin Books, 1986.

David, Saul. *Prince of Pleasure: The Prince of Wales and the Making of the Regency*. New York: Atlantic Monthly Press, 1998.

Doyle, William. *The Oxford History of the French Revolution*. New York: Oxford University Press, 1989.

Durant, Will and Ariel. *The Story of Civilization: Part IX, The Age of Voltaire*. New York: Simon and Schuster, 1965.

——*The Story of Civilization: Part X, Rousseau and Revolution*. New York: Simon and Schuster, 1967.

——*The Story of Civilization: Part XI, The Age of Napoleon*. New York: Simon and Schuster, 1975.

The editors of *American Heritage: The Magazine of History*. Narrative by Bruce Lancaster, with a chapter by J. H. Plumb. *The American Heritage Book of the Revolution*. New York: Simon & Schuster, Inc., 1958.

Einstein, Alfred. *Mozart: His Character, His Work*. New York: Oxford University Press, 1962.

Farington, Joseph. *Memoirs of Sir Joshua Reynolds*. With a new introduction by Dr. Martin Postle. London: Pallas Athene, 2005.

Ferrières, Marquis de. *Correspondance inédite 1789, 1790, 1791*. Paris: Librairie Armand Colin, 1932.

Franklin, Benjamin. *Autobiography, Poor Richard, and Later Writings*. New York: Library of America, 2005.

————*Silence Dogood, The Busy-Body, and Early Writings*. New York: Library of America, 2005.

Fraser, Antonia. *Marie Antoinette: The Journey*. New York: Nan A. Talese, 2001.

Gabler, James M. *An Evening with Benjamin Franklin and Thomas Jefferson: Dinner, Wine and Conversation*. Baltimore, MD: Bacchus Press, 2006.

————*Passions: The Wines and Travels of Thomas Jefferson*. Baltimore, MD: Bacchus Press, 1995.

Gay, Peter. *Mozart*. New York: Penguin, 1999.

Gibbon, Edward. *Memoirs of My Life*. New York: Penguin Classics, Reprint Edition, 1984.

Greville, Charles C. F. *The Greville Memoirs*. Edited by Roger Fulford. New York: The Macmillan Company, 1963.

Gutman, Robert W. *Mozart: A Cultural Biography*. San Diego, CA: Harcourt, Inc, 1999.

Hamilton, Alexander. *Writings*. New York: Library of America, 2001.

Hervey, Lord. *Lord Hervey's Memoirs*. Edited by Romney Sedgwick. New York: The Macmillan Company, 1952.

Hibbert, Christopher. *The Days of the French Revolution*. New York: Harper-Collins, 1980.

————*George III: A Personal History*. New York: Basic Books, 2000.

————*Nelson: A Personal History*. New York: Da Capo Press, 1994.

————*Wellington: A Personal History*. Reading, MA: Perseus Books, 1997.

————*Wolfe at Quebec*. Cleveland, OH: The World Publishing Company, 1959.

Hildesheimer, Rudolph. *Mozart*. Translated from the German by Marion Faber. New York: Vintage Books, 1983.

Hill, Aaron and William Popple. *The Prompter: A Theatrical Paper (1734–1736)*. Selected and edited by William W. Appleton and Kalman A. Burnim. New York: Benjamin Blom, 1966.

Hodge, Jane Aiken. *Passion & Principle: The Loves and Lives of Regency Women*. London: John Murray, 1996.

Holmes, Edward. *The Life of Mozart, including His Correspondence*. Original ed. 1845. New York: Cosimo Books, 2005.

Jefferson, Thomas. *Autobiography, Notes on the State of Virginia, Public and Private Papers, Addresses, Letters*. New York: Library of America, 1984.

Johnson, Paul. *George Washington, the Founding Father*. New York: Eminent Lives, 2005.

Johnson, Samuel. *Samuel Johnson's Dictionary: Selections from the 1755 work that defined the English language*. Edited by Jack Lynch. Delray Beach, FL: Levenger Press, 2004.

Kant, Immanuel. *Critique of Pure Reason*. Translated into English by F. Max Müller. Garden City, NY: Doubleday & Company, Inc., 1961.

Ketchum, Richard M. *Decisive Day: The Battle for Bunker Hill*. New York: Henry Holt and Company, 1962.

———*Saratoga: Turning Point of America's Revolutionary War*. New York: Henry Holt and Company, 1997.

———*The Winter Soldiers: The Battles for Trenton and Princeton*. New York: Henry Holt and Company, 1973.

Kronenberger, Louis. *Kings and Desperate Men: Life in Eighteenth-Century England*. New York: Alfred A. Knopf, 1942.

Lamballe, Princess. *Secret Memoirs of Princess Lamballe: Her Confidential Relations with Marie Antoinette*. Edited and annotated by Catherine Hyde, Marquise de Gouvion Broglie Scolari, in the Confidential Service of the Unfortunate Princess. Reprinted from the 1901 edition. Honolulu, Hawaii: University Press of the Pacific, 2003.

Lever, Maurice. *Sade*. New York: A Harvest Book, 1994.

Lichtenberg, Georg Christoph. *Lichtenberg's Visits to England as described in his Letters and Diaries*. Edited and annotated by Margaret L. Mare and W. H. Quarrel. Orig. ed., Oxford University Press, 1938. New York: Benjamin Blom, 1969.

Madison, James. *Writings 1772–1836*. New York: Library of America, 1999.

Mathiez, Albert. *The French Revolution*. New York: The Universal Library, 1964.

Maxwell, Sir Herbert, Bart., M.P., LL.D., F.R.S., ed. *The Creevey Papers: A Selection from the Correspondence and Diaries of the Late Thomas Creevey, M.P. Born 1786–Died 1838*. London: John Murray, 1905.

McLynn, Frank. *Napoleon*. New York: Arcade Publishing, 2002.

Melville, Lewis. *The Beaux of the Regency*. 2 vols. London: Hutchinson, 1908.

Michelet, Jules. *History of the French Revolution*. Chicago, IL: University of Chicago Press, 1967.

Mikhail, E. H., ed. *Goldsmith: Interviews and Recollections*. New York: St. Martin's Press, 1993.

———*Sheridan: Interviews and Recollections*. New York: Macmillan, 1989.

Murray, Venetia. *An Elegant Madness: High Society in Regency England*. New York: Penguin Books, 1998.

Niemcewicz, Julian Ursyn. *Under Their Vine and Fig Tree: Travels through America in 1797–1799, 1805*. Translated and edited with an introduction by Metchie J. E. Budka. Elizabeth, NJ: The Grassmann Publishing Company, Inc., 1965.

Olsen, Kirstin. *Daily Life in 18th-Century England*. Westport, CT: Greenwood Press, 1999.

Paine, Thomas. *Collected Writings: Common Sense / The Crisis / Rights of Man / The Age of Reason / Pamphlets, Articles and Letters*. New York: Library of America, 1995.

Pallain, M. G., ed. *The Correspondence of Prince Talleyrand and King Louis XVIII During the Congress of Vienna*. New York: Charles Scribner's Sons, 1881.

Picard, Liza. *Dr. Johnson's London*. New York: St. Martin's Griffin, 2000.

Pool, Daniel. *What Jane Austen Ate and Charles Dickens Knew: From Fox Hunting to Whist—the Facts of Daily Life in 19th-Century England*. New York: Simon & Schuster, 1993.

Randall, Willard Sterne. *Thomas Jefferson: A Life*. New York: Harper Perennial, 1994.

Rendell, Jane. *The Pursuit of Pleasure: Gender, Space and Architecture in Regency London*. New Brunswick, NJ: Rutgers University Press, 2002.

Reynolds, Sir Joshua. *Discourses on Art*. Edited by Robert R. Wark. New Haven: Yale University Press, 1997.

Robinson, Andrew: *The Last Man Who Knew Everything: Thomas Young, the Anonymous Polymath Who Proved Newton Wrong, Explained How We See, Cured the Sick, and Deciphered the Rosetta Stone, Among Other Feats of Genius*. New York: Pi Press, 2006.

Robiquet, Jean. *Daily Life in the French Revolution*. Translated from the French by James Kirkup. New York: The Macmillan Company, 1965.

Rogers, Samuel. *Recollections of the Table-Talk of Samuel Rogers. To Which Is Added Porsoniana*. Edited by Alexander Dyce. The Michigan Historical Reprint Series, n.d. New York: D. Appleton and Company, 1856.

Schama, Simon. *Citizens: A Chronicle of the French Revolution*. New York: Alfred A. Knopf, 1989.

Solomon, Maynard. *Mozart: A Life*. New York: Harper, 1995.

Suskind, Patrick. *Perfume: The Story of a Murderer*. New York: Vintage International, 2001.

Thomas, Nicholas. *Cook: The Extraordinary Voyages of Captain James Cook*. New York: Walker and Company, 2003.

Turner, Thomas. *The Diary of Thomas Turner, 1754–1765*. Edited by David Vaisey. New York: Oxford University Press, 1984.

Vickery, Amanda. *The Gentleman's Daughter: Women's Lives in Georgian England*. New Haven: Yale University Press, 1998.

Vidocq, Eugène-François. *Memoirs of Vidocq*. New York: Ayer Publishing Company, 1976.

Walpole, Horace. *Memoirs and Portraits*. Edited by Matthew Hodgart. New York: The Macmillan Company, 1963.

Washington, George. *Writings*. New York: Library of America, 1997.

Weber, Caroline. *Queen of Fashion: What Marie Antoinette Wore to the Revolution*. New York: Henry Holt and Company, 2006.

Woodforde, James. *The Diary of a Country Parson 1758–1802*. Passages selected and edited by John Beresford. New York: Oxford University Press, 1949.

Wordsworth, Dorothy. *The Grasmere and Alfoxden Journals*. New York: Oxford University Press, 2002.

CHAPTER EIGHT

From the Mid-Nineteenth to the Mid-Twentieth Century: The Age of Technology

The Industrial Revolution Changes the Theater

In 1849, George Sand (1804–1876) published one of her most beautiful romantic love stories, *La Mare au Diable* (The Devil's Pond). She wrote:

> For, alas! everything vanishes. Merely since my own existence began, there have been more changes in ideas, and in the customs of my village than had been seen for centuries before the Revolution. Already, half the Celtic, pagan or medieval ceremonies, which I saw in full vigor during my childhood, have disappeared. In one or two years, perhaps, the railroads will erect their trestles in our deep valleys, carrying away, with lightning rapidity, our ancient traditions and our marvelous legends.

She was absolutely right: in the course of slightly less than fifty years, the world had seen more technological changes than it had in 500. Beautiful things were gone, lost forever, and what had replaced them, with the harnessing of steam and coal, was the ugliness of the factory chimney and the griminess of the mill towns, just as Charles Dickens (1812–1870) portrays them in *Hard Times*. On the other hand, streets, restaurants, theaters, and homes were now lit with gas lamps; and insulated ice boxes, lined with tin or zinc, were now indispensable fixtures in restaurant and home kitchens. Religion and piety were still of paramount importance, but some inroads into unquestioning faith were made by the advance of science—notably, in mid-century by Charles Darwin's (1809–1882) theory of evolution, which rocked the religious world to its foundations, and late in the century, by the iconoclastic ideas of Sigmund Freud.

The pace of technological change was almost dizzying. Only thirty-two years after George Sand penned those wistful, nostalgic lines, Gilbert and Sullivan's publicity-seeking producer, Richard D'Oyly Carte (1844–1901), replaced the gas lighting at the Savoy Theatre in London with electric lights, onstage and off, during the run of Gilbert and Sullivan's latest success, *Patience*. The new arrangements were not quite ready when the theater reopened on October 10, 1881, after its temporary closure allowing time to install the electric lighting and repaint the scenery. The delay was explained in a handout given to the audience: "It has never before been attempted to light nearly so many as 1,200 incandescent burners at a single undertaking." In a prospectus for investors, Carte had written:

> The greatest drawbacks to the enjoyment of the theatrical performances are, undoubtedly, the foul air and heat which pervade all theatres. As everyone knows, each gas-burner consumes as much oxygen as many people, and causes great heat besides. The incandescent lamps consume *no* oxygen, and cause no perceptible heat.

When everything was finally in place some nights later, Carte went in front of the curtain after the performance holding a lit electric bulb on a long wire, "and a hush fell upon the audience, who thought that electricity was always fatal," reported the *Electrical Times*. Carte put a piece of muslin around the bulb and smashed it with a hammer. He then held the muslin up, to show that it had not been burned, and the audience burst into wild cheering and applause.

Acting Styles in Melodrama, Realistic Plays, and Comic Opera

In the nineteenth and early twentieth centuries, the theater meant something in people's lives. Parisian theatergoers rioted in 1830 outside the Théâtre-Français (now the Odéon) when Victor Hugo's *Hernani*, a romantic melodrama later turned into the opera *Ernani* by Giuseppe Verdi (1813–1901), had its premiere, challenging the neoclassical unities of Racine and Corneille. The partisans of romanticism and classicism actually beat each other up!

Then there were the frightening, violent Astor Place Riots in New York City in 1849 between the supporters of the great British actor William Charles Macready (1798–1873) and Edwin Forrest (1806–1872), his muscular, temperamental American rival. In 1845, on Forrest's appearance in London, Macready had toasted him at a dinner at the Garrick Club, but Forrest was incensed when a member of Macready's party supposedly booed him at a performance. On his 1849 tour of the United States, Macready was received with all the hostility anti-British prejudice could muster. After the riots, Forrest was ostracized by New York society, but the mass of theatergoers were on his side, simply because he was an American. Macready describes what happened in detail in his *Reminiscences* (published posthumously in 1855). He suffered terribly, although he remained brave and stoic in the face of the disgraceful treatment accorded him.

The nineteenth century was the golden age of the star actor-managers, such as Irving and Booth. Demanding leading lights such as Bernhardt and Duse could be very difficult to be around. Eleonora Duse, for instance, may have been as pure in her approach to acting as the virgin priestess of an ancient cult, but she was also temperamental and moody—not that the vocation of priestess and unpredictable behavior are necessarily mutually exclusive. According to Guido Noccioli (1883–?), a young actor who kept a diary during the 1906–07 tour on which he accompanied her, Duse could be incredibly irritable, imperious, and demanding, as well as highly judgmental about everybody. Sometimes she simply didn't want to rehearse, and she would take a ride in the country because it was a beautiful day; or if she did show up at the theater, she would rehearse a scene or two in a whisper and then flounce out—when she didn't storm out, criticizing her fellow performers on the way. Noccioli, incidentally, was not being critical when he wrote down all the details about her temperamental behavior: he was one of Duse's great admirers.

The standard dramatic form of the era was the well-made play, epitomized in the theater pieces and melodramatic opera libretti of the man who brought it to perfection: the more-than-prolific Eugène Scribe (1791–1861), best known as a librettist for Verdi, Bellini, Meyerbeer, Halévy, Donizetti, and Rossini. His complete works comprise seventy-six volumes. The well-made play usually lacks psychological depth and social criticism, and revolves around plot, plot, and more plot. Its hallmark is that every strand and plot thread is neatly and logically tied up at the end. But there is no reason why depth of character could not be included, and in the best authors, it was. Popular for more than a century, the form is exemplified in many plays and melodramas, such as Victorien Sardou's (1831–1908) star vehicle for Bernhardt, *Tosca*, better known as the opera by Giacomo Puccini (1858–1924). Sardou, who was witty and astute even if he was facile, was rather unfairly crowned the King of Sardoodledum by George Bernard Shaw.

Acting in melodrama was usually heightened, done with fierce commitment to extreme situations and with extravagant gestures, facial expressions, and indicated emotion. In her book *Helen Potter's Impersonations* (1891), Helen Potter (?–?), an American actress who toured the country doing impersonations of celebrities, provided instructions on how to do a scene from a play about Queen Elizabeth I that she had performed (in Italian), as it was done by Adelaide Ristori (1822–1906): "RENDITION: Breathe fast and heavy; voice sometimes aspirate, sometimes half guttural; hand to the heart, eyes wide open, and now and then turned upward in the sockets."

The classics were usually done in a similar vein. Potter's stage directions to actresses playing Ophelia include the injunction to "bob and moan softly" and "move the hands through the air, feather motion." Her general advice is to "assume a gentle madness, and make sudden transitions from sadness to lightness, and, in one or two instances, even frivolity." But there were famous exceptions to this shallow, external approach in the productions of, among others, Edwin Booth, whose company performed at his theater on the corner of Sixth Avenue and Twenty-third Street in Manhattan.

Booth's sonorous, deep voice was recorded by Thomas A. Edison (1847–1931) in 1890 in a speech from *Othello*, available on a Pearl CD. His acting has been described and even his speech patterns annotated—based on reviews, prompt books, and original accounts—in *The Hamlet of Edwin Booth* by Charles H. Shattuck (University of Illinois Press, 1969), which covers every aspect and detail of his productions and performance. As Hamlet, whose main psychological motivation he saw as his deep love for his father, Booth played as usual in a low-key, realistic way. He was one of the first actors to deliver the soliloquy "To be or not to be" while seated on a chair in the most natural manner possible. In act 1, scene 4, Booth had his back to the ghost and turned to see him. Then, as Shattuck tells us, Booth staggered back, "raising his left hand swiftly as if to clear his eyes." His bonnet slipped off at the same time, and he sank into Horatio's arms, saying "in a fearful whisper, 'Angels and ministers of grace, defend us!'" Breathing hard, he leaned against Horatio as the ghost spoke, then sank to his knees. The descriptions of his performance resemble those of Betterton's and Garrick's playing of the same scene.

Among the most popular well-made melodramas of the period were adaptations of Harriet Beecher Stowe's (1811–1896) antislavery novel *Uncle Tom's Cabin* and an adaptation of a temperance novel, written to expose the evils of drink: Timothy Shay Arthur's (1809–1885) *Ten Nights in a Bar-Room*, adapted for the stage in 1858 by William W. Pratt (?–?). This melodrama of melodramas held the boards all over the United States for who knows how many years; it even had a number of twentieth-century revivals.

Equally famous was Leopold Lewis's (1828–1890) *The Bells*, adapted from a French melodrama, *Le juif polonais* (The Polish Jew) by Erckmann-Chatrian—the name of the writing team Emile Erckmann (1822–1899) and Louis-Alexandre Chatrian (1826–1890), who collaborated on more than twenty-seven novels and short stories, a number of which were adapted for the theater. This was the first of Sir Henry Irving's great hits; his 1871 performance as Matthias, the murderer haunted by the crime he had committed fifteen years before, made his reputation. The stage designer Edward Gordon Craig (1872–1966), son of Irving's celebrated acting partner Ellen Terry (1847–1928) and designer of Stanislavsky's experimental production of *Hamlet*, saw Irving in the play "more than thirty times," as he tells us in his informative memoir, *Henry Irving* (Longmans, Green and Co., 1930): "The thing Irving set out to do was to show us the sorrow which slowly and remorselessly beat him down." Craig describes Irving's performance in a scene where he thinks he hears the sledge-bells he heard on the night he murdered and robbed the Polish Jew in the forest and dragged his body from the sledge to burn it in the nearby limekiln:

> Puzzled, motionless . . . he glides up to a standing position: never has anyone seen another rising figure which slid slowly up like that: with one arm slightly raised, with sensitive hand speaking of far-off apprehended sounds, he asks, in the voice of some woman who is frightened, yet does not wish to frighten those with her: "Don't you . . . don't you hear the sound of sledge-bells on the road?" . . . suddenly he staggers, and shivers from his toes to his neck; his jaws begin to chatter; the hair on his forehead, falling over a little, writhes as though it were a nest of little snakes.

Melodrama may have drawn crowds, but this was also the era of the iconoclastic August Strindberg (1849–1912) in Sweden, with his symbolist as well as realistic dramas; the realist Henrik Ibsen (1826–1906) in Norway; and later in the century, Anton Chekhov, whose plays would require the style that Stanislavsky's realistic approach to acting brought to them. Another realist—the didactic, verbose George Bernard Shaw, with his "theater of ideas" and comedies full of intellectual debates— also wrote plays in which loose ends are not always tied up and the audience is deliberately left to ponder the fates of the protagonists. All these plays had to be acted in a more real style than the Delsarte approach allowed for. Even the melodramatic comedies of Oscar Wilde (1854–1900), which follow the formula of the well-made play in their construction, required a more realistic approach.

In doing Wilde's late Victorian plays, you must take account not only of their satiric, epigrammatic style but also of the moral and sexual attitudes of the day. The characters may be passionately in love, but demure decorous custom dictates that they hardly touch each other until they agree to be married. The theatrical literature of the Victorian period clearly reveals its mores and attitudes. In Gilbert and Sullivan's first big hit, for instance—the one-act operetta *Trial by Jury*, produced in 1875—the plaintiff, Angelina, sues the cad Edwin for breach of promise of marriage and influences judge and jury by lifting the hem of her bridal gown and showing them her well-clad ankle. They are shocked and titillated, and the lubricious judge finds for the plaintiff.

Jacques Offenbach's (1819–1880) comic operas reveal the social and sexual attitudes of the politically repressive regime in France from 1852–1870 of Emperor Napoleon III (1808–1873), in which the ruling classes were much given to luxury and extravagance. The first Napoleon's nephew had little interest in governing the realm once he had fulfilled his ambition to be declared emperor, but the greatest interest in the chambermaids of the Tuileries Palace. And for them, indeed, he had an abiding lust, satirized in the character of the philandering Jupiter in *Orphée aux enfers* (Orpheus in the Underworld), which, like Offenbach's later hit, *La Belle Hélène*, sends up classical mythology. Henri Meilhac (1831–1897) and Ludovic Halévy's (1834–1908) sparkling libretti for some of his other comic operas, wedded so perfectly to Offenbach's witty and exuberant music, are outspoken about sex. Indeed, they move into their own contemporary times with *La Vie parisienne* (Parisian Life), which amused the usually stolid, bourgeois Parisian public, eager for a laugh at the repressive regime. The three collaborated also in 1867 on *La Grande Duchesse de Gérolstein*, an antimilitaristic satire that takes place in a fictitious, caricatural German duchy. Even the visiting Prussians lapped it up and were thrilled to visit its gorgeous star, Hortense Schneider (1833–1920), in her dressing room, where she received and apparently serviced so many crowned heads and aristocrats, including Edward, Prince of Wales, the future Edward VII (1841–1910), that it was dubbed *le passage des princes*—Princes' Alley, loosely translated.

Needless to say, stick-in-the-mud, pedantic classical scholars were outraged and thought the Offenbachian reworking of mythology supremely vulgar. But note that these comic operas assume the same classical education and knowledge on the part of even the most ordinary members of his Parisian audience that nineteenth-century writers assume when they quote Roman and Greek authors in their original languages.

In America as well, such an education was assumed by speakers at July 4 celebrations when they compared the president of the United States to various Roman emperors, as Edmund Lester Pearson (1880–1937) tells us was the regular custom in the nineteenth century. Pearson was a New York City public librarian and prolific author whose delightful, witty *Queer Books* (Kennicat Press, 1970, first published in 1928) concerns such subjects as the temperance novels of the 1850s, long-winded Fourth of July orations, books of etiquette, and romantic novels such as *A Short Account of the Courtship of Alonzo and Melissa*. Published in New York state in 1811, it was wildly popular all over the United States and went through almost countless editions for sixty years before falling into obscurity.

In 1882, in the more stolid, staid island across the channel, W. S. Gilbert (1836–1911) and Arthur Sullivan's (1842–1900) *Iolanthe*, which mocked the House of Lords, portrayed the repressed nature of a would-be Jupiter in the character of the Lord Chancellor. And in *Patience*, sexual ambiguity, decadence, aestheticism and the so-called fleshly school of poetry—exemplified by Dante Gabriel Rossetti (1828–1882) and Algernon Charles Swinburne (1837–1909)—are mocked. Aestheticism, the movement of which Oscar Wilde (a particular target of Gilbert's satire) was an adherent, is exemplified in the writings of the influential art critics Walter Pater (1839–1894) and John Ruskin (1819–1900). In *Princess Ida*, women's equality and emancipation from the Ibsenesque dollhouse existences they were compelled to lead are held up to ridicule. The unwieldy antifeminist libretto is one reason this comic opera is rarely done, despite one of Sullivan's most tuneful and effervescent scores. The stubborn Gilbert could be terribly reactionary in his views, which is why the Victorian establishment loved his work: they knew he posed no threat to the established order.

The style in which these works should be performed implies a certain arch, knowing humor where the performer is aware in the back of his or her mind that what is said is very funny. But you have to play everything absolutely seriously. The staid or sprightly rhythms of Sullivan's music and Gilbert's dialogue give you a great clue as to the well-mannered, almost distant and egocentric behavior that is expected. The cadences of the English accent as well as superb, clear diction are also necessary concomitants of the style: sharp, hard, nicely articulated consonants and beautifully shaped vowels are essential.

An extremely popular institution that lasted for more than a century, from about 1850 on, the British music hall began as a kind of musical evening in the "saloon" (salon) or "song and supper rooms" of pubs— "public houses," or bars, established around the 1830s. People paid a small admission fee to attend the musical or dramatic entertainment provided. This professional variety entertainment proved so popular among the working classes that entrepreneurs began to build separate theaters, some of which could hold as many as 2,000 people. Specialty acts, magic, juggling, ventriloquism, wrestling, feats of strength, impressions of famous people, comedy sketches, dances, and musical numbers, usually of a comical nature, were performed.

The entertainment could include solo or group minstrel numbers, or consist of a three-act minstrel show, with skits and songs purporting to be African-American, although they were demeaning, stereotypical, and of course inauthentic. Of American origin, these minstrel shows were popular on both sides of the Atlantic. They were performed by white actors in burnt-cork blackface makeup or, after the Civil War, sometimes by African-Americans in blackface. Racism and ethnic stereotyping were an unfortunate part of the entertainment scene.

But authentic African-American theater had existed since at least 1816, when the newly formed African Theatre in New York City presented contemporary plays—some of which dealt with slavery—as well as Shakespeare and other classics. The company would have its own theater in Greenwich Village in 1822. Born in New York, Ira Aldridge (1806–1867) first performed with the African theater. He became a celebrated Shakespearean actor and toured Europe, where his performances were much praised. By the end of the century, there were famous African-American companies in Chicago and other major northern cities. African-American performers broke the barriers of prejudice temporarily when they performed on Broadway in 1898 in a ragtime musical comedy called *Clorindy*, which was a huge hit.

Among the most famous music halls were the Canterbury in Lambeth; Wilton's in the West End; and the Old Bedford in Camden Town. The audiences could be quite rowdy, and they let the performers know how they felt in no uncertain terms, but by the early part of the twentieth century, music halls were respectable enough to be considered family institutions, and even royalty occasionally attended. Music hall songs proved an enduring form of popular music, as did cabaret songs in France. Vaudeville in America—similar to the music hall—was also an immensely enjoyable kind of entertainment, and vaudeville artists toured the country to great acclaim.

An important part of the theatrical landscape of New York City at the turn of the twentieth century were theaters that did plays in their own languages for Italian and Eastern European Jewish immigrants. The actors performed in all the styles then prevalent, from the heightened melodramatic to the realistic to the farcical to the arch-comedic style of comedies and comic opera. The Yiddish theater flourished on Second Avenue, and one of its greatest stars was Jacob Adler (1855–1926), who played Shylock in Yiddish on Broadway, while the rest of the cast performed in English, much as Salvini had played Othello in Italian with an English-speaking cast. Adler was the patriarch of a noted theatrical family. Known for his realistic acting, he wrote an informative biography, *A Life on the Stage: A Memoir* (Applause Theatre Books, 2001), to which his daughter, the famous acting teacher Stella Adler (1901–1992), wrote an introduction.

My great-uncle Herman Wohl (1877–1936) was a noted composer and conductor in the Yiddish theater. He wrote hit songs and comic operas, some of them on biblical themes, both on his own and with Arnold Perlmutter (1859–1953). In the year he was born, in the *shtetl* (town) of Ottynia in what was then the Austro-Hungarian Empire and is now the Ukraine, Stanislavsky was fourteen, and he was thrilled to be involved in productions of the Alexeyev Circle, his family's amateur theater group. That same year, Offenbach began working on his grand opera *The Tales of Hoffman*. Gilbert and Sullivan staged *The Sorcerer*; they hadn't even dreamed yet of *H. M. S. Pinafore* or *The Pirates of Penzance*. And my great-uncle's music is right in line with the Offenbachian and G & S traditions of gorgeous melody and vivacious, effervescent rhythms, to which he added a rollicking minor-key lilt that gives it his individual stamp.

By the time he died in 1936, the world had, of course, changed considerably. Movies, which didn't even exist when he was born, now talked, and radio programs and recorded music were taken for granted as popular forms of mass entertainment. The automobile was a widespread form of transportation. The airplane had been invented, and it had been used in the Great War, which ended in 1918. The map of the world no longer included the Ottoman Empire or the Austro-Hungarian Empire. Russia was no longer ruled by a czar but by the Communists. The Fascists and the Nazis were in power. Franklin D. Roosevelt (1882–1945) was president of the United States, and his progressive programs to help end the Depression, with its dust bowls, soup kitchens, massive unemployment and terrible poverty, were in force. In February of that year, the first Social Security checks were mailed. There were still unrest and terrible labor strikes. Roosevelt was nevertheless reelected by a landslide in November. In France, the Popular Front government of Socialist Léon Blum (1872–1950) took power.

Contrasts in the Lifestyles of Social Classes in the Nineteenth and Early Twentieth Centuries

From the Victorian (1837–1900) through the Edwardian (1901–1910) eras in England, class distinctions, as well as sexual and moral attitudes, did not change much—any more than they did in Sigmund Freud's (1856–1936) Vienna. In his essay "Some General Remarks on Hysterical Attacks" (1908), Freud described a hysterical woman's possible sexual fantasy, involving her reading on a park bench while lifting her skirt slightly to reveal her foot. Not only was women's dress in the late nineteenth and early twentieth centuries repressive, in that it covered the human body in formless attire, but so was the sociocultural environment of early twentieth-century Hapsburg Vienna and of Europe and America generally.

Stella Adler said in her book on Chekhov, Ibsen, and Strindberg that after 1850 or thereabouts, there was only the middle class, and that everything it aspired to and wanted was aped by the lower economic classes and the upper economic strata, though the aristocracy would never have admitted that this was the case. As one indication of how right she was, note that bows were on the way out, except in formal circumstances such as a presentation at an aristocratic ball. No longer did servants bow or make a deep curtsey on entering and leaving a room, although they might nod their heads and curtsey almost imperceptibly when presenting a visiting card on a salver to their employer. Bourgeois morality, reflected in the plays of the period, prevailed everywhere in Europe and America, and partly as a reaction to the sexual freedom implied in romanticism, sexual repression was the order of the day.

The urban slums of the working poor and the mansions of the idle rich and the wealthy capitalists, brewers, mill owners, bankers, stockbrokers, businessmen, and aristocrats described in the novels of Charles Dickens and Honoré de Balzac (1799–1850) testify to the creation in Britain and continental Europe of a massive, impoverished proletariat on a hitherto undreamed-of scale. The despair and hopelessness of child labor, portrayed by Dickens in *David Copperfield*; the debtor's prison, described in *Little Dorrit* and *Nicholas Nickleby*; the infamous workhouse for the destitute, depicted in *Oliver Twist*—these institutions ground the masses down into vile servitude.

Although his descriptions are heart wrenching, Dickens was writing fiction. The situation was actually much worse than what he described. For a real sociological source, full of interviews and reportage about the wretched living conditions of the poor in mid-Victorian England, read the thoroughly researched and fascinating *London Characters and Crooks* by Henry Mayhew. He published the first two volumes of his sociological analysis in 1851—the year of the Great Exhibition in Hyde Park, meant to show what marvelous technological strides and wonderful progress the British Empire had made—under the title *London Labour and the London Poor*. This was followed in 1861 and 1862 by two more volumes. The seamy underside of London comes vividly to life in their pages, and even today Mayhew's descriptions of beggars, prostitutes, scavengers, and "dust-sifters" (we would call them "garbage-pickers" in America) have the power to shock, and are all too reminiscent of contemporary conditions in urban areas worldwide.

Even those who were employable could inhabit the workhouse. Among its inmates, besides destitute boys like Oliver Twist, could be found chimneysweeps' apprentices, vagrant cotton-spinners, and out-of-work dock laborers, as well as tramps (the word was originally "trampers") and pickpockets. The unsanitary, unhygienic workhouses were filled with rats and other vermin, and disease was rife. Medical care was scarce, when there was any at all. According to a sneak thief who stayed in many of them for a fortnight, "They used to give the lodgers a piece of bread at night, and another in the morning, and a night's lodging on straw or boards." And Mayhew describes "bone-grubbers and rag-gatherers, the 'pure', or dogs'-dung collectors, and the cigar-end finders": "The majority [of these marginalized people] are, moreover, persons who have been brought up to other employments, but who for some failing or mishap have been reduced to such a state of distress."

But many middle- and upper-class Victorians, comfortably ensconced in their stuffy houses, did not want to know about all that. They averted their eyes from the miserable life of the prostitutes or the drug underworld, with its opium dens and corruption, portrayed, for instance, in Dickens's last, uncompleted novel, *The Mystery of Edwin Drood*, and preferred to ignore the squalor and degradation that were practically staring them in the face.

In France, conditions for the working class and the poor were not much different than they were in England, as Balzac and later the impassioned naturalist Emile Zola (1840–1902) made clear. The face of the city of Paris had changed considerably: the slums around the Louvre were cleared away. New water supply and sewage systems were installed. And the wide boulevards we know today were constructed under the direction of Napoleon III's chief urban planner, Baron Georges Eugène Haussmann (1809–1891), whose schemes were the most ambitious since Napoleon I had put through the Rue de Rivoli and contemplated reconstruction that was never completed. But there were horrible working-class slums in the eastern districts where life was absolutely miserable. The Franco-Prussian War of 1870 ended in the overthrow of the emperor and the siege of Paris, followed in 1871 by the Communard revolution, which began in the eastern sections of the city. This uprising testified to the abysmal life of the proletariat and the deep desire for change. But the Commune was brutally overthrown, and the bourgeois Third Republic established.

Throughout the century, the ruling aristocracy was a force to be reckoned with, even if their power was being eroded. In Germany—a united country since its victory in the Franco-Prussian war, under the hegemony of Prussia—the caste system of the militaristic Prussian Junkers held sway, and the army officer corps came from that class and opposed the admission of all others, no matter how much they might merit advancement because of their abilities. And in Czarist Russia, industrially underdeveloped and in the thrall of a semi-feudal system even after the freeing of the serfs in 1861, the division between the classes was so severe that it would lead to riots, assassinations, and in 1917, to revolution.

In the Dual Monarchy of Austria-Hungary, under the long-lived and paternalistic Emperor Franz Josef (b. 1830; reigned 1848–1916), court etiquette in Vienna was exacting, rigid, and stagnant, and an inflexible class system prevailed. Franz Josef's son, Crown Prince Rudolf (1858–1889), had shot himself in a joint suicide with the woman he loved because he was not going to be allowed to marry her since she was not an aristocrat. The emperor disapproved of his nephew, the new heir apparent, Archduke Franz Ferdinand (1863–1914). Because he had married an impoverished aristocrat, even though she was of ancient lineage, Franz Josef would not allow her to sit near her husband at public functions and refused to allow their children the right to succeed to the throne.

In Queen Victoria's (b. 1819, reigned 1837–1901) England too, the class system was well established. Yet nouveau riche parvenu capitalists were ennobled because of the wealth they gained from whiskey or coal or financial schemes. They were, of course, despised by the masses and the old aristocrats alike. And even in Republican France, class snobbery was paramount in the upper economic circles, and aristocratic privilege with its sybaritic lifestyle had by no means disappeared—as Marcel Proust's (1871–1922) epic novel *In Search of Lost Time* clearly shows. America too had its class divisions, its robber barons and its labor problems, and its myth of the American dream alongside them.

There was an ethnocentric, imperialistic, racist attitude that filtered down through all social classes: some people were simply superior, others inferior; this was normal; this was the way things were. Such attitudes, exemplified in minstrel shows and vaudeville sketches, enabled the white majority of Americans to enact Jim Crow laws that entrenched racism against black people, and to move westward, taking over territory, mistreating the immigrant Chinese who would build the railroads, and meting out brutal treatment to Native Americans throughout the nineteenth century and into the twentieth. Simultaneously, European powers indulged in murderous exploitative imperialistic ventures in Africa. In the eighteenth century, India had been virtually annexed by Britain and was mercilessly exploited, though many in England would have said that they were merely bringing civilization to a benighted country, just as the French claimed to have a "civilizing mission" in Algeria and other countries they occupied. The occupiers seemed not to understand why there were periodic uprisings against their rule. The United States and European powers variously occupied and exploited parts of Asia. And the century ended in what seemed ominous saber rattling that would prove indeed to presage the horrors of the twentieth century.

Newspapers and such magazines as *The London Illustrated News* are wonderful source material for the study of the era. For instance, on the day my mother was born, January 15, 1915, World War I was raging, and the *New York Times* for that day reports that the French had abandoned several hundred miles of trenches to the Germans; the

King of Italy was touring the site of a devastating earthquake; and the women's right-to-vote campaign was making headway in all the states. Winter clothing sales were advertised, and you could buy a three-piece suit with an extra vest for $49. On Broadway, George Bernard Shaw's *Androcles and the Lion* was running, and Vernon (1887–1918) and Irene Castle (1893–1969) were dancing. At the Metropolitan Opera that evening, Enrico Caruso (1873–1921)—unrivalled as a tenor even today, both for his gorgeous voice and his thrilling singing—was scheduled to sing in *La Gioconda*; and Alma Gluck (1884–1938) got a rave review for her recital at Carnegie Hall.

The Stylistic Elements: Clothing, Accessories, Movement, Manners, and the Art of Living

Clothing and Movement: In her delightful book *Chekhov in My Life: A Love Story* (Harcourt, Brace and Company, 1950), Lydia Avilov (1864–1942) gives us a touching picture of domestic life in late nineteenth-century Russia, which is actually much as it was and is lived everywhere in the Western world. After an evening at the opera, she climbs into a sleigh to ride home:

> I went up. Chekhov, however, had sat down on the sidewalk side, so that I had to go around the sleigh before I could get in. I was wearing a cloak and my hands were not free, particularly as under my cloak I had to hold the train of my dress, my handbag, and my opera glasses. My feet sank in the snow and I found it very difficult to get into the sleigh without any help.

She would also have been wearing corsets, an undershirt, a girdle, and wide, long underpants, further restricting her movement.

There have been many scenes in such films as *Gone with the Wind* (1939) where wealthy young ladies are laced into their tight corsets, and the actresses have had to learn how to move and breathe in the nearly unmanageable hoop skirts and crinolines that were ubiquitous in America and Europe in the mid-nineteenth century. The photographer and actress Joanna van Mulder told me that when she was playing the title role in *Hedda Gabler* in full nineteenth-century costume, including the tight corsets, the director wanted her to throw herself into a chair instead of sitting down simply and comfortably, and she was obliged to do so sideways and to lean into the chair; it was impossible to make quick movements in the binding, uncomfortable costume. And walking gracefully backwards out of a room in a floor-length gown with a train, as women were obliged to do when leaving the presence of royalty, for instance, required great dexterity in the holding and movement of the skirts—made more difficult because the lady was often holding a fan, a reticule or purse, and perhaps other accoutrements as well.

Clearly, nobody could get into such clothing without the help of servants, who in the antebellum South were slaves. At least two people were required to put on the incredibly wide petticoats, once the corsets had been tightly laced. To put on the actual overskirt, huge tongs were employed on one side of the hoop skirt by one servant to lift it over the wearer's head, while the other servant lifted and held the other side. The skirt was then lowered slowly and carefully down into position before being arranged over the petticoats, like the sofa slipcover it sometimes resembled.

Lady's and men's clothing went through a kind of evolution in the course of the nineteenth and early twentieth centuries, which eventually led to the lighter garments we wear today and to increasing informality. But from the late 1820s on through the end of the century, women's floor-length dresses were heavy and cut high up on the chest, revealing as little as possible. The human form was hidden behind massive dresses with puffed-out leg-of-mutton sleeves, and faces concealed by large bonnets.

You can see pictures of all the changing fashions through the century in *Godey's Lady's Book*, an American magazine published from 1830 to 1898; the French magazine *La Mode Illustrée*; and *Harper's Bazaar*. The illustrations in *Godey's* from the late 1830s through about 1880 show that women's floor-length skirts did not change much in width, and the bottoms belled out. Hoop skirts came and went in the 1860s, but slimmer silhouettes were not seen until the beginning of the '80s, when, however, the bustle made a temporary return. The bell-shaped skirt gave way in the '90s to the wasp waist and slim hourglass shape, when the puffy leg of mutton sleeve was also back, only to disappear by 1905. The bosoms of the gowns were cut lower in the 1850s, but they were cut higher as the century wore on. Working women's clothes, like those of men, were always more practical and made of coarser material as well.

In 1881, the Rational Dress Society shocked the Victorian public by approving of Amelia Bloomer's (1818–1894) principles that women's clothing should not be confined to the customary floor-length dresses and gowns. Instead, they should wear the baggy bloomers with frilly cuffs—worn under a knee-length skirt—that she devised, particularly for any strenuous activity such as cycling. The bicycle had been invented, and riding it in parks was a popular form of recreation, especially for men. But women also wanted to ride it, and suitable costumes with baggy trousers were designed, similar to men's bicycling outfits of knee-length knickerbockers and tweed jackets. Worn with this costume were *balmorals*, or "bals" for short, a kind of canvas or leather sneaker. But it was not until 1912 that the more comfortable brassiere and girdle began to replace the one-piece corset.

In men's clothing, short vests were worn under the coat, as they would continue to be through at least the first half of the twentieth century. By the middle of the nineteenth century, top hats and long heavy greatcoats were worn, with wide trousers replacing the form-fitting leggings of the early 1800s. You have only to look at the many photographs of the Civil War era in America and the Victorians in England to get a sense of the heaviness of the clothing. Outerwear for men could include not only a large coat with a fur collar but a formal cape or cloak over it as well. The deerstalker hat and Inverness cape that Sherlock Holmes wears are a product of the movies, not of the stories, and were made famous by Basil Rathbone (1892–1967).

Most men were conformist in their dress, and even Oscar Wilde wore the frock coat (with knee-length skirts) and wide cravat we see him wearing in many photographs, although early in his public life he had been known for his iconoclasm in dress, sporting a blue velvet jacket and knee breeches. In the United States, where D'Oyly Carte had sent him on a lecture tour in 1882 as a publicity stunt to advertise *Patience*, his friend Lillie Langtry (1852–1929), who was on tour in a play, saw him giving one of his lectures on aesthetics. He was dressed in a "black velvet suit with knickerbockers, silk stockings and black shoes with silver buckles, his neck embellished by a Byronic collar," just as photographs from the tour show. He also had a brown velvet suit in the same style and a large, flowing scarlet cravat that he wore with it. And he usually wore a large boutonnière as well. "I do not think I ever met him wearing gloves, but he always carried a pale lavender pair, using them to give point to his gestures," wrote Langtry.

Accessories: Women's usual accessories included fans, pretty much out of fashion by the end of the nineteenth century. Apparently, there was a coded language of signals through slow fanning and slightly faster flut-tering that, though lost to us today, was well understood at the time. This complicated language was supposed to be part of the training of all young ladies. But whether this is myth or history, and how much it was used, remains an open question. The coded language—like the "language of flowers" and the meaning of precious stones—was probably quite unknown to Victorian men, even if women did learn it. The fan could, of course, be used in flirtatious or coquettish ways that would be quite obvious to anyone.

Women often carried muffs. Fox or fur stoles and feather boas were also among the usual accessories. Gloves had to be worn whenever a lady left the house, and could be arm-length if they were worn with a sleeveless gown at a formal ball or at the opera; and parasols or umbrellas were carried. Women also wore hats, which, again, were de rigueur when they left their domiciles, and could be quite elaborate and stuck on with hatpins. And women always carried handbags, or little purses or reticules—the latter, which were worn with a strap around a wrist, being usual with formal wear.

Eyeglasses, which had been worn since the Renaissance, were now more widespread, especially since prescriptions could be provided as opposed to general magnification. They were often in the form of *pince-nez* (French for "pinch nose")—as we see, for instance, in photographs of Anton Chekhov—and were framed lenses on a ribbon worn around the neck or fastened to a lapel. If you have to wear them, you must practice balancing them so that they don't fall off, as I did when I wore them as the Lord Chancellor in *Iolanthe*. Monocles on ribbons were also fashionable, and they too require practice—I used one as Sir Joseph Porter in *H. M. S. Pinafore*. At the right moment, you can make it fall out of your eye by relaxing the tension with which it is held in place.

Ladies often used folding or stationary *lorgnettes*, which were tiny framed eyeglasses on a long stem. They could be taken out ostentatiously at a ball or in any situation and used to view a prospective bride or groom, or for general inspection. In act 1 of Offenbach's 1866 comic opera *La Vie parisienne*, the courtesan Métella is embarrassed when she is confronted by two rival admirers in a train station, where each has gone to await her. She has arrived accompanied by a third suitor, whom the other two do not know. Whipping her lorgnette out of her dainty reticule, she snaps it pointedly in their direction to unfold it and looks the men up and down. "Connais pas," she says, to their utter astonishment. "Don't know you." She then winks at them behind the third admirer's back, but they are by no means mollified.

The jabot, still seen as men's neckwear early in the nineteenth century, was superseded first by the large, tied cravat and then later by the ascot and necktie (also called a cravat) that we still see, and by men's batwing bow ties. Men's shirts had to be fastened with cufflinks, until, eventually, the cuffs were buttoned; studs with which to attach collars and fasten shirtfronts were also replaced by buttons, although in formal wear they continue to be used. Cufflinks and studs could be quite elaborate, and bejeweled sets were made with diamonds or pearls. Of course it took time to get into all this gear, the discomfort of which was added to by starched collars and shirts, and dressing could be rather tedious. Dressing for a party, ball, or other affair was often completed with a *buttonhole*, which was a flower stuck in the left buttonhole of the jacket. Women often wore small sprays of flowers as a corsage or pinned to the upper parts of one of their sleeves; lilies and the delicate lily-of-the-valley were popular. Tiepins did not make their appearance until the end of the century. Even during the Regency, the fashion of wearing spats was seen; it became more widespread later in the century and disappeared after the 1920s and '30s. Men wore top hats, and later fedoras, and wore gloves and carried canes. Later in the century, men carried tightly furled umbrellas, which, in England, replaced the walking-stick for businessmen going to the city.

The Early Victorian Period: Henry Colman's European Life and Manners: This delightful book is invaluable source material for the conditions of life, and the attitudes of Americans towards Europe near the beginning of Victoria's reign. Born in Boston, Henry Colman (1785–1849), who appears from his letters to have been a most pleasant and modest person, was a congregational minister and teacher in Hingham, Massachusetts; a Unitarian minister in Salem; then a farmer in Deerfield; and an expert writer on agricultural subjects. He traveled extensively in England, and more briefly to Scotland, Ireland, Italy, and France—often going by railway or stagecoach, and observing everything with a perspicacious eye. Mr. Colman published his exhaustive letters home to friends and relatives in two volumes the year he died. In a tragic irony, he perished shortly after arriving in England on a trip that he had made for health reasons.

He knew a number of English aristocrats and was invited to the vast country estates of the Duke of Devonshire, which he discusses in some detail. As an agriculturalist, he was much interested in English farms, and he attended agricultural shows. Mr. Colman describes life's daily routines and the conditions of different social classes. He discusses transportation, hotels, food, and the theater, of which he generally rather disapproved (as he did of tobacco and alcohol), except for certain edifying, moral plays. He visited prisons and attended such events as the horse races at Epsom—very exciting, "But one race is enough for me." In 1848 he had been in Paris, where he saw the conditions and events that led to the uprising that overthrew King Louis-Philippe and established another republic, itself soon to be overthrown in the coup d'état that put Napoleon III on the throne.

The letters begin in 1843 in London, which Mr. Colman found a confusing, amazing, almost overwhelming labyrinth. He had never seen anything to rival it in the cities of America, and he vividly evokes the streets thronged with people. His descriptions of the traffic jams of horses and carriages could easily apply to the congested thoroughfares of modern cities, where the cars are lined up bumper to bumper. Mr. Colman notes that the streets are muddy when it rains but otherwise nice and clean, like the shops and market stalls, and that the crossings are regularly swept. But he notes as well the great number of wretchedly poor people, especially women, wandering in the streets and surrounded by the luxury of the *noblesse*, as he calls the aristocratic class.

He attended church services and was deeply impressed by the formality and magnificence of the dress worn by the priests and other officials, "which is in itself all beautiful, and operates powerfully on the veneration, but which is very foreign from the naked simplicity to which we are accustomed." And he notes that the Anglican Church "is altogether a political establishment," the opposite of religious establishments in the United States, which at the time were resolutely independent of government affiliation, as indeed they are supposed to be, according to the Constitution.

His hotel was comfortable, clean, and neat, and he paid thirty shillings per week, which was $6.67 in American money, for a parlor and bedroom. The price included breakfast and tea, but candles and fire were extra, and he paid a shilling to have his boots blacked and errands done. He also tipped the chambermaid. He could have paid less if he had taken rooms across the Thames, but he preferred the central location.

From London, on June 1, 1843, he communicated the following details to "My dear A___":

> The neatness of the better class of women is quite striking. The majority of them wear white cotton stockings, without those dirty pantalets which you see bobbing about the ancles [sic] of our women, and they have too much good sense under an affected modesty to let

their clothes draggle in the mud; but they raise their skirts a little, and you will see them elegantly dressed, and walking through, and crossing the muddiest streets in the rain and not a speck of dirt upon their shoes or stockings. I wish our ladies at home could take some lessons from them. Another thing shows their good sense. They all, in walking, wear pattens or thick-soled shoes, as thick as cork shoes, or else galoshes. India rubbers are not seen. They have another practice which I greatly admire. They seldom wear false curls; but women whose hair is gray wear it gray, and seem to take as much pains with, and as much pride in their silver locks as the younger ones do in their auburn tresses. I have met a good many ladies in company, but I do not find them to differ greatly from those I left at home, among the well-educated classes. Manners, however, are certainly much more a study than with us, and, upon the whole, make society much more agreeable; for they are not put on for the occasion, but grow up with them as a matter of course. Every thing in society proceeds much more quietly than with us.

There are many other details of a similar nature that bring the period vividly and personally to life in these eminently readable letters. Speaking of letters, mail was delivered in London six times a day!

The Mid-Nineteenth Century: **The Greville Memoirs:** One of the most interesting sources for what we know about nineteenth-century English life, from the Regency through the middle of Victoria's reign, are *The Greville Memoirs* (see also page 231), in eight volumes, published posthumously in three series. The intelligent Charles C. F. Greville (1794–1865), in his capacity as clerk to the sovereign's privy council from 1821 to 1859, was an astute observer of George IV, William IV (1765–1837), Victoria, and their entourages—and of the other great personalities and high society life of the era, as well as of the politics of the age, as the country headed towards governmental reforms. Like Pepys, he knew everybody. In a letter of October 25, 1874, to her grandson, the Crown Prince of Prussia (1859—1941, the future Kaiser Wilhelm II), Queen Victoria characterized the memoirs as "most indiscreet":

[Greville] shows a nasty, and most ill-conditioned disposition towards my two Uncles in whose service he was and whose hospitality he enjoyed. And I am most indignant that I should be praised at the expense of my poor old Uncle and predecessor, who though not dignified or very clever—was very honest—most anxious to do

what he thought was right. But the accounts in many ways are full
of truth—and the one of my first Council wonderfully exact.

It is true that Greville characterizes William IV as a sort of burlesque
eccentric, but he also gives him credit for his good qualities: "Although
King William was sometimes weak, sometimes obstinate, and miserably
deficient in penetration and judgement, he was manly, sincere, honest
and straightforward."

William, Duke of Clarence, the third son of George III, had lived in
obscurity until his elevation to the kingship "altogether forgotten by the
great world." Because of his naval career, he was nicknamed the "Sailor
King"; because of his eccentricity, he was nicknamed "Silly Billy." His
seven-year reign, starting in 1830, saw the abolition of slavery throughout the British Empire (he had originally opposed abolition); restrictions
on child labor; the Reform Act of 1832, which democratized the British
electoral system; and the burgeoning of industry.

Greville's memoirs are filled with people whose opinions sometimes
display the arrogant attitudes of imperialism, class snobbery, repression,
and reactionary conservatism that form the background to the entire
period. And we see the workings of the technological innovation that
was part of the Industrial Revolution. Greville marveled on December 3,
1851, that "At twelve o'clock yesterday morning the wonderful Electric
telegraph brought us word that two hours before the President had
accomplished his Coup d'État in Paris with success." The president was
soon to be Emperor Napoleon III.

The anecdotes Greville retails have their amusing side. Here is one,
dated January 4, 1838, one year into Victoria's reign, that illustrates the
class consciousness of the period and shows us how the high and mighty
lived. Greville has been invited to Belvoir Castle (he describes it in detail
on the occasion of his first visit in 1834), on the estates of John Henry
Manners, fifth Duke of Rutland (1778–1857), to celebrate the duke's
fifty-seventh birthday:

> Today (the Cook told me) nearly four hundred people will dine in
> the Castle. We all went into the Servants' hall, where one hundred
> and forty-five had just done dinner and were drinking the Duke's
> health, singing and speechifying with vociferous applause, shouting
> and clapping of hands. I never knew before that oratory had got
> down into the Servants' hall, but learned that it is the custom for
> those to whom 'the gift of gab' has been vouchsafed to harangue the
> others, the palm of eloquence being universally conceded to Mr.

Tapps, the head coachman, a man of great abdominal dignity, and whose Ciceronian brows are adorned with an ample flaxen wig, which is the peculiar distinction of the Functionaries of the whip.

And Greville proceeds to excoriate the "Radicals" who claim "the selfish aristocracy have no sympathy with the people." He would like to see such people observe the "feasting in the castle," and he extols the virtues of the hundreds of servants and peasants in the countryside round about Belvoir who praise and celebrate the Duke, who is "as selfish a man as any of his class—that is, He never does what he does not like, and spends his whole life in a round of such pleasures as suit his taste, but he is neither a foolish nor a bad man." Greville dislikes equally "the High Church and the High Tory," who are all for privilege and would suppress dissent of any kind. He believes that in the middle between the two extremes lies the happy mean of constitutional monarchy as practiced in Great Britain, that paradisiacal country where "God's in his heaven—All's right with the world!" as the Italian girl Pippa sings in the concluding line of Robert Browning's 1841 five-part verse drama, or dramatic poem, *Pippa Passes*.

Living Spaces and Furniture: Furniture, like clothing, went through an evolution in design and comfort throughout the century. From about 1815 to 1848 in Vienna, the "Biedermeier" style of furniture, constructed with simple, clean, curved lines, became popular with the middle classes. Among its hallmarks was the use of inexpensive woods such as cherry or oak, stained to resemble the more expensive mahogany. Some literature and music are also characterized as Biedermeier, because of their simplicity and accessibility. Schubert's lieder, for instance, can be played on the piano by anyone with only elementary training. Many people think the style was named after a particular person, but Biedermeier was a literary character whose name was used by several authors. The unsophisticated Biedermeier (the German word *bieder* means "virtuous"; the name Meier, or Meyer, is like Jones or Smith) typified the middle class, with its simplistic, narrow-minded morality. From being satirical, the term became descriptive.

By the Victorian era, heavy upholstered chairs and lots of cushions were the fashion. Victorian rooms could be dark, as curtained windows kept out the light, since airy rooms were deemed undesirable and unhealthy. Middle- and upper-class rooms were stuffed to bursting with knick-knacks, gewgaws, and bibelots. Photographs of Sarah Bernhardt's rooms attest to the hothouse atmosphere that was considered the mark of wealth and health, and the rooms could be ostentatious in a cramped way.

But there were those, such as the aesthetes, who wanted no more heavy draperies clogging the windows; the airless atmosphere of a drawing room invaded by family photographs and the framed, braided hair of the departed; dried flowers under glass and ornate clocks on elaborately carved mantelpieces; antimacassars on the back of every chair and lace doilies topped by little, chaste statuettes—no sex, please—on every table. Spare, trim, beautifully graceful open designs and plenty of wholesome air were to replace the stodgy, stuffy, unhealthy miasma, and a healthy flush born of outdoor exercise was to drive away the deadly pallor of the denizens of these Victorian parlors.

By the time 1914 rolled around, the atmosphere had lightened, partly because of technological innovations. Whereas in 1880 it was rare for a home to have indoor plumbing and hot-water heating, twenty years later, it was usual, as was the indoor flush toilet. Even toilet paper had been invented, by the British Perforated Paper Company, in 1880. The use of the telephone changed communication as much as the automobile, which required paved roads and streets; the train and then the airplane were to revolutionize transportation. Home refrigeration, in the form of the icebox—the iceman driving round neighborhoods in his truck delivered great blocks of ice to every house—changed to the electric refrigerator. These, of course, become increasingly sophisticated, as did the gas or electric stove and oven, which replaced the coal or wood-burning stove, and all of these changes naturally made servants' and women's work in the home much easier.

Mid-Victorian Domesticity and Mrs. Beeton: Before Mrs. Beeton, there was Alexis Benoit Soyer (1810–1858), a naturalized Englishman from France and the virtual inventor of the modern English army field kitchen. He was one of the most famous of Victorian cooks, and he published several books, including the popular *A Shilling Cookery Book for the People* (1855).

Mrs. Isabella Beeton's *The Book of Household Management Comprising Information for the Mistress, Cook, Housekeeper, Kitchen-Maid, Butler, Footman, Coachman, Valet, Upper and Under-Housemaids, Lady's-Maid, Maid-of-All-Work, Laundry-Maid, Nurse and Nurse-Maid, Monthly Wet and Sick Nurses, etc. etc.—also Sanitary, Medical and Legal Memoranda: with a History of the Origin, Properties and*

Uses of All Things Connected with Home Life and Comfort was a very popular book that went through innumerable editions. It is an invaluable resource for the Victorian period. If you have to play any of the servants listed in the delightfully unwieldy title, a veritable who's who of servants, this book is a necessity. It tells you all about the duties servants have to perform, as well as informing you about the etiquette and procedures of life in the upper- and upper-middle-class Victorian home, and how to give dinner parties, aside from containing almost countless recipes. This perennial classic was written by Isabella Mary Mayson (1836–1865), who was married to the publisher Samuel Orchard Beeton (1831–1877). She wrote articles in her husband's magazines, and in 1861 they were published in book form. Such was the parlous state of medicine that the poor woman died of puerperal fever at the age of only twenty-eight, a week after giving birth to her fifth child. *The Secret Life of Mrs. Beeton* (2007), produced by the BBC Masterpiece Theater, is superb, not only for the moving story it tells of her life, but for its accurate, detailed recreation of the Victorian era.

Victorian Country Life as Seen by the Reverend Francis Kilvert: The *Diary* kept from 1870–79 by Reverend Francis Kilvert (1840–1879), vicar of Bredwardine, a country village in Hertfordshire, is a great Victorian classic, and it places him in the first rank of diarists, along with Samuel Pepys, John Evelyn, Frances Burney, Thomas Turner, Rev. James Woodforde, and Dorothy Wordsworth.

This sweet-tempered, loving man died tragically young, just after his return from a honeymoon trip to Scotland. His wife Elizabeth survived him by thirty-two years. The diary presents a fascinating picture of the rural life of the times. Neither unworldly nor uncritical, he loves to laugh at the comedies and pantomimes he attends at the theater in London, to which he makes frequent trips. His interests are wide-ranging: he enjoys art exhibits and is a bit of a romantic sentimentalist. One of his favorite poets is "dear old Wordsworth." His rhapsodic descriptions of nature in fact remind one of the Wordsworths. Kilvert's enthusiasm for life and his affection for people, many of whom he describes with an eye to the telling detail, are infectious. This wonderful diary is replete with details of how life was lived and with a certain almost sentimental Victorian piety that the good clergyman took for granted. Although he was unquestioningly patriotic to a fault, he did sometimes look on life and people with a bemused, judgmental eye. There is a broad range of real-life, delightful characters; many incidents; and wonderful pictures of country fairs, flower shows, picnics, farm people and their interests and love for their animals; and much more besides.

Manners and Etiquette; Greetings and Salutations: Throughout the Victorian and Edwardian eras there were hundreds of books of etiquette published. And there is no doubt that their prescriptions as to what was considered "good form" were followed, as Victorian realist novels alone attest. One dared not be guilty of "bad form"; wearing the wrong size cufflinks could be considered "frightfully bad form," as Lord Lilburne, one of the characters in the film *The Shooting Party* (1985), which takes place in 1913, avers. Among the books is a diminutive volume called *The Young Man's Own Book; A Manual or Politeness, Intellectual Improvement and Moral Deportment*, published anonymously, probably in the 1850s, and virtually stolen, with no credit given, from Lord Chesterfield's letters to his son. Equally anonymous is the pervasively prescriptive *Decorum: A Practical Treatise on Etiquette and Dress of the Best American Society* (1879), which even has home health remedies for every condition known to humanity, much like *Mrs. Beeton's Book of Household Management*. And *The Correct Thing in Good Society* (1902) by Florence Howe Hall (1845–1922), daughter of Julia Ward Howe (1819–1910), who wrote "The Battle Hymn of the Republic," is positively exhaustive. Its convenient facing pages are headed "It is the correct thing" and "It is not the correct thing." Peruse the prolific Professor Thomas E. Hill's (1832–1915) popular works, *Manners and Morals Illustrated* and *Manual of Social and Business Forms*, or his highly respected *The Essential Handbook of Victorian Etiquette*—readily available because it has been republished in a charmingly illustrated paperback (the book went through many editions between 1873 and 1890)—and you will have a perfect guide to Victorian propriety.

In the United States, among the upper classes of both North and South, staid etiquette was the order of the day, with Southern high society having a reputation for gentility and Northern robber barons and magnates for more rigid formality. The growing West had its own set of rough-and-ready frontier manners, but once such cities as San Francisco were settled, the upper-class establishment observed the same kind of civility and politesse found among its counterparts in the East.

Florence Howe Hall's book covers how to write letters properly; how to send and receive invitations; what to do when paying calls; what to do when walking in the street (men should walk on the curb side, to protect women); how to converse and what to converse about (no politics or religion or any unseemly subject having to do with sex; and, please, no personal remarks, as even Alice remarks to the Mad Hatter when he observes that her hair wants cutting); how to behave at parties, receptions, dinners, lunches and dances; how a gentleman should behave at his club (don't demand too much attention from the waiter; don't propose someone for membership after he has been turned down; do behave with decorum and speak quietly). She also tells us that it is not the correct thing "to try to 'pump' people, or to ask questions about their personal or private affairs." Many of the same subjects are also dealt with in the anonymous books mentioned above. All that was left in the way of conversation, I suppose, is summed up in the ladies' chorus in Gilbert and Sullivan's *The Pirates of Penzance:* "Let us shut our eyes / And talk about the weather." On the other hand, if you must discuss something less anodyne, it is the correct thing "to think before you speak" and to be an attentive listener. But it is not the correct thing "to affect a foreign accent." And don't, by any means, express strong opinions either of approbation or disapprobation about the food you eat at a dinner you are invited to. In fact, don't express strong opinions about anything!

One did not call on someone without presenting a printed visiting card, which was brought on a tray by a servant to the person one desired to visit. And cards were used on every conceivable occasion. As the anonymous author of *Decorum* informs us, "It is becoming more usual for visits of ceremony to be performed by cards; it will be a happy day when that is universal." (Can you imagine a card "performing" a visit? No doubt Lewis Carroll could have: this is very *Alice in Wonderland.*) If you were going abroad and wished to say goodbye, you presented your card in an envelope with the initials "p. p. c." written on it: *pour prendre congé,* French for "to take leave"; but as the author of *Decorum* tells us, the initials "may with equal propriety stand for *presents parting compliments.*" Also, "Gentlemen ought simply to put their cards into their pocket, but ladies may carry them in a small elegant portfolio, called a card-case." And Professor Hill admonishes us never to examine the visiting cards placed in a "card basket" in order to see who else had been calling, on pain of being considered rude—unless, of course, you are "invited to do so."

Ladies had their "at home" days, and one knew which they were, and knew too that visiting hours were usually in the middle of the afternoon. But it was not improper to call in the morning, when necessary and appropriate. The following advice under the heading GENTLE-MAN'S MORNING CALL from *Decorum* should prove useful:

> Gentlemen would do well to bear in mind that, when they pay morning calls, they must carry their hats with them into the drawing room; but on no account put them on the chairs or table. There is a graceful manner of holding a hat, which every well-bred man understands.

You could, however, put your top hat on the floor, if you needed to use both hands! In any case, as we are informed, "Morning visits are always very brief, being matters of mere ceremony." Ladies could call on each other, but "A lady never calls on a gentleman, unless professionally or officially. It is not only ill-bred, but positively improper to do so." Gentlemen, however, "are permitted to call on married ladies at their own houses. Such calls the usages of society permits, but never without the knowledge and full permission of husbands." And of course, ladies were never to be seen in public unless accompanied by other ladies or by their husbands. Florence Howe Hall's *The Correct Thing in Good Society* has twenty-three pages devoted to what one may and may not do "When Making Calls."

Note that people did not call otherwise than on an official at-home day, except for some particularly compelling reason or if one were such a close intimate that it did not matter, and then one could be friendly and informal and even dress informally. But even when a visitor was making a friendly call, if the servant informed him or her that the master or mistress was "not at home," the visitor tactfully and discreetly went away, perhaps leaving a note or a card before doing so.

In the afternoon, tea would be served. The tea service was brought in by a servant, but the mistress of the house, or the master, if he were a bachelor, served her or his guests, who did not help themselves unless invited to do so. The opening scene of *The Importance of Being Earnest* takes place against the background of this well-established social custom, and all the characters would know the elaborate system of etiquette that was de rigeur. In Paris high society, there was a certain Anglomania that developed during the latter part of the nineteenth century: ladies served tea in the afternoon and used English phrases, as Proust's character Odette does in *Swann's Way*. For Parisian men, it was the highest privilege to be a member of the Jockey Club, founded in 1833 in Paris by the eccentric Lord Henry Seymour-Conway (1805–1859). In London, men went to their club frequently, and some spent as many evenings there as they did at home.

The etiquette books discuss how to deal with servants. Florence Howe Hall tells us that it is the correct thing "to be dignified but always courteous in one's demeanor towards servants," but it is not the correct thing "to be familiar with servants or to joke or laugh with them." And you mustn't gossip with servants either, nor must you rebuke them in the presence of other people.

There was a terribly elaborate, formal system of address that people used throughout the era in Victorian England. Husbands and wives often addressed each other as Mr. and Mrs. when they were in the company of others, and even in private; this was the case on the Continent as well, where old married couples in France or Germany called each other "Monsieur" and "Madame" or "Herr" and "Frau." In many cases, married couples did not use first names with each other for their entire lives. There was thus a certain respect displayed, but also a certain distance. And this custom had prevailed for a very long time. Even near the beginning of the nineteenth century, the parents of the eligible young ladies in *Pride and Prejudice* address each other as Mr. and Mrs. Bennett.

When talking of others or when talking to them, it was de rigeur to use titles and/or last names. It was the custom even in public schools for the boys to call each other by their last names. Only within the family circle were children addressed by their first names or by nicknames, but once they had grown to adolescence, they were addressed as "Master" or "Miss," titles that would also be used by servants when the children were younger. Above the age of fifteen, a boy was addressed as "Mister." Young women and girls addressed each other as "Miss" unless they became intimate friends, when they were said to "propose," meaning to suggest using first names with each other. It was customary to refer to the eldest unmarried daughter in a family by the title "Miss" and her last name; the other daughters were called "Miss" followed by both names. If one did not know a child's name, it was all right to address the child as "My boy" or "My girl." Read Jane Austen and Henry James (1843–1916), and you will see this sort of formality clearly.

The hierarchy of titles in the English aristocracy, and the forms of address associated with them, would be known to all the characters in that milieu. The king was addressed as "Your Majesty" and then as "Sire" for the rest of a conversation, although "Your Majesty" could be used throughout. The queen was addressed as "Your Majesty" and then as "Ma'am." The princes and princesses, children and grandchildren of the sovereign were (and are) addressed as "Your Royal Highness" and then as "Sir" or "Ma'am." Royal great-grandchildren are addressed as

"Lord" or "Lady," followed by their first names. In descending order of rank, a duke and duchess are both "Your Grace" or "Duke" or "Duchess"; a marquess (marquis) and marchioness; earl and countess; viscount, viscountess, baron and baroness are all "My Lord" or "My Lady" or "Lord" or "Lady," followed by their titular name. The same form of address is used for the eldest children of all these nobles. In Scotland, the heir presumptive is addressed as either "Lord" or "Lady" or "Master" or "Mistress." A baronet and his lady are addressed respectively as "Sir" or "Sir" followed by the first name; and "Lady" or "Lady" followed by the first name. Knights of the realm, whose titles are not hereditary, are addressed as "Sir," and dames (of orders other than the Thistle or the Garter) as "Madam" or "Dame" followed by the first name; knights' wives and ladies (of the order of the Thistle or the Garter) as "My Lady" or "Lady" followed by the first name. Kings George IV and William IV were called "Sir" by their prime ministers in private converse, as opposed to the public occasions during which they were addressed as "Your Majesty." Victoria was "Ma'am" in private to her ministers of state and ladies in waiting. A courtesy title was conferred on a duke's eldest son, who could be "Viscount," but all the other sons were "Lord" followed by their first names. The aristocrats, like the schoolboys, usually talked about each other and called each other by their last names; they also signed letters using only the last names connected with their title.

The Anglican clergy were mostly addressed by their titles—Bishop, Dean, Canon, and so forth. But an archbishop could also be addressed as "Your Grace." In the Roman Catholic Church, the Pope was and is addressed as "Your Holiness," "Holy Father," or "Most Holy Father"; cardinals as "Your Eminence"; archbishops and bishops as "Your Grace" or "Your Excellency"; a monsignor as "Monsignor"; and a priest as "Father"; a nun as "Sister"; and a mother superior as "Mother Superior."

Conditions were similar in the rest of the European monarchies. In France, Germany (once it was united in 1871) and Austria, the sovereign was often addressed in the third person, which translates as "His" or "Her Majesty": "If His Majesty would deign to command his humble servant..." The king could also be called "Sire" or "Your Majesty" by those who were more intimately acquainted.

In the United States, where such titles were constitutionally prohibited, Florence Howe Hall tells us that it is not the correct thing for an American citizen even to have a coat of arms on his visiting card. Less formal manners prevailed in America, although the conventions of etiquette were still quite prevalent, obviously, and the titles "Mr." and "Mrs." were customary even among intimates and married couples. The 1947 film *The Heiress*, based on Henry James's novel *Washington Square*, demonstrates American Victorian period manners quite clearly and shows us the etiquette of making calls, as does *Life with Father*, made in the same year.

In an age when smoking was considered daring and usually indulged in only in private, and when women were not supposed to do it at all, men often carried cigarette cases, sometimes quite ornate and made of silver and engraved. Oscar Wilde used to present them as gifts. Cigarette holders were also quite common. Queen Victoria forbade smoking, even on the grounds of all her royal residences, and in any room she might be expected to be in at any time, which effectively meant that smoking was confined to the servants' quarters. She had actually tried smoking herself at picnics, in order to drive off the insects, but she didn't care for it.

Much went on in private life behind closed doors that was considered scandalous, and aside from private encounters on the street between prostitutes and their clients, there were heterosexual and homosexual brothels. These are described by Marcel Proust in *Sodom and Gomorrah* and elsewhere in his novel, and were publicized in such affairs as the Oscar Wilde trials or the Cleveland Street scandal, regarding a homosexual establishment in that street, in which several aristocrats were implicated. In 1893, the Eulenburg affair in Germany shocked all of Europe: the homosexuality of one of the Kaiser's closest friends, who was married with children, was exposed, and Wilhelm himself was implicated.

Nevertheless, the public atmosphere was one of distant formality. People showed themselves in their carriages in the Bois de Boulogne in Paris or on the avenues and nodded to their acquaintances; the courtesans were whispered about and ogled, the aristocrats presumably admired—or at least their clothing was. In England, people went for Sunday strolls after attending church dressed in their Sunday best. The same sort of custom prevailed in the other cities of Europe. In Vienna people strolled on the Prater, in Berlin on Unter den Linden or in the parks, in order to see and be seen. In the United States, too, there was the formal Sunday stroll after church in cities and towns.

Bows and curtsies were also de rigeur. By the 1840s, men bowed from the waist or inclined the head without putting either hand over the heart. By the end of the century, men would nod to each other in the street, and perhaps doff their hats to a superior. But it had been customary before that for friends and acquaintances to do a bow from the waist. And men were advised to remove the cigars from their mouths when bowing to a lady in the street, to whom they always doffed their hats.

Women's curtsies were a bit less elaborate than they had been, except at court functions, where women still curtsied to the floor when making obeisance or upon being presented to the queen. Female servants curtsied slightly from the waist when entering and leaving a room, and particularly if they were talking to their employers.

Bows and low curtsies on entering a formal party or ball were required. Men could still "break a leg," and women did deep curtsies. In military fashion, German aristocrats and highly placed officers added to the bow the custom of following it with heel clicking.

There was even a proper way for gentlemen to shake hands: you were supposed to offer the whole hand and to grasp the other's hand firmly but not too hard, as Professor Hill informs the avid reader. And, he tells us, you must only shake the hand for two or three seconds at most. And you must shake with the right hand, unless it is impossible to do so because you are holding gloves or a hat, in which case you must say, "Excuse my left hand."

You were supposed to sit without crossing your legs—impossible for women to do in any case—and to remain upright. At dinner, you were never supposed to place your elbows on the table or to chew with your mouth open. "Eccentricity should be avoided as much as possible," warns Professor Hill, when talking of conduct at the dinner table.

The Salons of the Victorian Era: Home Entertainment: In Europe and the United States, in the upper economic strata, there were literary and artistic salons and luxurious society parties, with servants passing among the guests with trays of food and drink, just as you see them in many films and in popular genre paintings of the Belle Époque by the impressionist Jean Béraud (1849–1935). Refreshments could also be served at a buffet table, where the guests helped themselves.

At some of these events, young ladies made their debuts in society and were presented to their highly placed host and hostess after making an entrance. In France, attending a particular salon had political and social implications. During the Dreyfus Affair, for example, those who believed in the innocence of the only Jewish officer on the French General Staff—Alfred Dreyfus (1859–1935), accused in 1894 of spying for the Germans and later exonerated—hardly spoke to those who believed he was guilty; there were Dreyfusard and anti-Dreyfusard salons. The latter were often rigidly reactionary, and stood for *la vieille France* (the Old France), meaning the virtues of France under the Bourbon monarchy, which was to them a paradise. Among its finer attributes, as far as they were concerned, was that Jews, Napoleonic aristocrats, and anyone not of ancient lineage were simply excluded from all social consideration.

François Delsarte's system became so popular that even nineteenth- and early twentieth-century society ladies studied it. Anna Morgan's *An Hour with Delsarte: A Study of Expression* (Lee and Shepard, 1889), for instance, illustrated with figures, was meant not for actors but for the general public, and in particular for the society belle. In chapter 2, "The Importance of Correct Bearing," we read:

> One of the most deplorable faults of bearing is produced by giving an undue prominence to the abdomen, and is emphasized by carrying the hands directly over it (see Fig. 1). Observation need not be confined to the lower classes for this glaring fault; one would have no difficulty in finding it in the higher grades of society, where it is unpardonable...
>
> Two forms of bearing which one frequently observes, and which are certainly not attractive, are the habitual attitudes of arrogance and self-conceit: the first is produced by throwing the weight on the back leg and carrying the shoulders upward and backward (see Fig. 4); the second by a conspicuous presentation of the chest...
>
> A natural poise is shown when one stands with one foot slightly in advance of the other, the weight resting easily on the balls of the feet.

The book is full of exercises meant to instill gracefulness. How to sit and move, how to hold your head, and what to do with your hands are also covered, and—this is important for anyone doing plays set in this period—she tells you "How to Bow":

> In polite usage, the pretentious formal bow is no longer decorous; it has been superseded by the mere graceful inclination of the body, bending slightly from the ankles; and this form prevails on the platform and in the parlor. Out of vogue too is the familiar nod of the head in recognizing another. An inclination of the body is the genteel form of recognition, which has the merit of being graceful as well.

In salons in Europe, and in the United States, where they took this sort of thing seriously, the society hostesses and hosts provided a great deal of artistic entertainment, from vocal and instrumental concerts to "tableaux," in which the hostess and her male and female friends would don costumes and create a famous scene from history or art. Delsarte gestures and poses in these tableaux were as de rigueur as the French phrases thrown into conversation in English and American drawing rooms. The salon devotees were also very fond of poetry recitations and interpretive dances, and the hostess or someone invited to perform would dance or give recitations using the appropriate Delsarte gestures.

The art of "statue posing" was especially popular, lending particular piquancy to an acid remark of Proust's friend, Madame Geneviève Straus (1849–1926), about a woman who had gained an enormous amount of weight: "She's no longer a statue, she's a group!" Madame Straus, the daughter of the composer Fromental Halévy (1799–1862), was a notable personality of the era—a committed Dreyfusard, like Proust, Zola and Anatole France (1844–1924), and a witty cultivated salon hostess. Offenbach's librettist, Ludovic Halévy was her first cousin, and she was the widow of the composer Georges Bizet (1838–1875)—whose uncle, incidentally, was Delsarte. In 1887, after eleven years of widowhood, she married the lawyer Emile Straus (1844–1929), who adored her. Some of her friends said, "You're marrying Straus? What a crashing bore!" "What do you want?" she replied. "It was the only way I could get rid of him."

One can hardly imagine a staid Victorian lady across the channel making such a joke, except, perhaps in a play by Oscar Wilde. But compare Madame Straus's remark with one made to Samuel Rogers in the Regency period, when he lamented the fact that he was unmarried: "If I had a wife, I should have somebody *to care about me.*" "Pray, Mr. Rogers," said Lady J., "how could you be sure that your wife would not *care more about somebody else than about you?*"

Food and More about Table Manners: The formality extended, of course, to dinner parties, from those given by Queen Victoria (who often wrote of herself in the remote third person as "the Queen") on down to the less sumptuous affairs of the middle class. Food for the wealthier classes was abundant, extravagant, and lavishly prepared and presented.

Among the many well-known restaurants opened in London by the end of the nineteenth century were the Café Royal, established by a French wine merchant in 1865 in Regent Street, and Kettner's, established by a former chef of Napoleon III in 1867 in the heart of the Soho district. In 1890, the renowned Auguste Escoffier (1846–1935) refined and expanded classic French cuisine at the Savoy Hotel in London, where he set up the kitchens and oversaw the cooking under the management of Richard D'Oyly Carte, who was expanding his fortunes using the money he had made in the theater. Escoffier later went to work at the Ritz Hotel in Paris, where he established the kitchens in 1898 for the Swiss entrepreneur, César Ritz (1850–1918). All four restaurants still exist in all their ornate Victorian splendor, but Kettner's is now a pizza and champagne bar.

In 1903, Escoffier wrote the greatest book of classic French cuisine, *Guide Culinaire* (translated as The Escoffier Cookbook), a perfect guide to the food of the period. Escoffier invented such dishes as melba toast and peach melba (a peach poached in sugar syrup, then set on a scoop of vanilla ice cream, with sweetened raspberry puree poured over it, surmounted by whipped cream), in honor of the much acclaimed Australian opera singer Nellie Melba (1861–1931). Her farewell speech at Covent Garden in 1926 was recorded, and you can hear the diction and style of the period when she had been so admired and idolized for her heavenly voice.

All over Europe in the early nineteenth century, until around 1850, food was presented to diners using the French service—everything was served at the same time, usually in three courses comprising many dishes each. Platters were placed on the table, and the guests helped themselves. In the Russian service that prevailed after 1850, the food was cut up and plated and then put in front of the guests, or else they served themselves from platters held out to them by footmen. The Russian service, which was soon more popular, is what we generally know today at most restaurants and family meals. A repast is served in discreet courses: starter, main dish, and dessert, followed by coffee and perhaps petits fours. But in Victorian days there were often twelve courses, with different soups, fish, and roasts following in succession. In the great houses of the Victorian, Edwardian, and Georgian eras, in both Europe and America, men and women separated at the end of the meal: women remained in the dining room for such delicacies as elderberry wine; men retired to the billiard room for port and cigars and perhaps a card game.

Through the beginning of the First World War, the upper economic classes ate a great deal of food at any one meal: courses of clear and cream soups, shellfish, fish, poultry and meat; salads and cooked vegetables mounded on platters; puddings, trifles and a great variety of fresh fruit, from the farm or raised in the hothouse. And they drank wine and champagne by the ton, much in the manner, it would seem, of Rabelais' Gargantua. Later, the Americans invented the predinner cocktail, much to the horror of many Europeans, who preferred an aperitif of straight Scotch whiskey, perhaps with a splash of soda (but never with ice cubes, as was the fashion in the United States); or gin with a dash of tonic or bitters; or the ubiquitous sherry of Victorian England.

Mr. Colman informs us that in June 1843, during his trip to London, he partook of "a very substantial meal" when he "breakfasted with a large party of gentlemen, members of Parliament and others. This is a charming mode of visiting and very common. You go at ten and usually sit until twelve."

In Queen Victoria's household, four separate dinners were given every evening: one for the lower servants, one for the upper rank of servants, one for the official members of the household (when they were not dining with Victoria), and one for the queen and her guests. The menus were lavish, but the queen ate very quickly and consumed in a trice the copious helpings she insisted upon being served. The brown Windsor soup she loved was made not only with a base of ham and calves' feet to give it body, but also with shellfish and game, and flavored with Madeira. She also adored cream of chicken soup. Fish and four kinds of meat were usually offered at every dinner. Victoria had a great appetite for roast beef, boiled chicken, and Scottish haggis served with potatoes. For dessert there were hot and cold puddings of various kinds—she especially loved trifle—chocolate cakes, and biscuits, and she ate masses of pears and apples. She also adored oranges, which she ate with a spoon after the top had been sliced off. Throughout the meal she drank several kinds of wine, and Scotch with mineral water or soda.

Behavior and manners at these dinners were stultifyingly formal, and the atmosphere depended entirely on the queen's mood. She could be depressed and silent, or in a mood to cross-examine the members of her family. And if she were obliged to invite a minister of state whom she disliked, the mood could be chilly at best, or positively glacial. Everyone was expected to be on his or her best behavior, of course. These dinners are very well depicted in *Mrs. Brown* (1997), with Judi Dench as Victoria setting the perfect tone. Similar grand occasions among the upper bourgeoisie are described in all their hilarious solemnity by Charles Dickens in *Dombey and Son* (1848) and other novels, well before the era portrayed in *Mrs. Brown.*

Conversation, initiated by the queen, when she chose to do so, could be dull and solemn and entirely unmemorable, according to a number of people who were there and who kept journals. As soon as the queen finished eating a course, not only was her dish removed, but those of the assembled company as well, whether they had finished eating it or not. Often they had not finished, since the queen ate so rapidly, but that was etiquette, and it had to be observed. One evening, the queen was talking with the distinguished diplomat and government minister for various departments at various times, Spencer Compton Cavendish, Lord Hartington (1833–1908), who was so engrossed in the conversation that he had not finished his mutton and green peas, whereas the Queen had finished hers. Both plates were removed, and Hartington, apparently unacquainted with the ritual, was unpleasantly surprised. "Here," he cried to the servant, "bring that back!" Everyone at the table was immediately terrified. The servant did so, much to the genuine amusement of the sovereign, who was famously not amused but who was very fond of Hartington, as she makes clear in her journals. She actually smiled, and the company relaxed—a little. In fact, the atmosphere could as often be jovial and pleasant as miserable and solemn, since it depended on how the queen was feeling. Sometimes she liked jokes and laughter and could laugh quite heartily, particularly in the last few years of her life.

As the nineteenth century drew to a close, food had improved in Europe and the United States for all social classes, and it was better distributed as well. The automobile was so popular by 1900 that the Michelin Tire Company published the first edition that year of its guidebook to French hotels and restaurants. The intrepid motorist, in long duster and goggles, wearing a cap and driving gloves, could find gas stations and repair shops that sold Michelin tires wherever he or she went in France.

Marcel Proust, born in 1871 in Auteuil—then a village just outside Paris, where his pregnant mother had fled during the brief and bloody episode of the Commune—extolled the cuisine of his childhood and wrote mouthwatering descriptions of boeuf à la mode (braised beef with carrots in a rich brown sauce redolent of white wine, thyme, bay leaf, parsley, and onions), roast duck with red wine sauce, and pineapple with kirsch. The Parisian working class, on their way home from the job, stopped in at cheap, crowded restaurants called *bouillons*, where they got a hunk of delicious bread and a bowl of bouillon with meat and vegetables in it.

By the end of the century, the food in Vienna, influenced by Austria-Hungary's vast empire, had never been better: Viennese pastry, like French baking, was world renowned. The Viennese, again like the French, loved their coffee and cake. And there were dumplings and roast duck with red cabbage from the future Czechoslovakia, soups and goulashes from Hungary, and Austria's own boiled beef, a delicious dish made in a great variety of ways, which Emperor Franz Josef ate for dinner almost every day.

Social Dancing: At a party or a ball, a gentleman conducting a lady to the dance floor or in to dinner was never supposed to offer his hand, gloved or not, but only his arm, on which the lady was supposed to rest hers lightly. The typical dances of the period include the waltz in three-quarter time, considered quite scandalous, even in staid Vienna where the Strauss family held musical sway; the polka, which Queen Victoria thought so licentious that she forbade it; the galop; and the quadrille, with figures very much like that of American square dancing. In Lewis Carroll's *Alice Adventures in Wonderland,* as you may recall, there is the famous "Lobster-Quadrille," danced by denizens of the sea: "Will you walk a little faster?" said a whiting to a snail, / "There's a porpoise close behind us, / And he's treading on my tail."

The etiquette observed at a ball or dance was very strict. Florence Howe Hall even tells us that it is not the correct thing "for women with ugly scraggy necks, shoulders and arms, to display them in a way that is painful to the beholders." Cover up, ladies! And be sure to wear your "richest jewelry!" A lady entered first, followed by her husband. The host and hostess received their guests with a bow, and the guests returned the bow and, sometimes, shook hands with the host and hostess. Men asked women to whom they had been presented to dance with them, but women were not supposed to ask men or even to hint that they would like to dance. It is not the correct thing "for a gentleman to enter into conversation with a lady he does not know." Nor must a lady refuse an invitation from a man and then immediately accept one from another: "Duels have been fought for smaller matters than this."

Dueling in the Nineteenth Century: The first treatise on dueling was published in Venice in 1553, when it was already an old and established practice. Atavistic and reprehensible in the eyes of many, it was also illegal almost everywhere. Alexander Hamilton, Mikhail Lermontov (1814–1841), and Alexander Pushkin (1799–1837) are among the well-known victims killed in duels, and many dueling scenes in literature are famous: *Hamlet*; Pushkin's *Eugene Onegin*; Alexandre Dumas' (1802–1870) *Three Musketeers* and *The Count of Monte Cristo.* The etiquette of dueling is graphically depicted in the latter in the scenes involving the duel between the Count and young Albert de Morcerf.

By the nineteenth century, the etiquette of dueling had become complicated, formalized, and codified. *L'Art du duel* (The Art of the Duel, 1885) by the art critic, collector, and writer Adolphe Tavernier (1860–1922), detailed the code of conduct to be followed. The journalist and novelist Aurélien Scholl (1833–1902) maintained in his preface to that beautifully illustrated book that "the duel is superior even to the law, since a judge can satisfy only one of the parties.... The duel is to wounded honor what the band-aid is to cuts and open sores." The duel was meant to be a fair fight between two equal adversaries, refereed by objective outside parties—the seconds—who also served as witnesses in case of legal complications. And it was only to be fought once—no second duel for the same offence, whatever the outcome. Usually, the offended party—the challenger—chose the type of weapon to be used; neither adversary could use weapons he owned, because in the interests of fairness, the weapons had to be unfamiliar to them.

There were three degrees of offense: a simple offense in the form of a remark, drawing, or gesture; an offense accompanied by insulting behavior; or an offense accompanied by physical assault—a slap, throwing a glove or a glass of wine in someone's face. In the first case, the offended party had the right to choose only the weapon. In the second, he could choose both the weapon and the conditions of the duel (one or two shots, for instance). If a victim of the third kind of offense, he chose those and, in addition, the distance (fifteen, twenty, or thirty paces, for example) that would be allowed between the duelists—the choice of the conditions and the distance applied only to a duel with pistols. Also, "the prescriptions of the dueling code are not absolute... and a certain liberty in evaluating the facts is always left to the seconds and the arbitrators," whose "imperative duty" is, in fact, to discourage a duel and to refuse to participate if they consider the reasons for it to be frivolous.

Tavernier goes into the nice question of who has the right to choose the weapon in certain cases:

> To a slap, you reply, I imagine, with a blow from your cane that breaks your aggressor's right arm. What should one decide in such a case? As the offended party, the first one assaulted, you choose the epee. You will certainly have to wait for your enemy to be completely cured before measuring yourself against him.

But while he is recovering, you have plenty of time to improve your skill in fencing, which he obviously cannot do. You therefore lose the right to choose the weapon! After all, "You could have slapped him back, instead of breaking his arm."

Cards were exchanged (as opposed to the gauntlet or gloves of an earlier era being thrown down and picked up), and the four seconds—two for each duelist—met in solemn conclave; the opponents would henceforth communicate only through them. Anyone had the right to refuse to participate in a duel (dueling was illegal, after all) even at that point in the proceedings. And it was the seconds' duty to try to discourage the affair altogether. But if explanations, apologies, and excuses were offered but not accepted, they arranged the time, place, and details of the duel and then informed the two opponents, who accepted the conditions or might demand changes. The duelists' seconds and a doctor, sometimes two, stood by as the duel proceeded. The duelists first saluted each other. Sometimes, an apology might suffice for the duel to be called off even at that point. If pistols were used, the duelist chose their arms from a selection presented by the seconds, who loaded the guns. Then the two opponents stood with their backs to each other, and on a signal from one of their seconds, chosen by lot, they walked ten or more paces from each other, turned, and fired either at will or on a word or pre-arranged signal (the dropping of a handkerchief, for instance) from one of the seconds. If the weapons were swords, a similar procedure to that in judging a fencing match was used, and on the first blood, the duel was usually over—although if that had not been stipulated, it could continue. Wounding with a pistol or drawing blood with a sword was generally sufficient for satisfaction.

Painting and Photography

The era of photography began around 1839, when the daguerreotype process was perfected by Louis Daguerre (1789–1851), a scene painter at the opera. The extensive photographs of the American Civil War by Matthew B. Brady (ca. 1823–1896), who traveled with the Union armies, still have the power to startle us in their starkness and candor, as we see the sad bodies of slain soldiers on the battlefields. And the French portraits by Félix Nadar (1820–1910) (who was also a military balloonist, and led a company of balloonists during the siege of Paris in the Franco-Prussian War of 1870–71) of such notable people as Victor

Hugo, George Sand, and Jacques Offenbach bring his sitters vividly to life, especially since his aim was to capture their personalities, so that he photographed whole series of portraits of a single sitter.

For the first time, theatrical productions were photographed in detail, and every aspect of the original mounting of such plays as *The Seagull* or Henry Irving's or Sarah Bernhardt's productions, and almost all the Gilbert and Sullivan and Offenbach comic operas, are available. We get a sense from these photographs of what those productions must have been like, and when we couple that with some recordings that were made by actors such as Bernhardt or Irving and singers who worked with Offenbach or Gilbert and Sullivan, we have a real sense of nineteenth-century performance style.

But of course the art of painting did not disappear with the advent of photography. As a result of the realism of photography, it changed considerably, as painters felt they could get away from stuffy, academic, ultrarealistic canvases—photographic realism, as it began to be called—and experiment with effects of light and shade. Eventually, they dispensed even with those, as they turned to abstract forms of art. Romanticism, in fact, endures in painting for the entire century and more. Its various schools include those of the German fantasists; the Victorian Pre-Raphaelites, who admired the so-called pure art of painters before Raphael; and such precursors of impressionism as Camille Corot (1796–1875), with his gray-green, blurred landscapes, mesmerizing in their dreaminess. The grand vastness of Eugène Delacroix (1798–1863), and the fantasist Gustave Moreau (1826–1898), whose canvases of such subjects as the beheading of John the Baptist could be positively frightening, are typically romantic. And the impressionists themselves fall into this category.

A precursor of impressionism, the English artist Joseph Mallord William Turner (1775–1851), painted on a thick white ground and laid in the sketch of his painting in bright, light colors thinned with turpentine. He then began to paint over them in thick layers, and the final effect of his overlaid glazes and washes is luminescent, particularly when you stand well back from his paintings. His contemporary, John Constable (1776–1837), was more conservative and more realistic in his peaceful, evocative landscapes depicting the beauty of the English countryside.

Experimenting with color and light, and making shadows reflect purples, greens, and other colors instead of the simple, classic black, was what Claude Monet (1840–1926), Edouard Manet (1832–1883), and the other impressionists had decided to do, and they shocked the conformist academic realists of their day, who considered them slightly unhinged. The revealing portraits of Jacques-Emile Blanche (1861–1942)—a friend of Proust, whose portrait he painted—are very typical of the more standard art of the late nineteenth century, although they borrow impressionistic techniques; he also wrote very informative memoirs. His paintings stand in sharp contrast to the unique, iconoclastic, innovative style of Vincent van Gogh's (1853–1890) evocative, broad landscapes and strange night skies, as well as his still lifes and the portraits of the people he knew.

In the United States, the huge, magnificent canvases of Albert Bierstadt (1830–1902), glorifying and aggrandizing the soaring mountain landscapes and billowing clouds of the wide open spaces of the American West, and the splendid romantic paintings of the Hudson River School of Upstate New York portray an unspoiled country, untouched by the ravages of man's presence, that existed mostly in the painters' imaginations.

In the area of graphic arts, the caricaturist Honoré Daumier's (1808–1879) satiric prints are still highly amusing and allow us a glimpse into a vanished world, which we can nevertheless recognize and understand because, despite changing times and customs, there is a universal psychological element in his pictures of life in school, in the law courts and hospitals, in the political arena, and at home.

Music

The nineteenth century is the era of the early and late romantic schools of music and the flowering of the opera. There are, of course, a vast number of recordings of the operas of Karl Maria von Weber (1786–1826); Gioacchino Rossini, a great gourmet in his retirement; Gaetano Donizetti (1797–1848); Vincenzo Bellini (1801–1835); Giuseppe Verdi; Giacomo Puccini; and the repulsive Richard Wagner (1813–83), a perfect horror, whose bigotry, pretensions, and bombast did not preclude his writing operas that many people adore. Offenbach's and Gilbert and Sullivan's comic operas, all of which belong musically to romanticism, have been previously mentioned. The manically obsessive anti-Semite Wagner envied Offenbach his lightheartedness while despising him for being a Jew, albeit one who had converted to Catholicism in order to marry the woman he loved.

Another Jewish convert, to Lutheranism this time, Felix Mendelssohn (1809–1847)—like Mozart a child prodigy—died at the age of only thirty-eight, but his prodigious output of memorable pieces has rarely been surpassed. Everything he composed is magic, like his famous incidental music to Shakespeare's *A Midsummer Night's Dream*. The octet he composed at the age of sixteen is still considered a mature masterpiece, as is the unsurpassed Violin Concerto in E minor, Op. 64. And as conductor of the Gewandhaus Orchestra in Leipzig, he made that city the musical center of his day. He premiered symphonies by Robert Schumann (1810–1856) and Franz Schubert (1797–1828), and in his "historical" concerts, he kept alive the music of Handel, Haydn, Mozart, and others, and was single-handedly responsible for the revival of Bach's music. It is to Mendelssohn also that we owe the preeminence of the conductor in contemporary music.

Among the two or three supreme melodists of the romantic or any other age is Franz Schubert. Every great composer has contributed memorable melodies to the corpus of music, but it can only be said of a few (Mozart, Mendelssohn, Offenbach, and Schubert among them) that they were melodically so prolific that nearly everything that came from their pens was delightful and extraordinary, and bewitches the listener on first hearing. The astounding *lieder* (songs) of Franz Schubert are ultraromantic, glorying in individualism as an ideal, and exalting yearning and unrequited love and the glory and beauties of nature. The prolific Schubert also composed trios, quartets, and symphonies.

The late romantics include Pyotr Ilyich Tchaikovsky (1840–1893) in Russia, whose ballets, symphonies, violin concerto, and string pieces are constantly performed. Claude Debussy (1862–1918) in France—nonconformist, but with a firmly romantic sensibility nonetheless—composed impressionistic pieces, such as *La Mer* (The Sea), which imitates the surging waves. And one must not leave out the arch-romantic Johannes Brahms (1833–1897) in Vienna, and the German Max Bruch (1838–1920), whose *Scottish Fantasia* and Violin Concerto No. 1 in G minor, Op. 26, have been much recorded.

Aside from the art song, this period also sees endless potboiler ballads and parlor songs—many of them quite sentimental—by Sullivan and other composers, such as Stephen Collins Foster (1826–1864) in America. Popular composed music included music hall and vaudeville songs that added a rich texture to the culture. Vaudeville comedians and comedy teams would even go on to radio and then television.

Literature

Public school education in the United States and all over Europe, as well as private and religious schools and the spread of universities, made the population at large more knowledgeable and cultivated than at any other time in history. In the nineteenth century, literature was produced in previously unheard of quantities, as literacy rose and reading became one of the most popular pastimes. Literary styles changed with the sociocultural and political evolution resulting in part from public education, and the romantic, realistic, and naturalistic schools overlap each other.

The now classic *Diaries* of Irish poet William Allingham (1824–1889), who knew just about everyone in the Victorian literary world, provide invaluable insights and pictures of life and people. The diary began as an attempt at autobiography, never completed and turned into posthumously published daily journals that start in 1847. Through Allingham's narration and the actual conversations he reproduces, Tennyson; the irascible, opinionated Thomas Carlyle (1795–1851); and other major and minor literary figures come vividly to life with all their faults, foibles, prejudices, concerns, and humanity. All these writers came to maturity in the romantic age that shaped their outlook on life.

The hallmarks of romanticism are idealism; yearning, and unrequited yet faithful love; the late eighteenth-century concept of life as *Sturm und Drang* (German for "storm and drive," or stress, or strife); *Weltschmerz* (literally "world pain"), the agony of being alive; the exaltation of discontent, melancholy, grief, despair, pessimism, and depression as sacrosanct values; emotionality over rationalism; new forms over classical models; the idealization of nature; a distrust of civilization; and the importance of the subjective, the imaginative, and the irrational, as opposed to rationality and level-headedness.

All these characteristics are found in French author Benjamin Constant's (1767–1830) beautiful love story *Adolphe*. Convoluted, flowery prose, heightened effects, and lurid melodrama are further occasional romantic characteristics, found, for example, in Mary Wollstonecraft Shelley's (1797–1851) thrilling *Frankenstein*. The *Memoirs* of the archromantic author of *Atala*, Viscount François-Auguste-René de Chateaubriand (1768–1848) are the incarnation of the romantic spirit of sensuality, longing, and melancholy; and they paint a vivid portrait of contemporary France as well. The Brontë family produced some of the supreme English romantic literature, and there have been excellent films made of Charlotte's (1816–1855) *Jane Eyre* and Emily's (1818–1848)

Wuthering Heights. Again we see fine, sometimes extravagant, but compelling writing, and riveting, passionate stories—high emotion and evocative thrilling episodes set against wild landscapes of mountains and crags and in mysterious, labyrinthine houses. But there are also novels that we associate with all the stylistic faults of unwieldy, convoluted Victorian writing, where one word is never used if two will do—for example, the now obscure *Paul Clifford*, published in 1840 by Edward George Bulwer-Lytton (1803–1873), reads like an unconscious parody. Everyone knows the opening line, and nobody remembers where it comes from: "It was a dark and stormy night..."

Individualistic attitudes, inexact words, and occasionally an overblown style of expression are typical of the romantic novels of the American James Fenimore Cooper (1789–1851), whose prose sagas of the Leatherstocking series and novels of the sea, popular in Europe as well as the United States, can be rather leaden. The same overdone style prevails in the poetry of Robert Southey (1774–1843), once enormously popular as well, and we now find the novels of Nathaniel Hawthorne (1804–1864) ponderous. On the other hand, the American romantic Washington Irving (1783–1859), considered the first great American litterateur, wrote beautiful tales, such as "Rip van Winkle," which we still read with pleasure. And Hawthorne's sometimes overly serious friend, Herman Melville (1819–1891), wrote with supreme craft and imagination. The important philosophical New England essayists Ralph Waldo Emerson (1803–1882) and Henry David Thoreau (1817–1862), with the ideas of the latter on civil disobedience, are also important reading for the period.

One of the greatest American masters, Edgar Allan Poe (1809–1849), led a complicated, tortured life, and his vivid mind spawned memorable grotesque and arabesque tales (some of them, perhaps, induced by alcohol or drugs) that are still riveting and that speak to the depths of our unconscious minds. He was erudite, read Latin and Greek, and studied ancient and modern languages. People were fascinated by his public readings of his most famous and popular poem, "The Raven."

Among the notable romantic poets, Sir Walter Scott, whose engrossing historical novels are typically romantic in tone and story; the poet laureate, Alfred, Lord Tennyson (1809–1892); and Robert (1812–1889) and Elizabeth Barrett Browning (1806–1861) are particularly inspiring, not to say glorious.

Germany found a voice in the works of the historian Friedrich von Schlegel (1767–1845), as well as in the lyric poetry and satiric sensibility of the restless, cosmopolitan Heinrich Heine (1797–1856), some of whose poems were set to music by Schubert. One, "Die Lorelei," about an alluring, seductive siren that dwells on the Rhine, became so famous that even the Nazis dared not eliminate it from school textbooks, although they chose to label the work of this Jewish poet "anonymous" and claimed he had stolen it. Heine is considered Germany's greatest lyric poet, along with Friedrich Hölderlin (1770–1843).

And Russia's greatest romantic poet, Alexander Pushkin, penned two memorable narratives that give a true picture of attitudes and life in Russia of his day, *Eugene Onegin* and *The Queen of Spades*, both of which were turned into passionate operas by Tchaikovsky. The ardent and romantic Polish patriot Adam Mickiewicz (1798–1855) was perhaps his equal, with his national poetic epic *Pan Tadeusz*, among many other works. For a novel about the Russian conquest of the Caucasus, read the arch-romantic *A Hero of Our Time* by the poet Mikhail Lermontov, which so inspires Solyony, who takes himself to be the hero of our time (which he misunderstands profoundly) in Chekhov's *Three Sisters*. The satirical wit of Nicolai Gogol (1809–1852) has already been mentioned in connection with Stanislavsky's production of Bulgakov's adaptation of *Dead Souls*. Later, the century saw the work of Feodor Dostoevsky (1821–1881), with his deeply pessimistic, dark view of life and mordant sense of humor, and of the prodigious humanitarian genius Leo Tolstoy (1828–1910).

The English actress Fanny (Frances Anne) Kemble (1809–1893) had a long and distinguished career. She retired from the stage—temporarily, as it turned out—after an American tour, when, in 1834, she married Pierce Butler of Georgia, who inherited his grandfather's plantation and slaves in 1838. Kemble was horrified when she went to the plantations, and she left her husband, who refused to give up his slaves. She became a noted antislavery activist, divorcing Butler in 1849. Her various volumes of memoirs and reminiscences, including *Journal of a Residence on a Georgian Plantation 1838–1839*, are invaluable sources for information on the life and theater of the period. There is an excellent television film based on her experiences, *Enslavement: The True Story of Fanny Kemble* (2000), starring Jane Seymour as Fanny Kemble Butler and Keith Carradine as Pierce Butler.

There are numerous narratives by former slaves portraying the horrors they endured, among the most famous being Frederick Douglass's (1818–1895) *Narrative of the Life of Frederick Douglass, an American Slave*, published in 1845, and Sojourner Truth's (1797–1883) *Narrative of Sojourner Truth*. Both of them were ardent fighters in the abolitionist movement. Equally well known and admired is Booker T. Washington's (1856–1915) autobiography, *Up from Slavery*. The brilliant diplomat, intellectual, and writer James Weldon Johnson's (1871–1938) searing portrayal of racism in his novel *The Autobiography of an Ex-Coloured Man*, first published anonymously in 1912, is a great American classic and not to be missed. Also essential reading is the towering social and political activist W. E. B. Du Bois' (1868—1963) landmark work, *The Souls of Black Folk*. On its publication in 1903, it divided the black community: some wanted to pursue the more conservative policies of Booker T. Washington in quest of equality and civil rights; others wanted to protest more radically and actively.

Also important for a view of the developing political and social system in the United States is *Democracy in America* by Alexis de Tocqueville (1803–1859), a French traveler and writer who was sent to the United States in 1831 to study the prison system and was quite enthusiastic about what he saw. His is not a jaundiced view, unlike that of Charles Dickens in his *American Notes Written for General Circulation*, published after his 1842 trip to the United States. Dickens nevertheless provides some valuable sociological insights and some unforgettable portraits of frontier style, indecorous table manners, the prison system, New York City in the era of the gangs that ruled it, and conditions of life generally. Although replete with a romantic sensibility, his book is a herald of realism.

In the realistic and still later naturalistic periods, we speak of realistic writers' attitudes and style and of their values. These include the truthful portrayal of character and of nature, as well as rationality, objectivity, minimizing of subjectivity, and straightforward prose, containing real descriptions without flowery coruscation. The humanitarian naturalists, such as Emile Zola, went one step further than the realists and portrayed the seamy, grimy side of life teeming in the underbelly of Europe's great cities. They were crusaders who wanted social and political reform.

George Eliot (nom de plume of Mary Ann Evans, 1819–1880) produced some of the great realist novels of the age, among them her masterpiece about English rural life, *Middlemarch*, and *Daniel Deronda*, which deals with anti-Semitism in a way entirely sympathetic to Jews. Anthony Trollope (1815–1882), whose writings display a streak of anti-Semitism, produced a huge body of realist novels, among them the Palliser series and the Barsetshire novels. Benjamin Disraeli (1804–1881), an Anglican proud of his Jewish heritage, and a novelist before he became a politician and Victoria's favorite prime minister, penned perfervid romances such as *Coningsby* and *Sybil* in a combination of romantic and realist styles.

The great Italian literature of the period includes Alessandro Manzoni's (1785–1873) masterpiece, *I promessi sposi* (The Betrothed), a historical novel set in the seventeenth century; the poetry, theater pieces, and memoirs of the adventurer, writer, and soldier, Gabriele D'Annunzio (1863–1938); and the regional stories and novels of the Sicilian author Giovanni Verga (1840–1922), one of the leaders of the *verismo* (realist) school. Among his best-known tales is "Cavalleria Rusticana," made into an opera by Pietro Mascagni (1863–1945). And the innovative, influential plays of Luigi Pirandello (1867–1936), among them *Six Characters in Search of an Author*—precursive in some ways of both surrealism and the theater of the absurd—still hold the stage. He won the Nobel Prize for Literature in 1934.

The novels of the prolific Alexandre Dumas include *The Three Musketeers* and its sequels, with vivid portraits of historical personalities. *The Count of Monte Cristo* is based on two true stories; it begins in the time of Napoleon's exile on Elba, and it depicts life in nineteenth-century Rome, Paris, and Marseille. *La reine Margot* and his many other great classics are among the very best in world literature. His son, Alexandre Dumas, fils (1824–1895) was also highly successful as both a novelist and a playwright. He is perhaps best known for the play he adapted from his novel *La dame aux camélias* (*The Lady with the Camelias*, also known as *Camille*). France prided itself as well on the poetry and novels of the passionate, politically concerned, powerful, and virtuosic Victor Hugo, best known today for *The Hunchback of Notre Dame* and *Les Misérables*; and on the romantic novels of Stendhal (1723–1842), *The Red and the Black* and *The Charterhouse of Parma*.

George Sand rebelled against restricting, puritanical bourgeois morality—with its injustice towards the less fortunate and its rigid restraint of sexuality—in such novels as *François le Champi*, in which an orphan boy (the argot word from the country region of Berri, *champi*, means "an orphan found in the fields [les champs]," where he has been left by his mother) eventually gains happiness and overcomes all odds against him; and *La petite Fadette*, about a woman who is unjustly looked on as no better than a whore, but who, once again, finds happiness. And Balzac's *Human Comedy* series clearly show a different attitude about sex than Charles Dickens does, for example. Both wrote of love and passionate, often doomed relationships, but there is a priggishness and a repression in Dickens, for whom sexuality is only alluded to and hinted at as something prurient that leads to evil consequences (he was thinking unconsciously of his own problems in that domain), that is absent in the more frank and open writing of Balzac, who even dared to treat the all but taboo subject of homosexuality, albeit in a veiled way. For Dickens, emotional devastation, affliction, heartache, and wretchedness are the price of desire—these are dire warnings against indulging in sex, as, for instance in *Nicholas Nickleby*, where the chaste Miss Nickleby is almost sold into prostituting herself by her wicked uncle in order to facilitate his business ventures.

Honoré de Balzac's *Lost Illusions* (1837–43) and its sequel *The Splendors and Miseries of the Courtesans* (1843–47) together tell a complicated story that displays all kinds of sexuality and sexual passion and deals with their psychological complications, as well as showing the manners and etiquette and political attitudes of the period. Balzac was attempting to paint life realistically as he saw it, and to present a panorama of the society of his day that would be a lasting picture of nineteenth-century France, and he succeeded beautifully, even though he never lived to complete his project. Also important for a study of life in France at this time are the short stories of the troubled Guy de Maupassant (1850–1893) and the highly romanticized writings of Alphonse Daudet (1840–1897).

There were similarities, as well as differences, in sexual attitudes in France and England. Attesting to this are the scandal surrounding Gustave Flaubert's 1857 realist novel *Madame Bovary*—about a discontented bourgeois housewife who dreams of romantic love and, indeed, indulges her desires—and his subsequent trial for obscenity; and the controversy over the frank sexuality of Wilkie Collins's (1824–1889) *The Law and the Lady* (1875), which was serialized in a magazine, as novels often were in those days: the editors dared to rewrite certain sections without the author's permission, and successive episodes were received with increasing disgust by the puritanical public.

Karl Marx (1818–1883) maintained that the capitalist economic system was at the root of all of society's terrible problems and inequities, and that class conflict and warfare were the inevitable results of the socioeconomic power structure, pitting the ruling class against the proletariat. In 1848, he and his associate, Friedrich Engels (1820–1895), published one of the most influential books ever written, the *Communist Manifesto:* "Workers of the world, unite! You have nothing to lose but your chains!" Marx spent the rest of his life working on his masterpiece, *Das Kapital*, in which he expounded, among other things, his theory of dynamic social change. Read these books for some of the progressive social thinking of the period.

The Sherlock Holmes stories and novels of Sir Arthur Conan Doyle (1859–1930) are also excellent for studying the manners, mores, class system, attitudes, and decorum of the late Victorian and Edwardian periods. The novels of Emile Gaboriau (1832–1873), who was called the father of the detective novel by no less a person than Conan Doyle himself (Sherlock Holmes was inspired in part by Gaboriau's detective inspector of police, M. Lecoq, based partly on Vidocq) are a mine of information about the manners, fashions, social attitudes, class structure, daily routines of life, and living conditions of mid-nineteenth century France. His brilliantly plotted, deeply moving masterpiece is *Monsieur Lecoq*, one of the great nineteenth-century novels.

Victorian and Edwardian provincial English life is portrayed in the powerfully emotional realistic novels of Thomas Hardy (1840–1928) and the gentler, more sentimental, idealistic stories of historian and sociologist H. G. Wells (1866–1946), better known for his science fiction books such as *War of the Worlds*. And imperialism and imperialistic, jingoistic attitudes are evident in the works of Rudyard Kipling (1865–1936). For life in America, you could hardly do better than to read the works of Louisa May Alcott (1832–1888) and Mark Twain (1835–1910)—just as you would read the Yiddish Mark Twain, Sholem Aleichem (1859–1916) and Isaac Loeb Peretz (1852–1915) for their picture of Jewish life in eastern Europe. And read Count Leo Tolstoy, the stories and plays of Anton Chekhov, and the novels of Ivan Turgenev (1818–1883) and Feodor Dostoyevsky if you want a picture of life in Russia. And for a panoramic view of the Russian Revolution as it affected the Cossacks of southwestern Russia, read Mikhail Sholokhov's (1905–1984) long novel *And Quiet Flows the Don*, published in two parts between 1928 and 1940. The prolific Spanish novelist Benito Pérez Galdós (1843–1920), known as the Balzac or Dickens of Spain, wrote a forty-six novel cycle called *Episodios Nacionales* and his four-volume masterpiece, *Fortunata y Jacinta*, which depict nineteenth-century Spanish life in detail and with psychological depth. For life in Vienna, the psychological plays, such as *Anatol*, and novels of Arthur Schnitzler (1862–1931) attest to the influence of his friend Sigmund Freud's (1856–1939) ideas, as do the poetry and other writings of the tempestuous and depressive Rainer Maria Rilke (1875–1926). Freud himself was a superb writer who was proud to have won the Goethe Prize for Literature.

To get a feeling for the seamy, passionate side of the psychology of the mid- to late-nineteenth-century era, read Zola, and the poetry of Charles Baudelaire (1821–1867), often considered the greatest poet in the French language; as well as that of the iconoclastic symbolist lyricist Paul Verlaine (1844–1896) and his lover, Arthur Rimbaud (1854–1891), the bad-boy wonder and brilliant innovative symbolist poet who chose to give up the artistic life and moved to Africa, returning to France only to die. The leading symbolist poet was Stéphane Mallarmé (1842–1898). The decadent school is exemplified in some of the writings of J. K. Huysmans (1848–1907)—notably, *A rebours* (Upside Down), about a sybaritic nobleman who is so wealthy that he can gratify every whim and proceeds to do so; it inspired Oscar Wilde (1854–1900) to write *The Picture of Dorian Gray.* Huysmans went through phases, however; he ended up as a conservative, very religious Catholic, and his writings reflect the gamut of the nineteenth-century intellectual quest for truth and spirituality.

The quest for truth was also pursued by Charles Dickens's friend, Wilkie Collins, known as one of the fathers of the mystery novel. He wrote the intriguing classics *The Woman in White* and *The Moonstone,* but most of his novels were sociological, with such books as *The Law and the Lady* and *Armadale.* You might also read Dickens's *Great Expectations* (1861) and *Bleak House* (1853) for a study of the sociology of the period, as well as for their emotional love stories and much loved sentimentality.

With enormous courage, Marcel Proust dared to face painful truths about the illusions, prejudices, and hypocrisy that destroy individuals and pervade society. Writing more than half a century after Balzac, whom he admired, Proust thought of his own human comedy in psychological terms, and portrayed his characters' mental processes in minute detail. Sigmund Freud was a contemporary of Proust's, and although Proust probably never read him, their ideas often coincide.

In Search of Lost Time is a first-person narrative, and *Swann's Way,* its opening volume, presents a nostalgic view of the narrator's childhood, awakened for him years later by the taste of some crumbs of madeleine soaked in a spoonful of tea. The saga of his life's journey takes us into a world that has largely vanished, in which the pace of life was more leisurely. But the peace of Europe was shattered by the coming of the Great War in 1914, which also interrupted the publication of the book and changed its plan, as Proust decided to include the war in his novel. Thus, while presenting a vivid portrait of French society in the late nineteenth and early twentieth centuries, it also became a story about the shattering of the old way of life, and the coming of a new, less familiar, more frightening world.

Film and Television

Steven Spielberg's *Amistad* (1997) is a deeply moving film set in 1839, based on the true story of kidnapped Africans who staged a revolt aboard the slave ship *La Amistad* that was taking them to America. Arriving in the United States, they are put on trial, and eventually freed when the court declares that they should never have been abducted. They were defended by ex-president John Quincy Adams, played by Anthony Hopkins. The incident was one of many important catalysts that inspired the abolitionists to pursue their cause. For the Civil War era in the United States, don't miss Ken Burns's documentary, *The Civil War*, a television miniseries. John Cromwell's 1940 film *Abe Lincoln in Illinois*, with Raymond Massey as Honest Abe, and John Ford's *Young Mr. Lincoln* (1939), starring Henry Fonda in the title role, are classic. *Glory* (1989), with Denzel Washington and Matthew Broderick, is the story of the American army's first black unit, and it is magnificently done in all ways, from the photography to the writing and the acting. A grand epic, superb in its recreation, *Gettysburg* (1993) was filmed on location.

The BBC has made film and television adaptations of most of George Eliot's novels. And there are many adaptations for the screen of other nineteenth-century novels, and quite a number of films, for example, of Alexandre Dumas' *The Count of Monte Cristo*, Victor Hugo's *Les Misérables*, and Balzac novels, as well as the 1937 film *Camille*, based on the work of Alexandre Dumas, fils. All of these are worth looking into for the recreation of France from the end of the Napoleonic era up to the revolution of 1830. *The Story of Adele H* (1975) is based on the real-life story of Victor Hugo's daughter, played by Emmanuelle Béart. Possibly psychotic, Adele Hugo was obsessively, delusionally in love with a young English soldier, whom she followed to Halifax, Nova Scotia in the 1860s. And there are two notable Hollywood films of Tolstoy's *Anna Karenina*, one made in 1935 starring Greta Garbo, the other in 1948 with Vivien Leigh.

Mrs. Brown (1997), with Judi Dench as Queen Victoria and Anthony Sher as Disraeli, is a magnificent recreation of the period. Sher perfectly captures nineteenth-century oratorical style in his speeches to Parliament. Such films as Robert Altman's *Gosford Park* (2001) and the 1971–75 television series *Upstairs, Downstairs* admirably capture the styles and mores of the late Victorian and Edwardian eras.

Dreamchild (1985), about Lewis Carroll, captures the mid-Victorian era perfectly, as it goes back and forth between contemporary times and the childhood of the original Alice, Alice Liddell, who is being in honored in New York on the centenary of the publication of *Alice's Adventures in Wonderland* (filmed and adapted for television several times and made into the famous Walt Disney cartoon feature of 1951).

Topsy-Turvy (2000) and *The Great Gilbert and Sullivan* (1953) both tell the story of the famous team, but the older film is considerably cleaned up, although it has wonderful performances, including that of Martyn Green as George Grossmith. The later film really shows the conditions of the Victorian era, and it provides a wonderful glimpse into the making of *The Mikado* (itself filmed several times), including the decorum and rehearsal procedures in the pre-Stanislavskian theater.

Oscar Wilde (1960), with Robert Morley memorable in the title role, is particularly obnoxious in its moralizing and homophobia but still worth seeing for his and other performances. Much the same thing can be said of *The Trials of Oscar Wilde*, also known as *The Green Carnation*, with Peter Finch as Wilde, made in the same year. *Wilde* (1997), with Stephen Fry as Wilde and Jude Law as Lord Alfred Douglas, is a magnificent recreation of the late 1890s period and an excellent, very real version of the tragic story.

Simon Callow's "living biography" of Charles Dickens by Peter Ackroyd, *The Mystery of Charles Dickens*, first done in London, on tour in Britain, and on Broadway in New York, was taped for television at the Albery Theatre in London in 2001. The show includes many readings from the novels, and Simon Callow succeeds beautifully in his goal of having the audience "encounter" Dickens; a DVD is available from Kultur Video. Also excellent is the 1976 BBC television miniseries *Dickens in London*, with Roy Dotrice in the title role. In 1983 Emlyn Williams made a television program of his superb one-man stage show of Charles Dickens's public readings.

There have been a great many English and some American films and TV programs made from Dickens's novels, from the days of silent film on. They all represent the filmmaker's interpretations, and it is through their eyes that many people view the original material, as several writers in the collection of essays *Dickens on Screen* (Cambridge University

Press, 2003) have pointed out. That being said, some of the films and television programs—especially those produced by the BBC—have done an admirable job of recreating the mid-Victorian era. David Lean's *Great Expectations* (1946) is a masterpiece and one of the best Dickens films ever made. Although brilliantly done, Lean's version of *Oliver Twist* (1948) was accused of anti-Semitism because of Alec Guinness's outrageous caricatured makeup and performance as Fagin; but Guinness was only following the unfortunate original characterization in the novel—which is, to say the least, unsubtle. Roman Polanski's *Oliver Twist* (2005) is a much better reworking of the novel than Lean's in some ways, and Fagin, played by Ben Kingsley, emerges as a real human being. He is the first person to be kind to Oliver, which immediately makes us like him, although he is still a cowardly crook who condones violence even if he is not actually violent himself. Old Hollywood and British Dickens films include *David Copperfield* (1935), with W. C. Fields as Micawber; the previously mentioned *Nicholas Nickleby* (1947, nicely filmed again in 2002); and an excellent version of *The Pickwick Papers* (1952). The older films made from the novels Dickens set in his own era are better at recreating the period, because, for one thing, the filmmakers and actors were not that far removed in time from it; they had certainly grown up with parents and grandparents who lived through the middle to late 1800s, and would have passed on the manners and mores to their children (to the extent that they could, since, of course, these things had been changing rapidly since the end of the First World War).

Ingmar Bergman made two films that are set in nineteenth-century Sweden and that clearly show the culture and manners of the period. Both are delightful: *Smiles of a Summer Night* (1955) and the semi-autobiographical family saga *Fanny and Alexander* (1983), with sumptuous decors and costumes from the turn of the twentieth century and a glimpse of manners and etiquette that is unsurpassed.

Merchant Ivory films of Henry James and E. M. Forster novels are, as always with their productions, incredible period pieces, such as James's *The Golden Bowl* (2001) and Forster's *A Room with a View* (1986) and *Howards End* (1992). And see as well James's *The Wings of the Dove* (1997), directed by Iain Softley, and the 1947 film of James's *Washington Square*, *The Heiress*, with wonderful performances by Olivia de Havilland, Montgomery Clift, Ralph Richardson, and Miriam Hopkins. Among other period films, Martin Scorsese's *The Age of Innocence* (1993), adapted from Edith Wharton's novel, accurately portrays the formality and etiquette of the upper classes in early 1900s New York. The 1999 film adaptation of Wilde's *An Ideal Husband*, which shows authentic Victorian moral ideas on sexuality that now seem dated, does the same for London high society, but if you want to see *The Importance of Being Earnest*, look at the 1952 version with Michael Redgrave as Jack Worthing and Edith Evans as an unsurpassed Lady Bracknell, not the 2002 film. Like Wilde's, many of George Bernard Shaw's plays are available on DVD, mostly in BBC presentations that are uneven.

The Shooting Party (1984)—with superb performances by James Mason, Dorothy Tutin, John Gielgud, and James Fox heading a grand cast—is a depiction of genteel country life in England in 1913. The class structure, manners, and mores of the period are very well portrayed, with the snobbishness and anti-Semitism of some members of the upper classes quite blatant. *Oh, What a Lovely War* (1969) is a superb version of Joan Littlewood's stage musical. Based on a novel by Anthony Hope, the Hollywood films of *The Prisoner of Zenda* (both the 1937 and the 1952 versions use the same script), set in a fictitious middle European monarchy, shows the social attitudes and rigid etiquette that prevailed at the end of the nineteenth century. And both are lots of fun to watch.

In *Psychoanalysis and Anthropology* (International Universities Press, 1950), the Hungarian-born American founder of psychoanalytical anthropology, Géza Róheim (1891–1953)—who grew up in Budapest and was familiar with life in Vienna (he knew Freud)—says that Howard Lindsay and Russell Crouse's Broadway play *Life with Father* "represents society or the family...in [turn-of-the-century] Vienna as much as in New York." Michael Curtiz's 1947 film with William Powell and Irene Dunne is readily available on video or DVD, and *The Great Caruso* (1951), with Mario Lanza as the tenor with the unsurpassed golden voice, is a highly fictionalized, sentimental account of Caruso's life, but it does show turn-of-the-century life in New York in excellent detail. And for a film that shows New York in all its squalor and primitiveness sixty years earlier, in the 1840s—much as Dickens described it in his *American Notes*, worth reading for his observations not only of New York but of all the places he visited—see Martin Scorsese's *Gangs of New York* (2002), overdone perhaps, but with much about it that is authentic and true to the period that he carefully researched. The 1936 Academy Award winner, *San Francisco*, set during the 1906 earthquake, is not only a superb movie musical typical of the 1930s, but it brilliantly recreates the earthquake at the end of the film.

An absolutely wonderful, heart-warming film, in a class by itself, is Danish director Gabriel Axel's *Babette's Feast* (the Academy Award winner for the Best Foreign Film of 1987), based on an Isak Dinnesen short story. The film is set in a remote village in Jutland in Denmark. Babette (Stéphane Audran) is a French refugee who has gone into exile to escape from war-torn Paris during the Franco-Prussian War of 1870–71. The war has been over for a while when she learns that she has won the lottery and will have enough money to go back to France, where she had been a renowned chef in her previous life. Instead, she decides to use all the money to create a feast for the simple people of the village, especially the two very religious daughters of a clergyman who have so generously helped her by taking her into their home as their servant. The banquet she creates is memorable and mouth-watering, and this slice of life is very sophisticated and shows varying social classes and conditions. Besides, it is just a delight, and frankly, it brings tears to my eyes every time I see it. Incidentally, the china she uses, sent for from Paris, is in the Haviland Impératrice Eugénie pattern, named for Napoleon III's empress, which would seem to be appropriate. But although it is in the style of the late 1860s, it is nevertheless anachronistic, having been created by Theodore Haviland in 1901 for the empress herself (she died in 1920). "Picky, picky," I can hear you saying, but such details are important for the sake of authenticity.

Starring Sam Neill in the title role, *Reilly: The Ace of Spies*, a 1983 television miniseries set in the era of the Russian Revolution, is based on the extraordinary true story of Sigmund Rosenbloom, who changed his name to Sydney Reilly and became Great Britain's first master spy. It is an astonishing saga, adventurous and full of telling period details. *Nicholas and Alexandra* (1971) depicts the fall of the czar and the events leading up to it in a very good recreation of the period. The revolution is also the subject of *Reds* (1981), based on the American John Reed's memoir of his participation in the uprising of 1917, *Ten Days That Shook the World*. And Serge Eisenstein's silent masterpiece *Potemkin* (1925), about a mutiny on the Battleship Potemkin that helped spark the abortive, bloody St. Petersburg riots of 1905, remains gripping and moving to this day. A highly fictionalized account, the entertaining classic film *Anastasia* (1956) stars Ingrid Bergman as the young lady who tried to pass herself off between the world wars as the czar's daughter who had survived the massacre of the Russian royal family. In real life, DNA testing proved that she was indeed an impostor.

If you are doing a film or a play set during World War I, don't miss the admirable 2006 Koch Vision DVD set *The Great War: The Complete History of World War I*, an excellent history of World War I. The first year of World War I, 1914, is the setting for a brilliant, heartbreaking film, *Joyeux Noël* (Merry Christmas, 2006), based on the true incident of a Christmas Eve ceasefire among German, Scottish, and French troops. And don't miss John Huston's great classic *The African Queen* (1951), starring Katherine Hepburn and Humphrey Bogart and set in Africa during the First World War, or *All Quiet on the Western Front* (1930), an antiwar film based on Erich Maria Remarque's novel. Errol Flynn and Basil Rathbone head an excellent cast in the moving *Dawn Patrol* (1938), a frank, harsh look at the lives of World War I British flying aces. For a satirical look at the war and the class system, see Rowan Atkinson in *Blackadder IV*, with Hugh Laurie and Stephen Fry as particularly obtuse officers—absolutely hilarious.

Parts of Marcel Proust's *In Search of Lost Time* have been remarkably poorly adapted for the screen, but then, the task of adapting his book is perhaps impossible. Harold Pinter's screenplay, done a number of years ago in London as a staged reading, reads silently better than it does out loud, and it is no wonder it was never filmed.

The films *Swann in Love* (1984)—Volker Schlöndorff's extravaganza, adapted from a section of *Swann's Way*—as well as Chantal Akerman's *The Captive* (2000), set in contemporary times and based loosely on *La Prisonnière*, are not well done, despite some fine performances. However, *Swann in Love* is sumptuous in its decors and costumes, and it recreates the period superbly.

Raul Ruiz's *Time Regained* (1999) is occasionally interesting as film-making, but confusing and obscure unless you have read Proust's final volume. Marcello Mazzarella looks amazingly like Marcel Proust, and the period, with its manners and style, is beautifully done. Paris under the threat of German invasion during World War I is very authentic in feeling. Still, the film is a disappointing attempt, with some egregious miscasting in major roles. Two biographical attempts are interesting, at least: Percy Adlon's German film *Celeste* (1981), based on the memoirs of Proust's housekeeper and general factotum, and Alan Bennett's television film, *102 Boulevard Haussmann* (1990), with Alan Bates as Proust.

Marcel Proust: A Writer's Life (Wolfe-Carter Productions, Inc., 1992), is an excellent documentary produced by the major Proust scholar and biographer Professor William C. Carter, of the University of Alabama in Birmingham. Aside from his magisterial biography, *Marcel Proust: A*

Life (Yale University Press, 2000), he has written several other wonderful books, including *Proust in Love* (Yale University Press, 2006). Since *Little Miss Sunshine* came out in 2006, he jokes that he must be the number three expert on Proust in the United States (he is number one).

The 1920s Through World War II

The universe of characters romping through the 1920s and '30s created by that supreme humorist P. G. Wodehouse (1881–1975)—whose perfectly crafted books are a window into the world of English stately country houses, men's clubs and jazzy carryings on—includes Jeeves, the wily, clever, well-read, knowledgeable, sophisticated butler and virtual governess to the feckless, charming, well-meaning Bertie Wooster, who is always getting into trouble with his girlfriends and with his galaxy of stern, battle-axe aunts. Just as hilarious are the "amiable and bone-headed peer" Lord Emsworth and the other denizens of Blandings Castle. Then there are Wodehouse's wonderful golfers and fishermen, as well as Mr. Mulliner, Psmith ("the 'p' is silent"), and many more from various walks of life. They attest not only to the continued repressive existence of the British class system but to the changing way in which it was now viewed. It is the smart, intellectual butler Jeeves who upholds the traditions of English decorum and correct behavior for Wooster, the naïve paradigm of the idle upper classes. The upper strata of society, as Wodehouse perceived them, were now a subject for satire in a more democratically minded world, which was also increasingly a prey to fascist demagogues, who preached their messages of hate, and despised Communism and progressive thinking everywhere.

This was the age when women were finally given the right to vote: the right was granted in 1893 in New Zealand, at the end of 1918 in Great Britain, and by the Nineteenth Amendment to the Constitution in the United States in 1919. That same year, the Eighteenth Amendment to the United States Constitution was passed, sanctioning the ill-advised experiment prohibiting alcoholic beverages, with the Volstead Act ushering in the gangsterism of the Roaring Twenties; prohibition would be ended with the Twenty-first amendment in 1933. Not until 1944 did women get the right to vote in France, but in Norway, they had been able to vote since 1913.

Throughout the twentieth century, there was an atavistic male chauvinist and patriarchal attitude on the part of men, which decreed that middle-class women stay in the home and take care not only of the children but of their husband's every need. The good middle-class housewife in the 1920s through the '40s cleared away the leavings of food and cigar butts and empty beer bottles the morning after, having retired and left her husband and his buddies alone on poker nights. Men and women went to baseball games, horse races, and other sporting events, but women were expected to be more reserved than men, depending on the event, and to dress with decorum. Of course, as the century wore on, women would wear slacks and scant bathing suits and shorts in public, so there was clearly a growing sense of freedom.

In the 1920s, women had been working in offices for several decades as secretaries, and like the machines, they were called "typewriters." And during World War II, they would work in factories and the armed forces. Once women ceased to wear the girdles and slips that many used even as late as the mid-1950s, and once the general style of clothing relaxed, so did manners and etiquette. But in high-society circles, there were and still are such customs as debutante balls and polo matches and, in England, hunts and royal receptions that retain a measure of the old-fashioned etiquette discussed earlier in this chapter. However, World War II saw the end, by and large, of the more rigid manners and deferential class attitudes that had survived even after the First World War had destroyed the old aristocratic system. Nevertheless, the many editions of Emily Post's books of etiquette sold very well; her first one was written in 1922.

While the projectionist was changing the reels in the old-time movie palaces and nickelodeons in the days of silent film, messages shown on the screen indicated the necessity of inculcating good manners: young ladies were admonished to remove their hats, which could be quite large and elaborate before the *cloche*, a beretlike hat, became popular in the 1920s, and gentlemen were enjoined not to "expectorate on the floor." Advertisements for soaps and other products were shown as well.

By the 1920s, advertising had come into its own, and a study of newspaper and magazine ads show just how life was viewed and how things changed over the decades. John Caples (1900–1990) started as an ad copywriter in 1927 for the company that became Batten, Barton, Durston and Osborne (B. B. D. & O.), the huge advertising firm in New York, and wrote four classic books on advertising. He spent fifty-six years at the company, most of them as vice president, and he was famous for full-page ads with an illustration at the top and a text that told a little story. Probably the most famous, written in 1925, was headlined

"They Laughed When I Sat Down at the Piano, But When I Started to Play!—," for the U.S. School of Music. Later, there was "They Grinned When the Waiter Spoke to Me in French—But Their Laughter Changed to Amazement at My Reply." Clearly, knowing French was no longer de rigueur.

A faster pace of life arrived as the automobile went beyond the stage where you had to crank the engine to get the car started. In the United States, the ubiquitous soda fountain, which had been around for a century, was modernized in 1903, and generations of teenagers enjoyed malteds or banana splits and shared ice cream sodas. And the first Horn & Hardart automat opened in Philadelphia in 1902. You could get wonderful freshly brewed coffee, and when you put coins into a slot, you lifted the little window and took out the sandwich or piece of apple pie resting behind it—fast food that you didn't have to wait for. Automats, like cafeterias and the bars where you could buy a meal for a nickel in the first decades of the twentieth century, were so popular that the last one closed in New York only in 1991. The beauty parlor and its masculine equivalent, the barber shop, with its famous red and white pole, had been around since the late Victorian era, and they came into their own in the 1920s and '30s. Men could get a shave and a quick haircut, and the children could play in a model motor car. Women had their hair bobbed or curled or made into stylish hairdos. All this, portrayed in the cinema of the times, lends the between-war decades a kind of innocent aura that they can hardly have possessed in reality (except among teenagers, the bobbysoxers with their raging hormones). This is particularly clear when one considers the Great Depression and the politics of fascism that was steadily growing in power and taking over parts of Europe with a frightening rapidity, and was even a threatening force, with home-grown movements and demagogues, in the United States.

And in fact, alongside these pleasant social institutions was a sinister undercurrent of class distinctions and prejudice, with secretly restricted admissions and quotas for Jews in some universities, for instance, and the snobbery of the question, "Did you go to the right school?" There were also restricted clubs, country clubs, and communities where Jews were not admitted. Laura V. Hobson's (1900–1986) 1947 novel *Gentleman's Agreement*, filmed that same year, is about a newspaperman, played by Gregory Peck, who passes himself off as a Jew in order to research anti-Semitism in exactly such situations.

Even more horrible was the ubiquitous racism directed against black people, so graphically portrayed, for instance, in Harper Lee's (b. 1928)

1960 novel *To Kill a Mockingbird*, set in a small town in Alabama during the Depression. It was made into a movie in 1962, starring Gregory Peck as a courageous lawyer who defends a black man accused of rape. Jim Crow segregation laws and the Ku Klux Klan in the South and prejudice and ghettoized communities in the North would continue to exist for many decades, and of course, the disease of racism is still with us.

The popular, politically conscious American author Sinclair Lewis (1885–1951), the first American to win the Nobel Prize for Literature, in 1930, dealt with such issues in his first commercial success, *Main Street* (1920), about the hypocrisy and narrow-mindedness that pervaded small-town life; *Babbit* (1922), concerning the rapacity of capitalists; and *Kingsblood Royal* (1947), one of his last works, about racism. *Elmer Gantry* (1927) dealt with the hypocrisy, bigotry, and cant of fake preachers and religious con men preying on a gullible population all too willing to believe in their sincerity, and *Arrowsmith* (1925) portrayed corruption in the medical profession. A scathing critique of the famously laconic thirtieth president of the United States, *The Man Who Knew Coolidge* (1928), was a comic departure from his usually serious novels. In *It Can't Happen Here* (1935), Lewis's fictional scenario of a fascist takeover of the United States government showed that this was indeed a frightening possibility. "When fascism comes to America, it will be wrapped in the flag and carrying a cross," he wrote.

It was no wonder that in the 1930s, years before Joseph Stalin's (1878–1953) shocking, disillusioning betrayal of the Russian Revolution was revealed, many selfless progressive people turned to Communism with the honest desire to reform government; reign in the unbridled destabilizing power of the capitalists; eliminate exploitation; institute economic equality; and improve the lot of working people, hit harder than any other socioeconomic class by the Depression. Had it not been for their efforts, we would not have had such necessary institutions as unemployment insurance or social security. Franklin Delano Roosevelt, accused by his obtuse opponents of "creeping socialism," stood for social justice. He realized that without some changes, the system would collapse: "Reform if you would preserve," he said.

In Europe, as in America, the 1920s and '30s were the Jazz Age. Jazz, which originated, like the blues, among the black population of the American South, particularly New Orleans, was hugely popular in Paris and Berlin (of course, the Nazis banned it as soon as they took over); and black American musicians and performers such as New

Orleans clarinetist Sydney Bechet (1897–1959) and singer and humanitarian Josephine Baker (1906–1975) had wonderful careers there, which they were denied in their own country because of the prejudice that pervaded American society. Paris was a haven for the "lost generation," as Gertrude Stein (1874–1946) dubbed her fellow American post–Great War expatriate writers (among them Sinclair Lewis, who spent some of the 1920s abroad): artists, musicians, and assorted bohemians, who flocked to Paris to find out what life was all about and to live free from the puritanical constraints of their native country. The pace of life was fast, if not in fact hectic, with all-night clubs and bistros, fast cars—in America, too—and fast and loose morals and sexual experimentation. This was a heady, exciting age, soon to emerge from the swamp of the Depression, only to sink pathetically and frighteningly into the horrible quagmire of the Second World War.

The Stylistic Elements: Clothing, Accessories, Movement, Manners, and the Art of Living

Clothing and Accessories: During the 1920s through '40s, it was de rigeur for women to wear gloves and hats—sometimes quite ornate, with feathers or small birds, and little veils that descended to cover the face—and to carry purses. The length of women's skirts varied with the decade, and the costume of the 1920s "flappers" was particularly distinctive: short skirts ending in fringes. Floor-length gowns and dresses were now worn only on formal occasions. Beautifully draped dresses, sometimes with pleated sleeves and stylish silhouettes emphasizing the graceful curve of the body, were now the norm. Ornaments could include large bows or ribbons, strategically placed, and brooches to set off the color of the fabric. Necklaces, bracelets and earrings, as well as finger rings, were all very popular.

From the 1880s through to the end of World War II and beyond, English men's clothing held the same preeminent position that French clothes still hold in women's fashions. The bespoke tailors of London's Savile Row catered to royalty, the wealthy, and celebrities worldwide. Their clothing was stylish, elegant, beautifully cut, sturdy, and long lasting; their shirts and often their shoes and hats were made to order, and their garments were imitated from New York to Vienna and points farther east. Cravats and jewelry could also be made to order. All the firms mentioned below still exist.

Among the most famous names in providers of gentleman's necessary accoutrements, Asprey, Ltd. in New Bond Street made luxury accessories, including business card holders, traveling alarm clocks, and jewelry boxes: its monogrammed silver cigarette cases were world famous around the time of the First World War. One of the most celebrated tailoring establishments, Henry Poole & Company, is also one of the oldest, having been founded in 1806. To receive his clients, Mr. Henry Poole (d. 1876), the son of the founder, had a large, leather-upholstered chair constructed, within which a scale was concealed, so that his customers could be weighed without having to discuss the matter or to feel embarrassed if they had put on a bit of weight since their last visit.

Sometime in the 1920s, Frederick Scholte (?–?), who was cutter to the Prince of Wales, the future Duke of Windsor, invented the London drape suit, an elegantly cut outfit soon to prove popular with movie stars and other celebrities. The double-breasted jacket's armhole is cut high and small, and the sleeve is wider at the top, with the jacket as a whole remaining close to the body and the arms free to move without any binding effect. It could be pin-striped or solid, or in the Prince of Wales's case, patterned in his personal plaid, and it might have pointed, flaring lapels. Its subtle inverted triangle silhouette, based on the shape of the uniform of the Royal Household Guards, emphasized broad shoulders and an athletic look. The suit is particularly associated with the Savile Row firm of Anderson & Sheppard.

For men, the starched, detached collars of the 1920s gave way by the 1930s to already sewn on, attached collars, which were much easier to wear; comfortable undershirts were always worn as well. In America, the first men's trousers with a zip-up fly, replacing the buttoned fly, was introduced by Hart, Schaffner & Marx in 1936. Upper-class Englishmen often wore ties with their regimental or school stripes and had, therefore, a small selection; that would change as patterns became more attractive and elaborate. In the 1920s, the three-piece tweed outfit of jacket, vest, and knee-length knickerbockers with knee-length socks, two-tone shoes, and a cap was popular for country wear. With a sweater and shirt instead of the jacket and vest, and with the knickerbockers wider than they were for walking down a country lane or hunting, this was the golf outfit that was de rigueur. Among the pieces of riding gear necessary in the open roadster—besides the duster, driving gloves, and goggles—was the "scarf helmet," invented by the firm of Herbert Johnson in New Bond Street. This consisted of a scarf, patterned or plain and made of any material, attached to the usual tight driving cap.

The three-piece single- or double-breasted suit—called a business suit in the United States and a lounge suit in Great Britain, with the vest worn with its lowest button unbuttoned and a pocket watch on a chain—was the usual wear until the 1950s, when the two-piece single-breasted suit replaced it.

In the Western democracies, especially in upper-class circles, and in the fascist lands as well, men's evening wear required white or black bow ties. How many scenes have you seen in period films where the incapable husband asks his wife to tie his bow tie when they are preparing to go out for the evening? Cuffs and shirt fronts were fastened with cufflinks and studs. For men, it used to be absolutely necessary to go to the opera or the concert hall wearing formal evening attire—especially if you were sitting in the expensive seats—including an old-fashioned Victorian top hat and perhaps an opera cloak, while women wore cloaks or stoles, elegant hats, gowns, and formal jewelry to the opera. Fur coats and fox or mink stoles were popular. For the less expensive seats, the rule was jackets and ties for men and nice dresses for women. For other theater events or dinner at a restaurant, men always wore a jacket and tie, and women dressed formally, with gloves and hats and good dresses.

Manners and Social Dancing: In the Victorian era, as we have seen, men sometimes took their hats, as well as their canes and gloves, into the drawing room where they were received. But by the 1920s they were expected to hand them to a servant or to leave all their paraphernalia in the hall before proceeding to the parlor. And they no longer bowed, nor did women curtsey, except on the most formal occasions. Instead, everyone shook hands on being presented to someone else or on meeting a friend. In England and America, a person of lower class, rank, or status was presented to a person of higher status, never the other way around. At a formal affair, particularly in the 1920s, when Edwardian etiquette was still almost as strong as it had been before the Great War, women were asked if they wished to be presented to a particular gentleman; they were free to decline. Men still doffed their hats or touched the brim when meeting someone in the street. But by the 1950s, not everybody wore hats, so a simple nod and a smile sufficed, and perhaps a word of greeting.

In general, from the 1920s through to about 1950, there was a greater sense of staidness, formality, and decorum, and less familiarity and informality, than there is now, as you can readily see in films of the era. In the Nazi and Fascist dictatorships, as the many films made about them show, there was an unsurprisingly rigid sense of protocol and fastidious, almost phobic manners, extremely pretentious and arrogant, with a psychopathic sense of entitlement on the part of the racist thugs who were in power.

Social and ballroom dancing were taught in dancing schools throughout the United States. In the 1920s, the Charleston, with its famous step of hands crossing knees, danced by the "flappers" in short, flaring skirts, was much in vogue, and so was the more staid fox trot. The exotic, sultry, sexy Argentine tango was considered daring and dangerous, and was adored. And the jitterbug, another freewheeling dance, in which the partners hardly touched, but gyrated and swung each other around, much to the shock of their staid elders, was also popular by the 1940s.

Painting and Photography

The early part of the twentieth century saw another artistic revolution, concomitant with the musical one. The incredibly prolific, innovative Pablo Picasso (1881–1973), who went through so many phases, is perhaps the most famous of the modern artists who decided to change painting and the way people look at it. As a very young man, he painted beautiful, realistic canvases, but he soon found that this was not satisfying enough, and he wanted to expand the parameters of what he could paint, how he could paint it, and how he could express himself.

Abstract expressionism as a general movement was an attempt to escape entirely from any kind of realistic approach. Even the canvasses of Henri Matisse (1869–1954) and the French post-impressionist school of the Nabis (the Prophets), such as Edouard Vuillard (1868–1940) and Pierre Bonnard (1867–1947)—all with recognizable people and objects— and the tremendous canvases of distorted figures painted by Fernand Léger (1881–1955) express their feelings, as opposed to a simple, photographic view of the world. Among the new approaches to art were Dadaism, surrealism and cubism.

Aside from the marvelous paintings, which give you an incomparable feeling for the period, the extensive photographic record is, of course, invaluable.

Music

This was the era of recording and of the big bands and popular songs such as those by Irving Berlin (1888–1989). At the Cotton Club in

Harlem, New York City, you could hear Josephine Baker before she left for Paris and Duke Ellington (1899–1974), among many other notables. Josephine Baker made several films, so you could hardly have better source material for the performance style of the period. Spanish zarzuela and Viennese operetta were still going strong. Listen, for instance, to Emerich Kálmán's (1882–1953) brilliant *Die Herzogin von Chicago* (The Duchess of Chicago), heavily influenced by jazz rhythms and textures. Produced in 1928, it features jazz bands in nightclubs, as well as Hungarian folk music rhythms and themes. It opens with the Charleston!

In the world of classical music, composers rebelled against the standard keys and scales and harmonies, and Arnold Schoenberg (1874–1951) invented the twelve-tone scale. Before him, Igor Stravinsky (1882–1971) had caused pandemonium in Paris in 1913 with his music for *The Rite of Spring*, danced by Serge Diaghilev's (1872–1929) famous Ballets Russes, with designs by Léon Bakst (1866–1924). The music of Maurice Ravel (1875–1937) and the Hungarian Béla Bartok (1881–1945), on the other hand, is much more standard in its approach, for all the occasional atonal touches. The prolific Bartok published collections of thousands of folk songs, aside from composing numerous orchestral and piano pieces.

Literature

Many of the great writers of English poetry, prose, and plays were Irish, including William Congreve in the Restoration period; Jonathan Swift, Lawrence Sterne, Oliver Goldsmith, and Richard Brinsley Sheridan in the eighteenth century; and Oscar Wilde and George Bernard Shaw in the nineteenth. The theater had long flourished in Ireland, and in the early years of the twentieth century, through the 1920s and '30s, with the independence of the Republic of Eire assured, it took a new turn. With the Celtic revival and the resurgence of pride in the Gaelic language and culture, memorable plays on Irish themes began to assume great popularity. The level of writing, acting, directing, and producing was exceptionally high. The Abbey Theatre, founded in Dublin in 1904, opened with a bill of one-act plays by W. B. Yeats (1865–1939), Lady Augusta Gregory (1852–1932), and John Millington Synge (1871–1909), who were joint artistic directors. The theater would later produce the plays of Sean O'Casey (1880–1964) and James Joyce's sometime secretary Samuel Beckett (1906–1989) as well.

John Galsworthy's (1867–1933) *The Forsyte Saga*, James Joyce's (1882–1941) *Portrait of the Artist as a Young Man* (1916), and Joyce's short stories, *Dubliners* (1914), are set in the Victorian through the Georgian eras. Helped by the American Sylvia Beach (1887–1962), ensconced in her Paris bookstore Shakespeare & Co. on the Rue de l'Odéon, James Joyce published *Ulysses* in 1922. Hard as it is to believe now, the book was considered highly controversial, and not just because of its literary innovative style and language, but because it supposedly contained obscene passages, notably Molly Bloom's outspoken and gloriously sexual soliloquy. It is very beautiful and a superb piece of writing, but quite mild by today's standards—much milder than the eighteenth-century writings of the Marquis de Sade.

London saw its own literary renaissance with the rise of the Bloomsbury group, headquartered at the houses of the Bell siblings in Bloomsbury. They were an informal literary, philosophical, and artistic coterie that included Virginia Woolf (1882–1941); her second husband, the avant-garde Fabian Socialist publisher and writer, Leonard Woolf (1880– 1969); the biographer and essayist Lytton Strachey (1880–1932); novelist E. M. Forster (1879–1970); and economist John Maynard Keynes (1883–1946).

At the Algonquin Hotel in New York City during the 1920s and '30s, a distinguished company of urbane humorists, witty litterateurs, sophisticated critics, and accomplished stylists calling itself the Algonquin Round Table met in not-so-solemn conclave to palaver, gossip, and have intellectual fun. They were wonderful raconteurs and polished writers, known for their bons mots. They included the delightful Robert Benchley (1889–1945), who made a number of short films, perfect viewing, therefore, for the period, as well as for himself; the acerbic, depressive Dorothy Parker (1893–1967); as well as the playwrights George. S. Kauffman (1889–1961) and Moss Hart (1904–1961); Sherwood Anderson (1876–1941), Russell Crouse (1891–1966), and Marc Connelly (1890– 1980); novelist Edna Ferber (1887–1968); and actor Harpo Marx (1888–1964) of the famed Marx Brothers.

Just as Noël Coward (1899–1973) captured the basic qualities of British life, the journalist Damon Runyon (1884–1946) was the quintessential New York writer. Runyonesque characters run the gamut from boxers, baseball players, gamblers, low-lifes, and hangers-on to Salvation Army girls and nightclub performers. Big Jule from Cicero, Illinois— which he pronounced Illinoise—Nathan Detroit, Sky Masterson, and Harry the Horse were brought vividly to life, not only in his short stories, but in that perennially favorite 1950 Broadway musical with music and lyrics by Frank Loesser and a book by Abe Burrows and Jo Swerling, *Guys and Dolls*, which combined Runyon's short stories "The Idyll of Miss Sarah Brown" and "Blood Pressure."

In the 1920s and '30s, New York City also saw the Harlem Renaissance of African-American intellectuals, writers, musicians, and artists, including poets and novelists Langston Hughes (1920–1967) and Zora Neale Hurston (1891–1960), among many other luminaries. And the novels of F. Scott Fitzgerald (1896–1940) portray the era of jazz and easy money and speakeasies. Thomas Mann (1875–1955) published his daring *Death in Venice* in 1912, the year the Nobel Prize for Literature went to the Indian writer Rabindranath Tagore (1861–1941). In 1924, Mann published the quintessential World War I Novel, *The Magic Mountain*. And Ernest Hemingway (1899–1961), acclaimed for his spare writing style, wrote *A Farewell to Arms* about his experiences in the Great War. *The Sun Also Rises* is about the 1936 Spanish Civil War that brought Francisco Franco (1892–1975) to power when the Phalangists brutally overthrew the republic.

Anatole France, who was not given much to experimenting with form, won the Nobel Prize for Literature in 1921 for his body of brilliant works, among them the allegorical *The Revolt of the Angels*; *The Gods Are Athirst*, a psychological novel about the French Revolution; *The Red Lily*, a beautifully observed novel about love; and the ingenious, satirical *Penguin Island*. But in the 1920s, there was a desire on the part of some writers, such as James Joyce, to experiment and expand the parameters of what writing could do, as there had been in music and painting, especially since many thought literature had come to the end of what could be achieved with the standard forms. After Proust, who could write a novel, or at least a novel as great, as all-encompassing, as vast as his panoramic portrayal of his society? But such pessimism, like the perennial prediction of the death of the theater, was misplaced of course. Franz Kafka (1883–1924) was breaking new ground with his surrealistic, bizarre allegorical works, such as *Metamorphosis*, while working in an insurance office in Prague. And the unique writer Gertrude Stein, along with others, was experimenting with language. If you read her aloud, she sometimes makes much more sense than if you read her silently to yourself. Stein and her life partner, Alice B. Toklas (1877–1967), held court at their salon on the Rue de Fleurus and received many eminent writers and artists.

In Austria, Robert Musil (1880–1942) published his dark novel of adolescence and coming of age, *Young Törless*, in 1906 while he was still a student, and wrote one of the great twentieth-century masterpieces, the unfinished *The Man Without Qualities*, the first volume of which was published in 1930 and the last of three in 1943, posthumously. As soon as the Nazis took over Austria, he escaped to Switzerland.

Memoirs, journals, diaries, and eyewitness accounts about World War II and the Holocaust abound and are essential for an understanding of what happened. After the war, Anne Frank's (1929–1945) world-famous journal, *Anne Frank: The Diary of a Young Girl* (Bantam Reprint Edition, 1993), was discovered by Miep Gies (b. 1909), the courageous woman who helped hide the Franks. She gave the diary to Anne's father, Otto Frank (1889–1980), the only survivor of all those who had hidden from the Nazis in a cramped attic apartment, until they were betrayed and taken to the concentration camps. Chaim Kaplan's (1880–1942/43) searing *The Scroll of Agony*, about his life in the Warsaw Ghetto, is the most revealing indictment of the inhumanity of the life the ghettoized Jews were forced to lead. The *Warsaw Diary* of Adam Czerniakow (1880–1942)—the unfortunate Chairman of the Jewish Council, ordered by the Germans to oversee the deportations from the Warsaw Ghetto—is also deeply upsetting; he committed suicide rather than obey. Wieslaw Kielar's (1919–1990) *Anus Mundi: 1,500 Days in Auschwitz/Birkenau* (Times Books, 1980) is a graphic, brutal portrayal of the camp. Victor Klemperer's (1881–1960) diaries, *I Will Bear Witness: A Diary of the Nazi Years 1933–1941* and *I Will Bear Witness: A Diary of the Nazi Years 1942–1945* (Modern Library paperbacks, 1999 and 2001), are among the most heartrending documents of the period. And Primo Levi's (1919–1987) brilliant books *Survival in Auschwitz* (Touchstone, Reprint Edition, 1989) and *The Drowned and the Saved* (Vintage; Reprint Edition, 1995) are essential. The children's author and illustrator, my friend Anita Lobel (b. 1934), wrote a graphic and moving account of her experiences as a child in war-torn Poland: *No Pretty Pictures: A Child of War* (HarperTrophy, 2000). Elie Wiesel's (b. 1928) books, among them *Night*, *Twilight*, and *The Forgotten*, are heart wrenching. Władysław Szpilman's (1911–2000) autobiographical memoir *The Pianist: The Extraordinary Story of One Man's Survival in Warsaw, 1939–1945* (Picador, 2002) was the basis for Roman Polanski's deeply moving film. The first volume of my friend Hans Sahl's (1902–1993) memoirs, *The Few and the Many*, was published in New York by Harcourt, Brace & World in 1962. As a young man in Berlin, he was becoming known as both a lyric poet and a theater critic. He recounts the saga of his escape from Germany, hiding in Prague, then in Switzerland, then in Paris, from which he fled to the southern unoccupied Vichy zone of France, where he was imprisoned. He escaped, made his way on foot across the Pyrenees, reached Lisbon, and caught one of the last ships to leave for New York in 1941.

Film and Television

The 1920s was the era of the failed Prohibition of alcohol in the United States, when speakeasies flourished—"speak easy" at the door of the "private" club, where you could get bathtub gin. There are, of course, hundreds of films about that gangster era and about World War II, made both during the actual period itself and afterwards. Among the many documentaries you should not miss are Claude Lanzmann's *Shoah* (1985) and Marcel Ophuls' riveting 1970 documentary, *The Sorrow and the Pity*, portraying the Nazi occupation of the French city of Cler-mont-Ferrand during World War II. People in all situations and condi-tions and walks of life are interviewed. For actors, the lessons are invaluable. And for a comprehensive overview of World War II, see the television documentary series *The World at War*, narrated by Laurence Olivier.

Period films: From the 1920s through the 1940s, Hollywood churned out film after film, prior to and during the Second World War, so that all you have to do to get a sense of the style of behavior and the manners is to learn from them. See, for instance, the enjoyable, humorous *Thin Man* series of detective films made between 1934 and 1947, a study in mores, etiquette, and archly decorous manners, with Myrna Loy and William Powell. Powell also played Florenz (Flo) Ziegfeld, Jr. (1867–1932), the Broadway producer of those famous extravaganzas, the Ziegfeld Follies from the 1890s through the 1930s, in two delightful films, *The Great Ziegfeld* (1936) and *Ziegfeld Follies* (1946). And the innumerable gangster films about the Prohibition and slightly later eras, starring James Cagney, Humphrey Bogart, or Edward G. Robinson, are still terrific, riveting entertainment. The Great Depression of the 1930s is perhaps most vividly depicted in the film adaptation of John Steinbeck's moving *The Grapes of Wrath* (1940).

The music hall figures largely in such films as Alfred Hitchcock's *The 39 Steps* (1939) and Charles Chaplin's *Limelight* (1952), set in London in 1914. In fact, Chaplin began his career as a music hall performer.

John Osborne's (1929–1994) *The Entertainer* (1957), set in 1956, stars Laurence Olivier as a seedy, passé music-hall comic. Early Warner Brothers Vitaphone sound films of real vaudeville acts (be prepared for some touches of the typical racism of the period) can be seen on the three-disc DVD edition of the first film "heard around the world," *The Jazz Singer* (1927). And the authentic performance practice of the early twentieth century is clearly seen in *Yankee Doodle Dandy* (1942), starring James Cagney as George M. Cohan, who was the technical adviser on the film.

It is fascinating to watch such films as *Red-Headed Woman* (1932) and the two versions of *Baby Face* (1933), one prepared for release before the Hays code of censorship and the one that actually was shown to the public after the antisexual code took effect. Along with the 1931 version of *Waterloo Bridge*—directed by James Whale, famous for the horror classic *Frankenstein* (also 1931) and the musical *Show Boat* (1936)—they are available on a DVD from the TCM Archives called *Forbidden Hollywood Collection*, volume 1. The films all show an outspoken attitude toward sex that was a product of growing sexual freedom in an era when the ideas of Freud were being popularized. With the Hays code, of course, this freedom was to be suppressed in favor of a rigid hush-hush attitude that prevails to some extent even today in certain circles, despite the so-called sexual revolution of the 1960s. Even the more famous 1940 version of *Waterloo Bridge*, starring Vivien Leigh and Robert Taylor, is less free about prostitution than the earlier film. Also notable in the 1931 film is the style of presentation: the acting is somewhat theatrical, and the makeup is very stagy, the film not having quite come into its own as a medium. The men's makeup in particular, with heavy eye shadow, mascara, and lipstick almost as heavy as the women's, gives the film an amusing air of androgyny.

One of the French filmmaker Jean Renoir's masterpieces, *Les Règles du Jeu* (1939, The Rules of the Game), presents the decadence of the upper strata of French society, oblivious to the looming disaster of the World War. His masterpiece, *Grand Illusion* (1937), which takes place during World War I, is a searing indictment of the class system and of war itself.

Among the most intriguing and instructive films set when the war was in full swing is the 1942 Academy Award winner *Casablanca*. There is the entertaining Sherlock Holmes series of films updated to the World War II era, with Basil Rathbone as Holmes and Nigel Bruce as a bumbling Dr. Watson (not at all Conan Doyle's character, but amusing nonetheless), among them *Sherlock Holmes and the Secret Weapon* and *Sherlock Holmes and the Voice of Terror*, both made in 1942. Alfred Hitchcock's thrillers *The Thirty-Nine Steps* (1935) and *The Lady Vanishes* (1938) give a great picture of the behavior, manners, and mores of the 1930s just before the war. Ernest Hemingway's *The Sun Also Rises* (1957), about the Spanish Civil War of 1936, is an important novel and film for the period, and the film captures perfectly the era and the war that took place only twenty years or so before it was made. Arthur Miller's *All My Sons* was filmed in 1948, so that the period feeling is, of course, absolutely authentic.

Several Michael Powell and Emeric Pressburger films, always beautifully made, are vivid depictions of wartime conditions and events. See, for instance, *The 49th Parallel* (1941), based on a true story about the attempted escape of Nazi pilots whose plane crashes in Canada, and the not-quite-contemporary *The Battle of the River Plate* (1956), about the pursuit of the pocket battleship Graf Spee. They made a number of somewhat sentimental but wonderful films about British life, among them *The Life and Death of Colonel Blimp* (1943), *A Canterbury Tale* (1944), and '*I Know Where I'm Going!*' (1945), but the producing/writing team is perhaps best known for the brilliant, fictional portrayal of the world of ballet in their riveting 1948 film *The Red Shoes*.

Modern Films and Television: Among the most amusing television shows set in the 1920s are the Jeeves and Wooster miniseries based on P. G. Wodehouse, and two different Lord Peter Wimsey miniseries based on the mysteries of Dorothy Sayers, one starring Ian Carmichael and the other Edward Petherbridge—both excellent, and each quite different. You can see them wearing the knee-length trousers called knickerbockers, long socks, sturdy shoes, caps, and tweed jackets. The 1920s is also well presented in *The Great Gatsby* (1949 and 1974) and the Edwardian era in two BBC series based on *The Forsyte Saga*, also adapted by Hollywood in the film *That Forsyte Woman* (1949). The 1948 version of Terence Rattigan's *The Winslow Boy*, adapted several times for film and television, is excellent for the Georgian period of the 1930s in England.

A truly haunting film, *The Wind that Shakes the Barley* (2006) brilliantly dramatizes events in Ireland in the 1920s. It is the story of the mortal conflict between two brothers who begin by fighting together, but end up on different political sides. One of the brothers supports the Anglo-Irish Treaty of 1921, which was viewed as a betrayal by the Republicans; the other continues to fight the British. The Irish War of

Independence that had begun in 1919 went on until Southern Ireland achieved its independence in 1922, leaving Northern Ireland a part of the United Kingdom. *Michael Collins* (1996), with Liam Neeson as one of the doomed heroes of the revolution, is equally effective and moving.

For the Prohibition era, see Francis Ford Coppola's film *Cotton Club* (1984), which recreates the nightlife in Harlem. *The St. Valentine's Day Massacre* (1967), with Jason Robards, Jr. as Al Capone, who has been portrayed as a film character more than sixty times, is one of the many violent films made about the Chicago gangs. *Road to Perdition* (2002) with Paul Newman is a powerful and moving look at the period; and *The Untouchables* (1987), with Kevin Costner as Eliot Ness and Robert De Niro as Al Capone, also recreates the period perfectly. So does Ron Howard's powerful *Cinderella Man* (2005), with Russell Crowe as James Braddock, the boxer who in 1935 beat the bruiser Max Baer to become heavyweight champion of the world. The film is a perfect recreation of the era of the Great Depression in New York, as my mother, who lived through it, told me. Based on Kazuo Ishiguro's novel, Merchant Ivory's *Remains of the Day* (1993), set largely in an English stately home, is the story of a discreet, self-effacing butler, proud to serve, played by Anthony Hopkins, and his relationship with the more assertive, principled house-keeper, Emma Thompson, both of whom serve a Nazi sympathizer (Edward Fox), who is later condemned as a traitor to his country. The Spanish film *Pan's Labyrinth* (2006), written and directed by Guillermo Torres, presents a profoundly affecting, sometimes horrifying view of events in the Spanish Civil War, and the brutality of Franco's Phalangists.

There have been almost countless films portraying the battles of World War II, usually in highly fictionalized versions. Among these are *The Longest Day* (1962), about the D-Day landings on the coast of Normandy; *Battle of the Bulge* (1965); *From Here to Eternity* (1953), adapted from James Jones's novel, which depicts the bombing of Pearl Harbor; *Pearl Harbor* (2001); *Tora! Tora! Tora!* (1970), which shows both American and Japanese views of the bombing; Terence Malick's *The Thin Red Line* (1998), about the battle of Guadalcanal; Clint Eastwood's excellent films about the taking of Iwo Jima, both made in 2006: *Flags of Our Fathers* from the American point of view, and *Letters from Iwo Jima* from the Japanese side. *The Battle of Britain* (1969) attempts the impossible task of portraying the epic air war over England, and it is worth seeing.

For the situation in Italy, see Vittorio de Sica's heartbreaking *The Garden of the Finzi-Continis* (1971) about what happened to Italian

Jewish families in Ferrara. And don't miss Franco Zefirelli's delightful, moving *Tea with Mussolini* (1999), based on his personal experiences, about a group of expatriate English women living in Florence during the war. The Academy Award winner for Best Foreign Film of 1988, *Cinema Paradiso*, is a painful film about the ravages of fascism and the horrors it caused.

Mrs. Henderson Presents (2005) is the heartwarming story of Laura Henderson (Judi Dench), who buys a London theater, renovates it, and reopens it as an all-nude music hall, with the help of Vivian Van Damm (Bob Hoskins). Together they keep it going through the blitz. In a story of survival against all odds, Adrien Brody's sterling, Academy Award–winning performance in Roman Polanski's suspenseful *The Pianist* (2002), based on the memoirs of Władysław Szpilman, is unforgettable. So is the altogether searing film *Fateless* (2004), based on a book by Imre Kertesz, about the fate of Hungarian Jews. There have been a number of films about Raoul Wallenberg, the Swedish diplomat in Budapest who saved thousands of Jewish lives by issuing Swedish documents to them—among them *Wallenberg: A Hero's Story*, made for television in 1985, starring Richard Chamberlain in the title role.

Both based on true stories, *Europa, Europa* (1991) is spellbinding, and *The Counterfeit Traitor* (1962) is magnificent. And don't miss three films by Spielberg that also capture the period perfectly: *Empire of the Sun* (1987), based on J. G. Ballard's autobiographical novel, which takes place in Shanghai as the Japanese attack and in a Japanese concentration camp; *Schindler's List* (1993), based on the true story of Oskar Schindler and how he saved Jewish lives from destruction; and the fictionalized account of actual historical events surrounding D-Day in World War II, the compelling film *Saving Private Ryan* (1998), the story of the attempt to save one American soldier's life after both his brothers have been killed. The last film presents accurately observed, terrifying details of the 1944 Normandy invasion and gruesome occurrences on both a massive and an individual scale.

The 2004 television series *Foyle's War*, with the supremely real Michael Kitchen as a police inspector and altogether wonderful casts, is excellent. It shows what life was like in Britain, with issues other than the war, although related to it, being important as people went about their daily lives.

Andrzej Wajda's *Korczak* (1990) is an emotionally searing account of the last days of Dr. Henryk Goldszmit, the innovative teacher and radio personality whose pseudonym was Janusz Korczak. He was a

Polish Jew dedicated to teaching and caring for children and to protecting Jewish orphans from the Nazis, and he heroically accompanied his young charges from the orphanage he had set up in the Warsaw Ghetto to Treblinka, where they were all murdered.

The Diary of Anne Frank (1959) is less convincing than it might have been, but the film is still a credible adaptation of the Broadway play made from the famous book; other versions, made for television, are better. But the best film on the subject is the 1995 Oscar winner for Best Documentary, *Anne Frank Remembered*, with rare film footage of Anne herself and interviews with, among others, Miep Gies.

Come See the Paradise (1990) with Dennis Quaid, who falls in love with a young Japanese-American girl at the point where the Japanese are being rounded up and sent to internment camps, portrays one of the more horrifying episodes in American history. These events are also dramatized in *American Pastime* (2007), about interned Japanese-Americans who organize a baseball team.

The Desert Fox: The Story of Rommel (1951), with James Mason as the doomed Field Marshall, is effective but highly fictionalized; he played the part again in *The Desert Rats* (1953), about the war in Africa.

There are many films with Hitler as a character, but few, aside from documentaries, that concentrate directly on him, as does *Downfall* (2004) with Bruno Ganz incredible as the maniac dictator, whose psychopathy he captures perfectly. This film is the only version of several about his last days in the underground bunker in war-torn Berlin that is worth seeing, although Alec Guinness in *Hitler: The Last Ten Days* (1973) does an excellent job in the title role.

Sidney Lumet's fascinating *The Pawnbroker* (1965), with Rod Steiger, is about a survivor who endlessly relives the memories of the camps, which we see in a series of momentary flashbacks.

Louis Malle's film *Au revoir les enfants* (1987), based on incidents from his childhood in occupied France, has a very powerful impact: three Jewish students who had been hidden at his school under assumed names by priests were taken away by the Gestapo, along with the school principal, and killed. Malle's film *Lacombe, Lucien* (1974), about a young man who gradually becomes a Nazi collaborator simply by not thinking and by allowing himself to slip into the role, is also heartbreaking.

Based on a true story, *Amen* (2002), a film by Costa-Gavras, is about the attempt by a priest, Riccardo Fontana, to help SS officer Kurt Gerstein get the news about the Holocaust to the Vatican in order to have them intervene and save lives.

The 1982 television miniseries *The Wall*, based on John Hersey's novel about the Warsaw Ghetto, is too didactic but, again, full of authentic detail. And the riveting 1974 miniseries *QB VII*, based on Leon Uris's novel about the unmasking of a doctor who assisted at the horrendous, so-called medical experiments in a concentration camp, has the ring of authenticity, even though it is, of course, fiction. But in the tedious, highly fictionalized miniseries *Holocaust* (1978), the writers did not really seem to grasp the enormity of the subject. On the other hand, the daring rescue of resistance fighters under the nose of the Gestapo in 1943 in Lyon, France, based on real-life events, is very authentically depicted in the stirring film *Lucie Aubrac* (1997). One of the reasons may be that the heroic Madame Aubrac herself (1912–2007), who rescued her husband with the help of other members of the Resistance, was the technical adviser on the film, which is based on her book *Outwitting the Gestapo* (University of Nebraska Press, new edition, 1994). *L'Armée des ombres* (Army of Shadows; 1969)—based on a novel by Joseph Kessel and directed by Jean-Pierre Melville, who wrote the screenplay—is a starkly real portrayal of the French Resistance, a story of fear, betrayal, and solitude. It is a masterpiece not to be missed.

Dealing with corruption and hardship in 1946 in war-torn Vienna, Carol Reed's brilliantly photographed *The Third Man* (1949), based on a story by Graham Greene, who also wrote the screenplay, is one of the great classic films. Reed's 1947 film, *Odd Man Out*, with a wonderful cast, is equally compelling. It is set in Belfast in 1946 and stars James Mason in the role of an IRA fugitive.

For More Information

Ackroyd, Peter. *Dickens*. New York: HarperCollins, 1990.

Adler, Jacob. *A Life on the Stage: A Memoir*. Translated with commentary by Lulla Rosenfeld. Introduction by Stella Adler. New York: Applause Theatre Books, 2001.

Adler, Stella. *On Ibsen Strindberg and Chekhov*. Edited and with a preface by Barry Paris. New York: Random House, 1999.

Allingham, William. *The Diaries*. Edited by H. Allingham and D. Radford. Introduction by John Julius Norwich. London: The Folio Society, 1990.

Anonymous. *Decorum: A Practical Treatise on Etiquette and Dress of the Best American Society*. New York: J. A. Ruth & Co., 1879.

Avilov, Lydia. *Chekhov in My Life: A Love Story*. Translated from the Russian and with an introduction by David Magarshack. New York: Harcourt, Brace and Company, 1950.

Baily, Leslie. *The Gilbert and Sullivan Book*. New York: Coward-McCann, 1953.

Beeton, Mrs. Isabella. *Beeton's Book of Household Management*. A first edition facsimile. New York: Farrar, Straus and Giroux, 1969.

Bernhardt, Sarah. *The Art of the Theatre*. Translated by H. J. Stenning with a preface by James Agate. New York: The Dial Press, 1925.

———*My Double Life: The Memoirs of Sarah Bernhardt*. Translated by Victoria Tietze Larson. Albany, NY: State University of New York Press, 1999.

Blum, Stella, ed. *Fashions and Costumes from Godey's Lady's Book: Including 8 Plates in Full Color*. New York: Dover Publications, 1985.

———*Victorian Fashions and Costumes from Harper's Bazaar, 1867–1898 (Dover Pictorial Archives)*. New York: Dover Publications, 1974.

Boehn, Max von and Oskar Fischel. *Modes and Manners in the 19th Century*. Translated by M. Edwardes and with introduction by Grace Rhys. 4 vols. London: J. M. Dent & Sons, Ltd., 1927.

Carter, William C. *Marcel Proust: A Life*. New Haven, CT: Yale University Press, 2000.

———*Proust in Love*. New Haven, CT: Yale University Press, 2006.

Clurman, Harold. *The Fervent Years: The Group Theatre and the Thirties*. New introduction by Stella Adler. New York: Da Capo Press, 1983.

Colman, Henry. *European Life and Manners in Familiar Letters to Friends*. 2 vols. Boston: Charles C. Little and James Brown, 1850.

Craig, [Edward] Gordon. *Henry Irving*. New York: Longmans, Green and Co., 1930.

Delsarte, François, L'Abbé Delaumosne, Angélique Arnaud, Marie Géraldy, Alfred Giraudet, Francis A. Durivage, and Hector Berlioz. *Delsarte System of Oratory: 1. The Complete Work of L'Abbé Delaumosne. 2. The Complete Work of Mme. Angélique Arnaud. 3. All the Literary Remains of François Delsarte (Given in his own words). 4. The Lecture and Lessons Given by Mme. Marie Géraldy (Delsarte's Daughter) in America. 5. Articles by Alfred Giraudet, Francis A. Durivage, and Hector Berlioz*. 4th edition. New York: Edgar S. Werner, 1893.

Einstein, Alfred. *Music in the Romantic Period*. New York: W. W. Norton & Co., 1947.

Ellmann, Richard. *Oscar Wilde*. New York: Alfred A. Knopf, 1988.

Escoffier, Auguste. *The Escoffier Cookbook: A Guide to the Fine Art of French Cuisine*. New York: Crown Publishers, Inc., 1969.

Flusser, Alan. *Style and the Man: How and Where to Buy Fine Men's Clothes*. New York: HarperCollins Publishers, 1996.

Fromkin, David. *Europe's Last Summer: Who Started the Great War in 1914?* Alfred A. Knopf, 2004.

Glavin, John, ed. *Dickens on Screen.* Cambridge, UK: Cambridge University Press, 2003.

Greville, Charles C. F. *The Greville Memoirs.* Edited by Roger Fulford. New York: The Macmillan Company, 1963.

Gutman, Robert W. *Richard Wagner: The Man, His Mind, and His Music.* New York: Time Incorporated, 1968.

Hall, Florence Howe. *The Correct Thing in Good Society.* Boston: Dana Estes & Company, 1902.

Hethmon, Robert H, ed. *Strasberg at the Actors Studio: Tape-Recorded Sessions.* With an introduction by Robert H. Hethmon and preface by Burgess Meredith. New York: Theatre Communications Group, 1991; (5th Printing), 2000.

Hibbert, Christopher. *Disraeli and His World.* New York: Charles Scribner's Sons, 1978.

———*Queen Victoria: A Personal History.* New York: Da Capo Press; Reprint Edition, 2001.

Hill, Professor Thomas E. *The Essential Handbook of Victorian Etiquette.* San Matteo, CA: A Bluewood Book, 1994.

Hite, John. *Czarist Russia, 1801–1917.* New York: Causeway Press, 1989.

Holland, Merlin. *Irish Peacock and Scarlet Marquis: The Real Trial of Oscar Wilde.* New York: HarperCollins, 2003.

Hyde, H. Montgomery. *The Cleveland Street Scandal.* London: Coward, McCann and Geoghegan, 1976.

Irving, Henry. *The Drama: Addresses.* London: William Heinemann, 1893.

Kift, Dagmar and Roy Kift. *The Victorian Music Hall: Culture, Class and Conflict.* New York: Cambridge University Press, 1996.

Kilvert, Rev. Francis. *Kilvert's Diary: Selections from the Diary of the Rev. Francis Kilvert.* Chosen, edited, and introduced by William Plomer. 3 vols. London: Jonathan Cape, 1938.

Kracauer, Siegfried. *Orpheus in Paris: Offenbach and the Paris of His Time.* New York: Horizon Press, 1983.

Lewes, George Henry. *On Actors and the Art of Acting (1875).* New York: Elibron Classics, 2005.

Macready, William Charles. *Reminiscences and Selections from His Diaries and Letters.* Edited by Sir Frederick Pollock, Bart. New York: Macmillan and Co., 1875; the Michigan Historical Reprint Series, n.d.

Mayhew, Henry. *London Characters and Crooks.* Edited and introduced by Christopher Hibbert. London: The Folio Society, 1996.

McCutcheon, Marc. *Everyday Life in the 1800s: A Guide for Writers, Students & Historians*. Cincinnati, OH: Writer's Digest Books, 1983.

Mikhail, E. H., ed. *The Abbey Theatre: Interviews and Recollections*. Totowa, NJ: Barnes and Noble Books, 1988.

———*Oscar Wilde: Interviews and Recollections*. 2 vols. New York: Harper & Row Publishers, Inc., 1979.

Mitchell, Sally. *Daily Life in Victorian England*. Westport, CT: Greenwood Press, 1996.

Morgan, Anna. *An Hour with Delsarte: A Study of Expression*. Boston: Lee and Shepard, 1889.

Noccioli, Guido. *Duse on Tour: Guido Noccioli's Diaries 1906–07*. Translated and edited with an introduction and notes by Giovanni Pontiero. Amherst, MA: The University of Massachusetts Press, 1982.

Olian, JoAnne, ed. *80 Godey's Full-Color Fashion Plates (1838–1880)*. New York: Dover Publications, 1998.

———*Victorian and Edwardian Fashions from "La Mode Illustrée."* New York: Dover Publications, 1997.

Olivier, Laurence. *Confessions of an Actor: The Autobiography*. London: Orion Books, Ltd., 1982.

———*On Acting*. London: Sceptre, 1987.

Pearson, Edmund. *Queer Books*. Orig. ed. 1928. Port Washington, NY: Kennicat Press, 1970.

Pool, Daniel. *What Jane Austen Ate and Charles Dickens Knew: From Fox Hunting to Whist—the Facts of Daily Life in 19th-Century England*. New York: Simon & Schuster, 1993.

Postgate, Raymond. *Story of a Year: 1848*. New York: Oxford University Press, 1956.

Potter, Helen. *Impersonations*. New York: Edgar S. Werner, 1891.

Proust, Marcel. *In Search of Lost Time*. Translation of *A la recherche du temps perdu* by C. K. Scott Moncrieff and Terence Kilmartin, revised by D. J. Enright. 6 vols. New York: The Modern Library, 1992.

Queen Victoria. *Queen Victoria in Her Letters and Journals*. A Selection by Christopher Hibbert. New York: Viking Penguin, 1985.

Robb, Graham. *Balzac: A Biography*. New York: W. W. Norton, 1994.

———*Victor Hugo: A Biography*. New York: W. W. Norton, 1997.

———*Rimbaud: A Biography*. New York: W. W. Norton, 2000.

Saint-Denis, Michel. *Theatre: The Rediscovery of Style*. Introduction by Sir Laurence Olivier. New York: Theatre Arts Books, 1960.

Shattuck, Charles H. *The Hamlet of Edwin Booth*. Chicago, IL: The University of Illinois Press, 1969.

Shattuck, Roger. *Proust's Way: A Field Guide to In Search of Lost Time*. New York: W. W. Norton & Co, 2000.

Sheehy, Helen. *Eleonora Duse: A Biography*. New York: Alfred A. Knopf, 2003.

Stebbins, Genevieve. *Delsarte System of Expression*. 2nd ed. New York: Edgar S. Werner, 1887; 6th ed. New York: Edgar S. Werner, 1902.

Strachan, Hew. *The First World War*. New York: Viking, 2004.

Strachey, Lytton. *Eminent Victorians*. New York: Penguin Classics, 1990.

——*Queen Victoria*. New York: Harvest Books, 2002.

Strasberg, Lee. *A Dream of Passion*. New York: Penguin Plume Books, 1987.

Weintraub, Stanley. *Uncrowned King: The Life of Prince Albert*. New York: Free Press, 2000.

World War II

Churchill, Winston S. *The Second World War*. 6 vols. New York: Mariner Books Reprint Edition, 1986.

Dawidowicz, Lucy. *The War Against the Jews, 1933–1945*. New York: Bantam Reprint Edition, 1986.

Friedländer, Saul. *Nazi Germany and the Jews, Volume 1: The Years of Persecution, 1933–1939*. New York: HarperCollins Publishers, 1997.

——*Nazi Germany and the Jews, Volume 2: The Years of Extermination, 1939–1945*. New York: HarperCollins Publishers, 2007.

Gilbert, Martin. *Auschwitz and the Allies: A Devastating Account of How the Allies Responded to the News of Hitler's Mass Murder*. New York: Owl Books, 1990.

Gruhl, Werner. *Imperial Japan's World War Two, 1931–1945*. New York: Transaction Publishers, 2006.

Shirer, William L. *The Rise and Fall of the Third Reich: A History of Nazi Germany*. New York: MJF Books, 1998.

Trunk, Isaiah. *Jewish Responses to Nazi Persecution*. New York: Stein and Day, 1979.

——*Judenrat: The Jewish Councils of Eastern Europe Under Nazi Occupation*. New York: Macmillan Publishing Company, 1972.

Yahil, Leni. *The Rescue of Danish Jewry: Test of a Democracy*. New York: Jewish Publication Society of America, 1969.

Recordings

There are innumerable audio recordings of the spoken word and of opera singers from the turn of the twentieth century, some of whom span the eras of acoustic and electrical recording, as well as early recordings of operas, operettas, and instrumental music. Here are some anthologies you will find especially useful for this period; you can hear the spoken accents of the period, as well as performance styles.

About a Hundred Years: The History of Sound Recording. (Includes voices of Arthur Conan Doyle, Sarah Bernhardt, Thomas Alva Edison, Johannes Brahms, Mahatma Gandhi, von Hindenburg, Neville Chamberlain, Winston Churchill, Leo Tolstoy). Symposium CD 1222, 1997.

The Art of the Savoyard: Singers Who Worked with Gilbert and Sullivan. Pearl CD, 1993.

Bay Mir Bistu Shayn: Great Songs of the Yiddish Theater, Volume 2. (Includes three songs by Herman Wohl.) Milken Archive: American Jewish Music CD 8559432, 2005.

Emma Eames: The Complete Victor Recordings (1905–11). (Includes a radio interview with Emma Eames, talking about early recording conditions.) Romophone CD 81001-2, 1993.

La Grande Epoque: Rare Recordings of Delmas, Héglon, Lafitte. Simon-Girard. (Includes Offenbach recordings of Juliette Simon-Girard, who worked with the composer.) Pearl CD, 1994.

Great Actors of the Past. Compiled by Richard Bebb. (Ellen Terry, Henry Irving, Sarah Bernhardt, Herbert Beerbohm Tree, Edwin Booth, Lewis Waller, Alexander Moissi, Julia Neilson and Fred Terry, Constant Coquelin, Joseph Jefferson, Tommaso Salvini, and Cyril Maude.) Argo Records, LP SW 510.

Great Shakespeareans. (Edwin Booth, Herbert Beerbohm Tree, Arthur Bourchier, Lewis Waller, Ben Greet, John Barrymore, Sir Johnston Forbes-Robertson, Sir John Gielgud, Henry Ainley, and Maurice Evans.) Pearl, Gemm CD 9465, 1990.

In Their Own Voices: The U.S. Presidential Elections of 1908 and 1912. (William Jennings Bryan, William H. Taft, Woodrow Wilson, and Theodore Roosevelt.) Marston Records 52028-2 CD, 2000.

The Jazz Singer. 3-disc DVD set. (Includes authentic early sound films of vaudeville acts.) Warner Brothers, 2007.

Nellie Melba: Farewell 1926. (Includes acoustic and electrical recordings and her curtain speech at her farewell at Covent Garden.) Eklipse Records Limited CD, 1992.

The Noël Coward Collection. 7 DVDs. (Includes interviews with Noel Coward, radio plays, and television versions of plays *Hay Fever, Private Lives, Tonight at 8:30,* and more.) BBC Video DVD, 2007.

Paris Was A Woman: A Film by Greta Schuller. (Documentary about the Paris literary scene of the 1920s through '40s; includes interviews with Sylvia

Beach, Janet Flanner, voices of Gertrude Stein, and many others.) Zeitgeist Video: DVD, 2001.

Poetry Speaks: Hear Great Poets Read Their Work from Tennyson to Plath. Book and 3 CDs. Narrated by Charles Osgood. (Includes voices of Alfred, Lord Tennyson, Robert Browning, Walt Whitman, W. B. Yeats, Gertrude Stein, T. S. Eliot, Ezra Pound, Dorothy Parker, Edna St. Vincent Millay, Langston Hughes, Ogden Nash, Dylan Thomas.) Sourcebooks MediaFusion, 2001.

Russian Revolution in Color. Cineflux International DVD, 2007.

Le Théâtre Parisien de Sarah Bernhardt à Sacha Guitry. 6 CDs. (Recordings of Sarah Bernhardt, Constant Coquelin Aîné [the original Cyrano de Bergerac], Yvette Guilbert, Sacha Guitry, and Jean Cocteau.) EMI France, CZS 7675392. 1992.

Index of People

About the Author

ROBERT BLUMENFELD is the author of *Accents: A Manual for Actors* (Limelight, Revised and Expanded Edition, 2002), *Acting with the Voice: The Art of Recording Books* (Limelight, 2004), and *Tools and Techniques for Character Interpretation: A Handbook of Psychology for Actors, Writers, and Directors* (Limelight, 2006), and the collaborator with noted teacher, acting coach, and actress Alice Spivak on the writing of her book *How to Rehearse When There Is No Rehearsal: Acting and the Media* (Limelight, 2007). He lives and works as an actor, dialect coach, and writer in New York City. He has worked in numerous regional and New York theaters, as well as in television and independent films. For ACT Seattle he played the title role in Ronald Harwood's *The Dresser*, and he has performed many roles in plays by Shakespeare and Chekhov, as well as doing an Off-Broadway season of six Gilbert and Sullivan comic operas for Dorothy Raedler's American Savoyards. He created the roles of the Marquis of Queensberry and two prosecuting attorneys in Moisés Kaufman's Off-Broadway hit play *Gross Indecency: The Three Trials of Oscar Wilde* and was also the production's dialect coach. Mr. Blumenfeld has recorded more than 300 Talking Books for the American Foundation for the Blind, including the complete Sherlock Holmes canon and *The Count of Monte Cristo*. He received the 1997 Canadian National Institute for the Blind's Torgi Award for the Talking Book of the Year in the Fiction category, for his recording of Pat Conroy's *Beach Music*, and the 1999 Alexander Scourby Talking Book Narrator of the Year Award in the Fiction category. He holds a B.A. in French from Rutgers University and an M.A. from Columbia University in French Language and Literature.